Christianity and Buddhism

FAITH MEETS FAITH

In the contemporary world, the many religions and spiritualities stand in need of greater communication and cooperation. More than ever before, they must speak to, learn from, and work with each other in order to maintain their vital identities and to contribute to fashioning a better world.

The FAITH MEETS FAITH Series seeks to promote interreligious dialogue by providing an open forum for exchange among followers of different religious paths. While the Series wants to encourage creative and bold responses to questions arising from contemporary appreciations of religious plurality, it also recognizes the multiplicity of basic perspectives concerning the methods and content of interreligious dialogue.

Although rooted in a Christian theological perspective, the Series does not limit itself to endorsing any single school of thought or approach. By making available to both the scholarly community and the general public works that represent a variety of religious and methodological viewpoints, FAITH MEETS FAITH seeks to foster an encounter among followers of the religions of the world on matters of common concern.

FAITH MEETS FAITH SERIES

Christianity and Buddhism

A Multicultural History of Their Dialogue

Whalen Lai
and
Michael von Brück

Translated by
Phyllis Jestice

ORBIS BOOKS

Maryknoll, New York 10545

Founded in 1970, Orbis Books endeavors to publish works that enlighten the mind, nourish the spirit, and challenge the conscience. The publishing arm of the Maryknoll Fathers and Brothers, Orbis seeks to explore the global dimensions of the Christian faith and mission, to invite dialogue with diverse cultures and religious traditions, and to serve the cause of reconciliation and peace. The books published reflect the views of their authors and do not represent the official position of the Society. To learn more about Maryknoll and Orbis Books, please visit our website at www.maryknoll.com.

English translation and abridgment of the German-language original edition copyright © 2001 by Orbis Books.
Translation by Phyllis Jestice.
Published by Orbis Books, Maryknoll, New York, U.S.A.

This book is an abridged translation of *Buddhismus und Christentum: Geschichte, Konfrontation, Dialog* by Whalen Lai and Michael von Brück, copyright © 1997 and 2000 by Verlag C. H. Beck, Munich, Germany.

Manuscript editing and typesetting by Joan Weber Laflamme.
Manufactured in the United States of America.

Library of Congress Cataloging-in-Publication Data

Brück, Michael von.
   [Buddhismus und Christentum. English]
   Christianity and Buddhism : a multicultural history of their dialogue / Whalen Lai and Michael von Brück ; translated by Phyllis Jestice.
      p. cm. — (Faith meets faith series)
   Includes bibliographical references and index.
   ISBN 1-57075-362-8 (pbk.)
      1. Christianity and other religions—Buddhism. 2. Buddhism—Relations—Christianity. I. Lai, Whalen. II. Title. III. Faith meets faith.

BR128.B8 B7713 2001
261.2'43'09—dc21

                                                                    2001024591

Contents

Foreword

On Buddhist-Christian Dialogue

HANS KÜNG

Times change, and not always for the worse: *interreligious dialogue*, for a long time a concern solely of specialists and esoterics, is today also a *political desideratum*. The propagation of the widely covered thesis of a "clash of civilizations," a "culture war," has alarmed both politicians and scholars and made them sensitive to the significance of "dialogue between the cultures." No modern statesman champions this cause in such varied and sustained fashion as the president of the Federal Republic of Germany, Dr. Roman Herzog. He regards this issue as "one of the most important of our time, a theme that inescapably unites Asia and Europe." As he has expressed it:

> History has by no means come to an end with the end of the Cold War. On one side the globalization of markets, technologies, the media, even of interacting cultures appears to be unstoppable. On the other side, we observe again and again, even in supposedly enlightened societies, the reflex to retreat into a national or cultural circling of our wagons, thinking in categories of power, the painting of images of enmity. The fashionable scenario of clash of civilization, which prophesies for the world a global cultural war in place of the Cold War, is a typical example of this mode of thought. I believe this scenario is scientifically and ethically questionable. If, however, it is spread by the media and is established in elite thought, it can easily become a self-fulfilling prophecy. America, Asia, and Europe have in like manner a single interest—also thoroughly an issue of national security—to resist the intellectual fallacies of this scenario.

Thus the federal president spoke on the occasion of our official dialogue meeting over which he presided on 3 April 1997, during his state visit to Kuala Lumpur:

> The theme of your meeting today, the question of whether a universal civilization is conceivable, plays a central role in concerns about intercultural peace. Professor Huntington, as we know, denies this possibility. That is

what is dangerous about his scenario. Does not civilization, throughout the world, mean at the least protection of peace, taming of force, the quest for knowledge? Do we even know what we unleash, if we give up thought of a minimum of common civilization?

Yes, how the situation has changed in the dozen years since the time when two young scholars, Dr. Michael von Brück and Professor Whalen Lai, began the research project *Balance and Perspectives of Christian-Buddhist Dialogue*, whose impressive results now appear in this book. Back then I had behind me four public dialogues on Christianity and Buddhism with the Göttingen Buddhologist Professor Heinz Bechert before a large audience in the Studium Generale of the University of Tübingen (1982), and had fundamentally reworked and published my "Christian answers" (1984).[1] I wrote on 15 July 1985 in support of the proposal to the German research society for support of this new project:

> Transfer of technology and ideas: communication in the realm of philosophy and theology has not kept step with the recent progress in world-wide communication in the scientific-technical and economic-political realms. Besides this, often political crises and even military conflicts (Near East, Iran/Iraq, India/Pakistan) have a religious subtext, which makes these confrontations especially fanatical. On the other hand, however, more and more political, scholarly, and economic leaders have begun to realize that a true understanding among the peoples cannot be brought about by pushing to one side the ethical and religious dimension. Upon this backdrop today dialogue between Christianity and the world religions takes just as important a place as earlier the dialogue between the Christian churches did for the pacification of Europe. The long-continuing transfer of technology must be expanded by a transfer of ideas.
>
> The difficulty now is that the state of interreligious dialogue up to this point, which has branched out unmethodically internationally, is hardly known in Germany. Because of this, the often acknowledged preeminence of *German theology* in the international realm will only remain if, like the Americans, they earnestly go into the problems of interreligious dialogue, and do not shove these problems to one side because of doctrinaire or confessional prejudice.
>
> No long explanations are necessary to show that East Asia plays a leading role in interreligious dialogue . Especially in Japan Christian-Buddhist dialogue has been encouraged, but also in China interest in religion is again evident thanks to recent political upheavals. In each case, to balance the work Dr. von Brück will undertake with concentration on India, Sri Lanka, and Southeast Asia, this must be expanded through investigation of the dialogue situation in the far east. Professor Lai, Chinese by birth, satisfies the

---

[1] Hans Küng, et al., *Christianity and World Religions: Paths of Dialogue with Islam, Hinduism, and Buddhism*, trans. Peter Heinegg (Garden City, N.Y.: Doubleday, 1986; Maryknoll, N.Y.: Orbis Books, 1993).

requirements for this research project in an excellent fashion, as is clear from both his bio- and bibliography.

In connection with public dialogue with specialists in Islam, Hinduism, and Buddhism, it has become apparent to me what Global Ethic had consolidated as a project in the years after I wrote that recommendation:
• No peace among the nations without peace among religions.
• No peace among the religions without dialogue between the religions.
• *No dialogue between the religions without fundamental research on the religions*.
These two specialists have now performed a fundamental work of this sort in regard to Christianity and Buddhism. And today, after many years I can thankfully declare: they have not fallen short of expectations!

Buddhism is commonly understood to be the radical opposite of Christianity. Despite this, a worldwide dialogue between Buddhists and Christians is underway—admittedly not between official representatives (with the exception of the Dalai Lama!). And even for two well-read and far-traveled observers of the scene it is hardly possible to study all the Christian-Buddhist dialogue undertakings in the whole world and to elucidate the problems discussed there; comprehensiveness cannot be their goal. But their expositions are highly representative in every case, in three respects:
1. Christian-Buddhist *encounters* in the central countries of dialogue are handled in their own historical contexts: in India, Sri Lanka, China, Japan, Germany, and the United States of America.
2. The central *tangible differences* are presented with their nuances and critically investigated. Everything is concentrated on three central problems: Jesus Christ and the Buddha Gautama, God and *dharma*, *samgha* and church.
3. Finally, the paradigm shift in the history of Buddhism and the *hermeneutic aspects* of current encounter are situated in reference to the Buddhist-ecclesiastical dialogue.
When one has been the first to discuss all these problems in public dialogue with a representative of Buddhism at a German university, he is naturally glad that a decade and a half later the proposed solutions have been widely adopted. For their part, the authors of this study may be glad that it has been possible for them, with unending effort, to offer both students of Buddhism and the interested public a convincing look not just at the status of dialogue, but also the points of possible convergence and agreement that now have emerged between Christianity and Buddhism despite all remaining differences. No other religions appear to be as widely separated from each other as Christianity and Buddhism. It is encouraging for all those engaged in the cause of peace between religions, since even between Christianity and Buddhism there is so much common ground and thus a solid basis for practical cooperation.

Both authors have now asked that I say something in this foreword about the *relationship between the paradigm shift in Christianity and Buddhism*. I comply gladly. Since the 1970s I have worked to apply Thomas S. Kuhn's paradigm theory to the history of theology, churches, and religions, and have also tested this application in the context of Buddhism, in order to work out the historical relativity as well as the historical context of different branches of Buddhism. And I made the personal acquaintance of Michael von Brück at a symposium held at the University of Hawaii in Honolulu in 1984, which had as its main theme "Paradigm Changes in Buddhism and Christianity." This was prompted by the successful International Ecumenical Symposium "A New Theological Paradigm?" sponsored in 1983 jointly by our Institute for Ecumenical Research in Tübingen, the University of Chicago Divinity School, and the international journal for theology *Concilium*.[2] One of the few at the Hawaii symposium who had already fully grasped how much paradigm analysis can contribute to the understanding of other religions, especially Buddhism (as can be seen with unity and multiplicity, constants and variables, continuity and upheavals in historical depth of focus, actual relationship and larger context), was the young Chinese professor from the University of California, Whalen Lai.

There is not "a" Buddhism, just as there is not simply "a" Christianity. The authors have undertaken a more carefully reflective paradigm analysis of the mighty and many-branched two and a half thousand year picture of "Buddhism" and its different paradigms and schools of thought, in which even the learned often find it difficult to see the forest for the trees, or the unity in face of all the differences. The authors confirm this balance in dialogue in a twofold fashion:

1. Rightly, the authors have not excluded *any of the historically developed great Buddhist religious forms* from the start as "unbuddhist." Often the Tantric Buddhism of Tibet has been viewed as a "re-Hinduization" and as a decline from pure Buddhism ("Lamaism"). Others have discredited the Japanese "Pure Land Buddhism" as fundamentally unbuddhist "Amidism." This came to pass in opposition to the believers of each branch, who regard themselves as authentic Buddhists despite all their differences from other forms of Buddhism. One will only do them justice by recognizing that they live their Buddhism in an entirely different general constellation, in another "paradigm" (according to Thomas S. Kuhn, another "general constellation of convictions, values, and procedures"). This is not a matter of different religions, but of different paradigms of one and the same religion (Buddhism). By heeding the different paradigms it is possible to surmount Christian-Buddhist dialogue's thus far all too exclusive concentration on Buddhism's meditation tradition and to neglect no longer the popular Buddhism of the villages, the state Buddhism of the nations of Southeast Asia, and the political-social history of Buddhism in general.

2. Also rightly, though, the authors have *criteriologically measured the new forms of Buddhism* in the final analysis on the basis of their origin with *Gautama, the Buddha*, and await a historical-critical investigation of their own tradition from the Buddhist partners in dialogue. In dialogue the different Buddhist paradigms

---

[2] See Hans Küng and D. Tracy, *Theologie—wohin? Auf dem Weg zu einem neuen Paradigma* (Zürich/Gütersloh, 1985); Hans Küng, *Theology im Aufbruch. Eine ökumenische Grundlegung* (Munich, 1987).

have not acted in competition against one another but have stressed the necessity of dialogue with all important Buddhist paradigms (from original Buddhism through the three vehicles to Zen and Shin). Indeed, despite all striking differences in Buddhism's long history, again and again certain fundamental constants have been maintained and generally accepted: taking refuge with the Buddha, taking refuge with *dharma* (instruction), and taking refuge with *samgha* (the monastic community). These form the permanent determinants that shape Buddhism through all centuries throughout the countries and continents and through all change in paradigm from the ground up.

A paradigm analysis will not now attempt to be as original as possible and to discover a new paradigm. In the history of religions there must first of all be an epochal great constellation: in Christianity as in Buddhism, a macro-paradigm, which naturally encompasses many meso- and micro-paradigms.

In *Christianity* (I have analyzed this for more than a thousand pages in *Christianity*, 1994) it is possible to distinguish six different general constellations, all of which still have adherents today:
   • the Jewish-apocalyptic paradigm of original Christianity,
   • the ecumenical-Hellenistic paradigm of ancient Christianity,
   • the Roman-Catholic paradigm of the Middle Ages,
   • the Protestant-evangelical paradigm of the Reformation,
   • the reason- and progress-oriented paradigm of modernism,
   • the ecumenical paradigm of postmodernism (sketched out since the end of World War I and emerged into full light since World War II).

There are also six great constellations of similar complexity in Judaism (*Judaism*, 1991) and in Islam (study underway). But what is the situation with *Buddhism*? In agreement with most historical portrayals, in Buddhism it is also possible to establish six (again purely coincidentally) great constellations. These are traditionally designated as "turnings of the wheel of instruction":
   • the original Buddhist paradigm of the Buddha Gautama and his monastic community,
   • the Theravada paradigm of the lesser vehicle ("Hinayana") or better, the vehicle of the hearer ("Shravakayana"),
   • the Mahayana paradigm of the greater vehicle; this leads eventually to the reforming schools of meditation Buddhism ("Zen"), of belief Buddhism ("Shin"), and of action Buddhism ("lotus sects"),
   • the Vajrayana of the diamond vehicle ("Tantrayana"),
   • the defensive Buddhism in conflict with (socialist or capitalist) modernism, menaced with persecution (China, Tibet, North Korea) or secularization (Japan, South Korea, Southeast Asia),
   • finally, perhaps also in Buddhism a paradigm of postmodernism emerging from conflict with European-American modernism.

Already a superficial look shows that there is not a simple parallel between the six Christian and six Buddhist macro-constellations (I will not here return to the argument with Oswald Spengler and Arnold Toynbee in "Project Global Ethic" in 1990). The differences between Christianity and Buddhism are in any event immense. Despite this, one should not overlook quite definite *structural parallels*. *In both religions* the central *fundamental constants* have been maintained in all variants: permanent determinants of specific teaching, praxis, and institutionalization run through all paradigm shifts. Similarly to how the Christian "takes refuge," "believes" in Christ, the gospel (the message), and the church, so the Buddhist takes "refuge in the Buddha, in *dharma* (teaching), in *samgha* (monastic community)." Believers on both sides thus orient themselves by the same "stars" ("stellae"), as they again and again create new epochal "constellations"!

There are striking parallels in regard to the fundamental principles, but also relative to individual *paradigms*, which run through both religions. This is particularly clear with the *first turn of the wheel of instruction*. Just as Christianity could never have become a world religion without the paradigm shift from the Jewish-Christian-apocalyptic to the Hellenistic-ecumenical paradigm, which finally peaked in the "Constantinian transformation," so too Buddhism had to change. Through its first paradigm shift, from the Buddha to the older "communion of hearers" ("Shravakayana") and to the "teaching of the heads of orders" ("Theravada") the elite religion was transformed into a religion of the masses, with a developed cult including rites and ceremonies (especially the cult of relics) that the Buddha himself had described as one of the "ten shackles" without value for salvation, but that now became a source of religious merit for a better rebirth. Thus what was offered was no longer a *nirvana*-Buddhism of meditation and the extinguishing of desire (only possible for a monastic elite) but a *samsara*-focused Buddhism of satisfaction of desire that now only offered a familiarity with the life history of the Buddha and the saints, the customary commandments of their religion, and the collection of religious merits to attain a better rebirth. From an original Buddhism, concentrated on the monastic community and on renunciation of power, now came a Buddhism that, under Emperor Asoka, could practically become a state religion all the way to Sri Lanka. And just as the structures of the Byzantine paradigm have persisted up to the present in the countries of eastern Europe, so too in Southeast Asia the structures of merit- and state-Buddhism have endured.

Similarly, it is possible to compare structurally the *second turn of the wheel of instruction*, from the Theravada paradigm of "orthodoxy" and the "monk" to the *Mahayana paradigm* of mass- and lay-religion, to the paradigm shift from the Hellenistic Byzantine to the medieval Roman Catholic paradigm. The highly pious, ceremonial, and clerical Mahayana has been called a magnificent universal church, with the Buddha as ever-present, omniscient, and almighty highest god, surrounded by a pantheon, a great number of saints. With this, the separate Buddhology and royal ideology "from below" were united to a Buddhology and royal ideology "from above" (high Buddhology). The wisdom teaching of a monastic elite was transformed to a cult—often assimilated to Hindu, Taoist, and Shinto representations and forms—around numerous mercy-bestowing buddhas and bodhisattvas as well as a devotional piety movement for the masses, as it still continues today in China, Korea, and Japan.

But Mahayana, too, like every macro-paradigm, embraces different tendencies and schools. From the circle of the Buddhism that predominated in China developed two *reforming Mahayana schools*. Both of these reached a high point in Japan in the Kamakura period, and are often compared to the Reformation in Christianity. On the one hand is a belief-focused Buddhism of the Pure Land ("Shin"), which proclaims a salvation not by one's own powers but on the basis of belief alone (in the promise of Amida Buddha). On the other hand is meditation Buddhism ("Zen"), which is based on a radical concentration, simplification, and spiritualization. Besides these, in Japan there was yet a third reforming movement. This was a social Buddhism going back to the prophetic Nichiren and based upon a radical interpretation of the Lotus sutra, which has been compared to the social movements of Christendom from the Middle Ages to the modern era.

Perhaps it is only in esoteric forms of Christianity that parallels can be found to the *third turning of the wheel of instruction*. This form came into being around the middle of the first Christian millennium (contemporaneously with Shin and Zen, about five centuries after the transformation to Mahayana), in India, Nepal, Tibet, and as far as Japan: the diamond vehicle, the *Vajrayana* or *Tantrayana*. This is, all in all, not a reforming but a syncretic paradigm, in which many ritual, magical, occult, and miraculous elements are central.

In Buddhism there is no talk of a further turning of the wheel of instruction. Still, just as Christianity—prepared by the Reformation—was confronted very early with European modernism, imprinted as it was with the ideas of reason, progress, and nationalism, so now Buddhism also faces the same challenge. But up to now hardly any effort has been made to develop a *modern paradigm* of Buddhism, with the exception of the Buddhist lay movements in Japan (Rissho Koseikai, Soka gakkai, etc.), in Thailand (Sulak Sivaraksas Center), and in Sri Lanka (Ariyaratnes Sarvodaya Movement). In the Southeast Asian countries traditional Buddhism has kept relatively distant from the problems of modern industrial society, if one disregards individual prominent monks. A historical critique of the Buddhist tradition would be necessary in this context, because only on such a foundation is a well-founded inquiry into the Buddha of history and a confrontation with the political history of Buddhism possible.

A transition to a *postmodern paradigm*, as it is currently distinguished in Christianity, will only be possible on the basis of an integration of the modern, insofar as this is human and not inhuman. This is admittedly not to be confused with a retreat to the premodern, as is aspired to in a reactionary "re-evangelization" or "re-islamification." I have already sketched out the postmodern paradigm in the "Project Global Ethic." It is a constellation that is not only postcolonial and postimperialist, but also postcapitalist and postsocialist. Economically and politically viewed, it contains an ecological-social market economy. Religiously, however, it is an ecumenical community of the no longer mutually excommunicating but instead united Christian churches and the no longer fighting but now peacefully living together world religions.

A hopeful omen for such an ecumenical paradigm is the movement for a *global ethic*, or a necessary minimum of common ethical values and standards. In a short time this movement has gained greatly in strength, as I have documented in my book *A Global Ethic for Global Politics and Economics.* It would be very desirable if the Christian churches as well as Buddhist authorities would subscribe to the recommendations of the International Commission for World-Order Politics (1945), the World Commission for Culture and Development (1995), and the declaration of the Inter Action Council of former presidents and prime ministers (1996). These propose that the universal declaration of human rights of UNESCO (1945) might be expanded with a universal declaration of human responsibilities, such as was already sponsored by the parliament of the French Revolution (1789).

For this development, the "Declaration of a Global Ethic" of the Chicago Parliament of World Religions (1993) was especially encouraging, a document that I had the honor and labor of composing. Here it was above all harmony between Christianity and Buddhism in regard to the four fundamental ethical imperatives that made it possible for me to construct this declaration of global ethic upon four essential commandments and to derive fundamentals for a new ecumenical culture in the postmodern world from their negative as well as positive formulations. The Buddhists, too (among them the Dalai Lama), agreed to these "essential commandments":

• You should not kill! Or positively stated: Have reverence toward life! In other words, a commitment to a culture of powerlessness and respect for life.

• You should not steal! Or positively: Act justly and fairly! In other words, a commitment to a culture of solidarity and a just economic order.

• You should not lie! Or positively: Speak and act truthfully! In other words, a commitment to a culture of tolerance and a life in truthfulness.

• You should not fornicate! Or positively: Respect and love one another! In other words, a commitment to a culture of equality of rights and partnership between man and woman.

I do not doubt that this forceful volume with all its information for Buddhist-Christian understanding marks a milestone. I wish the two authors every success in their further academic efforts.

Introduction

A half millennium of Eurocentrism is coming to an end. Will the twenty-first century experience a confrontation of cultures, one that will involve not only economic and political might, but also religious identities? Or will it be an age of dialogue and cooperation among both regions and religions? Certainly, religions today still leave their mark, directly or indirectly, on international disputes, affecting as they do world views, models of history, views of humanity, and concepts of value. But what are "religions" and "religious identities"?

Religions interpret and give meaning to the world based on a specific history of belief. They are, however, also social and political systems that have legitimated governmental structures and, for as far back as we have written history, have competed with one another. Religions deploy powers that are able to give identity and orientation, but at the same time they legitimate demarcation, exclusion, and violence.

What is new in the present situation is that the fates of peoples on a global scale are so interlocking that almost all of humanity's problems require a common solution. For these reasons there is no alternative to dialogue among religions. Dialogue is the middle course between refusing to acknowledge the relativity and plurality of religious reality, and a pluralism of preference that would level out all values to a common denominator. Dialogue among religions should also not limit itself to necessary debates about peace, justice, care for the environment, and human rights, but must also concern itself with the ultimate foundations of responsibility and values.

It remains to be seen whether religions in modern societies, through cooperation, can contribute to making value orientations possible, and to containing loss of identity, anxiety, and the disintegration of social ties by establishing a new consensus about what we value. In any case, religions bear an essential joint responsibility for shaping the future of humanity.

THE TASK

Mutual understanding among differing cultures requires an interreligious hermeneutics—which of necessity has political relevance. The current meeting of cultures is encumbered by the heritage of European and American colonialism, by the economic and political inequality between West and East (with the exception of Japan), and by the role of religions in the respective countries involved (whether they support or are critical of the state). The struggle for recognition of the universal validity of human rights shows the problem. Rulers, as they defend their practices to the general public, often justify the oppression of their people by invoking specific cultural and religious values. Interreligious dialogue must clarify the extent to which such arguments are legitimate and valid. In this matter dialogue under democratic or pluralistic conditions (as in Europe, India, or America) can reach the level of becoming a catalyst for change.

History is open, but present possibilities are limited by conditions that have been created by the past. Therefore, we can only inquire into these outlined problems in a meaningful way if we confront head-on the complex history of how religions and cultures have encountered one another. In this book, we will study the interaction of Buddhism and Christianity, and especially the developments of this communication in the modern era. We have several reasons for this focus:

First, Buddhism is a world religion that spans the entire continent of Asia and links such diverse cultures as those of South Asia (India, Sri Lanka), East Asia (China, Korea, Japan), and Southeast Asia (Thailand, Burma, Laos, Cambodia, Vietnam). These areas form, economically and culturally, one of the most dynamic regions of the earth. Will the twenty-first century belong to these lands? Will they be able to spread their cultural values, including Buddhism, so successfully in Europe and America that the traditional identities of the European and American peoples, until now strongly stamped with Christianity, will fade?

Second, Buddhism shares a common history with Christianity. This has indeed been deeply marked by the aspirations for power of Christian colonizers and the corresponding opposition of Buddhists. This is not the only shared historic ground between Buddhism and Christianity, though; contact has led also to an intensive cultural exchange, based on mutual respect. Therefore it is especially useful to study the dynamics of encounters among religions using the example of Buddhism and Christianity.

Third, Buddhism, over the past hundred years, has established a foothold in Europe and America. Although at first this was limited almost exclusively to intellectual circles, after the Second World War Buddhism reached Christians of all social classes through many-leveled meditation movements. Some of the Christians it reached converted to Buddhism, while some have remained Christian and thus live in a sort of "religious dual citizenship." By this means a model of religious identity new to Christian culture has come into being. It deserves our attention, since it has already incisively changed the cultural pattern of Europe and America, formerly (nearly) purely Christian regions. In China or Japan the model of "religious dual citizenship" has a long tradition, and Buddhism in these lands—not without tensions—has adapted, changed, deepened, or become shallower. Will this also come to pass in Europe and America?

The goal of this book is to trace these processes back historically in both their spiritual and political effects, in order to establish their relation to the modern encounter between Buddhism and Christianity.

It is naturally impossible to deal with all of the sociopolitical aspects involved in the encounters between Western cultures and Asia. Therefore we have limited ourselves to those aspects of political history of the nineteenth and twentieth centuries that have significance especially for interreligious encounters involving religious institutions. "Secular" and "religious" aspects of this interaction are of course not identical, but it is impossible to divide them. Understanding of other cultures and dialogue with them are also influenced by their respective historical experiences and political interests. In other words, the *textual* identification of traditions is reciprocal to the *contextual* search for identity. By *dialogue,* therefore, we mean the conscious arrangement of an interreligious communication, in which what we call *religion* appears.

We understand interreligious communication as a constantly and ever newly scrutinized "simultaneous translation," in which the formation of language and tradition is subject to constant change. We wish to show the factors through which communication among religions is influenced and under what conditions understanding or error come about in these encounters.

THE METHODOLOGY OF THIS BOOK

Our method is on the one hand *historical-descriptive*, on the other hand *comparative*. We differentiate between historical-individualistic narrative and paradigmatic comparison. The latter builds upon the former, insofar as contextual analogs can reveal generally valid or typical structures, through which the interpretation of historical events (including whether or not they are credible) becomes possible at a different level of understanding. At the same time, we must make it plain that comparisons do not reconstruct facts, but rather construct historical events from a modern perspective into contemporary levels of understanding, that is, in new contexts. In other words, we do not use a phenomenological method of comparison, which would neglect the historical context of events. Comparisons allow, on the one hand, differentiation of appearances in accordance with their specific backgrounds (the particular can only be understood by the relation of reference points to other particulars). On the other hand, comparisons make it possible to set up hypothetical analogies (about ideas and developmental processes) that can be tested in the processes of linguistic transformation. Interreligious dialogue also plays a role in such transformation processes, making understanding possible.

For this reason, in this book we work toward a historical hermeneutic that relates and explains sociohistorical processes and intellectual historical developments in relation to one another. Thus arise models of perception fields that allow us to grasp religions as a dynamic of cross-societal and religious communication.

THE PROBLEM OF "MUTUALITY"

European and American assumptions of superiority have substantially shaped and misguided the Western world's view of Asia's Buddhist cultures. Hegel's historical philosophy is a good example of this: Europe, founded on the absolute religion of human reason, can study the *first steps* of spiritual development in India and East Asia as *relics of the past*, having itself already reached a higher stage of religious evolution.

It took the sense of helplessness created as bourgeois culture collapsed in the wake of the First World War to drive Western intellectuals into spiritual exile in Asia, projecting on that culture their own hopes and wishes. An example of this is Hermann Hesse's *Siddhartha* (1922), which influenced an entire generation. Carl Gustav Jung turned Hegel's judgment of Asian religions on its head. Jung found in India's archetypical consciousness a wholeness that the West, with its one-sided rationalism and individualism, appeared to have lost. Still, Jung was not prepared to consider the realities of historical and contemporary India, or to confront its outstanding personalities. Therefore, up until World War II the Western view of Asia (including Buddhism) remained a sweeping projection of European wishes and intellectual historical shortcomings.[1]

This ambivalence in ideology is mirrored in the history of European research. German research has concentrated especially on the texts of Pali-Buddhism, for the most part rationalistically interpreted,[2] and has set this rationalism in contrast to a Christian theology regarded as irrational. The Belgian-French school of Buddhology, on the contrary, has attempted to maintain ideological neutrality; the Catholic scholars (such as Étienne Lamotte, 1903-83) have kept Christian beliefs and academic interest in Buddhism separate from each other. The Leningrad school, above all Theodor Stcherbatsky (1866-1942), linked itself to the Marxist interest in Buddhist "materialism." Stcherbatsky concentrated on the dialectic and logic of Buddhists and left the mystical, transrational, and magical-occult elements out of consideration. Edward Conze (1904-79) in England studied Mahayana as an authentic tradition in its own right, and achieved a breakthrough in Anglo-American discussion. The rationalistic prejudice in favor of Theravada was thus overcome above all through his studies of the Prajnaparamita literature with its *sunyata* philosophy. Conze and Suzuki Daisetsu (1870-1966), the eminent conveyor of Zen Buddhism to the West, became the strongest defenders of the mystical and transrational dimension in Mahayana Buddhism. Conze decisively influenced more recent Buddhology in the United States, which today is marked by scholars who often convert to Buddhism themselves (Richard Robinson, Jeffrey Hopkins, Robert Thurman, Luis Gomez, Francis Cook, Rita Gross). This tendency shows that textual studies no longer only follow the Western academic standards of the nineteenth century. Some of these scholars have undertaken an education in the traditions modeled much more after that of the Asian, especially the Tibetan schools, an approach that has also precipitated them into a new conceptual education.

---

[1] See W. Halbfass, *Indien und Europa* (Basel/Stuttgart: Schwabe, 1981). On the problem of the Other as mirror image and projection of one's own subjectivity and interests, through which the Other is not completely differentiated from the self, see M. Theunissen, *Der Andere: Studien zur Sozialontologie der Gegenwart* (Berlin, 1965); B. Waldenfels, *Der Stachel des Fremden* (Frankfurt, 1990).

[2] With the notable exception of Friedrich Heiler (1892-1967) and Rudolf Otto (1869-1937). Heiler (*Die buddhistische Versenkung*, 1918) regarded transrational meditation experience as the core of Buddhism, while Otto in several works emphasized the moment of contact with the "holy" or "numinous" in Buddhism. Max Müller's (1823-1900) editions of Buddhist Sanskrit texts in England in the late nineteenth century at first had less influence on the German philosophical-theological discussion.

Conze searched for parallels to Christianity and found them, stimulated by Suzuki Daisetsu, among the gnostics and mystics. Conze's students among the American Buddhologists still understand the Christian-Buddhist dialogue largely from this perspective. Starting from Conze's recognition of Mahayana's significance, Umehara Takeshi has broadened the discussion in Japan, leading it away from the narrow path of rationalism by awakening interest in Mikkyo, in relation to Japanese Tantrayana or Shingon.

On the Asian side, the historically conditioned problems of understanding are complex. Only one aspect of this, although certainly a significant one, is the fact that an imperialist West, with its military force and missionary aggression in Buddhist lands, provoked an anti-Western movement. This reaction has taken the form (especially in Sri Lanka) of a nationalist-Buddhist emancipation movement. Still, this emancipation movement affects both sides in a much more fundamental way than can be explained by nation-state or religio-nationalist thought. In our study we would like to contribute a more nuanced picture of the meeting between different cultures. To do this, we must lay bare the roots of a determined structure of legitimation, that is, the historical and spiritual origin of the religions concerned. Buddhism and Christianity have common roots in the unique experiences of their founders, through which it became apparent to each man that he was more than what his everyday perceptions taught him.

Both religions attest that a new life potential can be discerned in the actual followers of the religion's founder, which the world has adapted, and will continue to adapt. Buddhism and Christianity are, however, different in their respective tales of origin, idioms, political developments, and philosophical approaches. There can hardly be a sharper contrast than that between the suffering Christ on the cross and the smiling Buddha seated in the lotus position. But what is the significance of that for us today? Perhaps it has to do with the differing spheres of experience that each man had to integrate in his teaching.

The difficulty of mutual understanding in an encounter between religions already arises in the use of different languages, as well as different mythological and historical assumptions. These assumptions have also promoted specific developments within their respective traditions, by which in both religions formerly separate confessional practices have later been fused with each other.[3] Upon closer examination, one can see that the developments within each religion follow a certain inner logic. These developments have not produced a true history of ideas, but they can be seen in their social-historical sphere of operation as ideas and symbols. Comparative methods must take these systematic connections into account.

---

[3] While there are clear structural and thematic differences in the encounter between religions, depending on whether Theravada or one of the different forms of Mahayana is involved, this is hardly the case with the Christian confessions. In the encounter with Buddhism, the basic premises and specific issues can barely or at least not primarily be arranged according to Catholic or Protestant modes of thought. Much more, they bear the stamp of the individual, regional, and political experiences of particular experiences. The Orthodox churches do not yet play a role in dialogue with Buddhism.

THE STRUCTURE OF THE BOOK

In this book we investigate the history of the meeting of Buddhism and Christianity, arranging our findings by land and region. By using this approach we can only show the fundamentals of this complex history. We do not wish to reduce the history of these encounters to a pure history of ideas but to work out the specific social and political components in the definition of religions and their interaction. The basis for success or failure of interreligious communication depends on these factors, as we will show.

It would be impossible to deal with all countries or be exhaustive, so we have selected cases that serve as good examples. We begin with India, the homeland of Buddhism. Although Buddhism almost completely vanished from India for centuries, it had an essential impact on the religious culture of post-Buddhist Hinduism. Of particular contemporary significance, through Ambedkar's contemporary Neo-Buddhist movement as well as through the presence of Tibetan exiles, a unique situation for dialogue has arisen in India. The mostly Buddhist Tibetans who have taken refuge in India are inclined toward ecumenism within Buddhism and are also open to interreligious contacts.

The history of Sri Lanka shows with particular clarity the political implications of religious encounters in South Asia, along with the difficulties of dialogue. With this example, though, we will also show how fruitful dialogue can be when these obstacles are recognized and credible people fearlessly promote mutual understanding.

The lack of data for Southeast Asia is regrettable. Because of the political situation in Vietnam, Cambodia, and Laos, the encounter between Buddhists and Christians there is scarcely documented, except in the case of the politically engaged Buddhists gathered around Thich Nhat Hanh in Vietnam. So it is not yet possible to draw a comprehensive picture of historical encounters between the two religions in this region.

The situation is different in the countries that practice Mahayana Buddhism from those that follow Theravada. Here we limit ourselves to the contrasting history of religious encounter in China and Japan, because the relationship between state and *samgha* as well as experiences with Western-Christian colonialism were different in each land.[4] Unlike China, Buddhism in Japan divided itself

---

[4] We will not deal with Korea because of limited space, although it is an important country for interreligious encounter. One can see this in the Korean liberation theology of Minjung and also in the feminist-interreligious beginning made by Chung Hyun Kyung (*Schamanin im Bauch—Christin im Kopf: Frauen Asiens im Aufbruch* [Stuttgart: Kreuz, 1992]). For Minjung, see Ahn Byung-Mu, *Draußen vor dem Tor. Kirche und Minjung in Korea*, ed. W. Glüer (Göttingen: Vandenhoeck & Ruprecht, 1986); compare to this J. Moltmann, ed., *Minjung. Theologie des Volkes Gottes in Südkorea* (Neukirchen, 1984); and A. Hoffmann-Richter, *Ahn Byung-Mu als Minjung-Theologe* (Gütersloh: Gütersloher Verlagshaus, 1990). We hope to have the opportunity to discuss the history of dialogue in Korea in a later publication.

into strongly differentiated schools or sects. Of these, practitioners especially of Zen and Pure Land have been more inclined to enter into dialogue with Christianity than with each other. In other words, in Japan there is not yet an intra-Buddhist ecumenism. The opening of Japan to Western technology and culture, including religion, since the Meiji reform (1868) is the basis for a unique dialogue situation.

Germany is our main example for Europe, although people in other European lands such as England, France, Russia, Italy, and Hungary have also been fascinated by Buddhism and its philological and academic development, constituting in part a longer tradition that is at least as significant as that in Germany.[5] We have chosen Germany, however, because nowhere else has Christian, especially ecclesiastical, interest in Buddhism been so marked, a situation that has influenced the general intellectual and philosophical discussion of Buddhism in that country.

The United States of America is currently the most dynamic region for academic-intellectual encounter between Buddhism and Christianity. With the foundation of the Society for Buddhist-Christian Studies (1987), dialogue has been institutionalized at a high level. The reasons for this lie in America's own religious history and also in the present structure of its university system.

This work is itself the result of encounters that go back many years, and we owe thanks to countless friends and partners in dialogue on several continents. Above all, we thank Hans Küng, who suggested the project, made our collaboration possible, and who in the course of the years has repeatedly encouraged us with pointers and insights from his own work on interreligious dialogue. Karl-Heinz Pohl of Trier and Michael Pye of Marburg have read through the chapters on China and Japan and made useful suggestions. Perry Schmidt-Leukel of Glasgow worked through almost the entire manuscript and contributed important suggestions and corrections. All errors of course remain the responsibility of the authors. Michaela Perkounigg, Henrike Sievert, and Myong-Hee Kim, all of Munich, helped with the organization of material and corrected the text. Without their help the book would only have been brought to completion with great difficulty. We thank the foundation Weltethos for its generous assistance in publishing the German edition and in translating this book into English.

We hope that his book will encourage others to face the hurdles that stand in the way of understanding other cultures. May it contribute to peace among the religions of the world.

---

[5] Henri de Lubac has presented an overview of this history in *La rencontre du bouddhisme et de l'occident* (Paris: Aubier, 1952), esp. 151 ff. For Hungary, one should mention the important Tibetologist Csoma de Körös (1784-1842).

1

India

Interreligious dialogue in India is especially concerned with the encounter between Christians and exiled Tibetan Buddhists. Their suffering in a foreign land has created a unique situation for formal conversation, based on totally different premises than the dialogue between Christians and Buddhists that is typical in postcolonial lands. This case shows how necessary dialogue becomes in light of the political situation and economic problems. Widespread fears will be set aside, and an encounter between people on both sides of traditional religious roles and identities is coming. Here too, however, we can assess both Christian and Buddhist reluctance to engage in interreligious dialogue. In the opinion of its opponents, such a dialogue (1) would lead to cultural infiltration by foreign ideas, (2) would place the exclusivity of their own position in question, and thus create a crisis in identity, and (3) would undermine the legitimacy of religious power structures. Finally, they argue that human life span is at best sufficient to study the details of only a single religion.

The situation shows that dialogue in India can contribute to the democratization of religious institutions. A look at Ambedkar's Neo-Buddhists reveals yet another totally different dimension: religion (and conversion) can be used as a means to exert political pressure, to obtain the emancipation of the oppressed. Here dialogue takes a very different form from learned academic disputes about God and/or nirvana. In this chapter we describe the sort of dialogue situations that best exemplify the many-sided relationships between Buddhists and Christians in India and illustrate the whole breadth of interreligious encounter there. The potential of dialogue in India lies above all in its contribution to the social emancipation of the groups taking part.

HISTORICAL BACKGROUND

HELLENISM AND CENTRAL ASIA

There has been an exchange between the Mediterranean world and northwestern India ever since Alexander the Great and his army reached the Indus Valley in 326 B.C.E. Possibly the West has received more from Asia in this exchange than it has given—not just spices and manufactured goods, but also ideas.[1] Gandhara art as well as the Buddhist text *Milindapanha* bear witness to a spiritual exchange. Contained in this text are the questions the Greek-Bactrian king Milinda (Menandros) asked the Buddhist monk Nagasena, as well as the Buddhist answers to his fundamental questions about life.[2] In the Hellenistic period and also the later Roman Empire there was at times very considerable knowledge of India. The description of India by Megasthenes,[3] a man who spent time at the court of Chandragupta (c. 322-298 B.C.E.), the founder of the Mauryan dynasty and grandfather of the Buddhist ruler Asoka (ruled 268-39 B.C.E.), was for centuries a main source for Hellenistic knowledge of India. Indian philosophy and religion were known at least in Alexandria, the greatest center of knowledge, including early Christian theology, in the Hellenistic world. Clement of Alexandria mentions the Buddha in his writings, marveling at the philosophical depth and ascetic rigor of Buddhist monks.[4] Possibly there was even a Buddhist group in Alexandria itself. How deeply Buddhism influenced early Christianity in the first and second centuries of the common era is a matter of debate.[5] It is probable, though, that there was indeed a reciprocal influence between the two religions. Besides this, there were already Christian communities in northwest India by c. 200 C.E., and it is probable that the Christians had encounters with the Buddhist world there. At the least, the organization of religious orders, the rosary used by Christians at prayer, and other aspects of Christian monasticism are presumably of Buddhist origin. Granted, our evidence about such influences and possible exchanges is scant. The Hellenistic period did not achieve a true dialogue between Buddhism and Christianity but only had contact at the level of sporadic encounters.

Christianity already began to spread eastward in the first two centuries after its foundation, long before the mission to the Germanic peoples began. In the

---

[1] H. de Lubac, *La rencontre du bouddhisme et de l'occident* (Paris: Aubier, 1952), 9.

[2] There are two recent German translations: Nyanatiloka, *Milindapanha: Die Fragen des Königs Milinda,* new edition by Nyanaponika (Interlaken: Ansata, 1985): J. Mehlig, *Weisheit des alten Indien,* vol. 2, *Buddhistische Texte* (Leipzig/Weimar: G. Kiepenheuer, 1987), 336-439.

[3] Megasthenes (c. 350-290 B.C.E.) was the ambassador of Seleukos I to India and author of a "history of India." Seleukos I Nikator (358-281 B.C.E.) was one of the successors of Alexander the Great and founder of an Asian kingdom. See F. Jacoby, ed., *Fragment der griechischen Historiker* (Berlin, 1923–), vol. 3, C 715.

[4] Clement of Alexandria, *Stromateis* I, 71,6: "Among the Indians some follow the instructions of the Buddha, whom they have honored as a God (*hos theon*) because of his unusual holiness (*hyperbole semnotes*)."

[5] Recently Zacharias Thundy has studied again the possible Buddhist origin of nativity stories, many of Jesus' parables, the miracle tales, the motif of the harrowing of hell, and so on (in development of the rather skeptical studies of this issue by Richard Garbe in 1914). See Z. P. Thundy, *Buddha and Christ. Nativity Stories and Indian Traditions* (Leiden: E. J. Brill, 1993), esp. 147ff. R. C. Amore also argues for the significance of Buddhist influence on early Christianity in *Two Masters—One Message* (Nashville, Tenn.: Abingdon, 1978). Against this view, N. Klatt regards the influence as limited in his *Literarkritische Beiträge zum Problem christlich-buddhistischer Parallelen* (Cologne: E. J. Brill, 1982).

course of this expansion to the East it came into contact with Buddhism, which at about the same time had begun its expansion from India to the north (Central Asia) and northeast (China). Since the third century B.C.E. it had spread to the south (Sri Lanka) and the southeast (Southeast Asia). As is still the case today, the religions at that time already encountered one another through a process of economic and cultural exchanges. This situation came to pass through the discovery of new trade routes, which transformed cultures, originally distinct from one another, into world cultures that are identifiable by the process of amalgamation they underwent. Central Asia, above all the Persian, Syrian, Sogdian, Turkish, and Uighar enclaves along the Silk Road, were already important centers for Buddhist-Christian contact in the third and fourth centuries C.E. Manichaean missions were active in Buddhist India and Central Asia in c. 240/242 C.E.; gnostic influence in the Indian-Buddhist realm is also evident in many cases.[6] Also, documents from Turfan and Tunhuang (in the western part of modern China) prove the reciprocal penetration of religions that are elsewhere known to have been clearly demarcated from one another, especially in eastern and western Turkestan.[7]

Already in this period the relationship between the two religions was marked by two tendencies, which we will encounter again and again in the historical record, and which are still characteristic: on the one hand, adaptation to the point of partial fusion; on the other hand, demarcation and polemic. Our question must be: What can we learn from this historical situation that would be useful for the current encounter of the two religions, in Europe as elsewhere?

When the eastern Syrian (Nestorian) monk Alopen reached Changan-an (the modern Xian in central China) in the year 635, the acculturation of Nestorian Christians into the Chinese-Buddhist mental world had already made great progress. In contrast, though, the Syrian, Persian, and Sogdian Christian communities in central Asia emphasized the differences between themselves and Buddhists or Manichaeans. They stressed the contrast between Christian belief in creation and the Buddhist view of constantly forming and dissolving elements of existence *(skandhas)*. These Christians also emphasized the difference between Christian teaching about the resurrection of the dead and the Buddhist goal of transforming consciousness into Buddha-nature. By these arguments the Christians apparently wanted to prevent the spread of docetist teaching, in other words, to prevent the view that the bodily life of Christ or any other human being is unimportant or only apparently real. Nevertheless, even here there were considerable reciprocal influences in thought and art, which can so far be identified only approximately. Above all, Turkish-Christian texts show this tendency toward fusion: their representation of Christ as son of heaven, king, and doctor are reminiscent of both Central Asian and Buddhist traditions. As is well known, both Buddhists and Christians perceive their founder as a physician, in both the

---

[6] H.-J. Klimkeit, "Buddha als Vater," in *Fernöstliche Weisheit und christlicher Glaube*, ed. H. Waldenfels and T. Immoos (Mainz: Grünewald, 1985), 258f.

[7] See E. Zürcher, *The Buddhist Conquest of China*, 2 vols. (Leiden, 1959); K. K. S. Ch'en, *Buddhism in China. A Historical Survey* (Princeton, N.J.: Princeton University Press, 1964).

literal and spiritual sense.[8] In other texts, too, Central Asian–Turkish Christians fall back on Buddhist ideas.

In India itself, a centuries-long process assimilated important elements of Buddhism into Hinduism. Thus, although the Muslim destruction of the Buddhist cloister universities of Nalanda and Vikramasila in the twelfth or thirteenth century put the final seal on the end of Buddhism in India, Buddhist influence remained. In the south Asian subcontinent after that, Buddhist-Christian encounters were limited to the Buddhist Himalayan regions and Tibet. These areas had imported Mahayana-tantric Buddhism in the seventh century and had raised it to the level of state religion. Over the centuries Tibet has preserved Indian-Buddhist culture through careful translations and faithful maintenance of monastic discipline and ritual.[9]

TIBET IN THE EIGHTEENTH AND NINETEENTH CENTURIES

As early as the thirteenth century, the Flemish Franciscan William of Rubrück (c. 1215-c. 1270) crossed the mountains of Karakorum and reached the Central Asian city of Urumtschi; William's report on his mission included an account of Mongolian-Tibetan Buddhism. In 1624 the Portuguese Jesuit Antonio de Andrade (1580-1634) became the first European to reach Tibet itself. In 1625 he founded a pioneering missionary outpost there, in Tsaparang.[10] Italian missionaries in the eighteenth century followed in his footsteps, establishing missions in Lhasa (the Capuchins in 1707-11, 1716-33, and 1741-45, and the Jesuits in 1716-21). These missionaries built a church, studied Tibetan, and even wrote pro-Christian pamphlets in Tibetan. The effect of this activity was slight, however, and the undertaking was soon abandoned. Except for the reports that these missionaries to Tibet sent back to Europe, their activities there have left hardly a trace. The more Tibet closed itself off from the outside world in the nineteenth century, the less likely interreligious encounter became. Travelers and traders who came to Tibet from British India did not bother with religious and cultural exchange; at the

---

[8] See H.-J. Klimkeit, "Gottes-und Selbsterfahrung in der gnostisch-buddhistischen Religionsbegegnung Zentralasiens," *Zeitschrift für Religions–und Geistesgeschichte (ZRGG)* 35 (1983): 3, 236ff.; Klimkeit, "Das Kreuzessymbol in der zentralasiatischen Religionsbegegnung," in *Leben und Tod in den Religionen. Symbol und Wirklichkeit* (Darmstadt: Wissenschaftliche Buchgesellschaft, 1980), 61ff.; Klimkeit, *Die Begegnung von Christentum, Gnosis und Buddhismus an der Seidenstraße* (Rheinisch-Westfälische Akademie der Wissenschaften. Vorträge G 283) (Opladen: Westdeutscher Verlag, 1986), esp. 15-20.

[9] For a very short overview of this history, see R. and M. von Brück, *Die Welt des tibetischen Buddhismus* (Munich: Kösel, 1996).

[10] Thanks to P. Schmidt-Leukel for this reference. See H. Herbst, ed., *Der Bericht des Franziskaners W. v. Rubrück* (Leipzig, 1925); F. Risch, ed., *W. v. Rubrücks Reise zu den Mongolen* (Leipzig, 1934); Christopher Dawson, ed., *Mission to Asia* (Toronto: University of Toronto Press, 1980); A. de Andrade, *Novo Descobrimento do Gram Cathayo, ou Reinos de Tibet* (Lisbon, 1626); M. v. Brück, *Religion und Politik im Tibetischen Buddhismus* (Munich: Kösel, 1999).

time, the Tibetan government forbade possible cultural influences from abroad. Until the 1930s the government regarded with suspicion Tibetans who sent their children to northern Indian (missionary) schools. The power of the monastic authorities permeated the government and cabinet *(kashag)*, and blocked every exposure to ideas from either West or East. It is in this context that one must understand the murder of the modernist Tsarong on the steps of the Potala during the reign of the thirteenth Dalai Lama (1876-1933), as well as the Panchen Lama's flight from Tibet in 1923. Although the thirteenth Dalai Lama was able to strengthen his central authority and advocated a moderate opening up to the modern world, he was unable to do so because of opposition from the nobility and the monastic hierarchy. Until the Chinese occupation of Tibet in 1950, the clergy was thoroughly conservative.

Only in the west Tibetan cultural region, especially the British-Indian influenced provinces of Ladakh and Lahul, could the Herrnhut missionaries found a few communities without arousing the opposition of the Buddhist monasteries. The Christians founded communities especially in Leh and Sheh. These foundations still exist today and, with Kalatse on the upper Indus, constitute the main centers of Christianity in the region. Lacking converts, though, Christianity in Lahul has practically died out. In the eastern Himalayas (Darjeeling, Kalimpong, Sikkim) there is a Catholic diocese. The current Catholic and Protestant missions in this region operate schools, which are also attended by Buddhist students.

THE TIBETAN EXILES IN INDIA

China's annexation of Tibet in 1949 and the ensuing national and cultural genocide of its people led in 1959 to a Tibetan uprising, bloodily suppressed by the Chinese army. In 1960, as a result, about eighty thousand refugees fled to India. There, under the leadership of the XIV Dalai Lama (b. 1935), they have settled in several large settlements and villages. These settlements are spread over several Indian provinces (especially Uttar Pradesh, Himachal Pradesh, Orissa, Arunachal Pradesh, and the largest settlement, Karnataka). This new environment created new possibilities for Buddhist-Christian contact. Many Tibetans attended missionary schools in Moussorie and Darjeeling, where compulsory participation in prayers, Bible readings, and so on, spread a negative image of Christianity. Already in the 1960s Tibetan refugees protested against Christian efforts to convert them. A letter of 23 January 1962 from Triyana Vardhana Vilura (the Buddhist center in Kalimpong) to *The International Buddhist News Forum* in Rangoon, Burma, complained that the Plymouth Brethren misused their mission school, employing it to convert Tibetan children to Christianity and spread anti-Buddhist propaganda. In the letter, Bhikku Khantipalo and Sister Amita Nisatta ask that the activities of this "narrowminded and insignificant Protestant sect, that thinks it has the only path to salvation" finally be halted.[11]

---

[11] "Tibetan Refugees and Christian Missionaries," *The International Buddhist News Forum* 2/4 (April 1962), 16 (Rangoon: The World Fellowship of Buddhists).

Today the Tibetan exiles have gained greater self-confidence, a necessary prerequisite to their current readiness to engage in dialogue. This self-confidence is based on the high prestige the fourteenth Dalai Lama (winner of the Nobel Peace Prize in 1989) enjoys throughout the world, the economic success of Tibetans in India and Nepal, and the foundation of countless Tibetan Dharma centers in Europe, America, Australia, and Japan.

However, in India as a whole the conditions for religious dialogue have become ever more difficult over the past few years. The reasons for this include political tensions among Hindus, Muslims, and Christians aroused by political-nationalist agitation for a Hindu state *(Hindu Rashtra)*; Islamic fundamentalism in the Middle East and Pakistan, which is also trying to gain influence in India; Muslim infiltration into the Buddhist part of Kashmir (Ladakh); and aggressive missionary activity by American evangelical groups working hand in hand with the economic interests of American companies. In light of these and other problems, the little group of "neutral" Tibetan Buddhists is acquiring an ever more important position as catalyst. This tendency has crystallized in the person and moral authority of the Dalai Lama. It is especially effective because none of the rival religions or cultural-social systems has a history of power and delimitation comparable to that enjoyed by Tibetan Buddhism.

INTERRELIGIOUS MONASTIC EXCHANGE PROGRAMS

It was not this political-social background but a newly awakened Western interest in Buddhist meditation and spirituality that led in the 1960s to first contacts between (Tibetan) Buddhists and (Catholic) Christians at the monastic level. On the Christian side, the Second Vatican Council's *Declaration on the Relationship of the Church to Non-Christian Religions* created a new openness toward interreligious contact.[12] This was manifested especially in the experimental attempts by French, Belgian, and English Benedictines such as Henri Le Saux (1910-73), Jules Monchanin (1895-1957), and Bede Griffiths (1906-93) since the 1940s to live a Christian life in the style of the Hindu monastic tradition *(samnyasa)*.

In the same spirit the American Trappist monk and poet Thomas Merton (1915-68) undertook a journey to India in 1968. His goal was to become acquainted firsthand with the Asian spirituality he had already encountered through readings on Zen Buddhism. He wrote in his *Asian Journal*:

I need not add that I think we have now reached a stage of (long-overdue) religious maturity at which it may be possible for someone to remain perfectly faithful to a Christian and Western monastic commitment, and yet to learn in depth from, say, a Buddhist or Hindu discipline and experience.[13]

---

[12] See J. Zehner, *Der notwendige Dialog: Die Weltreligionen in katholischer und evangelischer Sicht* (Gütersloh: Gütersloher Verlagshaus, 1992).

[13] Thomas Merton, *The Asian Journal of Thomas Merton* (New York: New Directions, 1970), 313.

Merton spent several days in dialogue with Tibetan monks in Dharmsala, where he also met the XIV Dalai Lama. As Merton wrote, he felt that this direct face-to-face exchange could lead to a much deeper dialogue experience than is possible when contact is limited to the study of books or other writings. In a letter to a friend, he commented on his experiences:

> I have been dealing with Buddhists mostly. . . . It is invaluable to have direct contact with people who have really put in a lifetime of hard work in training their minds and liberating themselves from passion and illusion.[14]

On the Buddhist side, the fourteenth Dalai Lama himself is currently the foremost figure in seeking and promoting interreligious dialogue. He has presented his motives and views on this subject in the course of numerous trips to North America and Europe.[15] In 1963 he wrote in his memoirs:

> Concord between religions is no utopia. It is possible, and under present world conditions it is extraordinarily important. . . . With all possible emphasis, let me stress how urgently necessary a seamless unity between all religions is. For this reason, followers of every religion should know something about other religions.[16]

To contribute to this sort of mutual understanding, in 1981 the North American Board for East-West Dialogue (NABEWD) agreed with the Dalai Lama to form a Buddhist-Christian exchange program for monks and nuns. Since that time the program has been renewed several times, most recently in August 1993 in the course of the conference marking the centenary of the World Parliament of Religions in Chicago.

The Tibetan Buddhist monk Kunchok Sithar has written about his experiences visiting Benedictine monasteries in 1982. In his view, Christian nuns are more open to Buddhism than monks. He continued:

> I have discovered that the two monastic traditions have a great deal to learn from and share with each other. Both forms of life are founded upon prayer, meditation, work, and spiritual studies and readings. The main difference is that Tibetan monasteries place greater stress on religious studies and ritual, while Benedictine monasteries lay more weight on a life of labor. . . . The harmony between religions, as encouraged by the holy father John Paul II in agreement with his holiness the Dalai Lama is not a goal that can be reached immediately. But the day will come when the love and healing life preached by the Buddha and Christ will unite the world in a common effort to save humanity from senseless destruction and to lead to the light in which we all believe.[17]

---

[14] Ibid., 324.

[15] See Dalai Lama, *Logik der Liebe* (Munich: Dianus Trikont, 1986).

[16] Dalai Lama, *Mein Leben und mein Volk: Die Tragödie Tibets* (Munich: Droemer-Knaur, 1962; TB edition 1982, 189).

[17] *The Tibetan Review* (1982): 6-7.

This set the tone for future dialogue that the Dalai Lama had already proposed several times, including on the occasion of his visit to the pope in Rome and that he hoped would result in growing harmony between the religions through dialogue; dialogue to encourage the two religions to learn from each other, while maintaining their individuality; and making the goal of dialogue a common engagement to work for freedom and understanding between peoples. Kunchok Sithar's remark is particularly interesting—that humans would be led through active love to a light "in which we all believe." The community of religions is more than a common social and political engagement.

It is not surprising that the final reality should be described with the symbol of *light*. Buddhism uses this metaphor in many liturgies to describe what Christians call "God," and Christian language is also full of metaphors of light. In Tibetan Buddhism the expression "clear light" (Tibetan *'od gsal*) is applied to illustrate the deepest level of the spiritual continuum, in other words, the last reality that can be reached through awakening or enlightenment *(buddhatva)*. Common to both religions is the association of light with illumination and warmth, repeatedly connected to love and transformation in the human sphere.

This exchange program led to public appearances of Buddhist monks in Christian communities in the United States. Criticism of the dialogue program has not been wanting from Christian fundamentalists. A famous and much-quoted example is an evangelical visitor's provocation, when he asked the Buddhist guests in a reproachful voice whether they had met "the Lord Jesus Christ, king of heaven and earth." The reply was: "No, we haven't met the Lord Jesus Christ, but we enjoy the company of many of his followers, whom we love very much." This anecdote makes plain the essence of this basic condition for dialogue: community of religions is based on a sense of human community.

LUTHERAN EXCHANGE AND DIALOGUE PROGRAMS IN INDIA

In the fall of 1981 the faculty of the Gurukul Lutheran Theological College in Madras proposed a Buddhist-Christian dialogue program to the United Evangelical Lutheran Churches of India (UELCI). The proposal stated that such a program is overdue for a number of reasons: no Christian institution in India had yet taken up Buddhist-Christian dialogue; Lutheran theology had until then contributed little to interreligious dialogue; the social significance of Buddhism's growing influence in India (the Neo-Buddhist movement and the presence of Tibetan refugees) needed to be investigated; both Buddhism and Christianity are minority religions in India, and followers of both should exchange information about their parallel experiences; and dialogue would offer the opportunity for each side to bear witness to its religion in a comprehensive and practical fashion, without arousing enmity between India's religions by carrying out missionary work. According to this plan academic dialogue should be extended to include visiting exchange programs, joint meditation courses, joint work on social projects, and long-term studies of the changes in Buddhist theology in the face of the changed circumstances of Tibetans in India—the issue of acculturation.

This program was organized for the period 1982 until early 1985 and jointly financed by the Lutheran Churches of India and the Council for Religious and Cultural Affairs of H.H. the Dalai Lama. Other Christian confessions and institutions (Church of South India, Roman Catholic Church, Syrian Orthodox Church) later joined. Additional private grants financed separate projects.

The dialogues were less oriented toward classic theological or philosophical disputations than toward examining contemporary social, political, and cultural issues of interest to both partners. So, for example, the program sponsored the following events:

• a lecture series on perceptions of God in Christianity, Buddhism, and Hinduism given by a Lutheran instructor from Gurukul College in Sera monastery near Bylakuppe in Karnataka (October 1981);

• a seminar, "The Armaments Race, Power, and the Peace of Christ," in Madras, with the participation of Buddhist abbot Lati Rinpoche (November 1981);

• a conference, "Understanding God: A Comparative Analysis of Theological Paradigms," in Tibet House, New Delhi, at which Buddhists, Hindus, and Christians joined in discussion (July 1982);

• a dialogue conference in the Buddhist School of Dialectics, Dharmsala, about the Buddhist-Christian spirituality of confession (July 1982);

• a dialogue conference in honor of Luther's 500th birthday on the subject "Luther and Monasticism in India" (August 1983);[18]

• a Christian-Buddhist exchange program including the visit of nine Lutheran pastors in India to Buddhist monasteries and centers in North India, and the reciprocal visit of six Buddhist lamas to south Indian Christian centers (August-October 1983);

• a dialogue conference on the theme "Emerging Consciousness for a New Humankind" with the participation of the Dalai Lama, Christian bishops of all major confessions, Indian officials, and representatives of the international diplomatic corps (Madras, 3-8 January 1985).[19]

Coordinated with this dialogue program the Catholic Shantivanam Ashram (in the state of Tamil Nadu) held dialogue conferences annually between 1981 and 1986. These meetings, attended by Hindus and Buddhists as well as Christians, combined lectures, conversations, meditation, and above all, communal life, for several days. Bede Griffiths, OSB, directed these dialogues. The conference themes ranged from "New Paradigms in the Sciences and the Mystical Traditions of Asia" to the nature of consciousness and the final realities, to application of Gandhi's theories in contemporary economic and political circumstances.

In order to describe and evaluate the results of the whole program while doing justice to its individual elements, it is necessary to give a brief summary of the results of each part.

---

[18] M. v. Brück, ed., *Authentic Consciousness—Hope for the Future* (Madras: Gurukul Publications, 1985).

[19] M. v. Brück, *Emerging Consciousness for a New Humankind* (Bangalore: Asian Trading Corporation, 1985).

DIALOGUES IN SERA MONASTERY (OCTOBER 1981)

About seven hundred Tibetan monks attended the afternoon lectures, while in the mornings fifteen Buddhist geshes (a Tibetan equivalent to a doctorate in philosophy) held discussions with two Christian theologians. The Tibetan Buddhists' total ignorance of Hindu or Christian theology was noteworthy. For example, the monk who translated had studied at a missionary school and was under the impression that Christianity must be a religion that advocates force, since the students there had sung the hymn "Onward Christian Soldiers" every day.

The geshes were very willing to listen, especially to expositions of Christian eschatology. Still, though, the linguistic and hermeneutic barriers appeared to be nearly insurmountable.

The conversations centered on two themes: Buddhists asked what *motivation for social engagement* lies behind the impressive efforts Christians have made in education and health concerns, and whether it would be possible to reach a similar efficiency working with Buddhist principles; and the *eschatological question*: If perfection is only possible in heaven, then how can perfected people practice practical love and healing transformation toward all creation without the possibility of reincarnation?

Four issues, which call for wider discussion, aroused particularly lively interest:

1. The Buddhists rejected the Christian search for salvation of the soul as anthropocentric.

2. For the Buddhists involved in the discussions, reincarnation is so self-evident that they acknowledge doubt in it only with a smile, while considering "salvation in heaven" to be a form of salvatory egoism.

3. The uniqueness of an enlightened person, his or her "individuality," is not lost in a consciousness continuum, as many Tibetan Buddhists understand it. Rather, one is not dissolved completely into the indistinguishable. In *nirvana*, too, there is a subtle polarity of distinctiveness within non-distinctiveness.

4. World peace can be brought about through intensive prayer (understood as a positive radiation of subtle energy). Today, however, humanity's spiritual quality is sinking more and more. Because of this, the future of humanity will be dark, unless the various religions take heed of their responsibility to educate others in this regard with united strength.

"THE ARMAMENTS RACE, POWER, AND THE PEACE OF CHRIST" SEMINAR (MADRAS 1981)

The differing modes of thought of Buddhists on one side and Hindus, Christians, Muslims, and Marxists on the other side throw an indicative light on the uniqueness of Buddhism. In this case, Hindu, Christian, and Marxist participants analyzed political and economic structures without their religious framework playing an important role. The Buddhist contributors, on the contrary, considered above all the motivational structure lying at the base of every possible action. Unexpectedly, some Muslims took part in the communal prayers for peace that formed part of the program; only evangelical Christian groups declined to participate. All participants, including Muslims and Sikhs, advocated educational work on eliminating the divisions between religions.

Dialogue about Concepts of God and Theological Paradigms in Religions (Tibet House, New Delhi, 1982)

This dialogue led to the first serious disagreement in the series; for example, early Buddhists described the Buddha as *bhagavan*, that is, as a personification of the spiritual absolute. In addition, Buddhism does not speak of creation, but of *karma*, the net of interrelationships. Consideration of the two symbolic concepts, for example how they related to one another, would be a useful task for future dialogue. Third, Tibetan Buddhists refer to the ultimate reality sometimes as emptiness *(sunyata)*, sometimes as ultimate godhood, for example, as clear light *('od gsal)*. So they certainly do not use only negative metaphors. The Buddha nature (whatever it may be called) must be regarded as the origin of all things.

It became clear that the Christian Trinity and the Buddhist concept of *trikaya* are models resting on specific structures of how to think of unity within difference. They cannot and ought not be hastily reduced to bare principles. Overall, one should beware of a "potpourri of religions," because this would be fatal to intellectual clarity. But one must also beware of any sort of absolutism, since the reality is a "mesh of multiplicity and unity."

What caused the stir at this meeting, typically, was the political implications of the dialogue. Representatives of the Bharatiya Janata Party (BJP) and the Rashtriya Svayam Sevak Sangh (RSS), both of which stand for restoration of conservative Hinduism, saw in the dialogue a weakening of the purity of Indian-Hindu culture, which in their opinion must be revitalized for India to gain greatness and influence again as a Hindu state. The West, they argued, is stamped with imperialism, as witnessed by the fact that it brought forth a Hitler, and this imperialism is a direct result of Christian demands for absoluteness. Therefore the Christians no longer have the right to speak of dialogue.

The conference ended in subjective and dubiously historical polemics against Christianity. The Buddhist participants did not take part in this. Instead, they emphasized even more the necessity for Buddhist-Christian dialogue, a process that could also be significant as an example to other religions.

Encounter Programs in Buddhist Monasteries

Even though these programs remained marginal to the overall situation in India, we nevertheless wish to give a detailed description of the conversations and interviews that took place in the course of the exchanges. Through this, we wish to convey as vital an impression as possible of the personal level of dialogue and opportunities for exchange between Christians and Buddhists in modern India.[20]

Twelve Indian Lutheran pastors lived for several weeks in Buddhist monasteries, coming in contact there with Buddhist nuns, monks, and laypeople. Eighteen monasteries in Lahul, Zanskar, and Ladakh were included in the discussions, and there were more than 60 individual discussions and interviews. Besides

---

[20] A detailed report is printed in M. v. Brück, *Christian-Buddhist Exchange Program* (Madras: Gurukul Lutheran Theological College, 1983), 3.

this, the exchange program made it possible for the Christian participants to get an impression of the current state of Buddhism in these regions. The discussions did not follow prearranged themes or lists of questions, since this format was not familiar to the Buddhist participants. Instead, conversations followed the interests of the Buddhists taking part in each case. The major issues were the purpose and possibilities of Buddhist-Christian dialogue, the central theological questions, and especially the social and political significance of dialogue for the participants.

Introduction by the Dalai Lama

The starting point and high point of this program was a two-hour conference with the Dalai Lama in Dharmsala on 21 July 1982. He called special attention to the great significance of the *contemplative dimension* in Buddhist-Christian dialogue and suggested that this should provide the parameters for intellectual and theological exchange. From this arises the question of rationalism in Buddhist-Christian dialogue, for example, the whole question of the relationship between reason and meditation. The Dalai Lama asserted at length that the Buddhist experience is by no means antirational; logical thought can completely grasp the principle of *sunyata* (emptiness). In the Madhyamika school,[21] at least, logical thought has more than a preparatory function. The idea of *sunyata* must of course be deepened by meditation. By this means, though, meditative clarity and concentration is a precondition for the untroubled functioning of logical thought processes. In the normal course of events, the difference between meditation and thought is a matter of differing temperaments, but at a fundamental level the two always coexist. One should also interpret the plurality of religions in this way— the different religions correspond to different human temperaments. The theme of dialogue should therefore not focus on this supposed divide but rather on the strengthening of morality, the welfare of all, universal brotherhood, and above all, peace among humankind.

The Christian partners in this discussion asked about ways of understanding truth. The Dalai Lama replied that Buddhists do not recognize a revealed truth but rather aim toward a deepened insight into reality through reason and meditation. Under these conditions truth will be self-evident.

The Dalai Lama pointed to Christian teaching on creation as a fundamental difference between Buddhism and Christianity, since Buddhists, unlike Christians, are convinced that everything comes to pass through *karma*. In a certain sense, he added, perhaps *sunyata* can be regarded as a "creator." After all, "everything comes from *sunyata*, and everything is *sunya*, but naturally this is something completely different from the anthropomorphically conceived creator God of Christianity, who acts through his *will*." The Christian participants agreed to this, but with the suggestion of further investigation into what Christian creation

---

[21] Madhyamika ("the middle way," systematized by Nagarjuna in the second century C.E.) is one of the great philosophical schools of Mahayana; it is, however, not representative of all Buddhist traditions.

theology really entails. They suggested that this is indeed a case of analogous concepts. One must ask whether a deeper understanding might lie behind the analogy, an understanding that could perhaps center on the idea of *creativity* in Buddhist-Christian dialogue. The Dalai Lama agreed to this and advocated studies of the question.

But from what *particulars* of the two religions might each side learn? Both sides agreed that Buddhists could above all learn from Christians in the field of *organized love of neighbor* and social engagement, while Christianity could best learn from Buddhism in the area of *meditation*.

Theological comparisons of concepts or symbols such as the Trinity and *trikaya* should, in the Dalai Lama's opinion, be encouraged, especially to deepen understanding of each dialogue partner's own religion. This should not, however, either cover up or emphasize the difference between religions, if dialogue is to surmount the real barriers between religions. For this, spiritual practices are much more important than theological study—"If one lives what he believes, he has everything."

Unlike the Christian participants, most of the Buddhists disagreed with the premise that dialogue would bring about a change in their own theological perceptions. As the Buddhists emphasized, we are not wiser than the Buddha and cannot add to his teachings. The Christian argument focused on the historicity of knowledge, that is, that truth itself does not change, but its comprehension and transmission do. The Buddhists were able to agree to this formulation. The question remained open, however, on how, precisely, the criteria for truth can be defined. It was still more difficult to frame an answer to the question of whether there are criteria that transcend the individual traditions of Buddhism and Christianity, and that could make possible a general methodology for interreligious hermeneutics.

This is particularly well illustrated in the case of Christ himself. For Buddhists, such as the Dalai Lama, Christ can be understood without difficulty as a bodhisattva. This, however, does not automatically mean that Buddhists can integrate Christ's teaching into their own without further ado. Indeed, the Dalai Lama does not believe that the Buddha can play an important role in Christianity, or Christ in Buddhism. At the most one can perhaps adopt some of each figure's specific teachings, after careful examination, and only if they can really be integrated into the religious system. In another context the Dalai Lama expressed his caution about claiming Christ for Buddhism thus:

> From the Buddhist point of view, Jesus could easily have been an incarnation of Avalokitesvara, the bodhisattva of compassion. but we do not formally recognize him as such, because it could irritate other people. Some might protest that we were trying to steal Christ for Buddhism.[22]

---

[22] Dalai Lama, interview in "Tushita," New Delhi, 1977, cited by Doboom Tulku Rinpoche, "Buddhism and Buddhist Monasticism," in *Authentic Consciousness,* ed. M. v. Brück, 86.

The problem here is similar to that brought up by Karl Rahner's notion of an "anonymous Christ": despite the commitment not to act out of self-interest in this dialogue, the problem of making a theological classification of other religions remains to be overcome.

Most important, as the Dalai Lama added, is that the partners in this dialogue should first of all get to know one another much more thoroughly, especially each other's practices, as a means to break down the many biases that stand between the two religions.

Confession of Sin

The conference held at the Buddhist School of Dialectics in July 1982 in Dharamsala continued the dialogue with the theme of confession. Interestingly, the discussion of Christian understanding of sin and confession aroused intense interest among the approximately two hundred younger Buddhist monks who attended. Some monks explained it thus: The difference between claims and reality is usually not treated thematically in their monastic life, which they consider to be a point of tension. At least for those high up in the hierarchy, it is only with difficulty possible to speak of or assume concrete failings to reach the ideal of completion in Mahayana Buddhism. The Christian understanding of sin, they believe, could perhaps help them to find more tranquil honesty.

The Character of the Dialogue

The Venerable Losang Nyima, the director of the Buddhist monastic school, conceded that it is possible to carry out historical-critical studies of their own texts following the methods of textual criticism, but that this is not the Buddhist approach to learning. What is old is in itself authentic and therefore true. The question of whether this means of studying is sufficient was not deemed important. Nevertheless, younger monks, although they often spoke about the need to guard the "core learning," asserted that much "unnecessary ballast" should be thrown out. Up till now there have only been vague thoughts of the criteria for choosing between what is central and what is peripheral, and indeed there is not yet a plausible methodology for dealing with this issue.

This is also the sense in which Tsering Zangduk (Lochen) Rinpoche argued, the head of the Gelukpa monasteries of Lahul, Spiti, and Zanskar, who at that time was only twenty-three years old. He had studied at the Buddhist School of Dialectics and had gotten to know Christianity superficially through European and American converts to Buddhism who were his fellow students. Even this minimal knowledge of Christianity had already awakened his interest in interreligious dialogue. He had concluded that education is the key to successful dialogue. This would also enable each religion to see its own history in relative terms, which could be a liberating development. This would further make possible the loosening of false connections, which is the prerequisite for all progress in Buddhist praxis. Therefore, interreligious dialogue could itself be a direct and integral component of Buddhist praxis. He sees the foundation and sense of dialogue, however, above all in ethical objectives that must be the concern of all religions in common, concerning themselves with the well-being of all living things. One must wait and see whether the dialogue might change each partner's own religion. Accommodation with modernism (also made inevitable in Zanskar because of the construction of a road) will come inevitably through the upcoming generation.

A certain *tension between the generations* was noticeable in the dialogue at a visit to the Central Institute of Buddhist Studies in Choglamsar/Leh (Ladakh). Laypeople and monks, boys and girls, study the Tibetan language, politics, economics, history, Sanskrit, Pali, art, astrology, and philosophy here. Since Hindus and Sikhs are also active as teachers, the students get to know other religions at least casually. They would welcome Christian teachers, but even at this school hardly anyone has heard of religious dialogue. Older lamas, who send young monks from their monasteries to study at this central school, are mostly skeptical of these "new subjects," because they have imparted to the monks knowledge detrimental to the traditional monastic life. When students with such an education return to their old monasteries, tensions are inevitable, and it can even come to open controversies about religious-political questions and the concerns of monastic organization. Even obedience to elders could be put in doubt. Some lamas see with concern that dialogue with Christianity may accelerate this process of emancipation. The invasion of tourists from "Christian lands" is often an irritation because of their disrespectful behavior in monasteries. On this account the dialogue would be under considerable strain at least in the regions involved.

The highly educated abbots of various monasteries (Phuktal, Karcha, Thonde, Atitsi) were against interreligious dialogue especially because of the fear that it would distract from spiritual praxis. Their view is that the religions are so different from each other that the practitioners can learn almost nothing from other traditions. Besides, a whole lifetime is not sufficient to study and practice Buddhism fully, not even to speak of other religions. What then is the use of accumulating a superficial knowledge of other religions, when, because of available time, one cannot even hope to practice them? There would be a danger of confusion. Therefore one must choose a single religion and then live in accordance with it. On the further question of how a person can choose a religion without knowing the alternatives, the abbot of Karcha explained: "Buddhism is true, because it offers a complete and practicable teaching."

In other words, the dialogue groups often met with a sort of Buddhist exclusivity, which, to be sure, was mostly expressed with friendliness. As the abbot of Atitsi in Ladakh said, he was not in a position to say whether a non-Buddhist could attain enlightenment, and therefore salvation—but he did not close out the possibility. This exclusive demeanor could also take the form of actively rejecting conversation with Christians when questions and arguments focused on the central points of Buddhist teaching. This was especially true in the isolated villages and monasteries of the Himalayan valleys. This stemmed from a certain mistrust, which appeared when the motives behind interreligious dialogue were not expressed clearly enough. The lamas living in relative isolation saw the sense behind religious dialogue less clearly than those who live in the vicinity of Muslims in Kashmir. Appreciation of their own situation and existential suffering proved to be the decisive preconditions behind the Buddhist partners' readiness to engage in dialogue. Less frequently, Buddhists declined dialogue because of hierarchical interests. As the abbot of Thonde explained, dialogue is sinful, because the salvation of the world depends solely on the lamas and the state of the currently existing monastic order. He could not understand the Dalai Lama's interest in interreligious dialogue but naturally bowed to authority.

The themes of creation, grace, the existence of a personal God, reincarnation, Christ's sacrificial death, prayer, and meditation were central to the conversations. There was almost always agreement that the contemporary situation not only necessitates new concepts, but also demands new methods for solving theological questions. What that means in a concrete sense, however, remained mostly unclear. So, for example, at the Buddhist School of Dialectics, conversation centered on the issue of causality, a concept fundamental to Buddhism. The dialogue on this subject proved to be difficult, even impossible, because there are no corresponding categories in the Christian tradition to compare to a hierarchy of causal relations. Therefore the Christian visitors could hardly reach understanding of the issues. The Christian Indians, trained in European philosophy, could barely follow the structure of Buddhist argumentation, not to speak of translating these arguments into their own south Indian (dravidian) concepts. Since in this case also the hermeneutic problem was addressed but could not be resolved only by allusion, the dialogue group of pastors recommended the creation of study circles for the study of one another's holy writings. By this means the partners hoped to come to a thorough understanding of each other's hermeneutical methods.

Heresy

The problem of heresy was an important theme of the conversations. While this concept has laid a heavy imprint on Christian history and has also encumbered the practice of Christianity, in Buddhism the idea exists only peripherally. Buddhism does indeed recognize different schools of both philosophy and practice, which have fought bitterly with each other. Only relatively seldom, though, has anyone disputed the essence of the Buddha-Being.[23] Especially in Mahayana and Vajrayana one speaks of different steps in the Buddha's teaching. These steps have been used as a transmitted means *(upaya)* to teach the truth about human existence *(dharma)* in a way accommodated to the capacity of humans of a given time to understand.[24] This theory allows syntheses and presents the possibility of unity in the fact of difference. It is also well known that within Buddhism there have been and still are politically motivated tensions, and also power struggles between the different schools—even in Tibetan history. Nevertheless, the *upaya* argument could still be fruitful in creating future ecumenism. At all events, it is

---

[23] There have at times been attacks on Buddhist opponents of particular teachings. For example, in the Ceylonese chronicle *Mahavamsa*, in the *Lotus Sutra* (ch. 2, according to which the haughty opponents of the Lotus tradition forsake the Buddha, while the sutra argues that there is only a *single* vehicle of the Lotus sutra), and especially with the prophetic reformer Nichiren (1222-82) in Japan.

[24] See ch. 6 below; see also M. Pye, *Skilful Means: A Concept in Mahayana Buddhism* (London: Duckworth, 1978).

of more practical help (as in the case of interreligious prayer) than the Christian ecumenical attempt to win intellectual consensus as a condition for a practical religious community (for example, a common interpretation of the eucharist). Especially on this point the dialogue with Buddhist partners stimulated intra-Christian ecumenical discussion.

Prayer

The theme of prayer was already at the center of the theological dialogue, because the participants took part in the daily hour-long prayers of their Buddhist partners. In Tibetan Buddhism there are several forms of prayer: petitionary, intercessory, penitential, and so on. In all forms of prayer, though, altruistic motives are expressed. As Ling Rinpoche (1902-84), the elder tutor of the Dalai Lama and head of the Gelukpa school explained, only an unripe person expresses prayer wishes for himself. The ripe, mature human being should only pray for the well-being of others. Also, in Tibetan Buddhism prayer is regarded as a direct conversation with the absolute spirit, which can either manifest itself to human needs spiritually or corporeally (in other words, in a "godhood" to whom one prays). The Christian partners were impressed by the intensity of prayer they encountered and were of the opinion that in Christian communal and liturgical prayer there is not enough emphasis on the elements of concentration and silence. Some wanted to apply this deep impression right away to their own communal practice. (This was actually carried out in the case of a south Indian village community.) The Buddhist hosts and their Christian guests agreed to pray regularly for each other.

Vicarious Suffering

Discussion about the theme of vicarious suffering sprang from consideration of a statue of Nilantha the Lokesvara, who as a bodhisattva drains a goblet filled with the poison of the world, making himself a sacrifice. Sacrifice of oneself for others and, through that, purification of one's own consciousness constitutes the Buddhist motif of offering. The suffering bound up in this, however, has never had a salvific meaning in the Christian sense, at least not in the sense of the traditional Christology of Jesus as an offering for sin, which is at any rate no longer accepted by many Christians.

Mission

The dialogues did not ignore the explosive problem of mission. Some of the Buddhist partners expressed fundamental opposition to missionizing. Others belonged to the tradition of belief that they should share their religious experience with others (a "sharing of consciousness") and held that this process of sharing is the proper term for what has, very misleadingly, been called mission. In any case, they agreed in their condemnation of proselytization, aggressive preaching, public criticism of other religions to promote one's own views, persuasion by means of material and other inducements, and several other points. *True* conversion, on the contrary, was held in respect by all partners in the dialogue. The model used by Tibetan Buddhists in the West was also acceptable and exemplary for the Christian interlocutors: the establishment of centers in which small groups seek to live an exemplary life in accordance with their teaching and invite others to join in it.

Conscience and Authority

Especially the younger generation of Tibetan exiles is beginning to rebel against traditional authorities. This same spirit is spreading among the young monks in the monasteries. Often this emancipation process is linked to feelings of guilt, since the authorities are legitimated by religious belief and tradition. Few, however, have put themselves in opposition to the traditional sense of Buddhist identity. The dilemma is this: Younger monks appeal ever more to personal conscience and want this to be accepted as more important than the monastic rule in decision-making. They argue that, at the least, the rule must be newly interpreted (as has also occurred in the past). Such representations are, to monastic authorities, a case of clear rebellion. The "anti-authority" monks, though, argue that Buddhism is not in fact a religion but rather a philosophy of life that frees the individual for autonomous decision-making. In any case, the *samgha* and its discipline play a pedagogical role. Emancipation from traditionally recognized authorities is, in the meantime, a worldwide phenomenon. Therefore there is considerable interest in discussing such questions with Christians—more interest than in considering theories about God, the Buddha, or *nirvana*.

Politics and Religion

A further urgent theme was the question of the proper relation between politics and religion—that is, between power and spirituality. Thanks to economic modernization and nationalist fragmentation, political enlightenment and its corollary of readiness for action has also come to be of central importance for Buddhists in India. (Some examples of the situation are civil war in the Punjab and Islamic fanaticism in Kashmir, in which the Buddhists in Ladakh are involved.) In such a situation, preserving one's own identity becomes a problem. Dialogue pales to insignificance in light of this task. It may be, though, that the process of dialogue could be useful in reaching this goal. Conservative lamas oppose any political engagement, because it is detrimental to the practice of meditation. However, some, such as the former king of Zangla and some lamas of the monastery of Rangdum, encourage monks to engage in politics. They argue that this is useful because monks are relatively well-educated and besides are dedicated to the ideal of selflessness. Monastic meditation culminates in the conquest of anger, rage, and jealousy; today more than ever, these qualities are necessary in successful daily politics. Buddhists could certainly learn much from Christians about how to make a practical link between politics and religion. Above all, younger Buddhist monks must for this reason be educated for dialogue with Christians.

Conclusions

As a result of this dialogue program we wish to emphasize the following points:

1. The contemplative dimension is the indispensable foundation for theological discussion in Buddhist-Christian dialogue.

2. The universal brotherhood of humanity, our common social and ethical responsibility, and engagement for peace have proven to be the main goals of dialogue in India.

3. The problem of whether and how much the various schools of thought differ from each other (including how much they ought to or may differ) in the dialogue is itself an obstacle to Buddhist-Christian dialogue.

4. Views of humanity, the concept of sin, and the problem of freedom have proven to be important themes in which the partners can help one another to gain "calm frankness" among themselves and toward the dialogue partners.

5. Neither the Buddhist nor the Christian partners were completely informed about the religion of the other. Therefore the preconditions were lacking to carry out the dialogue in the way many had hoped. Thus, everything possible must be done to deepen an unprejudiced knowledge of each other's religion, so that mistrust can be broken down and meetings can come about on the basis of religion without aggression.

6. There is not a single Buddhism any more than there is a single Christianity. The dialogue partners always find themselves in a concrete historical situation, one that is constitutive for the character of the dialogue.

7. On the Buddhist side, there is opposition to dialogue, especially within the hierarchy; this opposition has its roots especially in desire to maintain the status quo. Some Buddhist partners explained that religion is so intimate and holy a matter that one ought not destroy it by talking too much about it in dialogue.

8. In the dialogue interchanges it was significant that there was little interest in discussing classical theological conflicts (such as creation-*karma*, grace-liberation of self). Instead, people wanted to speak about current issues and problems, above all, (a) the problem of secularization, including the alienation of youth from religion, which is also gradually becoming a problem in Tibetan Buddhism; (b) Buddhist and Christian views on the proper position of women, especially the role of women in these religions; and (c) the possibility of dismantling mistaken judgments about the other religion that are based on ignorance.

LUTHER AND MONASTICISM IN INDIA

Naturally, the Reformation was an incident that took place within the context of European history. But are there things that other religions can learn from its course? In Madras on the occasion of Martin Luther's 500th birthday in 1983, the starting point for discussion was the question of whether a critical examination of religious life in Hinduism, Buddhism, and Christianity, all more or less stamped with the monastic ideal, can contribute to the search for "authentic consciousness" in the present. The theological and structural reforms of the Lutheran

Reformation present themselves as points of crystallization. It is significant that a shift in paradigm runs through the different and historically separate religious traditions. This shift is apparently true of several religions, and therefore is of importance in the analysis of how historical development occurs. Important questions included: the relationship between religious experience and social structure; the influence of monasticism in changing cultures and societies; the significance of language (and new translations of classical religious texts) for change in social and political structures; the relationship between spiritual freedom and inevitable institutionalization; and the significance of interreligious radical communities for the future of religions as well as for the social and political emancipation process.

Those who attended the conference appealed for plurality in lifestyle, both intra- and interreligious, since there are many ways to pursue an authentic religious life. "Open monasticism," practiced in Indian ashrams for millennia, was particularly recommended as a possible way to build communities in modern societies; as a foundation for interreligious meetings on prayer, meditation, and reflection; and as an alternative to social structures that have been destroyed (such as the collapse of the extended family and the nuclear family in industrial societies).

Under the theme of "parity before God and the difference between monks and laypeople," participants lamented clericalization in all religions. Buddhism, like other monastic religions, has a problem with this issue, not dissimilar to Luther's criticism of the Catholic church of his time. Buddhist reform movements similar to the Reformation in terms of their social basis (for example, the Pure Land Buddhism of Shinran in thirteenth-century Japan) have taken place in all religions. Working through this process in each tradition, along with examining the controversies raised by such reforms, would be a worthwhile task for dialogue. Through this the possibilities for action in modern conditions could be made known.

The Buddhist lama Doboom Tulku Rinpoche pointed out, in this regard, that the expression *samgha* in the Buddhist tradition can be used in two different ways:

> The Sanskrit expression that is most commonly translated as "monasticism" is *samgha*. But this expression has two meanings in the texts. The first is the community of ordained monks and nuns (*bhiksu* and *bhiksuni*). This is designated as the *conventual samgha*. That means, though, that the true *samgha* encompasses all human beings who have set themselves upon the path of discernment of higher reality. These people are the *real samgha*. It is difficult to say, though, who has insight and who has not. Therefore there are some who wear a robe as outward symbol of the *samgha*. In the *real samgha* there is no difference between monks and laics.[25]

This interpretation of the Buddhist *samgha* makes the ears prick. It can be compared to the Lutheran concept of the priesthood of all believers, which simi-

---

[25] Doboom Tulku, "Buddhism and Buddhist Monasticism," in *Authentic Consciousness*, ed. M. v. Brück, 88.

larly is measured solely on a spiritual criterion—that of belief. In this way a democratization of religious institutions could be reached. This could also be a task for dialogue, because (a) the problem of tension between spirit and institution is common to both Buddhism and Christianity. Both can learn from their own and each other's history; (b) "universal grace" and "universal Buddha nature" stand in opposition to "specific calling" and "individual realization" in both traditions. Both religions have developed specific models for thinking of this polarity. The current historical situation, however, requires new modes of expression, which must be found in interreligious dialogue; (c) the concept of the *samgha* can, in Mahayana Buddhism, be interpreted in a way similar to Luther's "priesthood of all believers"—including the historic failure to carry it out in practice. This interpretation must be made fruitful in the necessary activation of the laity in *both* religions; and (d) socially liberating or indeed revolutionary tendencies can be found in both Buddhist and Christian monasticism. This is linked to the freedom that is possible through spiritual experience. It is not a coincidence that monks and nuns have often inspired liberation-theologically oriented communities. Therefore, the relationship between contemplation and action can reach a new and practice-oriented definition in an interreligious partnership.

Is There an Eastern Mysticism?

In conjunction with the encounter and exchange programs, the Catholic Dharmaram College in Bangalore, the Gurukul Lutheran Theological College in Madras, and the Shantivanam Ashram (Tamil Nadu) organized several conferences on the theme: "Is there an Eastern mysticism?" in which Buddhist-Christian engagement played a central role.

Mysticism

The works of the Catholic theologian Thomas Kochumuttom demonstrate particularly well the current state of discussion in India on the subject of the differences and complementarity between what both religions call mysticism.[26] He observes these differences:

1. While in Christianity "mystical experience" is usually regarded as an extraordinary gift of God that few people attain, this concept does not exist in Buddhism. Here, the human reaches the most accessible form of experience through individual efforts. This is because in Buddhism, completely unlike Christianity, the "mystical union" is necessary for salvation. Therefore it must and can be reached by everyone in the end.

2. In Buddhism, the experience of enlightenment signifies complete liberation from the entanglements of personal consciousness. The Christian, on the contrary, can never be certain of not falling from mystical experience back into a state of sin.

---

[26] T. Kochumuttom, "Buddhist-Christian Approaches to Mysticism," *Jeevadhara* 13/78 (November 1983): 402-9.

3. This difference is linked to Buddhist belief in reincarnation, through which gradual perfection is possible. Normally, the Christian only has this life as the sole chance for maturing and so is totally dependent on grace.

4. Christian experience is the experience of an inner I-You relationship. Identity symbols and metaphors of total fusion with God, although occasionally used by Christian mystics, are not to be taken literally. In Buddhism, however, one can speak neither of persons nor relationships, since *nirvana* is understood as an experience of one's own true identity.

That established, Kochumuttom proposes making associations between these differences. He argues that all the Buddhist positions are acceptable, if the Christian adds specifically Christian experience to them. So, for example, one can speak of enlightenment in a Christian sense, but only enlightenment "from" and "in" Christ.

In regard to agreements between the two systems Kochumuttom points out that both traditions emphasize the ineffable and transrational character of mystical experience. Also, the resurrection experience of Christ corresponds to the enlightenment experience of the Buddha, to the extent that both involve a total transformation of the individual. Naturally, the terms in which these experiences were expressed depended on the historical context of each, and therefore were totally different. In other words, both Christ and the Buddha transcended their own historical context, but had to make themselves comprehensible within the parameters of their own time and place.

The thesis of "completion" often put forth by Christians and repeated by Kochumuttom—that the Buddhist experience reaches its peak *through* the Christian experience—was repudiated by most of the Christian participants; for the Buddhists it is "more than they can chew." The Buddhists added that this was not their problem.

We would like to remark on this: the philosophical rationalization of mystical experience follows different paths of argument in the two religions.[27] This mirrors the methodological program of dialogue in general. As the Madhyamika philosophy of Nagarjuna already described it in the second century C.E., one cannot pursue analytical philosophy on the basis of statements of contradiction and then apply this method to an "absolute" (such as *nirvana* or *sunyata*).

Perception of the Absolute

Madhyamika accepts neither revelation nor logic as a source for knowledge of the absolute, but only *prajna* (wisdom, insight, direct experience).

The question for the early church was, How can the perception that Jesus the Christ and the Spirit are present be rationally expressed? Alongside *theologia negativa*, theologians in the Scholastic period especially developed *analogy* as a method for speaking about God, to the point of the so-called proof of God. Kant rejected this proof and showed that theoretical reason cannot lie at the foundation

---

[27] See M. v. Brück, "Buddhist *sunyata* and the Christian Concept of God," *Jeevadhara* 13/78 (November 1983): 385-402.

of a concept of God. With that, Kant in Europe reached a similar conclusion to that at which Nagarjuna in India had arrived fifteen centuries before him. There remains the method of *theologia negativa*. This also proceeds from experience of epiphany. This way inquires further into the reason behind manifestations of God and explains this reason as non-epiphany. One can say that the means of experience *(pramana)* is here always a closing procedure *(anumana)*, that at any rate leads to a negative expression. The Christian *theologia negativa* does not deal with a negation of closure procedure, but with the negation of experience as the content of closure. So this concept of God too depends on perception, although the experience is negated. In other words, a definite dualism is repeatedly implied—God is indeed "beyond" every verbal expression, but this is not "other-worldliness" in the sense of "this worldly and beyond." Of course, Dionysius and others did not claim that one could make a positive statement about God through simple negation of a conscious experience analogous to the figure. But the Christian *theologia negativa* has thematized less than did Nagarjuna the inadequacy of thought on the basis of the dualistic implications of this thought process.

Because in Christianity perception of God is transmitted by means of experience of God in Christ, perception of God means participation in Christ. Knowledge is here the existential connection of love: reciprocal "indwelling." It is a process of becoming one *(henothenai)*, in which there are steps that correspond to the levels of reality (*absolute* Father—*incarnate* Son—*indwelling* Spirit). In Buddhism the structural parallel is the theory of the three "bodies of the Buddha" *(kaya)*.

Karma *and Creation*

The contrast between these two concepts is often named as the fundamental difference between Christianity and Buddhism. But is this really true? *Karma* indicates a web of potentials bound together without beginning; it stands for the interdependent causation of all occurrences on all levels of reality. *Karma* is, however, limited by the concepts of *buddhatva* (Buddha-ness), *tathata* (thusness), or *sunyata* (emptiness). Thus it has a boundary that it has made for itself. Buddhism does not pose the question of what the reason for or cause of *karma* is. The web hangs, as it were, on itself. In dialogue, Christians must now answer the question, How can Christian creation doctrine be newly interpreted in light of the concept of *karma*?[28]

EMERGING CONSCIOUSNESS FOR A NEW HUMANKIND

A conference on this theme (Madras, January 1985) put the Buddhist-Christian dialogue in the context of newly developing universalist paradigms in religions, sciences, and political-economic structures. Thanks to the presence of the Dalai Lama and his lectures, meditations, and discussions, the question of

---

[28] See below (Consciousness—*karma* and creation).

developing consciousness and consciousness research was a central issue of exchange, since he is particularly interested in this issue. The arenas of changed conditions of consciousness have been exactly described and systematically discussed in Buddhism for millennia, but there is nothing comparable in Christianity. Here another field for Christian-Buddhist dialogue in conjunction with interdisciplinary consciousness research presents itself.

The Buddhist philosophy of consciousness is not limited to human life but sees awareness present in different forms in all regions of reality. Buddhists, Christians, Muslims, Sikhs, and Hindus have now sought to make fruitful a universal or ecological paradigm for understanding this Asian tradition. The concept of the unity of reality held by scientists (for example in the concept of fields in physics), the indivisibility of observer and object being observed in experimental science, the interrelationship of processes that can be described through systems theories, and more, refer to a world view that converges with certain Buddhist traditions.

At this conference participants discussed the implications of such questions on a new paradigm of education, for a holistic understanding of technological complexes and political as well as economic structures. It became clear that a new consciousness appears especially in a number of global movements currently being experienced by almost all religions and cultures: the meeting of Eastern and Western religions; the search for deeper consciousness being opened up through meditation; the environmental movement; and the feminist movement. Therefore it is necessary to see Buddhist-Christian dialogue within the parameters of these different movements. We can assert firmly that this conference had a number of results.

It was possible to agree unanimously upon and publish a statement composed jointly by Muslims, Christians, Buddhists, Hindus, Zoroastrians, and Sikhs. This presented in concrete terms both the spiritual and the socio-political dimensions of interreligious dialogue and set forth suitable recommendations.[29]

The very fact that it was possible for several days for representatives of different religions to live, pray, meditate, and work together was pointed to as an expression of a new consciousness that already exists.

The participants formulated as a central insight the belief that the greatest problem of our age is the "unjust, sinful, and suffering-filled situation" of a great part of humanity and joined in urging all religions to change this situation. Interreligious dialogue must have as a primary goal the need to safeguard this responsibility for social change.

There was discussion of the necessity to formulate and practice an integrated spirituality, a *social yoga*, that must be complementary to the path of self-realization. The Buddhist *karuna* (a healing turn toward all beings), the Muslim concept of the *'umma* (brotherhood of all believers), the ideal of *ahimsa* (nonviolence), which has its origins in Jainism and was interpreted politically by Gandhi,

---

[29] Printed in M. v. Brück, ed., *Dialog der Religionen* (Munich: Goldmann, 1987), 139ff.

and the Christian commandment to love of neighbor—all of these could serve as motivational models.

The congress emphasized the right of each religion "to share its insights with others and to exhort others to a true conversion as a return to the source of the good, beautiful, and true, to which all traditions bear witness." The participants objected to any sort of manipulation, including psychological and/or material pressure or persuasion, as part of "conversion," regarding even the use of the word *conversion* under these conditions as a misuse of the term. It is also important in interreligious dialogue to analyze the danger of manipulation by mass media with respect to religious concepts, a danger that must be confronted jointly.

It was stressed that, above all, interreligious dialogue must make visible the mechanisms of bondage that have been caused by the goals of the "technological system." Contemporary tasks are so complex that they can only be overcome by religions working together. The multiplicity of methods and traditions can be helpful in this way, if people learn openness toward other cultures through dialogue based on partnership. Intellectual keenness as well as human courage are necessary for this. This will help promote a new lifestyle, which can be expressed in traditional terms among various religions as a call to holiness.

Finally, the congress recommended the construction of a permanent "interreligious community for study and spiritual encounter" in order to remove the feeling of elitism from the dialogue and to supply continuity. However, hope for continuity has not yet been fulfilled; the Buddhist-Christian dialogue in India fell almost entirely silent in the late 1980s and has not yet been resumed.

THE BEGINNING OF DIALOGUE BETWEEN CHRISTIANS AND OUTCASTES IN AMBEDKAR'S NEO-BUDDHIST MOVEMENT

Gandhi recognized the problem of the caste system in India. He believed, however, that it was possible to eradicate the most oppressive part of the system, untouchability, through a reform of Hinduism while still retaining the caste system. For him, untouchability was a cancerous growth within Hinduism that had nothing in common with the reasonable caste divisions of the Vedic tradition. Similarly, Bhimrao Ramji Ambedkar (1891-1956)[30] in the 1920s still believed that a reform of Hinduism in regard to the caste question was possible. However, disappointment at the lack of results of all such reform efforts led Ambedkar to change his views and turned him into a determined opponent of Gandhi. Ambedkar

---

[30] A. K. Vakil, *Gandhi-Ambedkar Dispute* (Delhi, 1991); K. N. Kadam, *Dr. Babasaheb Ambedkar and the Significance of His Movement* (Bombay, 1988); W. N. Kuber, *B. R. Ambedkar* (Delhi, 1978); K. S. Bharati, *Foundations of Ambedkar's Thought* (New Delhi, 1990); M. L. Shahara, *Dr. Bhim Rao Ambedkar: His Life and Works* (New Delhi, 1988); S. R. Baksh, *B. R. Ambedkar, Statesman and Constitutionalist* (Delhi, 1992). The most recent and illuminating study of Ambedkar is the dissertation by S. Jürgens, *B. R. Ambedkar—Religionsphilosophie eines Unberührbaren* (Frankfurt a. M./Bern: Lang, 1994).

was himself an outcaste from Maharashtra. He had thus experienced the devaluing and self-esteem destroying ideology of caste and untouchability personally. Therefore, he wanted to give the outcastes back their self-esteem, presenting himself as a model of human dignity for them to emulate. In this resolve he came near to the Tamil reformer Periyar (E. V. Ramaswamy Naicker, 1879-1974). Neither divided the problem of untouchability from the more general caste system, upon which the entire Hindu social structure stands and falls. Therefore the abolition of untouchability for them was necessarily bound up with the renunciation of Hinduism. From 1925 on, Periyar in Tamil Nadu led an anti-theistic, indeed antireligious campaign for the freedom and equality of the outcastes, which attacked and weakened the whole temple cult and social position of the Brahmans. Unlike Ambedkar, though, Periyar never formally abandoned Hinduism, choosing instead to operate as a critical voice within the structure of the religion.

Ambedkar, though, announced in 1935 at the famous Yeola conference that he would not die as a Hindu. Twice he nearly converted to Christianity but backed away at the end. For eight years he was engaged in dialogue with Bishop Pickett and others in Bombay.[31] What finally made him decide against Christianity was the fact that the churches in India showed little sense of social responsibility; the alliance that Christianity, too, often made with the caste system; and the problem that Christian converts were alienated from their families and caste-community, and even from their entire Indian identity. Besides these, Ambedkar feared that the conversion of hundreds of thousands of outcastes to Christianity would strengthen the political position of the English colonial power. In his famous speech "Annihilation of Castes" of 1936 Ambedkar developed three criteria by which religion must be evaluated, since religion is by no means only a private matter but constitutes and legitimates the morality of a society. Therefore, he said, religion must agree with the judgment of reason; establish the principles of freedom, equality, and brotherhood, and put them into practice; and proclaim war against poverty and oppression.

After years of study Ambedkar finally came to the decision that Buddhism best agrees with these criteria. He asserted that, where Christianity embodied similar principles, it was historically dependent and a copy of the Buddhist original! Ambedkar decided in favor of Buddhism above all for three reasons: (1) the stress on *prajna* (wisdom) appeared to him to present intellectual sincerity and a general educational ideal; (2) *karuna* (healing transformation and compassion) forms a stark contrast to the demeanor demanded of untouchables; and (3) *samatha* (mental equilibrium) can and must have a social component and will become the foundation for equality between all human beings. Buddhism, in his view, has always preserved the freedom to reject dogmas and rituals that were not founded on rational examination and practical experience. It can also always integrate local traditions into the greater system, which is of great importance for most Indians.

---

[31] B. A. M. Paradkar, "The Religious Quest of Ambedkar," in *Ambedkar and the Neo-Buddhist Movement*, ed. T. S. Wilkinson and M. M. Thomas (Madras: Christian Literature Society [CLS], 1972), 52ff.

Ambedkar himself drew historical parallels to Asoka's introduction of Buddhism:[32] through Asoka, Buddhism was able to gain a socially emancipatory power thanks to its rejection of the caste system, and the same benefit would come from the conversion of the untouchables in the twentieth century.

Ambedkar gave a new interpretation of three aspects of Buddhism to fit with his goals. In this he could call upon the national-emancipation and social-ethical goals in the new interpretation of Buddhism developed by Anagarika Dharmapala in Sri Lanka and the Mahabodhi society he founded, which was already known to intellectual circles in India. Ambedkar made personal contact with these interpretations in the course of his trips to Colombo and Burma in the 1950s. These three new interpretations are:

1. Ambedkar interprets the central Buddhist concept of *samatha* in the sense of social equality. In its original sense, however, it means the equilibrium of consciousness in the face of pleasant and unpleasant sensations, through which concentration on a single point becomes possible, as a monk practices in meditation.

2. Ambedkar believes that self-denial for the rich can be good. This, however, does not mean that one may preach a socially undifferentiated ideal of poverty. Ambedkar created this social-psychological concept from the spiritual-psychological analysis of *trsna* (thirst for experiences) of classical Buddhism.

3. Ambedkar understands the *samgha* not primarily as monastic community. For him, every socially engaged and selflessly active Buddhist is a *bhiksu* (begging monk). Therefore, Ambedkar binds those entering the Buddhist community with twenty-two additional vows, above all concerned with social ethics. Laypeople, too, can undergo ordination in this way.[33]

This reinterpretation also explains Ambedkar's engagement with Marxism, the economic theory of which he wanted to unite with Buddhist ethics. However, he expressly distanced himself from the Marxist-legitimated use of force.

When Ambedkar finally converted to Buddhism in 1956, about 3.5 million untouchables followed him—about 5 percent of all outcastes, or 0.7 percent of the entire population of India. In the following years the number of Neo-Buddhists grew to about 4.5 million. The untimely death of Ambedkar is probably responsible for this relatively small number, because much of the movement was based on Ambedkar's personal prestige: he was styled guru, "savior," and even "the most important Indian since the Buddha."[34] The conversions were mostly concentrated in the state of Maharashtra, especially among the outcaste Mahars, who constitute 70 percent of the outcastes in Maharashtra.

---

[32] It is apparently due to Ambedkar's great influence in the drafting of the Indian constitution of 1950 that the *dharmacakra* symbol (the Buddhist wheel of learning) of Asoka was included in the Indian national flag. According to S. Jürgens, 31, Ambedkar wrote the constitution almost alone, and also the abolition of untouchability by India's constitutional assembly was more the work of Ambedkar than Gandhi.

[33] M. Baumann, "Neo-Buddhistische Konzeptionen in Indien und England," *ZRGG* 43/2 (1991): 104.

[34] *Dalit Voice* 2/10 (March 1983): 104.

Ambedkar wanted to compile a "Buddhist Bible" from the immense canonical literature, to change fundamentally the organization of the *samgha* in both purpose and structure, and to found a worldwide Buddhist mission. He was only able to fulfill the first of these self-imposed goals, by writing the catechetical book *The Buddha and His Dhamma*, which was published posthumously in 1957.

Except for academic study of the Neo-Buddhist movement at the Christian Institute for the Study of Religion and Society (Bangalore), until the 1980s there was hardly any dialogue between Ambedkar's Neo-Buddhists and Indian Christians. This was because the Neo-Buddhists of India still lacked a strong sense of identity and most of them have had little formal education. In addition, their leaders have feared that they will be accused of lack of patriotism by the Hindu majority if they seek an alliance with the Christians. This is because conservative Hindus still regard Christianity as foreign and Western, an attitude that has strengthened again in recent times. For their part, Christians have not forgotten that, especially in the late 1930s, Ambedkar was sympathetic to Christianity but ultimately rejected it.

Certainly, though, since 1981 the journal *Dalit Voice* has appeared in Bangalore under the direction of V. T. Rajshekar, proclaiming itself as the "voice of the oppressed minority." This journal calls for open warfare against the rule of the caste system and above all seeks to organize the untouchables along Ambedkar's spiritual path, but at the same time increasingly setting itself apart from Ambedkar's stance of nonviolence. This periodical is closely aligned to Marxist-influenced and socially engaged Christians, and it enjoys a growing influence among the urban middle class. The relation of *Dalit Voice* to Buddhist-Christian dialogue is distant when this encounter only takes place at an intellectual level. On the other hand, the relation is positive when the liberation of the untouchables becomes the central common program. Therefore, Christian Dalit theology since the late 1980s has received inspiration from both Ambedkar's ideas and *Dalit Voice*. Under the headline "Conversion to Buddhism Helps Dalits" the journal produced the following in 1982:

Bombay: The conversion of Dalits to Buddhism has blessed them with a new world of fresh air. This is particularly visible among the youth, who have completely thrown off the psychological servitude under which their fathers groaned. The Neo-Buddhist has not only given up the irrational and superstitious rites that are practiced by Hindus, but has also taken up a scientific point of view. He has foresworn the Hindu gods and thrown them into the nearest rivers and springs. Today, the followers of the Buddha have only pictures of the Buddha and Dr. Ambedkar in their houses. The Buddhist has also given up degrading forms of work, such as the transport of animal carcasses, the transmission of death announcements, the collection of fuel for kitchens and marriage festivals of the Hindus of caste, the cleaning of village streets, etc. The new generation, which has been exposed to the world of learning and knowledge, has become psychologically independent of its opponents, in both the city and the countryside. The conversion, linked as it is with intellectual training, has brought forth a class of writers, who are making a significant contribution to Marathi literature.[35]

This report presents itself as a contrast to the circumstances in Christian churches that the author described earlier.[36] There, the complaint was made that, especially in the Orthodox churches of Kerala, the Christians had by no means given up their caste privileges, and the outcastes remained untouchable after their conversion.

However, at the same time the liberating aspect of Christianity and its educational establishment were again brought strongly into prominence in the 1970s and 1980s as directly linked to independence. On the search for allies, an editorial in the *Dalit Voice* made little historical distinction between colonial power and Christianity:

[Ambedkar] lived a majority of his life in India under British rule. The English were well-intentioned rulers. They gave us not only the education that the Brahmans had kept from us, but gave us western, modern knowledge. Not only that. When it came to a struggle for freedom and leaders like Gandhi and Nehru defied the English, it was only possible because they had acquired their wisdom through that same British education, which gave them the courage to fight for freedom and brotherhood. Without British rule, which was in fact Christian rule, India would not be what it is today. And so Ambedkar too, despite his open criticism of the British government, received all his courage from the British.[37]

The current Hindu ruling class would be still more repressive than the British-Christian system was. Therefore today—unlike in Ambedkar's time—an alliance between untouchables and Christians is sought. So, for example, V. T. Rajshekar gave a speech at the Christian Conference of Asia in 1982 in which he praised the Christians for having played in important role in raising the consciousness of untouchables.[38] In this case, interreligious dialogue has totally political and social functions.

Since 1981, Bhagwan Das, one of the leading Ambedkar-Buddhists of the Asian Centre for Human Rights in New Delhi, has published the journal *Samata Sainik Sandesh* (News of the soldiers of equality). In this work both Jesus and the Buddha are claimed as proponents of an ethics based on the fundamentals of human equality. Despite this, though, until the end of the 1980s there was no formal dialogue with Christian organizations. However, in 1992 the Dalit Solidarity Program began, directed by Bhagwan Das and financed by the ecumenical assembly of the church. Its goal is to build a communications network among Buddhist, Christian, Hindu, and other Dalit groups, and through conferences to

---

[35] *Dalit Voice* 1/7 (1982), cited in the report in *Deccan Herald*, 3 November 1981.

[36] *Dalit Voice* 1/3 (November 1981).

[37] *Dalit Voice* 1/17 (June 1982).

[38] *Dalit Voice* 1/24-25 (1982): 3ff.

bring together the various stances of the Dalit movement. Christian Dalits as well as Buddhists criticize by this means discrimination against outcastes within the church as well as in other Indian religions.[39] A solidarity association, one that reaches beyond classical religious borders, is thus in the process of being created.

A further development is extremely interesting. The Buddhist society Friends of the Western Buddhist Order, founded in London in 1967 by the English Buddhist Sangharakshita (Dennis Lingwood, b. 1925),[40] is active among the Neo-Buddhists in India. There its members build schools and other educational centers, in order to spread literature, make possible deeper insight into Buddhism, and disseminate propaganda for the Neo-Buddhist movement.[41] Since 1979 the group has had its own goal in India, rejecting a rigidly tradition-bound Buddhism. Instead, it gives precedence to the individual and social elements of the Buddha's teaching over philosophical debates about different doctrines and rituals. These "missionaries" were provocative toward traditional ecclesiastical circles (and also toward conservative circles of the *samgha* in Sri Lanka and Southeast Asia). There are not yet any studies of this new phenomenon. Even the European Buddhists themselves speak little of their presence in India, not wanting to draw upon themselves the wrath of conservative Hindus. This risk is especially present because the conversion of outcastes (mostly to Islam and Christianity) has often served as a political springboard.

Now, to encourage inter-Buddhist community and solidarity, an exchange program has sprung up between Indian Neo-Buddhists and Japanese *Buraku* (a stigmatized and underprivileged sector of the population, especially in Osaka). For this purpose, in 1980 P. P. Garude, the general secretary of the Buddhist community in India, visited Japan in order to report on Ambedkar and his social interpretation of Buddhism. In 1981 two Buraku leaders returned the visit, after which several Dalit writings were translated into Japanese. In March 1982 four prominent leaders of the Dalit Panthers (Arun Kamble, Rameshchandra Parma, Bapurao Pakhinde, and Ramdan Athavle) went on a lecture tour through Japan.[42]

Also, since the end of the 1980s contacts have grown stronger between Indian representatives of a Christian Dalit liberation theology and the Neo-Buddhists following Ambedkar's tradition. Possibly this points the way toward a new form of cooperation between Christians and Buddhists that would signify a new era and level of Buddhist-Christian dialogue.

---

[39] See the report in *epd-Wochenspiegel* (Frankfurt a. M.: Evangelischer Pressedienst), no. 24 (15 June 1995), 18.

[40] Dennis Lingwood spent three years beginning in 1944 with the British army in India, Ceylon, and Singapore, and there received instruction from Buddhist teachers. After the war he stayed in India and in 1949 was ordained as a Buddhist monk under the name Sangharakshita. He joined with Ambedkar and until his death helped lead the Neo-Buddhist movement. In 1964 he returned to England.

[41] M. Baumann, 110ff.

[42] Report in *Dalit Voice* 1/9 (February 1982): 10.

CONCLUSION AND PROSPECTS

• Dialogue based on shared human experience in communal living and participation in the practice of the other religion in reciprocal partnership is fruitful and builds trust. It has not been enough, though, to create hermeneutic and theological clarity regarding each religion's different models for interpreting the world, which also influence spiritual praxis and daily life. This is because even the fundamental experiences of human society are always molded by a specific social and cultural context.

• The general goal of dialogue—that is, the common duty of the religions in peacemaking, moral renewal, and the safeguarding of ecological responsibility—meets with unconditional agreement in India.

• Subtle theological differences on individual points can hardly be made comprehensible to dialogue partners who do not have detailed understanding of the other tradition. Thus, academic dialogue is very different from the encounter situations that take place in villages, monasteries, and communities.

• The Buddhist approach of expounding theological-philosophical differences through the doctrine of *upaya* (transmitted means) can be helpful for the Buddhist-Christian encounter. According to this approach, the different doctrines espoused by religions are necessary because humans have different temperaments and find themselves in differing historical situations.

• The Buddhist partners still think for the most part within the parameters of their tradition, while the Christian partners are more ready to problematize their own tradition (and the content of their doctrine). This situation creates different psychological assumptions for Buddhists and Christians in formal conversation, which must be considered more carefully.

• The theme of mission cannot be pushed to one side of the dialogue. This problem appears to be solvable, as long as the duty to *witness* for one's religion is not understood as the need to convert others to one's own position and institution. Instead, *conversion* must be recognized as a true spiritual transformation. The proper form of witness should be discussed in dialogue with partners of other religions following the principle of equal entitlement.

• Indian Christians (and also Buddhists) often fear that dialogue will cause them to lose their own identity. As a result, dialogue efforts (especially in many Protestant churches) run up against skepticism or rejection. The dialogues in India, however, also brought about an insight for Christian pastors and priests: *all* ideas are symbolic, and as such are not absolute. This insight signifies a rejection of intellectually and institutionally amassed power, which could be perceived as a spiritual cleansing. Interreligious understanding is also evident as a *process* of common search for truth, which is politically the sine qua non for the national integration of India.

2

Sri Lanka

In this chapter we will show how the encounter of Buddhism and Christianity is encumbered by the history of colonialism. Buddhist-Christian dialogue in Sri Lanka has an eminently political character. Precolonial Ceylon was a society in which kingship was legitimated by Buddhism and the land was actually controlled in a sweeping fashion by a Buddhist monastic elite. This state was conquered by European imperialism, for which Christianity served as a new vindication for rule. Moreover, part of the native middle class, which served in the British administration, converted to Christianity. Still, the arrogant ideology of the missionaries, who dismissed Buddhism as "paganism," provoked a national Buddhist revival under Anagarika Dharmapala. The Sinhalese Buddhist revolution finally raised Buddhism to the level of a privileged religion. In postcolonial Sri Lanka there have been alliances between Buddhism and Marxism, both engaging in polemical warfare against colonialism and Christianity. Still, the quest for national identity has placed increased burdens on the minority—especially the Hindu Tamils. Although the Christian middle class is still a relatively prosperous minority, they have been on the fringe of this process of nationalization and have been forced to take the defensive. In part, the Christian demand for dialogue goes back to this loss of power. However, it is also in part an honest attempt to heal the wounds of the nation.

HISTORICAL BACKGROUND

SRI LANKA AS THE OLDEST THERAVADA LAND

Sri Lanka, formerly known as Ceylon, is one of the first regions in which the Buddha's *dharma* was preached. According to tradition, Emperor Asoka (c. 250 B.C.E.) sent his son as a missionary to the island; folk tradition even reports three visits by the historical Buddha himself.[1] Sri Lanka is still proud to be the custodian

---

[1] See K. Malalgoda, *Buddhism in Sinhalese Society, 1750-1900* (Berkeley and Los Angeles: University of California Press, 1976); W. Rahula, *History of Buddhism in Ceylon: The Anuradhapura Period*, 3d ed. (Dehiwala, 1993); R. F. Gombrich, *Buddhist Precept*

of the earliest canon of Buddhist scriptures written in Pali, and most Sinhalese are still convinced that Pali was the Buddha's own language. (In reality, the Buddha spoke the middle-Indian Magadhi dialect.) Without question, Buddhism shaped the cultural and political structure of the "golden island." Therefore the historical chronicles *(Mahavamsa* and *Dipavamsa)* quite understandably assume the principle that only a Buddhist can be king of Ceylon. Still further, all kings were accepted de facto as bodhisattvas (Buddhas in the process of becoming), which spelled for the Hindu Tamils a still more significant exclusion from power and starkly reduced their influence on Ceylonese culture. The Tamil destruction of Sinhalese culture through the southern Indian kings of the Chola dynasty in the ninth century C.E. is still a trauma in the collective consciousness of Sinhalese Buddhists, one that affects their attitude toward the Tamil minority on the island.

Samgha (the monastic order) and state have supported and legitimated each other since the time of the kings of Anuradhapura (third century B.C.E.–tenth century C.E.). It is the pride of modern Sri Lanka that it is the only Buddhist land that was able to shake off colonial rule through a successful Buddhist revolution. Sri Lanka understands itself as the strongest bulwark of Theravada Buddhism, and to the present day the Buddhist temple is the social center of the village. The monk *(bhikkhu)* in the village is for the populace the living symbol of the power of Buddhist *dharma* (Pali *dhamma*). The strength of Sinhalese Buddhism lies therefore in the heritage of the *bhikkhus* and in lay recognition of the monks' authority.

On the basis of this (mythological) history, Sri Lanka has a distinct Buddhist self-consciousness, and the contemporary orientation in terms of nationalist-Buddhist and Sinhalese-ethnocentric identity is its logical consequence. Dialogue with Christianity is marked by this. Today Sri Lanka is the most important location for interreligious dialogue in the world of Theravada Buddhism.

CEYLON UNDER COLONIAL RULE

One must, however, understand this cultural and religious self-consciousness against the backdrop of the humiliation Ceylon suffered first under Portuguese-Catholic rule (1505-1658), then under the Dutch of the Reformed Church (1658-1795), and finally under the Anglican British (1795-1948). However old cultural pride might be, it first reawakened as a reaction to the traumatic history of the recent past and grew from there to a political strength, a political Buddhism. The attitude of Buddhists toward Christianity, especially missionaries, is the fruit of

---

and Practice (Oxford, 1971; 2d ed. Delhi, 1991); R. F. Gombrich, *Theravada Buddhism: A Social History from Ancient Benares to Modern Colombo* (London/New York: Routledge & Kegan Paul, 1988); E. W. Adikaram, *Early History of Buddhism in Ceylon,* 2d ed. (Dehiwala, 1994); E. Bechert, *Buddhismus, Staat und Gesellschaft in den Ländern des Theravada Buddhismus,* vol. 1 (Wiesbaden: Harrassowitz, 1966), 363; for the representation of political Buddhism we especially rely on Bechert, but also on the numerous articles and comments in the journal *Dialogue,* published by the Study Centre for Religion and Society in Colombo (since 1963).

centuries-long servitude and frequently forced conversions to the religion of whichever colonial power was ruling at the time. At the same time, then as now, there were well-educated Sinhalese among the Christian minority, who, despite being Christians, have not forgotten their cultural heritage. These are people who, as it were, join together the light of both traditions in their inner dialogue. They are rare, but they hold the key to dialogue between Buddhism and Christianity in Sri Lanka. Among their number are the Protestant Lynn de Silva (1919-82) and the Catholic Aloysius Pieris (b. 1934). These have been the most important Christian dialogue partners in Sri Lanka over the past four decades. We will therefore discuss them at length below.

Portugal in the sixteenth century was "inspired" by a triumphalist and nationalist Catholicism. The conquest of great colonial regions in South America had brought about a religious justification for military undertakings and cultural expansion. In Ceylon the Portuguese sought to destroy the country's national-religious Buddhist identity. This is absolutely clear in their attack on the symbol of royal power: the relic of the Buddha's tooth. According to tradition, it had been brought to Sri Lanka from India in the fourth century C.E., and since then has been a symbol of royal legitimacy—whoever possessed the tooth was accepted as the rightful ruler. The Portuguese declared in the sixteenth century that they had taken the tooth to Goa and destroyed it there, thus underscoring their claim to rule. The Sinhalese contest this story.[2] Whatever the truth, as always Portuguese colonialism also legitimated itself through the dominance of the Christian religion. The fact that the colonial rulers forced the Ceylonese to take Portuguese family names and thus foreswear their own family and clan tradition was one of the bitterest experiences the Ceylonese suffered. Especially in the villages, people returned to Sinhalese names the moment political pressure abated. Compulsion to assume a Christian first name (whether one was a Christian or not) was the policy of mission schools in many lands. But coercion to subject oneself through giving up the family name marked a still deeper assault on cultural integrity.

The Dutch conquerors were less fanatical—at least as far as persecution of Buddhism was concerned. However, as zealous Protestants they pitilessly persecuted all vestiges of Catholicism that the Portuguese had left behind. The fact that Portuguese-baptized Christians continued to practice Buddhism was widely tolerated. On the other side, Buddhist monks appear to have accepted baptism as long as those concerned did not slack off in their veneration of the Buddha. Aggressive Christian exclusivism apparently first manifested itself only in the nineteenth century.[3]

British rule supported the interests of the British East India Company. This was a trading company that did not have to justify itself through the state Church

---

[2] R. F. Gombrich, *Buddhist Precept and Practice*, 2d ed., 122. We thank P. Schmidt-Leukel for the reference.

[3] E. Harris, "Crisis and Competition: The Christian Missionary Encounter with Buddhism in the Early Nineteenth Century," in *Buddhism and Christianity: Interactions between East and West*, ed. U. Everding (Colombo: The Goethe-Institut, 1995), 19.

of England. The British, therefore, developed almost no missionary fervor. On the contrary. Since they wanted to use the native power structures, the British administration opposed the expansion of missionary influence, because "one does not wish to destroy the native traditions." The British administration began to take over some of the functions of Buddhist kingship, ranging from custodianship of the tooth relic to ratifying the ordination of Buddhist monks. This position changed in 1841, when ecclesiastical circles won support for the view that the British crown's duty to defend the faith (embodied in the royal title *defensor fidei*) must also include the destruction of "paganism" (Buddhism) and the promotion of Christianity.[4] This development provoked active resistance from the Buddhists. In 1848 martial law had to be imposed, and a high Buddhist monk was executed before the temple of the holy tooth.

ENCOUNTER AND CONFRONTATION IN THE NINETEENTH CENTURY

Destruction of Native Tradition

In the nineteenth century the door was opened to missionary communities that operated in very different ways, starting in 1805 when the first Protestant missions were sent out. The Methodist Daniel Gogerly in 1838 wrote a treatise *On Transmigration*, based on a rudimentary knowledge of Pali, that had an entirely polemical character.[5] Thanks to the economic and technological superiority of the Europeans, most missionaries were unswervingly convinced that they also enjoyed religious and cultural superiority. "The colonial government counts profit, the missions count saved souls," wrote the biting essayist Anagarika Dharmapala in the Mahabodhi journal. The anger of the Ceylonese grew against this Western imperialism that was secular as well as religious, political as well as spiritual. They developed as a counter-model a Sinhalese-Buddhist liberation ideology that also fused their ethnic and religious, nationalist and historical pride into a single whole. This in time gave the new nation Sri Lanka its identity—at the price of closing out the Hindu Tamils.

The nineteenth century as an age of Christian missionary movements was (with few exceptions) sensitive neither to other religions nor to the feelings of the people whose religions were being trampled upon. Everything that was not Christian was heathen. This arrogant demeanor can only be understood when one considers the historical background of nineteenth-century Europe, especially England. The evangelical movements of the eighteenth century (precipitated especially by John Wesley), with their stress on personal piety, social reform, and individual conversion, stood on the one side of this missionary spirit, and the

---

[4] T. Vimalananda, *The State and Religion in Ceylon since 1815* (Colombo, 1970), 168. We thank P. Schmidt-Leukel for the reference.

[5] See E. Harris, "Crisis, Competition, and Conversion: The British Encounter with Buddhism in Nineteenth-Century Sri Lanka," dissertation, University of Kelaniya (Sri Lanka, 1993); D. Gogerly, "On Transmigration," *The Friend* 2 (1838) and following issues, cited by Harris.

ideology of colonial imperialism on the other. Unlike traditional Calvinism, for members of these new movements salvation was not decided by predestination but depended on individual acceptance of Jesus Christ. On the other side, the economic and military success of the "Christian nations" was taken as a sign of "divine election." The missionaries controlled the media, the presses, and the schools. Thus they had at their disposal the means to make Buddhism appear absurd. According to the dominant missionary ideology, this was an act of mercy, since one must save the souls of the pagans by any means possible, even through polemics and material inducements.

Most Buddhist monks reacted at first with tolerance and respect for the high morality that they found in the teachings of Jesus, as the missionaries themselves reported.[6] Missionaries were even invited to Buddhist temples to preach and hold rational debates.[7] However, it very rapidly became clear that the majority of missionaries had no respect at all for Buddhist temples, monks, or religious festivals.[8] It did not take long, therefore, before Buddhists struck back against Christian missions with similar methods—such manuscripts can be found dating back to 1849.[9] Dharmapala finally succeeded in bringing a printing press to Ceylon (a gift from the king of Siam) and was thus able to begin a counterattack on a broader front.

The Nineteenth-Century Disputations

There was little dialogue, but already beginning in c. 1820 there was confrontation, which grew in intensity in the middle of the nineteenth century. Buddhist monks fought with polished philosophical arguments against the Christian polemic, which was heavily emotional and denunciatory in nature.[10] "From a position of tolerance and welcome and the wish for religious coexistence and indeed for mutually helpful dialogue on philosophical questions, a spirit of retaliation now developed against those who wanted to eradicate Buddhism."[11] This spiritual confrontation peaked with the famous disputation of Panadura between the Buddhist Miguttavatte Gunananda and the Christian David de Silva in 1873. The Buddhist had the audience on his side, and he triumphed easily in bombast. This

---

[6] We follow here the sources made available in E. Harris, "Crisis, Competition, and Conversion"; in this context Harris especially mentions R. S. Hardy, *Eastern Monachism* (1850) and *The Jubilee Memorials of the Wesleyan Mission* (1965).

[7] Benjamin Clough reports such an occurrence in 1815 (connected to the Vesak festival in the temple of Kelaniya). See Harris, "Crisis and Competition," 21.

[8] E. Harris cites the sources and mentions the CMS missionaries G. Erskins (1816) and J. Selkirk (1836) who, with their arrogance, discouraged Buddhist interest in dialogue. Harris, "Crisis and Competition," 19ff.

[9] Oral communication of G. Obeyesekere, December 1993.

[10] Thus Harris's summary, "Crisis and Competition," 23. In 1826 the British colonial government attempted to forbid the distribution of tracts against Buddhism by missionaries, but without much success (*The Missionary Conference: South India and Ceylon*, 1880, 322).

[11] Harris, "Crisis and Competition," 26.

event is still recognized today as the first glimmer of awakening Buddhist self-confidence in Ceylon. The Christian David de Silva reproached his Buddhist fellow-speaker with the following: (1) Through the Buddhist doctrine of *anatta* (not-self), humans are degraded to a soulless state of being. (2) It is unjust if, according to teaching on *karma* and reincarnation, one person does something and another (after reincarnation) has to take the consequences. (3) It is a contradiction when Buddhists on the one hand claim that when a consciousness is reincarnated it precedes the individual psyche and material body (*nama*, individual representation, and *rupa*—form), while on the other hand consciousness is regarded as an aspect of *nama* (representation). These are all questions that still cause difficulties today for Christian theologians who grapple with Buddhism. They therefore rise to the surface again and again in dialogue.

Admittedly, the monk Gunananda had good canonical answers to these three questions: (1) The burden of proof for the existence of the soul, which cannot be found in the five existence groups *(skandhas)*, lies on the Christian side. (2) The recipient of karmic retribution in the next life is "neither identical nor different" from the perpetrator of a deed. (3) The consciousness that precedes name and form is the consciousness of the preceding life. The consciousness, on the other hand, that gives a designation and is thus an aspect of the name-form constellation belongs to the identity of this current life.

The counter-criticism Gunananda made against the Christian position was just as little troubled by detailed knowledge of the other's position as was de Silva's attack on Buddhism: How can God be jealous, since this quality (in Buddhism) is counted among the spiritual impurities that an enlightened person has overcome? How can an omniscient God have created Adam, when he must have known that Adam would sin? The missionary, too, had his traditional theological answers, which naturally remained completely incomprehensible to the Buddhists.

What does the experience of this dialogue teach us? What are its consequences for the contemporary encounter between Buddhism and Christianity? Lynn de Silva, for many years the director of the Christian Dialogue Center in Colombo, and the Buddhist Neville Gunaratna deplored the lack of communication at that time in their reflection upon the centennial of the disputation (1973) in the journal *Dialogue*. But how could real communication have come about, in view of the political interests of both sides and the lack of *hermeneutic* consciousness, which would have detected the different linguistic logic of each position?

ANAGARIKA DHARMAPALA AND THE MAHABODHI SOCIETY— COUNTERPOLEMICS AND THE INTERNATIONALIZATION OF BUDDHISM

David Hewavitarane (Anagarika Dharmapala, 1864-1933) brought the quest for Buddhist self-identity to the highest point of his time and carried it beyond the borders of Ceylon. On his initiative the holiest place of Buddhism in India was restored, the site in Bodh Gaya (in the Indian state of Bihar) where Gautama

Sakyamuni received enlightenment. Besides this, in 1891 he founded a journal in which he could issue counter-propaganda to attack Christian agitation against Buddhism: *Maha Bodhi*, supported by the Mahabodhi Society.

The missionary schools in nineteenth-century colonial Ceylon had created an educated Sinhalese middle class. It was from such a family that the later home-less one *(Anagarika)* and protector of Buddhist teaching *(Dharmapala)* came. Dharmapala grew up in provincial circumstances; he knew no other country than Ceylon and ended his education at the intermediate level. His father's wish was that his son continue in the family business. He could, however, speak excellent British English. He was also a layman *(upasaka)*, whose wish to become a monk *(bhikkhu)* was only fulfilled late in his life.

Dharmapala's revival of Sinhalese Buddhism was markedly different from the nearly contemporary renaissance of Hinduism in India, launched by reform-ers like Ram Mohan Roy (1772-1833) and continued without break up to leaders like Vivekananda (1863-1902) and Radhakrishnan (1888-1975). An important difference is that England conducted itself differently in India than in Ceylon. Ceylon was ruled from India by the British administration there. Also, the Ceylonese had fewer chances for a higher education at Oxford and Cambridge than did the Indian elite—at least not until the time of people like Ananda Coomaraswamy (1877-1947) and K. N. Jayatilleke (1920-70), the foremost lite-rati who supplemented the essayist Dharmapala. Dharmapala consequently did not discover Buddhism through university studies in England, where the works of Mrs. Rhys-Davids were read, works that played a decisive role in the Pali Text Society and that interpreted Buddhism as a totally rational religion. (Dharmapala first encountered Rhys-Davids much later, when he visited England. After that, they supported each other. She helped him by collecting for the Bodh Gaya project; he helped her by reporting in his journal on the progress of the Pali Text Society.) The young Dharmapala learned Buddhism neither through an enlightenment experience nor through studying the classical texts, but through the speculations of the Theosophical Society, in other words through Madame Blavatsky. He re-mained allied with her to the end, even after he had left the society. His original wish was to belong to the Order of the Himalayan Masters, which the theoso-phists had dreamed up as their spiritual lineage.

The Theosophical Society was founded in 1875 in Colombo. Dharmapala plunged into the group around Helena P. Blavatsky (1831-91) and Colonel Olcott (1832-1907) soon after their arrival in Ceylon. It quickly became apparent that the occult powers that Blavatsky claimed to have at her disposal were highly questionable. After a violent controversy, she was forced to leave the country. Christian missionaries made polemical use of this fact, but it made little impres-sion on Dharmapala. He belonged to Colonel Olcott's reading circle and appar-ently used Olcott's methods later for his own Buddhist missionary work. Blavatsky represented the occult and esoteric element. Olcott, on the contrary, stood for the rational-analytical spirit, which discerned still-undiscovered natural laws as the cause of all "marvels" and also wanted to interpret everything Buddhist in rational terms. Admittedly, Olcott knew little about historic Buddhism. His conversion was rather to a "Buddhist theosophy."[12] But the more deeply he studied Buddhism, finally writing the *Buddhist Catechism* in 1881 with the help of the monk Sumangala Thero, the more his path divided from Madame Blavatsky. Olcott's Protestant puritanism, coupled with a strict work ethic, joined with his rational-Protestant interpretation of Buddhism to create an independent religiosity of a new stamp. This would become a serious opponent to the Christian missionaries thanks to its ethically oriented rationality. However, it almost completely disregarded popular Buddhism, with its piety oriented on the tales of the Jataka and on veneration of the Buddha, its festivals, the appeasement of spirits through dances, and so forth.

Olcott and also Dharmapala borrowed ideas from Christian missionary polemics in order to purify popular Buddhism. By this means they laid the foundations for the reductionist view that Buddhism is not a religion but a philosophy. All later interpretations arguing a scientific or modern Buddhism were already present here, the heritage of the European Enlightenment.[13] It is interesting that Olcott had difficulties with the notion of *nirvana* as the total dissolution of the self. He believed that some sort of personal identity must remain intact, and comforted himself with the thought that there were different interpretations of this issue in Theravada and Mahayana, something that his Theravada Buddhist colleagues disputed.

Dharmapala remained loyal to the Colonel for a long time and even accompanied him to Japan. The two only parted ways when Olcott's theosophical interests threw Dharmapala's Mahabodhi ideals into the shade. Another reason for the break was that after Madame Blavatsky's death, theosophy increasingly inclined toward Hinduism, with its doctrine of the eternal nature of the soul, while the distinguishing characteristic of Buddhism is its denial of the existence of an eternal soul.[14]

So Dharmapala was neither an Oxford scholar nor did he have other academic credentials. In contrast to Gandhi, he also did not attract the attention of the London press. His audience and supporters belonged to the urban lower middle class and the peasantry. His editorials in the Mahabodhi journal are not deeply thoughtful but were extraordinarily broadly effective. In part this was because he manipulated the language of the colonial rulers with masterful satire in order to make the Christian missions appear laughable, to his readers' amusement. His diary testifies to unwearying and simple piety. He was no philosopher and never claimed to be one. Indeed, in this thankfulness for Japanese support of the Mahabodhi project and in the hope of creating closer ties with Japan, he even stated the opinion that Theravada is not a school of "Hinayana" but a form of original Mahayana Buddhism!

---

[12] See G. Obeyesekere, "Buddhism and Conscience: An Exploratory Essay," *Daedalus* (summer 1991), Religion and Politics, 219-39; and idem, "The Two Faces of Colonel Olcott: Buddhism and Euro-Rationality in the Late Nineteenth Century," in *Buddhism and Christianity. Interactions between East and West*, ed. U. Everding, 32-71.

[13] G. Obeyesekere, "The Two Faces of Colonel Olcott," 54f.

[14] The theosophists, like most Europeans in the nineteenth century, did not clearly recognize the difference between Buddhism and Hinduism.

This insignificant man now succeeded in piecing together an international network that encompassed both Hinayana and Mahayana Buddhism, although these two traditions had lost all regular contact with one another centuries before. And he did this only on the basis of his simple wish to restore Bodh Gaya's ancient and well-deserved fame!

Although Dharmapala worked for the emancipation of Ceylon, he had no political ambitions. He simply wanted to help restore the cultural pride of his people. He preached to them, "We Ceylonese are not barbarians" and especially opened the eyes of those who saw destiny in the higher ways of the English. For him, the real barbarians were the British, and therefore it was foolish to want to imitate them culturally.

He built schools and hospitals and dreamed of an international guesthouse in Bodh Gaya, even of a Buddhist university. All this was in imitation of the Christian West's history of success and was intended to turn the missions' own weapons against them. Despite these activities, however, his personal expectations remained simple and modest. For want of the philosophical training that only monks possessed, he brought together linguistic metaphors casually; for example, calling on Theravada practitioners to behave like Mahayana bodhisattvas. He did what all lay Buddhists want to do: to collect merit through service of the three jewels (the Buddha, *dharma*, and *samgha*) in order, late in life, to attain full ordination as a *bhikkhu*.

Completely unexpectedly Dharmapala was raised to the stage of world history, when he was invited to attend the World Parliament of Religions in Chicago in 1893. He made his debut without the colorful clothing of the other Buddhist representatives, without marked ability in meditation, and without charismatic gifts. All he had was thousands of printed cards with the five commandments of Buddhism *(pancasila)*, which he wanted to distribute among the delegates. Thus he won the heart of the auditorium! In this way he discovered his calling, and from then on dreamed of ever greater projects. Many friends and benefactors supported him, so he was no longer dependent on the theosophists. In Ceylon, he awakened national pride that it was the purest Buddhist land under *dharma*.

Dharmapala's Mahabodhi movement bestowed upon Ceylon a national symbol of identity. Dharmapala himself was more an internationalist than a nationalist, and he spent more time in Calcutta than in Ceylon. Indeed, he had so much support from influential Hindu families that he roused opposition to the Mahabodhi Society from Ambedkar, the liberator of the Indian outcastes. Dharmapala was not so much an opponent of the English as of the missionaries. The Mahabodhi journal appeared in English, although he also issued other publications in Sinhalese. He agitated in the countryside but spent most of his time in the cities. To his grief he received more support from foreigners than from his own Buddhist countrymen.

Certainly the monk *(bhikkhu)* has always been the preeminent figure in Theravada Buddhism. Dharmapala, however, broke down the traditional strict dividing line between monk and layperson. He became the central figure of the entire fourfold *samgha* of monks and nuns, laymen and laywomen, and thus gave an example for other reformers.

THE BUDDHIST-NATIONAL INDEPENDENCE MOVEMENT

The Buddhist-national independence movement drove the British colonial power from Ceylon and in 1948 founded the modern state of Sri Lanka. This movement was motivated by political and nationalist sentiment and led by activist monks, who could count on support from almost the entire populace. This was not a foundation upon which a Buddhist-Christian dialogue could have flourished, a problem that can still be seen today. The once privileged Christian minority found itself on the defensive after independence; after centuries of Christian missionary assaults on Buddhism as paganism and idolatry, the Christians now had to face the discovery that the other side is not really interested in dialogue. This is especially the case because the Christian motive behind dialogue is often not considered sincere, as long as at the same time missions still operate and stage evangelical "crusades."

Christian interest in dialogue is also a new thing in Sri Lanka. Doubtless it stems at least in part from the displacement of the Christians from the old power structures, but it is more than that. It is also based on the insight that the nation can only be established if all social, religious, and political groups work together. Viewed socially, Christianity still very strongly represents a middle class that was able to rise in the service of colonial rule. The politically active Buddhist monks, on the contrary, under the leadership of Bhikkhu Walpola Rahula, mobilized the masses in 1947 to hold a general strike against the British. The politicization of the *samgha* can nowhere be so clearly seen as in the thesis, generally accepted in Sri Lanka, that monks must call for armed struggle in defense of *dharma*, and can or even ought to bear weapons themselves. This of course is expressly contrary to the classical monastic rule *(vinaya)* with its command not to injure other living things.

To appreciate the difficult political climate for dialogue in Sri Lanka, one must recall that especially in the 1950s and 1960s not just Buddhists and Christians but also Marxists at least indirectly took part in dialogue. Buddhists even partially adopted the Marxist critique of Christianity. It served at least as an argument against *colonial* Christianity, which carries joint responsibility for the capitalist exploitation of the countries of Asia and Africa. We must therefore examine this element in somewhat greater depth, because without the polemics (and injuries) in this context, the difficulties in the way of Buddhists and Christians understanding one another in modern Sri Lanka are hard to comprehend.

BUDDHISM AND MARXISM

The politicized Buddhism of Ceylon/Sri Lanka has a social revolutionary component. In Ceylon, as in Burma, the British-educated intellectual elite accepted the idea of democracy. Indeed, they did this so much that the classical ideals of the *samgha*—a ban on private ownership, democratic right to self-determination—appear as Buddhist values that anticipated the modern ideal of democracy. These values, they argue, have only been newly discovered by liberalism and Marxism, and have been deployed against Christian hierarchical thought (a God and "lord" ruling the world monarchically), which justifies economic exploitation and dictatorship. For where there is a highest God there can be no human freedom, since Christianity has transferred the heavenly hierarchy to earthly society. The Christian slave-holder mentality, according to this theory, is a direct result of theism. Ultimately the colonial policies of "Christian" lands had their roots in this hierarchical Christian thought, and a Hitler, too, could only be conceived of against such a background. Lenin sought to vanquish human greed and self-interest by force, which is impossible. Only the discernment and praxis that stem from the Buddha *dharma* can reach this goal.[15]

To many Buddhist social reformers in Ceylon/Sri Lanka, as in Burma, Marxism appeared as a helpful ideology. They felt, however, that it must be expanded by Buddhism, because Buddhism in its radical analysis of evil and equality goes far beyond Marx: the Buddha did not rest content with dividing up the possessions of another class. "Buddhism frees humanity from its lust for possessions" declares the manifesto of the left-wing Buddhist "Revolt in the Temple, the Victory of Dhamma," which one of the most prominent abbots of Sri Lanka has called "the blueprint for the next 2500 years."[16] These reformers regard the *samgha* as the model for the socialist ideal state and Asoka as the Lenin of Buddhism. The goal of the "Revolt in the Temple" is to bring the Buddha's teaching "from heaven down to earth" and to make real happiness in the here and now of the socialist postcolonial society of Sri Lanka.[17] While Marxism might analyze economic suffering, Buddhism gives an answer to psychological suffering, which is not bound to social class but is universal.

The alliance of Buddhism and Marxism won great acceptance in both Sri Lanka and Burma in the 1950s. Buddhism's critique of the principle of the capitalist free-enterprise economy, in which the individual and individual self-preservation are the dominating factors, offered at the same time a possibility of demarcation from the former colonial powers and the creation of their own identity.[18] For the national building of a Buddhist-oriented society, Marxism can provide the "economic methodology." The Sri Lankans did not, however, want to adopt the totalitarian Marxist state. The Buddhist Marxists believe that they can regard the economic side as an aspect of the "lower truth" *(samvrti)*, naturally to be distinguished from Buddhist *nirvana*, which is "higher truth" *(paramartha)*. For the classical Marxists, though, this differentiation was not acceptable. This is why in 1958 the Burmese head of state U Nu distanced himself from Marxism and after 1959 declared Buddhism to be the state religion. This has had repercussions on discussion in Sri Lanka.[19] Correspondingly, in the 1956 election there

---

[15] U Ba Yin, "Buddha's Way to Democracy," *The Burman*, 12 April 1954, 7 (cited in E. Sarkisyanz, *Buddhist Backgrounds of the Burmese Revolution* [The Hague: Nijhoff, 1965], 193).

[16] D. C. Vijayavardhana, *Dharma-Vijaya oder die Revolte im Tempel* (Colombo, 1953), 431 and 15f.

[17] Ibid., 557.

[18] J. R. Jayawardene, *Buddhism and Marxism* (Colombo, 1957), 44.

[19] Sarkisyanz, 196 and 219.

were also strong forces in Sri Lanka that wanted a Buddhist state. The election victory of a Buddhist-Marxist coalition led the country on the road to neutrality in foreign politics.[20] Domestically, Buddhism was given preferential treatment by the state.[21]

THE POLITICIZED *SAMGHA* AND WALPOLA RAHULA

Already before 1946 the politicization of monks in part of the *samgha* had roused protest. It was only after independence, though, that public debates about this problem began. Walpola Rahula[22] was a spokesman of the politically active group. He replied to his critics that it is the duty of monks to stand up for the oppressed masses. Some monks even identified themselves with Trotskyites and Stalinists, so that the left-moderate Ceylon Labour Party forbade *bhikkhu* participation in its assemblies.[23]

Rahula's publications had a marked influence on the already-mentioned text "The Revolt in the Temple." The radicals also took a stand against Sri Lanka's still-remaining ties to England (dominion status). In the "language war" that began in 1954 they supported the official monolinguism (only Sinhalese) against the official bilingual stand the Tamils hoped for. In the process the war of the Buddhist Sinhalese prince Dutthagamani against the Tamil king Elar (second century B.C.E.) was raised to the level of a religious and national myth. This was, however, a very problematic connection, for *Mahavamsa*, the oldest Ceylonese chronicle, had declared "a non-Buddhist is not a human being."[24] Since the end of the 1950s radical Buddhists have been in favor of solving the nationality problem by the conversion of at least outcastes and the lower castes of Tamils to Buddhism. By the end of 1962, about 100,000 outcastes were said to have gone over to Buddhism.[25]

In the early postcolonial epoch immediately after Europe's collapse in the Second World War, yet another power, ideology, and "religion" exercised a great fascination in Sri Lanka and the Southeast Asian countries: Maoism in China. Until the occupation of Tibet in 1950—and in Tibet itself until the 1959 rebellion—Mao also attempted to demonstrate parallels and harmonies between his ideology and Buddhism. Since the individual lust to possess is damned by both Maoism and Buddhism, China commended itself as South Asia's natural political and cultural ally against the former colonial powers of Europe. Mao found no slight resonance. The annexation of Tibet, though, aroused a violent reaction in Sri Lanka. Chinese occupation of Tibet and the crushing of the 1959 rebellion,

---

[20] W. H. Wriggins, *Ceylon: Dilemmas of a New Nation* (Princeton, 1960), 342ff.

[21] Bechert, 295.

[22] He is the author of the influential works *History of Buddhism in Ceylon* (Colombo, 1956), and *What the Buddha Taught* (Bedford/New York, 1959).

[23] Bechert, 314.

[24] W. Rahula, *History of Buddhism in Ceylon*, 79f. (cited by Bechert, 121).

[25] Bechert, 368.

followed by the Dalai Lama's flight, moved the All Ceylon Buddhist Congress and a group of *bhikkhus* to international protest.[26]

In the face of all the political, cultural, and religious reorientation, it was difficult for the Christians to find their proper place in the building of this new nation, which (unlike India, which is pledged to secularism) wishes to define itself in terms of Buddhism. This is in antithesis to the earlier Christian-designated culture of the colonial rulers. The spiritual and emotional pressure behind the search for a "native theology" as well as efforts to create dialogue with Buddhism come from this context. Therefore, dialogue in Sri Lanka cannot be distanced in an academic approach, nor can it only want to be linked to a two-thousand-year textual basis. It is a political-intellectual dialogue in a national politically explosive climate!

NATION-BUILDING

Despite this complex situation, dialogue in Sri Lanka has the longest and most continuous history of any land, apparently because it has been born from a historical urgency that other regions have not had to deal with to the same extent. This dialogue has not only been concerned with metaphysics or belief systems, but much more with the question of political and social survival: How can *a nation* be created in which humans of *different religions* can live with one another, without perceiving one another as a threat?

BUDDHIST MODERNISM

Sri Lanka's desire for national self-standing and cultural identity was not conducive to dialogue, because many Sri Lankans despised the religion of the former colonial powers. Buddhism, therefore, was interpreted as the surviving established religion and way of life with which Sri Lanka could go its way in an age of technological and scientific development. University intellectuals as well as parts of the *samgha* have advocated a Buddhist modernism, or "Protestant Buddhism" (G. Obeyesekere). This should include on the one hand inspiration from the West and its Enlightenment ideals, and on the other hand provide a better answer to the questions of the age. K. N. Jayatilleke's concept of science is an effort to expound the frictionless unity of Buddhist religion and scientific rationalism in contrast to the old tension between religion and science in Christianity. In this way, he believed, the spiritual inferiority of Christian belief would be made clear.

British Buddhology and textual criticism stood the Buddhist modernists in good stead, since they tended to interpret Buddhism as a rationally perfect system, completely in alignment with European scientific thought of the modern

---

[26] U. Phadnis, *Religion and Politics in Sri Lanka* (London: C. Hurst, 1976), 279ff. It should be noted on the other hand that a Buddhist reaction did not take place against the dictatorship of the Catholic Ngo Dinh Diem and the subjection of Buddhists in Vietnam.

era. So it is not surprising that Sri Lanka's head of state, S.W.R.D. Bandaranaike (assassinated in 1959), avowed that he had his own conversion experience in the library at Oxford.[27]

However, modernism also had an explosive side for the Buddhists. For example, when in 1961 the famed archaeologist S. Paranavitana gave evidence in a lecture that the Buddha's three supposed visits to Sri Lanka were pious legends rather than historical fact, a storm of indignation broke out, and the media speculated that Paranavitana must have been bought as a Catholic agent![28]

DIALOGUE AS HEALING IN NATION-BUILDING

The Marxist analyst Hector Abbayawadhana in 1973 gave two reasons why a growing group of Sri Lankan Christians was endeavoring to enter into dialogue with the Buddhists: First, the Christian effort for interreligious dialogue must in part be seen as compensation to reduce Christian longing for prestige and power after the departure of British colonial power. And second, in part, though, it must also be the true effort of Christians to take part actively in the construction of a multireligious nation and to heal old wounds between the two religious groups.[29] The Methodist pastor Lynn de Silva (1919-82) was the initiator of the "Ecumenical Institute for Study and Dialogue" in Colombo and of the journal *Dialogue*, which was and is the most important catalyst of this development.[30] The journal has appeared since September 1963, financed by the Christian Institute for Buddhist Studies. At first it was a mimeographed publication, but since 1973 its new series has appeared in better print as the journal of the Study Centre for Religion and Society in Colombo.

The famed disputation of 1873 between Rev. David de Silva and Bhikkhu Gunananda[31] was the starting point for Lynn de Silva's efforts to promote Buddhist-Christian dialogue. Like a red thread, the unsolved questions of 1873 run through his lifework. Thus, a century after the great debate, he treated again the problem "*anatta* and rebirth." De Silva concluded that in the 1873 disputation the grave Buddhist misunderstandings of Christian belief rested in part on the difficulty of translation. The Bible text that Gunananda had presented is extremely easy to misunderstand. Therefore it was de Silva's foremost concern to develop a hermeneutics that could make the gospel comprehensible to Buddhists on the basis of Buddhist categories.

Lynn de Silva perceived that after independence Dharmapala's politically intended and understandably biting remarks about Christianity called for a Christian

---

[27] Bechert, 360f.

[28] Bechert, 363f.

[29] H. Abbayawadhana, "Buddhist Christian Encounter: A Marxist Appreciation of the Role of Buddhism and Christianity in Ceylonese Society till Now," *Dialogue,* new series [NS] 1/1 (1973): 11-16.

[30] P. Schmidt-Leukel presents an excellent summary and characterization of Lynn de Silva's theology in *Den Löwen brüllen hören* (Paderborn: Schöningh, 1992), 185-202.

[31] *Dialogue,* NS 2/1 (1974): 17-26, see also 82f.

answer. De Silva hoped, when he founded his journal in 1963, for "an end of diatribe and beginning of dialogue." The main problem of dialogue in Sri Lanka, however, was and is the question of the community between the two religions.

The Study Centre and the journal prove that de Silva could indeed inspire numerous and influential Buddhists to participate in dialogue. He also succeeded in putting together a group of Christian theologians who developed a theology of acculturation and with it freed themselves from Christianity's colonial past in Sri Lanka. This group of theologians exercised a strong influence in the World Council of Churches (WCC). This organization broke out of the Eurocentric thought of its governing board and furthered the dialogue program with people of other religions. The trailblazing 1974 WCC conference in Colombo gave impressive proof of this, advocating a world community of Buddhists, Hindus, Jews, Christians, and Muslims.[32]

Dialogue's program is clear: its goal is not to evangelize. Rather, it understands itself as an organ of a common search for truth. It wishes

> neither to find the smallest common denominator, nor to create a parliament of religions, nor to work for a homogenous world religion. . . . The goal of dialogue must be seen much more in the context of the common human search for community—regional community, national community, and world community.[33]

The Study Centre in Colombo aims to work for a "holy worldliness," in other words a union of spirituality and social affairs.[34] De Silva took the stand that the Christians crippled themselves when they fought the Buddhists. When they despised Buddhism, they were holding the Ceylonese nation and its people in contempt; the result of this foolishness was that now Christianity itself was scorned.[35]

THE DEBATE BETWEEN JAYATILLEKE AND LYNN DE SILVA

The high point of de Silva's old series of *Dialogue* was a debate between Lynn de Silva and the Buddhist philosopher K. N. Jayatilleke. Jayatilleke became known in 1963 through his book on the theory of cognition (epistemology) in Buddhism.[36] He is a modern Buddhist intellectual, who has an extraordinarily wide understanding of rationality and empiricism. This allowed him to lead the polemics of "Buddhist rationality" against "Christian irrationality."[37] It was therefore important to him to represent convincingly the traditional Buddhist refutation of theism. Jayatilleke belongs in the line of logical positivists that reaches

---

[32] *Dialogue,* NS 2/1 (1974): 18-38.

[33] De Silva, in *Dialogue*, NS 1/1 (1973): 2.

[34] Editorial *Dialogue,* NS 2/1 (1974): 1-6.

[35] *Dialogue,* NS 2/1 (1974): 7-14.

[36] K. N. Jayatilleke, *Early Buddhist Theory of Knowledge* (London, 1963).

[37] See G. Rothermundt, *Buddhismus für die moderne Welt: Die Religionsphilosophie K. N. Jayatillekes* (Stuttgart: Calwer, 1979).

back to David Hume. This shows how, even in South Asia, interreligious discourse is linked to and influenced by the religious-historical situation and intellectual history of Europe.

Jayatilleke builds (with great expert knowledge, like the earlier Rhys-Davids husband and wife team in England) on the foundation of Buddhaghosa (fifth century C.E.), the classical systematizer of Theravada Buddhism. Jayatilleke was thus an outstanding, fully qualified, but also difficult dialogue partner for Lynn de Silva from the time the latter started publication. We cannot report the debate in detail here, but wish to emphasize several points made:[38]

• On the basis of new empirical reports Jayatilleke regards the theory of reincarnation to be proven, a point Lynn de Silva contests (first issue).

• De Silva argues in favor of the historical consciousness in Christianity, which Buddhism for the most part lacks. Jayatilleke parried this with the argument that the Buddhist perception of a cosmic history corresponds to the Christian feature (fifth issue).

• Jayatilleke corrects the widespread perception of the Buddha as merely a normal human being and teacher. Although born as a typical human being, as a fully enlightened being he is greater than a god (issues 13 and 17).

• When de Silva commented on the Christian doctrine of a creator God (issue 16), Jayatilleke answered with a sharp critique of theism in the next issue.

THE CONTROVERSY OVER THE EXISTENCE OF GOD

Jayatilleke's short essay "The Buddhist Attitude to God"[39] argues that the Buddha was an atheist. Mahayana, too, recognizes neither creation nor creator. His stand is that the Buddha explicitly rejected the Brahman philosopher Makkhali Gosala's theism. The latter had argued that God is the creator, and his providence brings about the development of life in *samsara* until finally, after all karmic powers have been realized, at the end all being is extinguished. Jayatilleke points to two reasons for the Buddha's atheism: (1) theism undermines human freedom and thus morality, because it reduces human beings to puppets in the hands of an almighty God; and (2) a God who is supposed to be both almighty and benevolent could not have created a world so full of evil and suffering. Jayatilleke, then, argues against the classical proof of God. For him, Anselm of Canterbury's *ontological* proof of God is merely a tautology, in which existence (a thing) was falsely identified as an attribute. The *cosmological* proof, for its part, contradicts its own premises, insofar as it emanates from an "uncaused causer," in certain respects distorting the term *cause* to the point of meaninglessness. For Jayatilleke, the *teleological* argument disproves itself, if one considers the gruesomeness and waste in evolution, which is "red with blood on teeth and claws." To introduce into this the incomprehensibility of God begs the question of how a loving God

---

[38] For an analysis of several logical connections that cannot be investigated in a historical context, see P. Schmidt-Leukel.

[39] K. N. Jayatilleke, "The Buddhist Attitude to God," *Dialogue*, old series [OS] 17 (17 March 1969): 3-9.

could permit this gruesomeness, unless theologians wish to reject the concept of God's omnipotence.

The Christian faith, for Jayatilleke, is consequently unfounded. Admittedly, a belief can be based on error and despite that bear good fruit. However, he argues that Christianity has never borne good fruit. The cause for this is that a natural corollary of Christianity is human beings' delusions of omnipotence, leading them to identify themselves with their almighty God. Someone like Hitler, who regarded himself as an instrument of divine providence, has fallen into this delusion. This is only a single case from recent times, but Jayatilleke points out that the history of Christianity shows many similar aberrations. Buddhism's critique of theism does not, however, mean that the Buddhist is an atheist in the sense of materialism. This is because he sets himself off equally from the idea of personal immortality *(bhava-drsti)* and from its opposite, the idea of complete extinction *(vibhava-drsti)*.

The Buddha indeed designated certain theories as unsatisfying. This does not necessarily mean that they are false. To their number belongs the concept of a revealed religion. Every religion that knows at least an element of freedom of the will, moral causation (that every deed has consequences for the doer), responsibility, and so on, has its value. Therefore community with believers of such religions is for Buddhists completely possible and meaningful. Even the Buddha admitted as valid the idea of a good god (Brahma) who was not almighty. In the final analysis, however, Buddhism is a therapy against suffering and fear. God or not-God is simply not the problem.

Christians can respond that the subordinate god Brahma in Buddhism does not correspond to the Christian concept of God, because Brahma exists in time and is conditional, which is not true of the Christian creator God. But that leaves the question of whether the Buddhist *nirvana* is at least functionally comparable to the Christian idea of God. Jayatilleke answers: "If nirvana is God in the sense of a transcendent reality, then those who need such a remedy [concept] still do not understand, while those who have attained understanding no longer need it [the concept]."[40] In other words, the comparison of God and *nirvana* is superfluous.

Jayatilleke's arguments prepared the ground for Dharmasiri's book against theism (1974).[41] This work brings a still sharper tone to the controversy between Christians and Buddhists, although without noticeably greater hermeneutic clarity.

In the same issue of *Dialogue* as Jayatilleke's essay on the existence of God, an anonymous article entitled "Gautama's Search for That Which Unconditionally Fits" provided a direct response to de Silva. The author cites the Indian historian of philosophy T. R. V. Murti, who in his book on the Madhyamika system

---

[40] Ibid., 8.

[41] G. Dharmasiri, *A Buddhist Critique of the Christian Concept of God* (Colombo, 1974). In the nearly unchanged American edition of the book (Antioch: Golden Leafs, 1988), Dharmasiri added a chapter in which he sharpens his criticism of theism in light of the position of animals and the environmental issue in general—for him, theism is authoritarian and rips apart the unity of nature (reference provided by P. Schmidt-Leukel).

in Mahayana Buddhism (1955) had proposed the thesis that the Buddhist Madhyamika philosophy aimed above all to show the boundaries of reason.[42] The author borrowed this argument so that with Mahayana Buddhist arguments he could refute the views of the Theravada Buddhist Jayatilleke on the rationality of atheism, and so defend the possibility of the Christian idea of God!

In an essay on the question of God,[43] de Silva paralleled the concepts of Buddhist *dharma* and Christian God: both are transcendent, yet both are also personal. How is that possible? According to de Silva, the impersonal absolute, for one who "sees" it, is not impersonal. Ultimately, *dharma* in Buddhism is the object of love, a matter of understanding as well as the adoration of the heart—in other words, a personal reality. When the early Buddhist Theragatas (hymns of the Elders) extol *dharma* as that which accords protection, as that which—transcendent in this and every possible world—adorns the Buddha's body and itself appears as *dharmakaya* (*dharma* body) in Buddhaghosa, this is a personal relationship to *dharma*.

This argument of de Silva's is artificial. It is problematic, because the hermeneutic foundations for such paralleling of concepts remain unclear.[44] Presumably de Silva himself knows that he is in this case interpreting simplistically classical Theravada Buddhist classification as well as its concept of the person. In order to find a congenial basis of community with his Buddhist partners, de Silva searches unwaveringly for a theistic *telos* in Buddhism.[45] Toward this end, he cites the Mahayana interpreter Edward Conze and the English Buddhist Sangharakshita[46] to give evidence of how in the history of Buddhism atheistic and theistic trends have existed side by side, and continue to exist today.

CONTEMPORARY DEVELOPMENTS

CONFRONTATION

Social and Ethnic Tensions

Because of the linkage of national identity and Buddhist religion it was impossible for a spirit of religious tolerance to develop that could have left its mark on Sri Lanka's political climate in either the 1960s or in the Tamil-Sinhalese altercations of the 1980s.[47] The contemporary Tamil-Sinhalese conflict is also horribly instructive in a religious and hermeneutic sense. Since Ceylon/Sri Lanka sought to win back its cultural and national identity through the Sinhalese language and the legend of a *single state* (formerly a kingdom) as the true nursery of Buddhism, the Tamil minority was closed out. The historical chronicles do indeed

---

[42] T. R. V. Murti, *The Central Philosophy of Buddhism*, 3d ed. (London, 1980).

[43] L. de Silva, "Dharma as Ultimate Reality," *Dialogue*, OS 17: 14-20.

[44] Schmidt-Leukel has analyzed this problem in *Den Löwen brüllen hören*.

[45] L. de Silva, "Theistic Development in Buddhism," *Dialogue*, OS 19: 1-7.

[46] Sangharakshita, *Die drei Kleinode* (Munich, 1971).

[47] See *Dialogue*, NS 4/3 (1976): 80-86.

report the astonishing mildness with which for the most part the Buddhist kings ruled over their non-Buddhist subjects. But this attitude has unfortunately not been imitated by the current political ruling class. This class has, with varying accents and political preferences, opted up until the 1994 election for identity through the demarcation and exclusion of minorities. In Sri Lanka's multireligious situation this led inevitably to the use of force. Therefore there is no alternative to dialogue, no matter how politically difficult and both intellectually and hermeneutically thorny it still is. The government that has been in power since August 1994, headed by prime minister Chandrika Kumaratunga, appears to have recognized this. At this time the Buddhist-Christian dialogue could enter into a new and promising phase. But are the Christians of the 1990s, among whom fundamentalist groups are growing in influence, ready for dialogue?

In recent times new conflicts and confrontations have appeared. At their heart is fundamentalist or evangelical groups (mostly supported by missionaries from the United States) evangelizing among the Buddhists. Numerous village communities that have been founded by interreligiously organized peace initiatives (Christian Workers Federation, World Solidarity Forum, Women's Action Committee, Mothers of Lanka, Movement of Defense of Democratic Rights, and others), as well as school and development programs, carry on the struggle to prevent armed religious conflicts. But the imprint of North American evangelical and fundamentalist missionary groups, which use the political instability of civil war and economic poverty, currently grows ever stronger. Money from North America, Europe, and recently also Korea flows as investments exclusively to church buildings for fundamentalist groups, which also attract possible converts through the promise of employment. In a similar fashion Japanese money recently has been going to Buddhists and investment in the Gulf countries to Muslims; in other words, religion legitimates particular political and economic interests. W. P. Ebenezer Joseph, writing in *Crosspoints* in 1993, points out that today in Sri Lanka religion and economy are no longer innocent partners, operating in mutually exclusive realms of human life. They are interwoven in the closest possible way with one another and scarcely separable; often they are manipulative instruments for concealed national and international interests in both politics and economy. There is a danger that such developments will play out in an atmosphere of armed ethnic conflict. There is a possibility that religious fundamentalism may express and find its religious identity in arms. Our country, he writes, which must still find a way out of a predetermined framework of armed conflict, cannot afford to be plunged into another sort of armed conflict. Should that come to pass, the island of paradise will finally be lost.[48] The Christian dialogue centers (especially those of the Jesuits and Franciscans[49]) are therefore concerned to

---

[48] W. P. Ebenezer Joseph, "Armed Religious Conflict?" *Crosspoints* 3/4 (June 1993): xxvii.

[49] T. Balasuriya, *Right Relationships: De-Routing and Re-Rooting of Christian Theology* (Colombo, 1993). The author, an Oblate of Mary Immaculate, investigates the entire history of Christian theology for hidden power interests, and in the light of this analysis wishes to root Christian belief in a radically new fashion in the original message of Jesus.

expose the fundamentalist tendencies in their own religion and their political consequences.

The Jesuit Aloysius Pieris, an important individual in Sri Lanka's Buddhist-Christian dialogue and Lynn de Silva's successor as editor of the journal *Dialogue*,[50] since the 1960s has placed the social and political significance of dialogue in the foreground. On the basis of his sensitivity for the social role of the *samgha* in Buddhist communities, he interpreted the dialogue situation in Sri Lanka somewhat differently than de Silva,[51] although with similar goals. He shows how the Buddha explained the entire sacred brahmanic universe by recourse to a purely psycho-anthropocentric interpretation of holiness in the here and now. Later, of course, this explanation again accumulated a scholastic ontology, very similar to that of Christianity. And, argues Pieris, the erection of houses of learning in both religions reflected the real social power structure.

The ethnic and religious conflict between Sinhalese and Tamils in Sri Lanka shows that Buddhist-Christian dialogue cannot be limited to theological comparisons or psychological differences but is rather an aspect of political fact in Sri Lanka. Religion is unavoidably implicated in social and political realities—indeed it engenders and legitimates these realities. If this is recognized, dialogue must promote honest criticism and also self-criticism of religions; otherwise it only serves as camouflage for power structures. The mutual processing of each partner's history as well as the baring of ideological and historical images is therefore a goal of dialogue that is painful for all those taking part. Up until now almost nobody has dared to undertake this difficult task.

In a rare exception, Lynn de Silva confronted the widespread prejudice that Buddhism, in stark contrast to Christianity, has always been peaceful.[52] De Silva points out that a glance at Ceylonese history shows that force has also been exercised in the name of Buddhism. He gives evidence of this with a quotation from the historian E. W. Adikaram:

> *Mahavamsa*, the historical chronicle of the Sinhalese Buddhists, interpreted the worst murderers in Ceylon as protectors of *dharma*. King Dutthagamani, who according to the chronicle mercilessly slew millions of Tamils, did this in order to protect the Buddhist community from destruction! Was the author of *Mahavamsa*, a Buddhist monk, so completely ignorant of the Buddha's fundamental teaching, or was he a helpless offering to the doctrine of hate, which at that time was penetrating Buddhism?[53]

---

[50] See P. Schmidt-Leukel, 222ff.

[51] A. Pieris, "Some Christian Reflections on Buddhism and Secularization in Ceylon," *Dialogue*, OS 24: 3-8.

[52] L. de Silva, "The Christian Attitude to Buddhism," *Dialogue*, OS 13: 7-12.

[53] E. W. Adikaram, "Buddhism and the Doctrine of Hate," *Daily News* (Colombo, 25 May 1964), reprinted in *Ambassador, Journal of the Ceylon Rationalist Association* 1 (1966). This same historian in a controversy with Walpola Rahula in 1962 recommended a return to the historical origins of Buddhism, and with it a purification of contemporary practice. Rahula replied that Buddhism has not decayed, but has of necessity responded to changed circumstances; thus, the call for a return to origins is ahistorical idealism (see Bechert, 366f.).

What is more, King Dutthagamani was comforted by ten or perhaps eight arhats, who assured him:

> No ballast on the way to heaven will grow from your deed. Only one and a half human beings have been murdered by you, oh ruler over humankind. One [of those killed] took his refuge in the three jewels, and the other [who counts as a half-person] had sworn the five vows *(pancasila)*. The rest were infidels and people of evil life, who do not count for more than wild animals.[54]

Some of de Silva's Buddhist dialogue partners were wounded by this.[55] After all, the Tamil hordes had, in the final analysis, been intruders and not indigenous citizens. Therefore the guilt-ridden king could with full right be called "defender of the *dharma*," just as Winston Churchill was a defender of Christian civilization against Hitler's barbarism.

The exchange became heated, and one could feel that it was not only the interpretation of history that was being debated, but also the judgment of the *samgha*'s role in modern Sri Lanka! De Silva struck back with new arguments,[56] introducing to the debate Edward Conze's remarks on Buddhist power politics.[57] Above all he referred to the fact that the war against the Tamils had been understood as a holy war, in which five hundred monks incited the troops, although according to tradition there had been at least one true Tamil king among the enemy.

One can sense the emotional pressure behind these debates and the longing felt by each side to vindicate its history. There is also, however, the will to remain in conversation. It is striking that these historic and political discussions were repeatedly interrupted by dialogue partners who were concerned with theology. Still, it would be false to interpret this as merely an effort to get away from secondary issues. For we have seen that both sides were convinced that Christian belief in God as well as Buddhist atheism have consequences for each side's view of humanity, the establishment of social models of conduct, and thus for political reality. And for precisely this reason both sides have fought so uncompromisingly about interpretation of belief in God.

The Confrontation with Dharmasiri on Belief in God

Jayatilleke polemicized against theism using the arguments of the old Abhidhamma systematizers, especially Buddhaghosa. However, the Buddhist who really grappled with Christian theology on the basis of its own philosophical tradition and arguments was Gunapala Dharmasiri. He worked out the rational

---

[54] *Mahavamsa* 25, 109f., cited in *Mahavamsa or the Great Chronicle of Ceylon*, trans. W. Geiger, Pali Text Society (Oxford, 1912), 178.

[55] G. Vithanage, "Buddhist Attitude to Christianity," *Dialogue*, OS 13: 13-17.

[56] L. de Silva, "Christian Attitude to Buddhism," *Dialogue*, OS 13: 19-24.

[57] See E. Conze, *Buddhism: Its Essence and Development* (New York, 1951).

refutation of theism in his book *A Buddhist Critique of the Christian Concept of God,* which appeared in Colombo in 1974.[58]

Dharmasiri begins with a critique of the ontological proof of God. His logical arguments certainly do not surpass Immanuel Kant's critique. Dharmasiri based his critique on history, on the view that the Buddha rejected Brahman belief in an eternal *brahman* and an immortal soul. He then supported his argument with recent British linguistic analytical philosophy, in order to show how senseless certain Christian assertions about God are.

Dharmasiri's arguments are weighty. However, most Christian responses address them imprecisely, or only noncommittally. Here we can limit ourselves to some aspects of the discussion Dharmasiri's book provoked in Sri Lanka, because Dharmasiri's work itself and de Silva's counter-argument have recently been analyzed by P. Schmidt-Leukel.[59] Several authors (in both Sri Lanka and the United States) have rightly posed a question concerning methodology: Dharmasiri appears to expect that Christian theology does indeed want to prove the existence of God—something that more recent theology, for good reasons, does not do.[60] Lynn de Silva also responds[61] that Dharmasiri's critique of Christian teaching on the immortality of the soul draws upon a concept of a substantial soul that contemporary theology rejected long ago. One can, after all, not compare the original mythic language of one religion with the philosophically reflective language of another.

Aloysius Pieris associated himself with this analysis of language forms and suggested that a distinction must be made between *gnostic* and *agapeic* language.[62] Both appear in both religions, but with different weight: originally Christianity was *agapeic*, while Buddhism was *gnostic*. Pieris points out that one must compare these corresponding elements with each other, rather than playing off one against the other. Moreover, the intellectualization of Buddhism, represented by Dharmasiri, corresponds to the *abhidharmic* tradition. In this, *nirvana* itself has become an entity that can be experienced,[63] but which is cleanly divided from *samsara* through the empty space of consciousness, called the *nirodha-samapatti*. In Buddhism there has always been a strong distinction between the empirical experience of the world and the religious experience of wisdom *(panna, prajna),* in which the leap to the latter is possible through intuitive or meditative realization. This leap, as Pieris argues, is for Christians less an act of *gnosis* than it is the

---

[58] G. Dharmasiri, *A Buddhist Critique of the Christian Concept of God* (Colombo, 1974). The book originated in a dissertation with Ninian Smart (Lancaster, England).

[59] P. Schmidt-Leukel, 194ff.

[60] See G. W. Houston, "Review" (of Dharmasiri), in *Buddhist Christian Studies,* vol. 3 (Honolulu: University of Hawaii Press, 1983), 161f.

[61] *Dialogue,* NS 2 (1974): 4 and (1975/76): 5. See A. Pieris, *Theologie der Befreiung in Asien* (Freiburg: Herder, 1986), esp. 79ff.; and idem, *Liebe und Weisheit* (Mainz: Grünewald, 1989), esp. 15ff.

[62] See especially A. Pieris, "God-Talk and God-Experience in a Christian Perspective," *Dialogue,* NS 2/3 (1974): 116-28.

[63] Dharmasiri, however, argued very clearly that *nirvana* should not be interpreted as a mystical experience in the Christian sense, since it knows no "object."

essence of an I-Thou relationship. In other words, it is not the dissolution of the known in the knower but a merging together of the lover with the beloved. The mystical-monastic element can merge together with the prophetical-priestly, if one heeds the different levels. Pieris can accept Dharmasiri's critique, without, however, coming to the same conclusion—that Christianity is otherworldly oriented and in the final analysis incapable of founding a moral philosophy based on reason. Quite the contrary: for Pieris, the personal language of incarnational theology shows that this is very much the case.

Dharmasiri's responses to his critics show that he felt himself misunderstood by most Christian theologians. He had wanted to show that one must give up all conceptualization in respect to God, because through it arise accretions that are a hindrance on the path to liberation. This assertion, without a doubt, expresses precisely the Buddhist tradition.[64] It is, however, also nothing unusual for Christian mystics.

Cooperation

Collaboration as Social Duty

Above we have shown that in Sri Lanka's Buddhist-Christian dialogue Marxism is always present as a third partner. A consequence of this is that the two religions not only have to deal with the religions themselves in dialogue but have to enter into questions critical of religion overall. A Marxist-influenced author who surveyed the Buddhist-Christian dialogue wrote: It is not a question of whether Buddhism or Christianity is "better." Instead, as Erich Fromm said, the question is whether a religion develops or inhibits human potential, in other words whether and how it contributes to liberation.[65] In the nineteenth century Christian triumphalism obscured the social aspects of the gospel, but it was a small reform branch of English Christianity that finally produced a generation of fighters for national and social liberty. The progressives among the Buddhists and Christians worked together for this. Lynn de Silva created the institute in Colombo, Bishop Lakdosa de Mel erected a retreat house *(aramaya)* where Christians and Buddhist monks could engage with one another, and Aloysius Pieris founded the Tulana Centre for interreligious research and encounter in Kelaniya. As a result, Father Yohan Devananda worked with the Aramaya in forming labor unions, Pieris developed his Asian liberation theology, and the Christian association of laborers together with the Buddhist congress of Sri Lanka produced the book *Buddhism and the People*. However, one must be sobered by the fact that the mainstream of the *samgha* was not very active socially. But it was also not possible for the Marxists to radicalize and mobilize the masses. Christians and Buddhists should, together with Marxists, struggle against the antireligious and

---

[64] G. Dharmasiri, "Comments on Responses to a Buddhist Critique," *Dialogue*, NS 3 (1976): 20f.

[65] V. Vidyasagara, "The Marxist Movement and the Buddhist-Christian Dialogue in Sri Lanka: A Comment," *Dialogue*, NS 10 (1983): 2-3, 16-28.

dehumanizing powers that the quest for money has set free. They should also find common cause against the egocentric economic mindset and consumerism, through which the chasm between rich and poor grows ever wider. They should take a stand for a community defined by *dharma* or a kingdom of righteousness that is inspired by the kingdom of God.[66]

In this Marxist-inspired attitude toward Buddhist-Christian dialogue, typical Buddhist ideas are noticeable again in the valuation of economic processes. In this view the problem in modern societies is not so much the workers' right to the fruit of their labor, but the problem of greed, including attachment to the products of one's own labor. It is not the unbraked productivity and progress that Marx proclaimed that must be furthered, but rather contentment with what one has and with the things that for material reasons are absolutely necessary, so one can master the higher spiritual tasks of life.

Aloysius Pieris's liberation theology connects to these thoughts. He wishes to formulate the Christian gospel in a Buddhist culture under Marxist stimulus, so that it develops into an *orthopraxy*. The political background in Sri Lanka on one side and the liberation-theological stance on the other side is the basis for Pieris's warning[67] that Buddhist-Christian dialogue may not limit itself to theological theories or the levels of inner spiritual experience (as is unfortunately mostly the case in America and Japan). Instead, it must deal with social and ethical questions in the political context of both religions.

In Search of the New Personality—the Religious Path

Speculative debate about the concept of God or transcendence has brought interesting ideas to light, but it has not necessarily brought the discussants closer to one another. The situation is very different with the other dialogue theme in Sri Lanka: the practice of the human religious path.

Several authors recommend understanding the two religions as different paths to perfection, which are different because the psychological foundations for describing the human spirit are different. So another "psychological method" could prove fruitful for the future in both traditions. As especially Anthony Fernando[68] has proposed, this could be seen as a path toward the transformation of the self. In the 1960s and 1970s Anthony Fernando established himself as an important dialogue partner. Fernando sought to uncover the inner affinity of the two religions especially in psychological terms, rather than in metaphysics. He argues that a Christian could find a place in the Buddhist-developed ideal of personality, and vice versa. Fernando passes over the question of *how* the religions differ from each other, asking the more interesting question of *why* they differ. He asks about orientation: What does the liberation of *nirvana* mean for development of the personality? Fernando further proposes that the goal of missionary work should

---

[66] Ibid., 27f.

[67] A. Pieris, "The Zen-Christian Dialogue in Japan: The First Impressions of a Sri Lankan Christian," *Dialogue*, NS 3/3 (1975): 107-12.

[68] A. Fernando, *Buddhism and Christianity*, 2d ed. (Colombo, 1983).

not be seen as the conversion of people from one institution to another. Rather, its proper purpose is to bring the individual from a state of spiritual immaturity to a spiritual adulthood—in other words, to a state that in Buddhism is associated with the image of the arhat, and in Christianity with the saint.

This beginning is being developed and placed in a wider context by the religious studies scholar Shanta Ratnayaka.[69] With reference to Buddhaghosa's *Visuddhimagga* ("Way of Purification") on the one hand and John Wesley's writings on the other, she shows that their paths to salvation especially differ because Buddhism starts with the concept of suffering while Christianity begins with sin. Both religions recognize a final reality but describe this reality in differing fashions. Logically, then, the structures of salvation are different. In both cases the entire structure of human development toward holiness or perfection is a gradual process. In both cases it consists of surmounting the encountered human situation. Therefore the two paths can be paralleled as follows:

Buddhism	*Christianity*
nirvana	kingdom of God
purity of insight—wisdom	glorification
vanquishing of doubt	gradual sanctification
purity of perception	new birth
clarity of consciousness	justification
wisdom	prevenient grace
state of suffering	state of sin

Even if the practicality of this schema is seductive, certain limitations rapidly appear, issues that once again can only be overcome if terminology is clarified. What does it mean when, for example, clarity of consciousness and justification are interpreted as parallel steps on the spiritual path to perfection? Intellectual clarity through the arrangement of the terms within their historical background and context is itself an aspect in the process of maturing discussion. The current dialogue should therefore concentrate on these questions, which link together spiritual praxis and theoretical reflection.

Mutual Transformation—Vision of a New Culture: Lynn de Silva's Last Essay

Lynn de Silva's sudden death in May 1982 marked a turning point for dialogue in Sri Lanka, and his last essay, "Buddhism and Christianity Relativized," consequently excited particularly great attention.[70] In this work de Silva appealed

---

[69] S. Ratnayaka, *Two Ways of Perfection: Buddhist and Christian* (Colombo: Lake House, 1978); abridged version: "Two Paths to Perfection," *Dialogue*, NS 1/2 (1973): 44-47.

[70] L. De Silva, "Buddhism and Christianity Relativized," *Dialogue*, NS 9/1-3 (1982): 43-72 (de Silva memorial volume).

for a relativization, which for him meant a correlation of the religions. He saw this as necessary if we can ever hope to reach the necessary state of community. It is no longer a matter of demonstrating the superiority of one religion over another, or the inclusivity of one's own religion compared to the other. Instead, he argued, it is time to be aware of the plurality of religions, tolerating and making them fruitful for the common interest. From this could emerge a new culture based on different religions living together. Lynn de Silva demonstrates this hope, yet again thinking through the three most important Christian theological themes brought up in dialogue in the past decades, developing them in the spirit of relativization. These are the question of God, Christology, and the meaning of grace.

In his published books about the theory of reincarnation and the soul, de Silva did not explicitly delve into the question of God or theology as such. He did, however, treat it in other works[71] and also in this last essay. With Paul Tillich he says that concreteness gives rise to polytheism, the question of the absolute creates the One, but the union of the deepest thoughts from both perspectives leads to the Trinity. He cites the Mahayana Buddhist doctrine of the three bodies or levels of manifestation *(trikaya)* and remarks that the *dharmakaya* is both transcendent and immanent; that is, it is the essence of all appearances. This corresponds to the godhead in Christianity. The *sambhogakaya* contains an element of mutuality and corresponds more closely to the Holy Spirit. Finally, the *nirmanakaya* corresponds to Jesus as "God with us" (Emmanuel). This, as de Silva himself knows, is naturally not a complete correspondence in particulars, but it is in terms of structure.

New in de Silva's last contribution is his attempt to extend the anthropological analysis of *anatta-pneuma* to Christology. Very differently from the Kyoto school, which by means of the concept of kenosis (God's self-renunciation) also denies the being of God, de Silva does not wish to relinquish the "thou" in Jesus' process of self-renunciation. This comes far nearer to the original New Testament meaning of Philippians 2:7-8 (that Jesus took on the form of a slave and was of human likeness, even to death on the cross) than the Kyoto school's reading. According to de Silva, the paradox is that it was in this way that Christ became completely one with God. He writes:

> His *kenosis (sunyata)* was thus a *plerosis (purnyata)*. Emptiness *(sunyata)* is the unqualified identity of the conditional and the absolute. Because Christ was sinless, he was absolute, and therefore his identity with conditional and unconditional was a complete conjunction of opposites.
>
> Although this verse contains deep theological insights, Paul was more interested in the spiritual significance of Christ's self-renunciation *(kenosis, sunyata)*. So he admonishes his readers in the preceding verses "to have the spirit that was in Jesus Christ."

---

[71] Thus, for example, L. de Silva, *Why Believe in God? The Christian Answer in Relation to Buddhism* (Colombo, 1970), where de Silva, prompted by Buddhadasa, investigates the paralleling of God and *dhamma*.

The essential principle of divine *kenosis*, resting on the concept of self-renunciation, is this: that Christ renounced himself without losing himself. On the basis of his identity with conditional existence he denied himself; on the basis of his identity with the absolute (God), however, he did not lose himself. His identity was a relationship between the conditional and the absolute. However, this was unique, in as much as it dealt with a relationship between the unconditional identity of the conditional self and the absolute. This is the principle of *kenosis*, which has affinities to the Buddhist doctrine of emptiness *(sunyata).*[72]

This interpretation of kenosis by de Silva at the end of his life emphasizes relationship with a "thou," rather than grounding in an "it." For Paul, kenosis is essentially a matter of the will, corresponding to the Lord's Prayer's "thy will be done." The Kyoto school transformed this into a conquest of the personal will and God's conquest of a non-god. For de Silva, the will that denies itself in Christ remains bound to the willed love. In other words, it is linked to the overflowing love on God's side and Jesus' self-renunciation on the other side, so that Jesus can become the vessel of divine self-renunciation. De Silva's Christian theology insists that there has only been one such occurrence of self-offering or self-renunciation in history—that of Jesus of Nazareth. All later self-renunciations come to pass in his name, whether they take the form of taking the cross upon oneself or the loss of one's life. At this point the difference between this theory and Buddhism becomes very clear.

Immediately, however, de Silva searches again for common ground, when he turns to the theme of grace. Does Buddhism recognize grace or not? De Silva cites Edward Conze in order to refute Walpola Rahula's negative answer to this question.[73] According to this, the extreme of pure human exertion and receiving mercy through a totally separate power would not conflict with the Buddha's teaching. The Buddha rejected the idea that enlightenment or *nibbana* (Sanskrit: *nirvana*) is dependent on specific practices. Otherwise, *nibbana* would be conditional.[74] Buddhism distinguishes much more between relative (worldly) and absolute (transcendental) knowledge, in other words *lokya* and *lokuttara panna* (worldly and supernatural wisdom). If this is the case, one can view *lokuttara panna* as the absolute source of power or grace, which must precede human exertion and lie at its root.

These existentially important questions have not been fully clarified, de Silva believes. In dialogue, the religions could learn to understand their own intentions better, and thus help one another in the process of self-transformation. This would be dialogue's decisive contribution toward the creation of community.

---

[72] De Silva, "Buddhism and Christianity Relativized," 57.

[73] Ibid., 62; E. Conze, *Thirty Years of Buddhist Studies* (London and Oxford, 1967), 38-50.

[74] M. Palihawadana, "Is There a Theravada Idea of Grace?" *Dialogue*, NS 9/1-3 (1982): 91-103.

RESULTS AND PROSPECTS

RESULTS

• The historical confrontation of the two religions because of colonialism remains the main impediment to dialogue. The religions regard and judge one another not only philosophically and hermeneutically through each's established patterns of thought, but also each follows the pattern of historical experiences. An honest analysis of the historical and political offenses committed by each religion is therefore still very difficult.

• The dialogue in Sri Lanka and the periodical *Dialogue* have reached their self-appointed goal, the progress from diatribe to dialogue. This dialogue, though, has until now only overcome the "logic of apologetic comparison" in a rudimentary fashion. For example, Lynn de Silva remained oriented toward the contrast, synthesis, and eventual toleration of chosen concepts.[75]

• Dialogue shows itself to be a form of community building that goes beyond traditional boundaries. Language is only a factor of this. Philosophical and theological agreement alone does not create a community, and it may be asked whether people in a single community cannot speak several different religious languages. The sociological, economic, and political impediments to interreligious understanding and the fundamentalist opposition to dialogue on both sides must be more clearly analyzed.

• Comparison of concepts brings insight not just into what is foreign but into each partner's own religion. Matters concealed by linguistic forms will be uncovered as well as the pluralism within each religion. It is important that each religion's language levels be examined more closely. Ideas from the popular religiosity of one tradition cannot be contrasted to philosophical and theological abstractions in the other.

PROSPECTS

• The Western myth of cultural and religious evolution has been overturned. Also, many Christians as well as Buddhists engaged in dialogue perceived Western technology and the economic structures to which it is linked to be unsalutary. Discussion of God or of spiritual liberation must, in this new context, find a new language if it is to be authentic. It can therefore be expected that the dialogue in Sri Lanka will take the form of a dialogue-based liberation theology.

• Ethnic tensions are also supported by religious demarcations. The anticolonial Sinhalese nationalism could and had to support itself on a political interpretation of Buddhism in opposition to British-Christian dominance. Through this, however, the country's Tamil Hindu minority was also excluded. A Buddhist-Christian agreement through dialogue can and must gain immediate political

---

[75] P. Schmidt-Leukel, 200.

significance to solve ethnic tensions in the sense of acceptance of religious pluralism and the partnership of ethnic groups.

• Certainly, dialogue in the 1980s and 1990s turned again toward open confrontation. The reason for this is the advancing Christian fundamentalism that comes especially from the United States. This phenomenon, with its "unethical methods" (gifts of money, promises of employment, and so on) systematically pursues the conversion of Buddhists and once again preaches a "colonial Christ."[76]

• Still, dialogue in the past decades has led to a visible result, despite all difficulties caused by historical baggage: numerous Christians and Buddhists encounter one another as individuals or at institutional levels with critical tolerance.

---

[76] A. Pieris, "Dialogue and Distrust between Buddhists and Christians: A Report on the Catholic Church's Experience in Sri Lanka," in *Buddhism and Christianity: Interactions between East and West*, ed. U. Everding, 205ff. This work also analyzes the role of the Catholic church in the ethnic conflict between Sinhalese and Tamils and bemoans the fact that church efforts to mediate are lacking in credibility to Sinhalese Buddhists because of the colonial Christian past. Pieris warns the Catholic church against the new proselytizing "evangelizations" in the spirit of "Euro-ecclesiastical expansion efforts" (209). For the evangelical missionary movement, see the report about the efforts by evangelical groups to distribute literature aggressively to four thousand Buddhist monks at a Buddhist festival, since "they are ripe for conversion" ("Religious Tensions Averted at Mihintale," *Crosspoints. A Quarterly Publication of the Commission for Justice and Peace of the National Christian Council of Sri Lanka* 3/4 [June 1993]: 1).

3

China

In China other conditions for dialogue prevail than those in India or Sri Lanka. These factors cast an instructive light on every possible dialogue between the religions: China is a multiethnic state that has always been characterized by a multireligious situation (Taoism and Confucianism, with the addition of Buddhism from the third century c.e.). In the Neo-Confucianism of the Sung Dynasty these traditions had already greatly influenced one another. The "sinification" of Buddhism in this process corresponded to a search for national identity through cultural and religious integration. Christianity opposed such an integration, and its enemies feared that it could undermine the order of the state. All philosophical-theological polemics must therefore be seen in this framework. We must ask: Does the contemporary quest for cooperation between cultures through common appreciation of the cultural identity of each require a totally different self-perception of the religions concerned than we find in the history of China?

In the nineteenth century, Europeans perceived China as an undeveloped civilization, one that required a government ordered by the European powers. Religion, too, served to bolster this response. At the same time, China (unlike Sri Lanka or India) was not only subjected to European-Christian powers in the twentieth century, but also to Japan, which, like China itself, had Confucian and Buddhist traditions. For this reason the Chinese struggle for independence could not support itself solely on religious identity. Instead, it drew its arguments from the European Enlightenment and later from Marxism, which was critical of every religion and was linked to Confucian humanism. Today, too, in China the question of interreligious dialogue is two-tiered: it searches for a humanism that can form the basis of national identity and simultaneously make international cooperation possible. Have the religions here made themselves superfluous through their history of force and constraint?

HISTORICAL BACKGROUND

Since the sixth century c.e. there have been encounters between Christianity and Buddhism in China, thanks to the migration of Nestorian Christians from eastern Syria. Among the Chinese people Christianity was at first perceived as a Buddhist sect. This view was encouraged on the one hand by the acculturation of Nestorian Christianity into Buddhism, and on the other hand by the similar characteristics in the two religions (withdrawal from this world for the sake of salvation in an otherworld, ascetic morality, monasticism). Thus Christianity was included when Chinese authorities persecuted Buddhism in the eighth and ninth centuries C.E. This created a community of interest, which after the persecutions led both Buddhist and Christian scholars to translate Nestorian and Buddhist texts into Chinese.[1] The Nestorian church in China had its own symbolism and liturgy, which were influenced by Buddhism. Thus the Franciscans who came to China in the late thirteenth century sought first to convert these "renegade Christians" to Rome. On the other side, however, the Nestorian Christians had almost no lasting influence on Chinese Buddhism, and Christianity in China died out with the Islamization of the Mongols and eastern Turkic peoples. Therefore we will not pursue this theme further here.

THE JESUIT MISSION IN CHINA

The Italian Jesuit missionary Matteo Ricci (1552-1610) and his companions arrived in China in 1582. Their missionary style was not confrontational but rather diplomatic.[2] They dressed like Buddhist monks, referred to themselves with the word used for Buddhist monks *(seng)*,[3] and established themselves in or near Buddhist monasteries. This was very meaningful for Chinese sensibilities, since the celibate Catholics already resembled Buddhist monks. In both cases, however, the monastic ideal was incomprehensible to most Chinese, who built their lives around the desire for descendants and the piety of children toward their parents. For this reason, and because he recognized that Buddhist monks did not enjoy particularly high social prestige, from 1595 on Ricci turned to the Confucian culture of the upper classes, dressing accordingly and joining in the Neo-Confucian critique of Buddhism. Despite this, the Buddhists still remained in general friendly toward the Christians.[4]

Although the Ming Dynasty (1368-1644) was not the most creative period of Chinese Buddhism, the Christian missionaries in China had to reckon with the Buddhists. This was not just because the monks were politically active, but also because some scholars from their ranks accepted the Jesuit challenge to engage in formal disputations about religion. In Nanking in 1599 Ricci debated with the famous Buddhist monk San-huai Hsüe-lang. In a meeting with the Buddhist scholar Huang Hui, Ricci debated about evil, and Chu Hsing (1535-1615) defended the cosmological myth of the Sumeru Mountain against Ricci's exposition of the

---

[1] G. Rosenkranz, *Die älteste Christenheit in China in den Quellen-Zeugnissen der Nestorianertexte der T'ang-Dynastie* (Berlin, 1939).

[2] H. Küng and J. Ching, *Christentum und chinesische Religion* (Munich: Piper, 1988), 259; I. Kern, "Matteo Riccis Verhältnis zum Buddhismus," in *Monumenta Serica* 36 (Nettetal: Steyler Verl., 1984/85), 65-126.

[3] In similar fashion the Jesuit Roberto de Nobili adopted the appearance of a Hindu wandering monk *(sannyasin)*.

[4] I. Kern, *Buddhistische Kritik am Christentum im China des 17: Jahrhunderts* (Bern: P. Lang, 1992), 2.

Christian doctrine of creation.[5] Buddhists and Christians agreed in their valuation of the emptiness of the world and in the need to strive for another world, which they proclaimed to be the true goal of humanity. The Buddhists sought to recognize such Christian doctrines in their own scriptures. This was nothing new, because the different Buddhist schools had also been brought into harmony with Confucianism and Taoism in this way. For Buddhists, this is regarded as "the skillful means" *(p'an jiao* or *fangpien*, Sanskrit *upaya)*,[6] in other words, a pedagogically important path to deeper understanding of Buddhism.

Ricci saw the essential opposition between the two religions in the fact that Buddhists (and Confucians) blurred the distinction between God and human, and wanted to identify themselves with the highest essence. The Buddhists took up this argument and turned it against the Christians. One must of course recognize that neither the Christians around Ricci nor his Buddhist opponents had the slightest understanding of the multiformity of the other's religion. Each made use of the other side as it represented itself, which created the simplistic image of "the Christian" or "the Buddhist." Christian mysticism, for example, was totally unknown to the Chinese interlocutors.

The Jesuit missionaries discovered in China a culture that they considered more economically developed and politically enlightened than their European homeland. The only thing lacking, as Ricci believed, was that China did not know God, or rather, appeared to have forgotten God. Ricci knew that the Chinese in the early dynasties of Shan (eighteenth-twelfth centuries B.C.E.) and Chou (twelfth century–249 B.C.E.) and also later had venerated *Shang-ti*, the highest lord. It was first in the context of the twelfth-century Neo-Confucian reform, he thought, that the educated had not exactly lost their sense for the absolute, but had reinterpreted it and placed the impersonal Supreme Ultimate *(t'ai-chi)* in place of the personal *Shang-ti*. By this means the personal God and the many gods and spirits in general were relegated to the lower realms of reality. Therefore, China only had to be reminded of its original monotheism through a corresponding interpretation of the classics. Ricci sought to do precisely that.

Ricci could without great theological difficulties greatly esteem Chinese culture and at the same time hold to a Christian higher good, the Christian theology of grace. The Thomistic two-storied image of reality divided into nature and grace made this combination possible. The Neo-Confucian idea of an ultimate rational principle, *li*, could also be accepted completely under the category of natural reason. One only had to expand this Chinese reason with Aristotle's still higher rationality. This would then be a natural preparation for the Christian faith. Faith, in turn, would then so enlighten natural reason that it would finally attain clear insight into the existence of the soul, which clearly separates humans from the lower life forms such as animals and plants as the unique crown of creation. The soul is in the final analysis immortal and so cannot be dissolved in

---

[5] F. P. Brandauer, "The Encounter between Christianity and Chinese Buddhism from the Fourteenth to the Seventeenth Century," *Ching Feng* 11/3 (1962): 30-38.

[6] For an understanding of this central concept for Mahayana, see M. Pye, *Skilful Means*.

the breath of heaven and earth, as the Neo-Confucians claimed. Ricci did not deny the value of Confucian reason, but he wanted to put it in the place that he as a Christian regarded suitable: in the realm of nature, which will be lit by the grace of Christian revelation. Ricci believed that, just like Aristotelian philosophy in Europe, Confucian thought in China could serve as a handmaiden of theology, as a preparation for divine revelation.

Ricci was certainly not an advocate of dialogue in the modern sense. However, he was also not dishonorable in his attempt to imitate Chinese customs, to ally himself with the Confucian classics, and above all to leave Chinese understanding of Jesus Christ unclear. This is because the Thomistic theology of nature and grace, undisputed at that time, lent complete credibility to such a position.[7]

EARLY POLEMICS

After Ricci's death, greater disagreements between Buddhists and Christians soon developed. These came for the most part in two waves, between 1608 and 1615, and from 1634 to 1643.[8] The Buddhists hesitated at first to get involved in polemics, because such action contradicted their ideal of world renunciation. But the lay Buddhist Huang Shen from Fukien wrote a treatise against Christianity between 1633 and 1635 and finally called for resistance against the Christian mission. He justified this by pointing out that for over fifty years the Christians had spread their teaching of the lord of heaven, destroyed statues of the Buddha, and burned copies of the sutras and scattered their ashes to the winds without the Buddhists doing anything to resist. The Buddhists who took part in polemics, however, clearly had to defend themselves against attacks from their own ranks, because lowering oneself to the level of controversy over words appeared to testify to an I-centered attachment. Despite this, ever more Buddhists took part in polemic, because they distrusted the dialogue between Christians and Confucian officials. They feared that these two groups could form an alliance and take action against the Buddhists.

The first phase of the Buddhist critique after 1608 was launched by the layman Yü Shun-hsi (d. 1621) and the monk Yün-ch'i Chu-hung (1535-1615). Significantly, they began their critique of Ricci with a practical question. This issue had been by no means central for Ricci, but for the Buddhists touched a nerve of their way of life: the Buddhist prohibition against killing animals and eating meat. Ricci had criticized this prohibition, but for the Buddhists it was an expression of their merciful attitude toward all living things. The Buddhist critique was matter of fact and was not yet tinged with bitterness. But the dispute, waged through writings and counter-writings, led to the first government persecution of Christians by imperial order in Beijing or Nanking in 1617. This persecution, which lasted until 1621, was the background for a change in the tone of dispute between Buddhists and Christians, which became sharper in the second phase,

---

[7] H. Küng and J. Ching, 260.

[8] I. Kern, *Buddhistische Kritik am Christentum,* 5ff. The following information on early Buddhist critique of Christianity in China is indebted to Kern's book.

which began in 1634. This was no longer limited to theological questions, because the Buddhists had recognized the political aspect of the Jesuit mission. Now they criticized the missionaries for desiring to change the political and social power structures by means of their religion.

Huang Shen, the above-mentioned lay Buddhist from Fukien province, composed a treatise against Christianity between 1633 and 1635, wrote a letter to the government asking it to take steps against the Christians, and encouraged Buddhist monks to criticize Christianity.[9] To appeal to politically influential circles he also advanced Confucian viewpoints and mixed them with Buddhist arguments to produce five charges against Christianity:

1. Christianity rejects the substantial unity of creator and created and in this way rips apart the harmony of the world.

2. The Christians wish to discredit the preeminent spirits of China (including the Buddha).

3. The Christians destroy cult images.

4. The Christians reject the Buddhist doctrine of reincarnation. By doing so they seek to destroy the interconnectedness of all living things, and therefore are willing to kill animals.

5. The Christians are trying to win more and more influence, so that they can undermine the order of the state through foreign penetration.

Finally, in 1638, the Christian missionaries were expelled from the province of Fukien to Portuguese Macao. The message was clear: Christianity was no longer just a partner in discussion, to be opposed more or less benevolently. Instead, because of its foreignness, Christianity had been identified as a dangerous religious and political power.

EUROPEAN REACTIONS

Ricci's enthusiasm for a China enlightened by natural reason, which only had to be reminded about God, infected Europeans. The Figurists, a group of French missionaries within the Jesuit order who were active in China between 1700 and 1750, went even further than Ricci. They believed that not only had ancient China venerated God as *Shang-ti* (highest lord) or *T'ien* ([lord of] heaven), but the Chinese had also had a knowledge of what in the Old Testament is called *wisdom*. So they considered that the truth of Christianity had from the beginning been foretold in the ancient books of China. Now the missionaries saw their task to be the revealing of this latent knowledge and making Jesus Christ comprehensible to the Chinese.[10]

However, Ricci's enthusiasm also had a totally different effect in Europe. He accelerated the Enlightenment critique of Christianity. For if the light of natural

---

[9] Ibid., 16ff.

[10] The Figurists, whose name comes from figurative exegesis of the Old Testament as opposed to allegorical or typological, understand the Christian history of salvation to begin before Christ (see C. v. Collani, *Die Figuristen in der Chinamission. Würzburger Sino-Japonica*, vol. 8 [Frankfurt a. M./Bern: P. Lang, 1981]).

reason could produce such a marvelous humanistic society in China as was described in Jesuit reports, why did human beings need God? Where the Enlightenment was not articulated in the form of atheism, at least the question resounded: Under such circumstances, are mission, church, and priest still necessary? China became for many Enlightenment thinkers a model of human civilization without the restrictive authority of the church. The philosopher Gottfried Wilhelm Leibniz's (1646-1716) fascination with China is an eloquent testimony to this attitude.[11] While Ricci had wanted to bring the church to China and pour out grace over nature, the China-fascinated Enlightenment at home in Europe worked for the liberation of reason from the tutelage of ecclesiastical authority.

The Enlightenment's love affair with China finally ended with the first industrial revolution and the colonialism of the nineteenth century. China now appeared to Europeans as an underdeveloped civilization that required the ordered rule of the European powers. Was not Europe far superior to the Chinese in democracy and technology? G. W. F. Hegel (1770-1831) no longer agreed with Matteo Ricci's praise for the benevolent monarchy of China. Instead, in his judgment Chinese culture was characterized by the enslavement of free individualism. It was at this time, two hundred years after the Jesuits, that Protestant missionaries came to China, expecting to find paganism and barbarity. It was in this spirit that the new encounter between Christianity and Buddhism began. It was marked by an enmity that left deep wounds. Even today there is no prospect of a healing dialogue.

THE SILENCE OF BOTH SIDES

There are no reports of encounters between Buddhists and the Protestant missionaries in the early nineteenth century.[12] The old idealization of China had faded, and China's economy was weaker than in the seventeenth century.[13] The few Buddhist monks whom the missionaries encountered were probably occupied with the numerous popular rituals, giving an impression of superstition. And since the Protestant Pietists did not value intellectual education nearly as much as the Jesuits do, they had hardly any point of contact with Chinese culture.

In addition, Buddhism in China had already been weakened for a long time, and the most significant scholars were no longer in the monasteries. Since the days of P'eng Te-ch'ing (1740-96) in the Ch'ing dynasty, the intellectual elite

---

[11] See G. W. Leibniz, "Das Neueste von China (1697)," *Novissima Sinica*, ed. H. G. Nesselrath/Reinbothe (Cologne: Deutsche China-Gesellschaft, 1979).

[12] W. Glüer, "The Encounter between Christianity and Chinese Buddhism during the Nineteenth Century and the First Half of the Twentieth Century," *Ching Feng* 11/3 (1962): 41.

[13] Ho Koon-ki, "Where Is the Utopia? A Comparative Study of the Responses of China and the West to Each Other during the Seventeenth and the Eighteenth Century," unpublished lecture at the conference *China, the Chinese, and the West*, University of Hong Kong (March 1986). See also Whalen Lai, "Chinese Buddhist and Christian Charities: A Comparative History," *Buddhist-Christian Studies* 12 (1992): 5-33.

had gathered much more around certain learned lay Buddhists. There were several reasons for this development. For example, monks were forbidden to be socially active, because the government for a long time had been trying to bring the "Buddhist revolutionaries" of the White Lotus sect under control. This movement was an offshoot of Pure Land Buddhism and had developed chiliastic and revolutionary elements. Most notably, in accordance with the Maitreya mythology they believed that the coming Buddha Maitreya would, after the end of the age of decay of *dharma*, establish a kingdom of justice. Inspired by this belief, Buddhist political-awakening movements since the end of Mongol rule in the fourteenth century had sought to found a state built upon Buddhist ideals. They had played a significant role in bringing down the Mongol Yüan dynasty and helped bring the first Ming emperor to power in 1368. Then, however, they were persecuted by the Ming rulers.[14]

Besides this, one must consider that in the nineteenth century only Pure Land and Ch'an (Zen) had survived from among the classical schools of Buddhism. These had little interest in learning and still less in intellectual debates with Christians. Pure Land was marked by rituals and religious devotion; Ch'an (Zen) was oriented toward silent meditation.

Nor were the Protestant missionaries of the nineteenth century open to new ideas and lifestyles. The majority of them were Pietists and Traditionalists, who sincerely believed that China must be conquered for Christ and Chinese souls be saved for God's kingdom—by military means, if necessary. This "missionary militancy" was indivisibly linked to the foreign military encroachment in China.[15] Even the American missionaries preferred to trust the British for defense rather than the Japanese and Germans, because Britain had an army and warships ready for action.[16] For the Protestants, the dissemination of the Bible was the appropriate and infallible tool to civilize the Chinese and win them for their own churches. Unlike the sacramentally minded Catholics, the Protestants, especially Robert Morrison (1782-1834), worked above all on a translation of the Bible into colloquial Chinese. When the Chinese authorities finally forbade Morrison to set foot on Chinese soil, he had chests full of Bibles thrown into the sea near the Chinese coast in the hope that they would drift to land and fall into grateful hands. The goal was mission, not dialogue.[17]

The hands of the Catholics were tied, because despite Jesuit successes in winning converts at the Chinese court, Rome had decided against the Jesuit method of

---

[14] For the problem of the White Lotus sects in China and their continuing political significance to the end of the nineteenth century, see the detailed study by B. J. ter Haar, *The White Lotus Teachings in Chinese Religious History* (Leiden: Brill, 1992).

[15] C. S. Song, *Theologie des Dritten Auges: Asiatische Spiritualität und christliche Theologie* (Göttingen: Vandenhoeck & Ruprecht, 1989), 184.

[16] J. K. Fairbank, ed. *The Missionary Enterprise in China and America* (Cambridge, Mass., 1974), 271, cited by Song, 185.

[17] Donald W. Treadgold, *The West in Russia and China: Religious and Secular Thoughts in Modern Times,* vol. 2, *China 1582-1949* (London: Cambridge University Press, 1973); John Young, "Comparing the Approaches of the Jesuit and the Protestant Missions in China," *Ching Feng* 22/2 (1979): 107-15.

accommodation to Chinese culture. In 1704 the papacy had issued regulations against the practice of accommodation, which were made still stricter in 1710 and 1742.[18]

Unlike the Jesuits, the Protestants had from the beginning turned to the lower classes rather than the nobility and higher officials. Morrison's Bible translation was for the most part read to illiterate Chinese, who regarded the text as the infallible word of the highest God. These missionaries appealed to a naive fundamentalism that was extraordinarily critical of the abuses in old Chinese culture, including the oppression of women. Liang A-fa, a poor printer's apprentice whom Morrison converted, passed on a Christian tract to Hung Hsiu-ch'üan, who believed himself to be Jesus' brother. In this role he destroyed the statues of the gods in Buddhist temples. Later Hung founded a "community for the worship of God." When the government forcibly suppressed this group, it spawned the revolutionary T'ai-p'ing movement (1850-66), which had as its goal the establishment of "a heavenly kingdom of great peace." It became a violent peasant revolt, linked to intellectuals, which sought to abolish private ownership and establish the equality of women. In a certain sense this movement was the fruit of a union between Christian eschatology and old Buddhist-Taoist traditions in the White Lotus sect, whose members had yearned for a chiliastically inspired revolt. We cannot here go into the details of this complex and still-debated revolt.[19]

First Modern Encounters

Toward the end of the nineteenth century some English Protestant missionaries began to study Chinese cultures and religions with greater seriousness and greater competence. James Legge (1814-97) joined the Confucian classics with Buddhist and Christian ideas to create an idealistic internationalism. After his return home he became the first professor of Sinology in England. Joseph Edkins (1823-1905) was the first scholar of Chinese Buddhism to grasp its significance for the entire cultural history of China; he saw the Pure Land school as paving the way for Christianity. However, the first real encounter began with Timothy Richard (1845-1919). He worked for many years in China with the lay Buddhist Yang Wen-hui (Jen-shan, 1837-1911). In his work Richard found Christian concepts in Chinese Buddhism, and through their cooperation Yang was exposed to Western ideas.

Yang, as the overseer for technical projects in Nanking, had been a member of the first Chinese diplomatic mission to London. There he made the acquaintance of the German scholar of India Max Müller (editor of *Sacred Books of the East*) as well as the Japanese Buddhologist Nanjo Bunyu. Yang studied English and came to value Christianity as well as British democracy and Western science. He brought a microscope and a telescope home with him from England, and he also began to work for reforms. He stressed the importance of a spiritual renewal for

---

[18] H. Küng and J. Ching, 262ff.

[19] See especially F. Michael, *The Taiping Rebellion: History and Documents*, vol. 3 (Seattle, 1971); see also Whalen Lai, "The First Chinese Christian Gospel: Liang Ah-fa's 'Good Words to Admonish the World,'" *Ching Feng* 38:2 (1995), 83-195.

China's political future. After Yang's reform efforts met with opposition from the Manchu government, he dedicated the rest of his life to the spread of *dharma*. Above all, he supplied temple libraries with a new edition of the Buddhist canon, which he published on his private press. When Anagarika Dharmapala returned to South Asia by way of China after the 1893 World Parliament of Religions, he encountered Yang, who apparently was inspired by Dharmapala to encourage a reform of Buddhism. Thus one can with justice call Yang the father of modern Chinese Buddhism. Through a chain of circumstances Yang became involved in Chinese politics; he also took part in the early world Buddhist movement.

The Baptist Timothy Richard was by no means a theological liberal. Despite this, he knew that China needed more than the bare salvation of souls for the life in the world to come, because social conditions in China were catastrophic. Richard became a pioneer in the modern effort to relieve hunger. In 1898 he became an advisor for the reform interests in Beijing, which wanted to explore the possibilities for a constitutional monarchy (modeled on the British system) in China. Before this, in 1893 he had taken part in the Chicago World Parliament of Religions. There he met Anagarika Dharmapala, who wanted to spread his Mahabodhi Society worldwide. When Dharmapala visited China the next year, Richard introduced him to Yang. Yang was fascinated with Dharmapala's idea of a world Buddhist mission and wanted to construct a modern Buddhist college-academy, which could combine Buddhism and Western education.

Yang had read the treatise *Ta-ch'eng ch'i-hsin lun* (Awakening of belief in Mahayana). This is not an Indian sutra but a Chinese text from the mid-sixth century C.E. that had great influence on the development of Chinese Buddhism. Apparently it was Yang who introduced Richard to this text, as well as to the Lotus sutra. Richard and Yang then worked together to translate them into English. Yang saw this as an opportunity to spread *dharma*, while Richard had other motives. He believed that *Awakening of Belief in Mahayana* and the Lotus sutra constitute together a "New Testament of Buddhism," thus supporting Edkins's idea that Pure Land Buddhism leads logically to Christian belief. He was convinced that the Mahayana tradition, which so thoroughly transformed Theravada's a-theism, must have been ultimately inspired by the apostle Thomas's mission to India. There was a bitter break between Richard and Yang when the latter discovered that Richard wanted to translate *chen-ju* or *tathata* (thusness) with the word *God*, and wanted to understand the three fundamental concepts of Chinese Mahayana as they are taught in *Awakening of Belief in Mahayana* (substance, form, and function) as a trinitarian God. As a result of this quarrel, Yang withdrew from the joint translation project, and Richard later published the work alone (the Lotus sutra only in the form of extracts). Thus the first effort at a dialogue-oriented translation and a comparison of Christianity and Mahayana Buddhism by Christian missionaries in China ended in a debacle. What was missing was a hermeneutics of dialogue that could have dealt with the truth of both traditions while allowing for historical differences and theological development.

During the period in which he worked with Yang, Richard also supported the reform of 1898, which was led by K'ang Yu-wei (1858-1927). K'ang strove for a reform of the state based on the spirit of Confucianism; however, he was also inspired by ideas of a universal spirit that were Buddhist in origin. On the basis of his Zen exercises K'ang had had an enlightenment experience, to which (since he did not have the direction of a teacher) he gave varying interpretations. So at one point he believed he had discovered himself to be a bodhisattva. On another occasion he understood his experience in the light of the cosmotheistic totality of the Hua-Yen school. According to this view the world is a completely interconnected totality, which he interpreted to mean that all national and international borders should also be set aside.[20] For his publications K'ang must have relied on Yang's Ching-ling press and for his studies of Hua-Yen philosophy on this press's earlier publications. In his personal piety, however, K'ang was and remained dedicated to the beliefs of the Pure Land school. K'ang was also swept up in the new general interest for the two Buddhist schools *Wei-shih* (in India *Yogacara*) and *Hua-Yen* (in India *Avatamsaka*), which can be seen in the fact that he also wrote a commentary on *Hua-Yen*. K'ang's most important work, the utopian *Ta-t'ung-shu* (Book of the great community) champions the thesis of the unity of religion and science. Richard had indeed made Western science known but had never linked faith and reason together. Since Yang, too, had kept a clear divide between worldly knowledge and transcendental experience in Buddhism, it is unclear what the source of K'ang's view was. Possibly in this he followed the young reformer T'an Ssu-t'ung (1866-98).[21] In any case K'ang was a life-long advocate of Confucian humanism. K'ang's most important disciple was Liang Ch'i-ch'ao (1873-1929), who had studied with Yang. He was one of the first scholars to analyze Chinese Buddhism using the tools of modern critical theory.

Meanwhile a third reformer, the young T'an Ssu-t'ung, joined the group around K'ang in 1894 in Beijing. In 1893 he had discovered Christianity for himself. T'an studied first with the missionary John Fryer (1839-1928), whose spiritual orientation was close to Richard's. Then from 1896 on he continued his studies with Yang. T'an became familiar not only with *Hua-Yen* but with *Wei-shih* (the philosophy of *Yogacara*), which had been forgotten in China for centuries, and which Yang had reintroduced from Japan. T'an also had intensive contact with Richard. All this finally inspired him to write his own masterwork, *Jen Hsüeh* (Treatise on the good). In this work T'an combined matter and spirit, science and religion, a theory of the ethereal realm and all-encompassing humanity, universal brotherhood and the endless *dharmadhatu* (realm of *dharma*)—in other words, the teachings of Confucianism, Buddhism, and Christianity. He believed that these three religions teach the *unity of all being*, *selfless love* that flows from a cosmic unity, and the *courage of moral action*, which seeks to heal a shattered reality. T'an spoke of an ultimate unity of matter (ether) and spirit (love), by which the ether is at the same time an immaterial medium that draws together all of

---

[20] Whalen Lai, "K'ang Yu-wei and Buddhism: From Enlightenment to Sagehood," *Ching Feng* 26/1 (1983): 316-43.

[21] It is still unclear who influenced him on this issue. See Chan Sin-wei, *Buddhism in Late Ch'ing Political Thought* (Hong Kong: Chinese University Press, 1985).

reality in a similar fashion to Christian *agape*, Confucian *jen*, or Buddhist *karuna* (mercy). The science of magnetic forces and psychology, for T'an, testified to the power of higher consciousness, which the Indians had named *citta* and the Greeks *pneuma*. On the basis of psychological *Yogacara* idealism on the one hand (according to which all things proceed from a consciousness—*citta*), and on the other hand the cosmological vision of unity of *Hua-Yen* (according to which all occurrences completely permeate one another), he expected that a new unified world would come into being, of which Confucius was the ideal fore-runner. T'an regarded Luther's Reformation as an important step toward this new world, one that brought into the world the great good of freedom to follow individual conscience. Finally, he argued that the French Revolution added the ideal of civil freedom. T'an thus blended the idea of religious martyrdom with the theory of a bloody revolution. When the dowager empress Tz'u-hsi (d. 1908) brought to nothing all the reform attempts that K'ang had sought in 1898 with the "hundred-day reform," T'an believed that he was called to be a martyr. Therefore he refused to flee from governmental authorities and was subse-quently executed.

Admittedly, T'an's syncretic philosophy was a private belief that was autho-rized neither by the Buddhist *samgha* nor by a church. Still, it had grown from T'an's contact with three other cosmopolitans who were at home in the worlds of both East and West. These were the Baptist missionary Timothy Richard, who came into contact with the Chinese modernist movement nearly by accident; the Buddhist K'ang; and finally the Confucian monarchist Yang, who had himself fought for reform in the name of tradition. To understand K'ang as a Buddhist requires an explanation: He was indeed oriented toward a religious variant of Neo-Confucianism (*chin-wen*, the New Text school), but, like most Neo-Confu-cians, took Buddhism as his starting point, with roots in the Pure Land school as well as inspirations from Zen. The Neo-Confucians left Buddhism behind them, because it depended too heavily on the legendary miracle tales of bodhisattvas and credited Neo-Confucianism with a higher rationalism. This alliance of the two religious currents led to the renewal of modern Chinese Buddhism, and K'ang played a role in this development.

K'ang's 1898 reform was indeed a product of the Confucian ethos, but it was also inspired by Christian elements (*agape* = love), Buddhist praxis (*karuna* = healing turn toward all being), the Lutheran Reformation, and the French Revo-lution. All these were the building blocks for a social and spiritual renewal of China, so desperately needed in the eyes of the idealistic utopians around K'ang. Like Gandhi in India, K'ang attempted to join together tradition and modernism, national awakening and internationalism, the sacred and the secular. That Em-press Tz'u-hsi broke up this attempt after a mere hundred days, before it had a chance to become reality, thrust China into an epoch of further and much more radical revolutions. The political developments followed hot on one another's heels, so that there was no more room for dialogue of any sort.[22]

---

[22] See Chan Sin-wei.

INTELLECTUAL WRESTLING
FOR THE RENEWAL OF BUDDHISM

Yang Wen-hui died in the same year that the Manchu dynasty fell (1911). K'ang Yu-wei remained a Confucian monarchist who could not come to terms with the republican principle of human equality. His student Liang Ch'i-ch'ao, however, joined the cause of Sun Yat-sen (1866-1925), a Christian product of the mission schools, who was able to make a compact of Chinese of all "confessions" (Confucians, Buddhists, Taoists, Christians, and so on) in the national revolution of 1911/12. The revolution guaranteed freedom of religion. For Christians, however, that meant that from 1924 Christian doctrine could not be taught in their schools, so that the non-Christians who studied at the many and excellent missionary schools could not be compelled to undergo Christian religious instruction. So now the missionaries who came to China from Germany and America were people dedicated to the theological liberalism of the Social Gospel.

The result was a period of unusual collaboration between liberal Christians and liberal Chinese humanists. This lasted until the iconoclastic, anticlerical, and anti-traditional May 4 Movement of 1919 (part of the Cultural Revolution of 1917-23) attacked all religions. In the name of science and democracy the revolutionaries repudiated Confucianism as feudal, while Christianity and Buddhism were rejected as unscientific. The Marxists, for whom religion was not just antiquated but a dangerous "opiate of the masses" that must be eradicated, grew ever stronger.

During these tumultuous years of the early twentieth century, as China sought a new identity, there was a largely ignored movement of intellectuals who recommended Buddhism as the solution to China's problems. Here, too, Yang Wen-hui played an important role.

Yang had remained a pious follower of the Pure Land school. Despite his modern learning, he thought little of an alliance of Buddhism with science and democracy. His *Collected Works* mirror this reserve well, even though the small Buddhist college he founded included instruction in all modern sciences. T'an Ssu-t'ung and the Buddhist monk T'ai-hsü thought otherwise; for them, Buddhism was in agreement with modern science. Therefore they wanted to reach a synthesis of the two.

Characteristically, these modern Buddhists displayed particular interest in *Wei-shih* philosophy (the consciousness-only school, *Yogacara*). We have already mentioned that Yang rediscovered this system in Japan and reintroduced it to China. In this tradition, the functions and factors of consciousness are analyzed in their particulars by means of subtle observations and clear classifications. The followers of *Wei-shih* perceive such a method as *the* rational philosophy. It can be compared to Western rational systems, but is of a greater depth than they. From the perspective of such an analysis of consciousness Christian theology appeared old-fashioned and speculative as well as irrational.

In order to understand Buddhist modernism in China more clearly, we must also mention several other developments.[23] Yang had a great number of direct and indirect disciples, and K'ang Yu-wei was also influenced by him, especially in the light of interest in *Wei-shih*. K'ang's *Utopia* begins with an analysis of thirty-eight varieties of suffering that must be overcome—not to attain the Pure Land spiritually but to cleanse this dirtied present world. Buddhist doctrines were reinterpreted politically, and psychological analyses were transformed into social ones.

Liang Ch'i-ch'ao returned disillusioned from Europe in 1920, after he had witnessed at first hand the consequences of the First World War. After his return he developed a philosophy that depended heavily on the *Wei-shih* system. We have already mentioned T'an Ssu-t'ung's synthesis of Buddhist, Confucian, and Christian elements with its focus on a philosophy of history that climaxed in the coming revolution. Besides these figures, this group that was especially interested in Buddhism also included Yen Fu (1854-1921). He was one of the greatest translators of Western philosophies of his time and an important bridge between East and West. One of the most important thinkers of this movement, though, must be singled out for special study: Chang T'ai-yen.

CHANG T'AI-YEN (PING-LIN) AND HIS CRITIQUE OF CHRISTIAN BELIEF IN GOD

Chang T'ai-yen (Ping-lin, 1868-1936), an expert in the Chinese classics, had also supported the reform of 1898 and declared himself for republicanism in Sun Yat-sen's sense, for which the Manchus in 1904 imprisoned him for the next three years. He found comfort in Buddhism; in the light of the concept of the bodhisattva's suffering for the sake of other beings he learned to bear the harshness of his imprisonment. In prison he occupied himself with *Wei-shih*. Against the background of these experiences, Chang united the Buddhist concepts of non-self or selflessness *(anatman)*, the contrary interdependence of all being *(pratityasamutpada)*, and emptiness *(sunyata)* with the idea of democracy, filling this synthesis with his revolutionary vigor. He never lost a sense of the tragic entanglement of humanity, as finds expression in the idea of *karma*. Despite this, though, he dreamed of the brotherhood of all humanity, believing that people could live with one another in peace without requiring the power of a state. His Buddhistically argued essay "On Atheism" (1906) was written long before the atheistic propaganda of the May 4 Movement. It is a defense of critical reason against the opposition of Christian belief in God.

Chang's essay attests to a new Buddhist self-consciousness. There are, he argues, only three basic types of religious philosophy—theism, materialism, and atheism. In India all three are manifest in their pure form: the theistic *Vedanta* school, which regards *brahman* as the only thing with full being, and that would reduce all reality in the end to God; the materialist *Vaisesika* school, which, while

---

[23] Lou Yulieh, "Fo-hsüeh yü chung-kuo chin-tai che-hsüeh" (Buddhology and modern Chinese philosophy), *Shih-chieh Tsung-chiao Yen-chin* (Journal of world religions) (Beijing, 1986): 1-17.

recognizing nine elements (earth, water, fire, wind, ether, time, space, will, consciousness), finally derives all from matter; and the atheistic *Samkhya* system, in which objective reality opposes subjective consciousness and in the end reduces all to an abstract principle. For Chang, Christianity is an incomplete form of brahmanical theism, while the *Yogacara* school (in Chinese, *Wei-shih*) can be understood as the most highly developed form of an "atheistic idealism." Here the existence of God or the soul is rejected, but the materialist critique is only used to show the universal insubstantiality of reality. In this way *Yogacara* avoids both the errors of theism and the undeveloped one-sidedness of materialism.

Chang's critique of Christian belief in God concentrates on the following problems: Theism, according to Chang, holds that God is eternal, omnipotent, omniscient, self-sufficient, and all-encompassing. But if God is without beginning, how can one speak of creation? If God is eternal, how can there be a judgment? For a God who creates and then destroys has changed himself, which is contrary to the idea of unchanging eternity. If an omnipotent and omniscient deity had wanted good for humanity, how could such a deity have created a human being who was susceptible to evil? If, however, sin is actually foreign to humanity and was only prompted by Satan, why should God have created Satan? If God created Satan in order to test humans, then God did not exclusively will good for humanity. But if God did not create Satan, then God was not the creator of all. If Satan only became evil because he did not obey God, God must have created this servant defectively. If all of this was only intended to serve humans as a test in the choice between good and evil, it cannot be understood why an all-knowing God needed a test, when he must have known beforehand what the outcome would be. Otherwise God would not be all-knowing. But why should a self-sufficient God have created something beyond himself in the first place? If the created was nothing other than God himself, then creature and God are identical, and there was never a time when the world did not exist—a position that Christian theism rejects. If indeed creation comes from God alone, one cannot speak of creation at a particular time, when God of his free will created something. If, however, the world came into being on the basis of a divine impulse of will, it must pass away when that impulse ends. But if this is so, one must compare the divine will to a child's mood. And such a concept accords with the Buddhist teaching—founded on enlightenment—of a transitory reality, which is brought into motion by a blind impulse. If, however, creation is separate from God, as the Christians believe, then they must be divided eternally. But then God would not be the sole reality, and he only molded a previously existing substance. If one speaks, like the Christians, of a *creatio ex nihilo* (creation from nothing), however, one must assume an insufficiency in God that could move him to create something. If this "something" were good, that means that God himself was not sufficiently good, because logically he would only create something good if he had need of it. Therefore, for Chang, Christian theism and especially the doctrine of creation are totally contradictory and not compatible with scientifically trained thought.

Chang believed the *Wei-shih (Yogacara)* philosophy to be the appropriate philosophy for the modern era. And this judgment ought to make a school. His Comtian positivism—not, however, Comte's nihilism or pessimism—made him interesting to socially critical intellectuals, especially since Chang placed bold religious models and social governmental structures in relation to each other: polytheism corresponding to oligarchy, monotheism to monarchy, and atheism to democracy, even following one another historically. According to this model, atheistic China properly had to surpass theistic Europe spiritually and culturally, which according to Chang would come to pass, unless China should suffer a setback because it passed directly from primitive polytheism (Taoism) to radical atheism (Buddhism). The necessary transitional stage of a monotheistic purification of idols was missing from Chinese history. Pure Land Buddhism, though, was according to Chang in a certain sense such a theistic relict, which watered down a pure Buddhist atheism. For Chang, the more quickly modern China surmounts belief in Amitabha and the host of deified buddhas and bodhisattvas, the better.

In this case, admittedly Chang misunderstood the religious situation of Buddhism in China. His self-conscious Buddhist-rationalist atheism had no backing in the living tradition of Buddhism in China. The two great traditions, Ch'an (Zen) and Pure Land (Ching-t'u) are anything but scientific and rational in their orientation.[24]

CHRISTIANITY AS THE RELIGION OF BONDAGE

Probably the most original thinkers were Hsiung Shih-li (1882-1968) and Liang Shu-ming (b. 1893). Both regarded themselves as Confucians, but like K'ang and other Neo-Confucians they also had roots in Buddhism. Hsiung became a disciple of *Wei-shih* after 1911 and developed a personal "new consciousness-only philosophy." Liang won esteem with a first comprehensive comparison of Eastern and Western culture based on *Wei-shih* analysis. According to this study, the Christian West is extroverted, India is introverted, and only China has reached a desirable balance of both elements.

Another student of Yang Wen-hui, Ou-yang Ching-wu (1871-1944) defined his position in the debate concerning the religion of reason (Buddhism) against the religion of belief (Christianity). He interpreted belief in God, following *Wei-shih* categories, as a state of consciousness in which consciousness is stalled on the seventh step of the way of eventual enlightenment. The concept of God is still an I-related form of consciousness *(adana-vijnana)*, in which an erring self-perception projects an erroneous concept of God. Only those who free themselves from this egocentric consciousness of full psychic dependence can achieve enlightenment. In Christianity, human beings subject themselves to a God who is nothing but the projection of their own psychic inadequacy. So, as a result, belief in God leads to human bondage.

In public lectures Ou-yang differentiated between scientific Buddhism and an unscientific religion such as, for example, Christianity. Such a religion promotes submission to God, belief in the founder of the religion in question, as well as

---

[24] For a detailed discussion of the philosophical developments and for literature about Chang T'ai-yen (Ping-lin), see Fung Yu-lan, *A Short History of Chinese Philosophy* (New York: Macmillan, 1948).

acceptance of an inerrant scripture. Buddhism, on the contrary, is not a religion in this sense, because it recognizes only this single maxim: rely only on the truth, rather than a person; pay heed to the meaning, rather than the word. For Ou-yang, the Buddha was no god, but a role model on the path to self-understanding. Since the Buddha-nature is within, in the final analysis a person relies on himself or herself. The words of Buddhist scriptures are only a skillful means *(upaya)* to lead people to liberating realization through their own efforts. When Buddhists take refuge in the "three jewels"—Buddha, *dharma*, and *samgha*—they mean by this each person who is enlightened *(buddha)*, the all-encompassing order of reality *(dharma)*, and the spiritual community of those who want to undergo liberating realization *(samgha)*.

Ou-yang continued with a contrast:

> Christianity signifies the inequality between the venerated object (God) and the self-humbling (the human being). Buddhism, on the contrary, proceeds from the equality of all things, since reality is not dualistic. Christianity articulates itself in a narrow net of statements of belief. Buddhism, on the contrary, is dedicated to the ideal of rationality, which promotes freedom. Christianity sets limits upon itself, and is therefore not competent to discern the cause of all. Buddhism, on the contrary, is open and ready to test the truth of every assertion. Christianity generates fear and makes people dependent on others. Buddhism, on the contrary, is a heroic personal struggle.[25]

The "new Buddhists" of the early twentieth century thus found themselves less in dialogue with Christianity (except in the negative sense) than with scientific rationalism and Western philosophy (which they regarded favorably). Thusness *(tathata)*, for example, was compared to Kant's thing-in-itself or with the transcendental I. These reform-minded Buddhists were far removed from the anti-intellectualism of Ch'an (Zen) or the stress on belief in Pure Land Buddhism, and they complained that these traditional schools had undermined true Buddhist rationality. Their rational and individualistic interpretation of the doctrine of *karma* also meant that they taught the complete moral accountability of human beings. They ignored or reinterpreted the Mahayana Buddhist concept of mighty superhuman redeemer figures in the form of bodhisattvas, who could convey their positive powers of consciousness to others. Instead, these Buddhist reformers were concerned with a Buddhism that could transform the present. From the bodhisattva ideal they derived only a call to social engagement and protest against the political status quo.

It should come as no surprise that no alliance appeared between this movement and the Christians in China. Similarly, no Buddhist-Christian dialogue developed. The fact that the two great thinkers Hsiung and Liang rejected Bud-

---

[25] Ou-yang Ching-wu, "Fochiao fei tsungchiao" (Buddhism is not a religion), published lecture from 1912, in *Fok Touhui, Fo-hsüeh* (Hong Kong: Chinese University of Hong Kong, 1983), 2: 96-100. This rationalistic understanding of Buddhism was and is upheld by both Theravada and Mahayana Buddhists in China.

dhism in favor of Confucianism shows, as earlier with K'ang Yu-wei and many Neo-Confucians, that even a Buddhism "modernized" in the self-understanding of these reformers could not really represent the "soul of China."

KARL LUDWIG REICHELT AND HIS MISSION TO THE BUDDHISTS

It was the Norwegian Lutheran missionary Karl Ludwig Reichelt (1877-1952) and another Buddhist reformer, T'ai-hsü (1890-1949), who encountered one another in a way that finally made dialogue possible.

T'AI-HSÜ

The monk T'ai-hsü was a student of Yang Wen-hui.[26] The layman Yang had interpreted Buddhism for the twentieth century, and T'ai-hsü as a monk wanted to transmit this reformed Buddhism to the *samgha*. T'ai-hsü supported modern education and in 1921 established his own Buddhist college in Wu-chang. He created several Buddhist communities (that admittedly for the most part existed only on paper), founded two Buddhist journals, called together a national Buddhist congress, and undertook lecture tours both in China and abroad. He also supported monastic reforms, especially wanting to see monks engaged in social issues, particularly in the fields of education and health. He also recommended that the Buddhist *samgha* support the struggle against Japanese aggression. While his disciples admired him, T'ai-hsü had many opponents among the conservative monks. He has a prominent place in the history of recent Chinese Buddhism.

T'ai-hsü's *Collected Works* have a considerable range. He came from the lower class and joined the *samgha*—but the Chinese monks of that time were above all concerned with rituals and magical practices, and had little to do with study and meditation. So it is not surprising that T'ai-hsü's writings display less intellectual clarity or originality than those of someone like Yang or other Buddhist lay scholars, with perhaps the exception that he reclassified the old schools according to *Wei-shih* philosophy. T'ai-hsü also came to believe that Buddhism is scientific and democratic. He even drew diagrams intended to show that Buddhist *dharma*, as a universal wisdom, encompasses all knowledge and all experience. In a manifesto of 1918 he proclaimed that only Buddhism teaches and practices human brotherhood and universal peace on the basis of the universal brotherhood of all humanity; therefore Buddhism is entitled to a significant role in world politics.[27] T'ai-hsü criticized Christian theism and believed that Buddhism could give to Christianity what it desperately needs: a religious spirit that is not in opposition to modern science and that could be a foundation for trust and community.[28] Conversely, China

---

[26] For T'ai-hsü, see Holmes Welch, *The Buddhist Revival* (Cambridge: Harvard University Press, 1968).

[27] H. de Lubac, *La rencontre du bouddhisme et de l'occident* (Paris: Aubier, 1952), 239.

[28] D. A. Pittman, "The Modern Buddhist Reformer T'ai-hsü on Christianity," *Buddhist-Christian Studies* 13 (1993): 79.

also, according to T'ai-hsü, needs an impulse from Christianity, to the extent that Christianity motivates individuals to bring about harmony and community beyond ethnic boundaries on the basis of the universality of its belief.[29]

T'ai-hsü was able to make use of "clerical" authority, an attribute that the other Chinese Buddhist modernists did not have. Therefore his influence on other monks was considerable. He published popular tracts, especially in the journal *Hai-chiao-yin* (Sounds of the tide). In these he repeated again and again, in a strongly simplified form and without great clarity, the similarities and differences between Buddhism and Christianity. As he saw it, these were:[30]

Buddhism	*Christianity*
Similarities	
ten precepts	ten commandments
ten virtues	eight beatitudes
ten schools	ten churches
mercy	love
humans as the children of the Buddha	rebirth in baptism
recitation of the Buddha's name	prayer
Pure Land	kingdom of God
bodhisattva vows	Lord's Prayer
Differences	
atheism	theism
human autonomy	divine omnipotence
original enlightenment	original sin
causation in mutual dependence	creation
analysis of consciousness	transcendence
awakening in the Pure Land	last judgment

It is striking that the list of similarities is much more hazy and questionable than the differences T'ai-hsü points out. However, T'ai-hsü's significance as father of modern Chinese Buddhism is not founded on a philosophical accomplishment. It lies much more in the fact that he was able to give countless Buddhist monks a new confidence in their calling in light of the modern world.

KARL LUDWIG REICHELT

The missionary who finally entered into dialogue with Buddhist monks— admittedly hoping to convert them—was Karl Ludwig Reichelt (1877-1952). He, too, sought his own special duty in rapidly changing China. It was not long

---

[29] Ibid., 78.

[30] See Chang Yu-chin in vol. 15, 3-39, of this journal, reprinted in Chang Yu-chin, *Anthologie: Midwest China Oral History* (1980): 3-39.

before Reichelt's time that Timothy Richard had attempted enthusiastically to demonstrate the parallels between Buddhism and the New Testament, as we have shown above. Reichelt followed Richard in this endeavor. An accidental encounter with the young monk Kuan-tu in the Buddhist Wei-shan monastery became for Reichelt a decisive experience: Kuan-tu, a monk from the monastery of Pi-lu, was deeply impressed by the gospels. He became a disciple of Reichelt, accepted baptism, and eventually Kuan-tu converted his abbot and many of his fellow monks to Christianity. Reichelt founded a study center for the monks in the city of Nanking; later he relocated it to a hill in the north, before the gates of the city. He named the place Ching Fong (Feng) Shan. This missionary success would not be repeated. The center, however, was later transplanted to Shatin near Hong Kong under the name Tao Fong (Feng) Shan (Mountain of the Tao-wind), which was understood as Mountain of the Holy Spirit.[31] This place developed into a center for dialogue that remained controversial for some Buddhists as well as conservative Christians.

Reichelt studied Chinese Buddhism and began to develop a theology that could vindicate his undertaking. He adopted Richard's belief that Mahayana Buddhism had been influenced by early Christianity. Pure Land Buddhism, too, thought Reichelt, was dependent on Nestorian Christian influences. Thus, for Reichelt, the Nestorian church in China had not died out but lived on buried within some schools of Buddhism. (Reichelt possessed a Chinese manuscript with an account of Jesus' life, which he believed had not been influenced by more recent Christian missions.) As a result, his mission was based on an effort to make it clear to the Buddhists that their teaching led naturally to the cross, which ultimately, so Reichelt believed, stood at the source of their own Mahayana tradition. So, too, all fear of "pagan" symbols was unnecessary, because Buddhism had in its own manner and under other names maintained the living gospel in China. For the sake of consistency, Reichelt used the Nestorian cross, which grows out of a lotus. Besides this, Reichelt introduced liturgical elements based on those of the Buddhist liturgy at Tao Fong Shan (cymbals accompanying recitation, incense, and so on), so that the converted monks could feel at home in their new community. In this way Reichelt advocated the classical form of an inclusive theology of connectedness. Matteo Ricci had already sponsored some of its basic elements, which had later run into opposition in Rome. But this new effort by Reichelt to free the gospel from European cultural elements through inculturation and to make it understandable for the Chinese on the basis of their culture came under harsh criticism from neo-conservatives. Attacks came especially from the Christians influenced by the Dutch missionary theologian Hendrik Kraemer (1888-1965), whose ideas were based on the theology of Karl Barth. They saw such inculturation as a danger to the purity of God's word and raised an outcry against religious syncretism.

To how great a degree was Reichelt's "Christianized Buddhism" really syncretic or synthetic? Was his "Buddhist form" of prayer to God inspired by a vision of a *single* truth present in *both* religions? Or was this inculturation only a

---

[31] Eric J. Sharpe, *Karl Ludwig Reichelt: Missionary, Scholar, and Pilgrim* (Hong Kong: Tao Fong Shan, 1984).

clever means of adaptation in order to win converts? Opinions are divided.[32] Perhaps Reichelt himself reflects the complexity of the issue: He studied Chinese Buddhism, but criticized its myths. He had theoretical as well as practical concerns, and cited Rudolf Otto and Nathan Söderblom as authorities, but also referred to the comments of the Buddhist D. T. Suzuki on liberation through one's own efforts (Japanese *jiriki*) or through the other power (Japanese *tariki*) of grace, which both play a role in Buddhism, in his reflections. He spoke using expressions like "universal and special revelation," "impersonal and personal absolute," "limitless emptiness and immediacy of grace through *tariki*," in order to relate Buddhism and Christianity to each other in a fashion allowing for dialogue. However, Reichelt's *praeparatio evangelica* and his adoption of the early church doctrine of the *logos spermatikos* (the divine logos, which is also spread in the germ among non-Christians) could not hold out against the uncompromising missionary theory of a Hendrik Kraemer, in which "and" as well as every "as well as" appears suspect. The Kraemer group had the majority (and the financial support). So this modest initial step toward an understanding between the religions had no future; it remained an isolated attempt.

For T'ai-hsü, Reichelt was only another missionary who wanted to convert the Chinese. Despite this, he invited Reichelt to lecture at his college, because he was certain of the superiority of his own religion. In comparison to the Buddha *dharma* he believed Christianity to be scientifically backward and metaphysically naive, so it certainly could not prevail. The problem with such a judgment, of course, is that in this case—as so often—the *ideal* of one religion was compared to the *reality* of the other! Many Christian theologians had juxtaposed the reality of ritualistic popular Buddhism with its magical rites and corruptible monks to an ideal of the church that was far from reality. Now T'ai-hsü turned the tables by comparing the Buddhist philosophical systems to the primitive and still barely formed beliefs in Bible stories, with their miracles and supernatural occurrences. Reichelt naturally knew that the practiced belief of Buddhists in villages and cities had little to do with the rational systems of the Buddhist modernists—there was a mass of non-Buddhist superstition, false teachings, and unconsidered practices. T'ai-hsü's assertion that Buddhism is rational and democratic simply did not correspond to reality. Both knew this difference clearly, and with a mutual though unarticulated tolerance they dealt with each other in a friendly fashion, at least publicly.

---

[32] H. Eihart, *Boundlessness: Studies in Karl Ludwig Reichelt's Missionary Thinking with Special Regard to the Buddhist Christian Encounter* (*Studia Missionalia Upsaliensia* 24) (Uppsala, 1974) practically makes Reichelt into a contemporary theologian. For Eihart, Reichelt was a student of Mahayana, who interpreted Christian theology anew based on the insight in *sunyata* and the two levels of truth in wisdom and healing turn to all beings. Eric J. Sharpe's biography, *Karl Ludwig Reichelt: Missionary, Scholar and Pilgrim* (Hong Kong: Tao Fong Shan Ecumenical Centre, 1984), gives a more realistic picture. According to this work Reichelt was at heart a conservative missionary who (like other missionaries) used certain Buddhist forms in order to spread the gospel more effectively among the monks. This work also makes use of Buddhist criticisms, and the ambivalence of the cross on the lotus is justified.

But this unexpressed problem is of vital importance for the methodology of dialogue and has still never been adequately grasped in a comprehensive fashion: each side is convinced that the other includes more or less "superstition" or "false religion," in comparison to which their own religion appears more outstanding.

Thus again and again we find this Buddhist argument against Christianity: since *karma* is to be understood individually, a divinely effected general remission of sins makes no sense. As if this early Buddhist doctrine had not been substantially modified within Buddhism itself—in Mahayana—so that "savior figures" such as Amitabha can bestow their boundless wealth of merit on others. Through this the law of *karma* (that each deed reacts on the doer) is not rescinded but is certainly relativized and loses much of its force! Buddhist popular belief in China lived (and lives) essentially in the hope that through trust and devotion people can have a share in the merciful deeds of these bodhisattvas (Amitabha, Avalokitesvara [Chinese Kuan-yin], and others).

And from Christians we hear the argument against Buddhism that since one can only attain *nirvana* through meditation, Buddhism is founded on an ideal of self-extinction and thus places totally unrealistic demands upon humans. As if the just-mentioned developments in Buddhism had never happened, and as if in Buddhism the talk of "self" and "I" was not avoided with good cause, because a person cannot "do" meditation, but rather *nirvana* is exactly the state of consciousness in which the "I" is finally let go!

From the already-described encounters between Buddhists and Christians in China we can recognize that the difficulties in the way of a deeper dialogue lie on the one side in *political relations* and *historical experiences*, but on the other side in *projections* and *false perceptions* that hinder communication and understanding, that is, in an unapproachable *hermeneutic*. Among these, one should especially call attention to the unreadiness of either side to look beneath the surface of the other religion; the error of comparing the ideal of one's own religion with the reality of the other religion; the conviction that one's own belief is sensible, while the other's is superstition; and the hasty reference to contradictions in the other religion, where perhaps ambiguities that lie in reality itself should be left untouched. These factors stand in the way of a real dialogue between Buddhists and Christians, and by no means only in China.

THE INFLUENCE OF THE NEO-ORTHODOX

Toward the end of his life Reichelt had to defend himself against the attacks of neo-orthodox Christian theology. This shows how much Europe's spiritual climate had changed after the First World War. Kraemer had sharply set off the gospel from all other religions and had taken a stand against any sort of "connectedness theology." Karl Barth, in the face of European culture's collapse in the First World War, had sharply criticized liberal "cultural Protestantism," proclaiming God's negative judgment of every culture, including its religion. For Barth himself, Christianity as a religious institution also fell under this verdict of unbelief, and thus, like all other religions, it needed the unmediated "grace from above" that could only be given in the name of Jesus Christ.[33] But "off in the mission field" this was often simplified to the old formula: "them against us— the religions against true revelation." In this way truth and revelation were made special attributes of Christianity, while falsehood, superstition, and human pride were the properties of other religions. Today this concept remains stamped upon many Protestant mission theologies and churches (especially in Japan).

Reichelt's theology, though, rested on other principles. He believed in a universal divine revelation that had been made to all religions (Söderblom), which was reflected in the experience of the holy (Otto). In Buddhism, Reichelt held, the holy found concrete expression in the limitless godhead (the emptiness of Ch'an) that indeed transcends the personal but still does not close out but instead encloses (Pure Land). To many modern theologians this formulation no longer sounds provocative, especially since Reichelt added that, just as the formless *dharmakaya* of the Buddha finds its concrete form and completion in the grace of the *sambhogakaya*-Buddha Amitabha, so can this Amitabha indicate the path to the complete and unique revelation of God in the man Jesus. But in his own time Reichelt remained isolated, except for the support he received from Anglican Bishop Hall in Hong Kong. For his interlocutors among the Chinese Buddhists this language also remained incomprehensible. They did not understand Nathan Söderblom's or Rudolf Otto's theologies, rooted as they are in the Christian mystical tradition. Nor were they interested in subtle considerations about the different bodies of the Buddha *(trikaya)* or emptiness *(sunyata)* in Mahayana Buddhism. For them, Buddhism was a thought structure that must illumine every rational thinker without intermediary.

So Reichelt's ideas found no resonance. His center Tao Fong Shan became a transit camp for Buddhist monks fleeing from Maoist China, who received free board and lodging there. Some of them were also baptized, and Reichelt was criticized for once again in this way winning conversions through material incentives.

One of Reichelt's better-known students and converts was C. C. Wang. In 1945 Wang wrote and published the book *A Look at Buddha and Christ.*[34] In this work he portrayed the lives of both figures objectively. Jesus, for Wang, is self-offering love even to the cross, in obedience to the Father. He is the complete revelation of cosmic truth and the only path to salvation. The presentation of the Buddha, similarly, is canonically orthodox. Unlike Reichelt, for Wang there is no discussion of similarity between the Buddha and Jesus or a link between the two religions (either historically or in content).

Another early manuscript, however, in which Wang attempted to defend Buddhism against Christian calumnies, was not approved by the mission board of directors and could not be published.[35] Wang had done no more than to present a

---

[33] See M. v. Brück, *Möglichkeiten und Grenzen einer Theologie der Religionen* (Berlin: Evangelische Verlagsanstalt, 1979), 45ff.

[34] The text of 1945 can no longer be found. This study of Wang's on the Buddha and Jesus is however apparently identical to the text that was published in 1967 by Tao Fong Shan under the title *Shih-chia yü Yeh-su* (Sakyamuni and Jesus).

[35] His life is described in "C. C. Wang," *Midwest China Oral History and Archives Collection*, 1980, with accompanying documentation of the texts.

new interpretation of some Buddhist concepts. For example, he explained the Zen doctrine of the "original face" of humanity, the Buddha nature, as not necessarily in opposition to the Christian doctrine of original sin, since it is related to Adam's condition before the Fall. For Wang, the Buddhists mean a "face" that can no longer be seen until the human being becomes aware of his sins. Wang must, however, have later gone over to the missionaries' viewpoint. In a new edition of his book, published in 1963 under the title *Yeh Fo Ko-san* (A comparison of Jesus and Buddha), he mocks this same Ch'an metaphor and interprets it as the essence of Buddhist denial of the soul. He also mentions the Pure Land school, but only cites the criticism of this school within Buddhism itself, in order to prove that the Pure Land is nothing but a pious fable. As a pastor, Wang repeated the usual Christian attacks against Buddhism: it is pessimistic, fatalistic, teaches flight from accountability in the world, and devalues God's good creation.

In the mid-twentieth century this discussion had made hardly any more progress than just described. The results of new research into the history of Buddhism were only available to Chinese Buddhists and Christians through translations from Japanese or English. Since most of these texts related to early Buddhism, it is hardly surprising that discussion in China hardly has gone beyond considering the positions of South Asian Theravada Buddhism and reducing them to a rationalistic interpretation of Buddhism.

Overall, in the debates some (abstracted) parallels between the two religions were demonstrated. There is hardly a trace of exchange that would lead from heart to heart into the existential depths of both religions. Instead, participants were content with supposedly literal interpretations of dogmas. The question was never posed of what a dogma or rule might have *signified* for the people in a specific historical situation.

On the basis of the comparison of the two religions that T'ai-hsü had published, Buddhist authors after the Second World War turned Reichelt's fulfillment hypothesis (according to which Christianity would bring the hidden disposition within Buddhism to completion) on its head:[36] they argued that it was rather Buddhism that would bring Christianity to fulfillment.

This is clear in a tract that Chang Chüeh-i published in 1958 under the title *Yeh-chiao yü Fo-chiao* (Christianity and Buddhism).[37] Chang had attended a mission school and was converted there to Christianity. He had prayed intensively for divine guidance, once when he was twenty-seven years old to the point of unconsciousness. When no revelation came to him, he turned in disappointment to Buddhism. At the age of seventy he discovered that in the final analysis Christianity is only comprehensible when interpreted in the context of Buddhism. For the apostle Thomas had not inspired Mahayana Buddhism, but the reverse. Asoka had indeed sent missionaries to the West, and Jesus could well have journeyed to the East. The Buddha was commemorated as Josaphat in Christian calendars of saints, and no less a figure than Schopenhauer had discovered that Indian elements appear to have had an influence on Christianity. This well-known argument led

[36] Chang Yu-chin, 40-69.

[37] Chang Chüeh-i, *Yeh-chiao yü Fo-chiao* (Christianity and Buddhism), 1958. (Page numbers in text refer to this edition.)

Chang to construct his own: that baptism and anointing are related to Tantric initiations. The name Christus, according to Chang, came from Sanskrit, just as *omega* as a term for God is a corruption of *om* (3). For Chang, Jesus had been a celibate monk who taught the Buddhist laws, performed Tantric miracles, and experienced a yogic resurrection (5f.). Penance, incense, and the rosary, moreover, came from Buddhism (7). The Lord's Prayer is an appeal to *dharmakaya* through the Buddha's sons, who recite the Buddha names ("hallowed be thy name"), so that the heavenly guest will finally come from the Pure Land ("thy kingdom come") (8). According to Chang, Jesus taught the law of *karma* when he said that his disciples should "bring fruit." But Jesus had shortened the chain of reincarnations and only spoke of a *single* next life—the "life of the world to come" (12). The Holy Spirit, it was clear to Chang, is the Buddha nature. A God juxtaposed to humanity must be pure projection but is still a means to cleanse the spirit (15). The kingdom of God is within. The Christian creator God is identical with the demiurge Brahma, and the creation nothing other than the beginning of a new world cycle. God's words are in this sense efficacious *mantras*, which allow all things to come to being. Satan, who as a serpent tempted Eve, is for Chang the *kundalini* power, which is presented as a serpent in the Indian Tantras, coiled up resting on the base of the spine (16f.). Chang identifies original sin as the "fundamental ignorance" of Buddhists, which suddenly (without cause) appears when a "differentiating consciousness" develops in the otherwise pure Buddha-spirit (18). *Karma* is the unalterable consequence of one's deeds, which each individual has to bear and make amends for. Thus, for Chang, Jesus could not really forgive sins. Jesus was, however, the outstanding example of a human being who totally and with perfect consistency lived with his own Buddha nature. This Buddha nature, in Christian terms, is the God who lives in every heart. In this sense not only was Jesus the Son of God, but all human beings are God's children (21f.). Chang ended his short treatise with the following Buddhist-Christian prayer:

> Christ Jesus our lord, let your precious blood flow through our bodies, that it may wash away our sins and cleanse our hearts, so that we see God and can recognize our true self, in order that we can prevail over the pain-filled cycle of rebirths and attain the step of complete freedom along with all other beings. (23)

One might laugh at this unhistorical syncretism, but Chang was entirely earnest and honorable in his position. It was an attempt to join together the two worlds, worlds that in China before that time were almost always unwilling to come to mutual understanding or were at downright enmity. China had suffered under the dominance of foreign powers that had laid claim to Christianity, and people like Chang now attempted, in their own way, to heal these wounds.

RELIGIOUS-POLITICAL FACTORS OF DIALOGUE

In the Theravada lands (Sri Lanka, Burma), nineteenth-century opposition to colonialism took the form of nationalism. In China, too, as we have shown above,

Buddhism was included after 1898 in the current of hope for a national reorganization. The reformers' vision of Buddhist internationalism did not last long though. In the revolution of 1911/12 Buddhists and Christians both stood on the side of the republic, and Buddhists and Christians were also united in their support of national defense against Japan's aggression. But China sought for national integrity, and the presence of foreign missions (some of which controlled large territories) kept awake images from the colonial past. For the growing Marxist movement, patriotism and class struggle were the new slogans, and after the foundation of the People's Republic in 1949 the foundation of a native church, independent of the missions (and of Rome) was both necessary and possible.[38] Admittedly, dialogue between all religious institutions and the communist state now had priority, since the state increasingly suppressed the free practice of religion. Even within the community of the independent Chinese churches hardly any exchange took place; the already inherited divide between confessions was now strengthened even more through pressure from the communist state.

In Taiwan (the Chinese Republic), too, where in principle there was greater freedom of religion, all encounters and confrontations with Christians stood in the context of the question of national identity. In this environment the polemic of both sides could take on sharp forms. A good example is the controversy between the *dharma* master Chu-yün and his opponent, the evangelical pastor Wu (Cantonese Ng) Yin-po, in 1955. Chu-yün gave a series of lectures in Tai-nan that was intended to confirm to the Buddhists that, despite some Christian missionary successes, the existence of the Buddhist *dharma* was not imperiled, as one can learn thoroughly of Christianity in the sphere of social work. Chu-yün had not intended to begin an open conflict with the churches when he remarked more with sadness than with reproach that the Christians built their churches in the vicinity of temples so that possible converts could easily enter the other doors. He said, what is more, that Christian evangelicals had disturbed Buddhist assemblies and waved around Bibles to champion their truth loudly against the falsehood of the *dharma*. But, said Chu-yün, one should have patience and need not fear these attacks. Christianity, he pointed out, is "the new shop" in the marketplace, which must hawk its wares aggressively since they are not of proven quality. On the other hand, he compared Buddhism to the traditional well-established market shop, which needs no advertising because it offers the genuine article and can count on regular customers and those who know it.[39] Therefore, he said, monks should avoid unnecessary disputations, and practice whatever they could learn from Christianity, that is, occupy themselves with education and healthcare.

Chu-yün was a traditionalist. It was clear to him that Gautama Sakyamuni was superior to the man from Nazareth, because good *karma* had helped one to birth as a prince, while bad *karma* had made the other a carpenter's son.[40] High birth, he assumed, is the sign of a coming buddha, and a noble teacher would also

---

[38] H. Küng and J. Ching, 270ff.

[39] Chu-yün, *Fo-chiao yü Chi-tu-chiao te pi-chiao* (A comparison of Buddhism and Christianity) (Taipei, 1956), 4-7.

[40] Ibid., 8-19.

not end on a cross like a thief. Besides this, the Buddha had more than twelve disciples and was doubtless better educated, because there are many sutras in comparison to a downright meager Bible. Chu-yün, who like his opponent Wu took the miracles stories literally, was also certain that the Buddha had undertaken spiritual journeys to much higher heavens than Jesus. Chu-yün believed in *karmic* responsibility—that the individual suffers the consequences of his or her earlier deeds. Therefore he argued that God could not simply forgive, and prayers cannot blot out sins. Chu-yün made no mention of the obvious discrepancy between this interpretation of Buddhism and the Mahayana teaching of Amitabha and Kuan-yin (Avalokitesvara). Besides this, for him Buddhism was Chinese, while Christianity was foreign and unsuited to China—the fact that Buddhism originated in India made no difference to him.

For Pastor Wu all this was pure blasphemy. He wrote a rebuttal called *Kao Fo-chiao yü Chi-tu-chiao te pi-chiao* (A critique of the comparison of Buddhism and Christianity) that appeared in 1956 in Taipei. On the book's cover was a resplendent shining cross, whose beams drove away two pairs of foxes and serpents, that is, deceitful and poisonous liars. As a biblical fundamentalist Wu cited biblical passages by the page that were supposed to refute Chu-yün. And he promised a reward of a thousand Taiwanese dollars for anyone who could show that he was wrong. Wu demonstrated the same confrontational spirit in two other books in defense of the faith that appeared later. The debate was at times very personal and injurious.[41]

A critique of Wu's critique, written by Chang Chia-mi (Chiung-sheng),[41] sought to support Chu-yün. In this work it became clear what the chief issue had been all along: the question of which religion corresponds to China's national interest. The "old shop" of Buddhism, argued Chang, suits the spirit of modern China much better. Therefore it could be regarded as "true Chinese," something one could not say of the "Christian shop," imported as it was from the West. He said that Buddhists had proven themselves to be loyal nationalists, while Christians had declined to bow before the flag.[42] According to Chang, Buddhists had even excelled the Confucians in filial piety, while Christians had been slack in this regard. Further, Buddhists, he believed, are more comprehensive in the practice of mercy and hold the ideals of freedom, equality, democracy, science, and universal love in higher regard. In short, Buddhism corresponds more closely to Chinese sensibilities, while Christianity had disparaged the teachers of wisdom from China's past. The Christians (especially Catholics) were, thought Chang, too closely linked to foreign lands, and it was impossible to be sure that they would always be loyal to the state.

Wu had already responded to these accusations. However, the most dangerous charge against the Christians, that they are not patriotic and their religion is unsuitable for the political and national integration of China, continued to be levied against them.

---

[41] Chang Chiung-sheng, *P'ing Fo-chiao yü Chi-tu-chiao te pichiao kao* (Critique of the comparison of Buddhism and Christianity) (Taipei: Hing-fang Book Store, n.d.).

[42] Ibid., 20ff.

DIATRIBE INSTEAD OF DIALOGUE?

In China there has rarely been any exchange between Buddhists and Christians, and when it has occurred it has mostly been accompanied by more or less bitter polemic. And time after time theological-philosophical dialogue has been influenced by the problem of how China can find its political and national identity in the modern world without giving up its cultural identity. A further example shows this strain upon dialogue between the two religions.

The monk Yin-shun (b. 1906), T'ai-hsü's best-educated student, can be designated as the first modern Chinese scholar of Buddhism. In his youth he was close to Taoism and also at times felt attracted to Christianity. In retrospect, in two articles under the general title "Does God Love Humanity?" published in the Buddhist journal *Hai-chao-yin*, he reported on his difficulties with the Christian faith.[43] These works are among the most intelligent contributions yet seen by Chinese Buddhists in regard to Christianity.

He returns to the old question: How can an omnipotent and loving God have created a hate-filled world and permit Satan? Yin-shun further asks: Why must God demand Job's subjugation as the price for his renewed favor and love? The "slave mentality" must, argues Yin-shun, reflect the relationships of an undemocratic community. Adam and Eve wanted knowledge of good and evil when they ate the fruit. They were punished, and similarly Job's case confirms that the Bible extols blind submission to God and ignorance as preferable to knowledge. In Taoism, indeed, ignorance can also be valued as a virtue, but this is reached by means of knowledge. Besides this, the Taoist utopia of a last condition of happiness is clearly more civilized than the garden of Eden. As a rationalist, Yin-shun rejected reference to the unfathomable will of God. Belief, for him, desires knowledge. A God who so humiliates Job and punishes the technical achievements of the tower of Babel must have been jealous of human success. Besides, this God is bloodthirsty, as the Bible reports when in his name thousands of Canaanites were murdered.

Yin-shun was very deeply struck by the Buddha's pacifism but also regarded Jesus highly. He just could not comprehend why there should be belief in this sort of mindless subjection to a despotic God. He did not want to present a *Buddhist* critique of Christianity; instead, he understood himself as a *humanist* attacking Christian denial of human worth. For with such a view of humanity it would be impossible to create the independent China of the future.

Once again Pastor Wu reacted, this time to the verge of political denunciation. He called Yin-shun a "turncoat Christian" (referring to his conversion to Buddhism) who had eaten "Christian rice"—an allusion to the four dollars of pocket money that monks who fled from communist China received from Reichelt's mission on the Tao Fong Shan. Yin-shun defended himself, declaring that he had

---

[43] Yin-shun, "Shang-ti ai shih-jen" (Does God love humanity?) and "Shangti ai shih-jen te tsai tulun" (Again: does God love humanity?), *Hai-chao-yin* 44, 7-8; 45, 6-8, reprinted in Chang Man-fu, ed., *Ta-cheng wen-fu* (Taipei: Ta-cheng wen-hua, 1971), 163-244.

never received the monthly four dollar stipend from the "mountain of evil wind" (a nickname for Tao Fong Shan). On the basis of his sociological analyses Wu then denounced Yin-shun as a "leftist" communist sympathizer. Yin-shun asked Pastor Wu to retract such politically dangerous words—for in Taiwan this constituted treason.

The evangelical pastor Kung T'ien-wen saw Yin-shun's honorable doubt in another light. Kung had studied at the Japanese universities of Bukkyo Daigaku (Tendai) and Otani (Jodo Shin-shu)—both Buddhist-supported institutions—and was director of the Institute for Christian Research. He wanted to refute Yin-shun's arguments, and the result was an unbiased exchange: Kung's argument was that Christianity distinguishes between subjection to God and to a political power. But Yin-shun could not understand how the concept of "subject in Christ" (as in Luther's 1520 treatise "On the Freedom of a Christian") could lead to freedom. So the two sides had differing views of the Reformation's contribution to the development of modern individual and political freedom. Yin-shun did not accept the thesis that Luther's struggle for freedom had paved the way for the civil freedoms of the French Revolution. Instead, he believed this to have been a product of the Enlightenment, which in his view had fought against the Christian mentality. China must join itself to the humanism of the Enlightenment, which can already be found in the Chinese classics.

Thus this at first intellectually above-average exchange also ended in bitterness. The contemporary Buddhist newspapers like *Hsiang-kang fo-chiao* (Hong Kong Buddhism) or *Young Buddhist* in Singapore avoid confrontation with Christianity. On the Christian side, the corresponding publications also report hardly anything relating to a Buddhist-Christian exchange.

There are, however, two noteworthy exceptions: *Ching Feng* (published by Tao Fong Shan) and the *Collectanea Theologica Universitatis Fujen* (issued by the Catholic Fujen University in Taipei) both concern themselves regularly with Buddhism. Pastor Peter Lee is the director of the Christian Ecumenical Center that publishes *Ching Feng* and is himself a committed partner in Buddhist-Christian dialogue. To be sure, the conservative Lutheran Norwegian missionary directorate has since 1988 prohibited Buddhist-Christian dialogue at Tao Fong Shan because of lessening missionary activity. Thus, at least at this location, it has thwarted a process that Lee describes as a transition "from mission to the Buddhists to possibilities of a comprehensive religious dialogue."[44]

Ecumenical thought and interreligious dialogue are only very weakly developed in the Chinese churches. For many missionary societies the enormous China is one of the last white areas on the missionary map, and the competition for mission successes is great. American and Australian evangelicals and fundamentalists are especially active. They present themselves as a bulwark against communistic atheism. Chinese adolescents are especially susceptible to this form of Christianity, perhaps in part because Confucian culture is thoroughly moralistic.

---

[44] Peter Lee, "From Mission to Buddhists to Possibilities of Multifaceted Religious Dialogue," *Ching Feng* 16/3 (1978): 115-25.

Besides this, however, it can offer a refuge or spiritual home for those denied access to traditional moral teachings. But a Buddhist-Christian dialogue in light of this aggressive Christian missionary politics would be nearly impossible.

SPIRITUALLY BASED EAST-WEST EXCHANGE

Traditionally, Chinese Catholics were more open to the Buddhist heritage and in this respect often have also been better informed than the Protestants. Thus one of the best books on the history of Zen Buddhism comes from the pen of the Catholic John C. H. Wu, with a foreword by Thomas Merton.[45] Another example is the Jesuit Yves Raguin. For decades he taught Buddhism at the Catholic seminary of Fujen University. In his book *Buddhism: Sixteen Lectures on Buddhism and Christianity* (1975) he appeals to the openness of the Second Vatican Council and writes:

> If we wish to enter into dialogue with Buddhism, it is not enough to talk to Buddhists. Much more, we must bring our own theology and philosophy into contact with Buddhist thought. The dialogue must begin within ourselves. . . . Certainly there are similarities between Buddhism and Christianity. Some only see the points where we meet, others only see the differences. We must seek to understand where differences *and* similarities lie. In this fashion it will be easier for us to grasp what is particular to Christian revelation. Finally it will become clear to us what sort of difference lies in the fact that the Buddha simply wanted "to show the way to *nirvana*," while Christ proclaimed "I am the way." The mysteries of incarnation, the Trinity, salvation through Christ's death and resurrection appear in a new light.[46]

The book compares theism and atheism, soul and *anatman*, personal God and impersonal absolute, community of love and extinction in *nirvana*. In the process, Raguin argues that Buddhism's rejection of God must be interpreted in the specific context of Indian historical philosophy at the time of the Buddha.[47] Still, almost all non-Christian religions have distinguished between an impersonal absolute and a personal God. It is unique to Christianity to blend together these two planes in a single concept of God. Nevertheless, the history of Buddhism shows, according to Raguin, that later Mahayana developments (bodhisattvas like Avalokitesvara and buddhas like Amitabha) drew closer to the Christian concept of God.

While the theological-conceptual dialogue requires sharper distinctions, an entry to greater harmony between the two religions appears to lie in the spiritual

---

[45] John C. H. Wu, *The Golden Age of Zen* (Taipei: Hua-kang, 1975). Wu Yi made a Chinese translation of this work.

[46] Yves Raguin, *Buddhism: Sixteen Lessons on Buddhism and Christianity* (Taipei: Ricci Institute, 1975), 3.

[47] Ibid., 44f.

praxis to which we have alluded. Recent Japanese interest in spiritual exchange between Christians and Zen Buddhists, as practiced above all by Hugo M. Enomiya-Lassalle and his students, has also spurred some Catholics in Taiwan to similar endeavors. Father Chang Chiung-shen, on the occasion of meditation courses for nuns, has given lectures (later published).[48] He remarks that it is a historical irony that Zen first attracted the attention of Catholics in Japan, while it originated in China.

There are, however, reasons for this situation that shed a light on the dialogue situation in China. As an institution, Zen in Japan was passed on in a purer fashion than Ch'an in China. In Japan the practice of *kung-an (koan)* and understanding of emptiness were also transmitted with few compromises. In Taiwan or Hong Kong, for example, there is hardly a pure Ch'an center. The mainstream of Chinese spiritual culture was fed much more from Taoist and Confucian streams. So, too, Chang's understanding of Ch'an is on the one side colored by Christianity and on the other side is characteristically Chinese. For him, the *personal* aspect of God best came to expression through the rational, extroverted tradition of the West, while the *complementary impersonal* aspect of God is thematized by the rational but introverted wisdom of China. There, devotional prayer based on objective images gave rise to personality and society as well as representation and emotional engagement; here, on the contrary, are consciousness of the flow of all forms and a greater inner transparency. The Greco-Christian inheritance of a dualism of body and soul sees in spiritual exercises a flight from the physical form. But Eastern anthropology, based on various types of yoga, uses body position (the lotus position) and concentrates the energies on the stomach *(t'an-t'ien)*. Although the East neglects the furthest contact (with God) and runs the danger of falling into a not-self nihilism, still it goes untiringly along the path of driving out of oneself the "ungodly" and reveals the godhead as in the final analysis transpersonal and ineffable.[49]

When we analyze Chang's West-East, *yin-yang* style of harmony in retrospect, certain problems do indeed appear. Did he not simplify the conquest of the word in Ch'an on the one side and the affirmation of the logos in Christianity on the other? His lectures lack the existential experience and depth that can be found in Lassalle, who contrasted two self-contained meditation systems that demonstrated structural parallels, as he had experienced in his decades-long practice of both. While Chang begins with the differences in theological teaching, for Lassalle these were completely secondary issues. Chang shows little understanding of the subtlety of the dialectic in Mahayana or for the essence of *kung-an (koan)*. So he repeated many particular points of the Confucian critique of Ch'an relating to the doctrine of emptiness. Admittedly, moralistic Neo-Confucianism, arguing as it does in dualities, is certainly not the most reliable authority for questions about Buddhist meditation practices.

---

[48] Chang Chiung-shen, *Chung-kuo ling-shu ka-ni* (Discussion of Chinese spiritual exercises) (Tai-chung: Kuang-chi, 1978).

[49] Ibid., 9-38.

Also, Chang is isolated in China. Only a few Christians practice Buddhist meditation. And, for example, unlike Japan, there is no Buddhist answer to this form of appropriation of Buddhist meditation by Christians in China.

The Presbyterian theologian Choan-Seng Song (b. 1929 in Tainan, Taiwan) is striving for connection with a Christian political popular theology while remaining conscious of China's classical spiritual values. He studied in Europe and the United States and wrote his dissertation on Karl Barth's and Paul Tillich's theology of religions in 1964.[50] From 1965 on he taught at the Presbyterian theological high school in Tainan. In 1970 he emigrated to the United States for political reasons (the problem of Formosa/Taiwan's self-determination in relation to mainland China).[51] He worked from 1973 to 1981 as assistant director of the commission for belief and church constitution at the ecumenical council of churches in Genf. After that he returned to Asia as a teacher of theology for a time. Since 1986 he has been a professor at the Pacific School of Religion in Berkeley, California. Song begins with the view that it is impossible to know God. This is attested throughout the Christian tradition, in what is called the dark or hidden side of God (for Luther, the *deus absconditus*). In Buddhism, a similar insight is expressed through the concept of emptiness *(sunyata)*. In interreligious dialogue, however, Song believes that one must leave these abstract theological concepts behind and work for a communication "from heart to heart."[52] Certainly in Asia, too, Asian spirituality is being more and more superseded by the materialism of the consumer society—the religions must join together to combat the "trivialization" of human problems by the mass media.[53] Song speaks very generally of "Asian spirituality" without making it clear what he means by this expression. In general, it is decisive for him that, in contrast to Europe where society is composed of more or less autonomous individuals, Asian sensibilities rest on the preeminence of community over individual. In Buddhism, to be sure, this aspect is not so distinct.[54] Confucian and Buddhist elements are thoroughly mixed in Song's views, but this corresponds to the religious situation in Taiwan. In Buddhism, for Song, one can doubtless find "traces of salvation,"[55] but Christ cannot be understood as a fulfillment of the Buddha or as a bodhisattva. Instead, he argues that bodhisattvas are comparable to Old Testament prophets, inasmuch as both carried out a spiritual catharsis in the societies of their time. They are

---

[50] C. S. Song, "The Relation of Divine Revelation and Man's Religion in the Theologies of Karl Barth and Paul Tillich," dissertation, Union Theological Seminary, New York, 1965. Further works of Song include *Christian Mission in Reconstruction* (Madras: CLS, 1975; reprint Maryknoll, N.Y.: Orbis Books, 1977); *The Compassionate God* (Maryknoll, N.Y.: Orbis Books, 1982); *Tell Us Our Names: Story Theology from an Asian Perspective* (Maryknoll, N.Y.: Orbis Books, 1979); *Jesus and the Reign of God* (Minneapolis, Minn.: Fortress Press, 1993).

[51] See L. Vischer, "Nachwort," in C.S. Song, *Die Tränen der Lady Meng. Ein Gleichnis für eine politische Theologie des Volkes* (Basel: Friedrich Reinhardt Verlag, 1982), 81ff.

[52] Song, *Theologie des Dritten Auges* (Göttingen: Vandenhoeck, 1989), 28ff.

[53] Ibid., 45f.

[54] Ibid., 15.

[55] Ibid., 144.

both ambassadors and conveyors of the hope that God has not abandoned the world.[56] Song differentiates between two sorts of spirituality: a "Buddha-type" and a "Christ-type." The first is more transhistorical, life-denying, and legalistic, and thus related to the Latin type of Christian redemption doctrine [*sic*]. The second culminates in God's self-renunciation on the cross.[57] According to Song, the lotus and the cross symbolize on the one side unity with nature and on the other side opposition to nature—in other words stand in contrast to one another.[58] In a similar contrast, while Jesus is the "incarnation" of God's love, the Buddha can only be understood as the "incomplete reflection" of the same.[59] Song takes this difference for granted in Christian theological self-understanding, giving no evidence of how he might support it in argument. Elsewhere he gives a more nuanced judgment. Thus, for example, he finds in Buddhism a thorough political engagement and action on behalf of the oppressed, as in Vietnam where Buddhist monks placed themselves on the side of the needy through their self-offering (self-immolation during the Vietnam War).[60] In light of such Buddhist experiences, Song came to the decision that in God's judgment Buddhists can be counted among the righteous, since they have helped the needy without even knowing that Jesus himself had done so (cf. Mt 25:40).[61] Both Jesus and Gautama Sakyamuni have become models to the poor; both opposed the religious hierarchies of their time and fought against their privileges.[62] This must be a part of the modern cooperation between Buddhists and Christians. As a result, for Song, the role of Christian mission is no longer "to claim people who consider themselves members of another religious community, but to grow together in knowledge and experience of what God effects for the salvation of this world."[63]

Song, with this dialogue-friendly approach, is an exception among Chinese Christians. The reasons for the very weak dialogue between Buddhists and Christians in China lie, as we have shown, in the general mistrust of both sides and the resulting lack of communication.

BEYOND OLD CONTROVERSIES—A BELIEF IN HARMONY?

For most Chinese it is clear: Buddhism is spiritually more sublime than Christianity. For example, a widely disseminated textbook by Lin Shih-mien, which compares the two religions,[64] is completely typical in depicting Christianity in an unfavorable light. For example, he makes the following comparisons:

---

[56] Ibid., 147.

[57] Ibid., 72ff.

[58] Ibid., 135ff.

[59] Ibid., 141.

[60] Ibid., 150ff.

[61] Ibid., 147f.

[62] Ibid., 135ff.

[63] Ibid., 148.

[64] Lin Shih-mien, *Pi-chiu tsung-chiao hsin-yang* (Comparison of religious beliefs) (Taipei: T'ien-hua, 1981).

• Buddhism is concerned with enlightenment, while Christianity focuses on God, who sends his son.

• In one religion a person can become a buddha; in the other the human being can never become God.

• Buddhism includes belief in universal reason, while Christianity is based on the idea of a unique revelation.

• Buddhism leads to spiritual openness and self-confidence, while Christianity generates fear and demands belief.

• In one religion the Buddha as teacher has employed clever means and leads pupils with mercy and love but cannot upset the right law of cause and effect. The other religion has an almighty, omniscient God who loves whom he will and damns whom he will.

• One upholds the equality of all beings in a common Buddha nature; the other has a creator to whom all beings are subject, so that they in turn force others into subjection.

• In one religion there is a pluralism of doctrines and ways that all lead to liberation and that are not limited to human beings (but also include animals, and so on). In the other is a solitary doctrine that is focused exclusively on humans and even among them only claims to save those who believe in it.

• Buddhism has the sutras, which can be rationally examined; Christianity has an inerrant Bible.

Only at the end does the author make a concession: Christians, fortunately, reject the veneration of all idols, while most Buddhists are not free of this. Still, for Buddhists too, images are only a means that at times can help the unenlightened. In truth, however, he asserts that all idols are empty and every attachment to them is an error, which is unfortunately not always clear enough to many simple Buddhists.

Here we see yet again that in China most Buddhist attempts to understand Christianity do not go beyond such superficial contrasts.

The first steps toward changing this predicament came in the 1980s. Growing interest in the academic field of religious studies, also present in Hong Kong and Taiwan, has brought scholars into the discussion, among whom it is possible to see appreciation of both religions. Their opinions are hardly encumbered at all by historical prejudices and religio-political considerations.

Thus in 1982 the young Christian scholar Liang Yen-ch'eng (Cantonese Leung In-shing), who had studied with Fok Tou-hui, the leading scholar of Buddhism in Hong Kong, wrote the widely disseminated book *Hui-ching shen-yao* (A spiritual journey to different regions of intellectual experience).[65] In a mythical journey whose literary form is related to Buddhist pilgrimages *(Gandavyuha)* through different realms of *dharma (dhatu)* this book depicts with existential pathos how the author travels through Western rationalism, then Taoist nothingness, and comes to know Buddhist emptiness and Confucianism's endless ethical creativity, so that in the end he can finally see human fallibility. An encounter with the church father Augustine brings the pilgrim to eternal life. On this journey each religion

---

[65] Leung In-shing, *Hui-ching shen-yao* (Taipei: T'ien-tao, 1982).

is taken seriously, and the author does not construct a hierarchy of "better" and "worse." As in the Buddhist view of the fluctuation of various horizons for perspective, so also here different entries to reality appear based on differing perspectives in the different religions, typologized pluralistically. Here and there Buddhism and Christianity meet one another in a significant way: the unfruitful Theravada issues of self versus not-self or theism versus atheism no longer stand in the way of deeper understanding. Where this problem appears again in Mahayana (especially from the Chinese perspective) as the doctrine of emptiness *(sunyata)*, Leung interprets it as the sense of "impressions of the state of being." Further, he believes that the Buddhist distinct consciousness that attaches to objects anticipates Adam's "eating the fruit of the tree of distinct knowledge." Or turned around, for Leung, the Christian opposition to all forms of veneration of images credits Buddhist doctrine that the consciousness confers on (empty) objects an absoluteness *(svabhava)* that they do not really possess. Even the Christian concept of original sin can appear in Buddhist form as *pen-chüeh* or not-yet-known enlightenment. This is because the latter, it is said, is nothing other than the still-unfreed Buddha nature or "*tathagata-garbha* in slavery." In this way it is possible for Leung not to be mired down in the often-repeated oppositions but instead to pose questions based on their existential significance and thus issue an invitation for *encounter*.

Leung also took part in Christian-Confucian dialogues in 1985; the results were published under the title *Hui-t'ung yü chuan-hua* (Understanding and transformation).[66] In this work he speaks of the need for Christianity to be "de-Hellenized." Although T. Fang and others had already brought the opposition between static Greek ontology and dynamic Taoist evolution to attention, Leung sought a new vocabulary that could avoid the problems of translating Greek and Greco-Christian terms. He first broke Western metaphysical constructions to pieces, so that he could build up new categories on the basis of an Eastern "rationalism" and "perspectivism." Although the issue here was a Confucian-Christian dialogue, Buddhism is included when Leung speaks of China's "rounded, complete, harmonious world view." For this is a metaphor of the Buddhist T'ien-t'ai school. Can this metaphor in fact open new perspectives of the "Christian doctrine of humanity's alienation" from its origin? Is harmony among the peoples and the religions possible?

Leung's spiritual journey follows a path that many Chinese intellectuals since the nineteenth century have traversed. The intra-Chinese struggle over the relationship among Confucianism, Taoism, and Buddhism in the formation of a Chinese identity is, however, much older. The Chinese, and by no means only the intellectuals, had been dominated by a Neo-Confucian influence since the twelfth century. This reshaped Buddhist thought so strongly that it is no coincidence that the Buddhist modernists hardly employed central expressions such as *not-self,* *emptiness,* and so on. Some (Buddhist) modernists then saw in Western rationalism a new possibility for the still incomplete synthesis of the Chinese traditions. Others retreated to traditional Neo-Confucian/Buddhist positions. Yet

---

[66] *Hui-t'ung yü chuan-hua* (Taipei: Yu-chiu, 1985).

others attempted to find a middle way. Still, almost all Chinese intellectuals were and are fascinated by the theme of the unity of "spirit and human nature" *(hsin-hsing)*. From this point they throw a bridge across to ethics, which in turn for someone like Leung, can lead much more smoothly to Christianity than would have been possible for a typical practitioner of Zen Buddhism in Japan.

Although Buddhism is not at the center of European-Chinese encounters, still the Buddhist components of Chinese culture are so significant that they cannot be neglected. Above all, one must shun the oversimplified catchwords of supposedly atheistic Buddhism, theistic Christianity, and agnostic Confucianism. It may be that with deeper analysis the three will be shown to have more in common than appears to be the case on the surface. In the final analysis, the nature gods that Buddhism opposed are totally different from the God of monotheistic Jewish and Christian belief. Buddhism and Christianity prevailed over the old conceptions of the divine that they met with in different ways. They developed philosophical-theological systems intended to protect adherents from a lapse into idolatry of expressions or images: in Christianity this is the dogma of creation from nothing *(creatio ex nihilo)*; in Buddhism the corresponding idea is the formula of not-self *(anatman)*. The corresponding doctrines are only meaningful in the context in which they were formulated. Besides, someone who is not attached to an immutable self (and the Christian concept of person does not mean this) need not feel attacked by the Buddhist doctrine of not-self. Besides each religion's concepts, in other words, their metaphysical dogmatizing must also be taken into account if there is to be hope for a meaningful Buddhist-Christian dialogue. This is all too clear from the example of China's history.

CONCLUSION AND PROSPECTS

• Buddhist-Christian dialogue in China is only very weakly developed. A reason for this is the fact that Buddhism—compared to its position in countries like Korea or Japan—is not at the center of Chinese culture. Chinese Christians, who work to create a native theology, thus mostly look to Confucianism rather than Buddhism and, in the People's Republic, occasionally to Marxism.

• Against the backdrop of colonial history the Chinese reformers of the nineteenth and twentieth centuries have looked toward Western secular science and democracy, which must be linked to the quest for national identity. Thus many interpreted native Buddhism as the suitable partner for a modernization oriented on rationality, while Christianity was portrayed as antiquated and opposed to science and democracy, especially since it was associated with the colonial powers.

• The Christian Chinese churches (except in the People's Republic) have little ecumenical cooperation. This is because different missionary societies generate divergent loyalties among the Chinese Christians and are rivals for conversions. The union of the Protestant Chinese Christian Association is directed outward rather than inward, because narrow loyalties continue without check. The high churches (Catholics and Anglicans, especially in British Hong Kong) developed a greater self-confidence and are therefore more open to assimilation—it is not a coincidence that Reichelt found his best support from Bishop Hall of Hong Kong. Biblical fundamentalism, American revivalism, pietistic evangelicals, and the mentality they share as a bulwark against communism make ecumenical efforts appear suspect and offer no basis for a dialogue with Buddhism.[67]

• So how might the future look, or what would be the necessary conditions for a more fruitful encounter between Buddhists and Christians?

However important the rational humanism of the liberal twenties may be for modern Chinese Buddhist self-understanding, still there can be no doubt that Chinese Buddhists must overcome the narrow interpretation of their tradition as based on scientific and democratic values. This is not because such an interpretation is completely false, but because it too starkly simplifies, especially in a world that more and more questions the premises of a rationalistic scientific faith. Besides this, such an interpretation has never been appropriate, especially for Chinese Buddhism. From this self-understanding emerges the caricature of Christian belief in an almighty God that is just as shallow as most Christian interpretations of Buddhism. Dialogue has rarely grown from a polemical confrontation of one belief system against the other. To find a way out of this dead end, the Buddhists must first learn to regard more realistically their Mahayana tradition as it has developed in China. The Christians for their part must acquire a new historical and critical perspective on their own religion, so that historically and linguistically conditioned views can be recognized and an interreligious hermeneutic can take shape. There are still not enough educational possibilities for Chinese Buddhists available in the Chinese language. Christian theological instruction in Chinese is best accomplished within an institutional structure, but most seminaries are concerned with little besides pastoral theology. To this point the study of Buddhism (especially by the circle around Fok Tou-hui in Hong Kong) has had little influence in creating a more accurate understanding of Buddhism on either side, with the noteworthy exception of Leung In-shing, whom we have discussed. With him it is possible to trace the direction in which Buddhist-Christian dialogue could develop.

• Dialogue must be based upon existential encounter and experience. The Chinese debate, on the contrary, has to this time been played out almost exclusively on the level of speculative reason. The result has been the confrontation of traditional doctrinal views. However, when ideas are not related to the real life of human beings, they remain abstract. The struggle for personal and national identity that already shaped the Chinese debate in the nineteenth and early twentieth centuries will be influential in a very different way in the future for Chinese Christian-Buddhist encounter. Whether this will be cooperative or confrontational remains to be seen.

---

[67] For a characterization of Chinese Christianity, see Wu Liming (Cantonese Ng Lee-ming), *Chi-tu-chiao yü Chung-kuo she-hui pien-ch'ien* (Christianity and social change in China) (Hong Kong: Theological Education Press, 1984).

4

Japan

Japan is one of Europe's and America's most important competitors in the world market. This fact gives rise to anxiety. There are countless studies that seek the reasons for Japan's success. In them it is clear that the unique combination of Japanese traditions and its economic-technological opening to the West offers a key to understanding Japan. These traditions include not only Confucianism and Shinto but also Buddhism. Christianity, on the contrary, is a part of the Western transmission of modernization in its attitude toward humanity, social systems, science, and technology. Is it then possible that the structures of dialogue between Buddhism and Christianity could be illuminating for the relationship between Japan and Europe/America in the future?

In Japan, too, Christian missions were regarded in the sixteenth to nineteenth centuries as politically dangerous agents of Western imperialism. Still, with the end of national seclusion in Japan in the second half of the nineteenth century, Buddhism and Christianity faced a religious search for identity in a materialistic and atheistically oriented industrial and consumer society. Therefore it was not a coincidence that dialogue emerged that focused on Christian experiences with European nihilism and atheism (Kyoto school). This dialogue is still philosophically fruitful today but remains highly abstract. Questions about the position of humanity in the cosmos and in society still have direct relevance for every person in face of modern civilization's threat to the future. Can we expect answers from Japan, especially since Japanese Zen meditation is spreading rapidly in formerly Christian lands and presents itself as an answer to individuals who have been uprooted from their traditions and who are threatened by fear of the future? Do tendencies appear in this cultural exchange that will also change the European mentality? Is that the point of dialogue between Buddhists and Christians in Japan?

HISTORICAL BACKGROUND

Japan's cultural and religious situation is with good reason described as "archaic modern."[1] This attests to the readiness to assimilate that has marked the

---

[1] T. Immoos, *Japan—Archaische Moderne* (Munich: Kindt, 1990).

land for more than two millennia in regard to ethnic, linguistic, artistic, religious, and technological matters, with the expectation that Japan would have forfeited its own identity in the process. On the contrary, though, this singular mixing created an ethnic and cultural as well as a linguistic homogeneity that can hardly be compared to any other culture. That which is peculiarly Japanese is immediately obvious in religion as well as art—unlike China, for example—but is difficult to isolate. Perhaps at its heart is the aesthetification of religion that has so assimilated Shinto, Buddhism, and Confucianism that they flow into one another, or the complementary nature of conceptual differences to create an unconfused expression of "mood." This has made their different traditions completely effective in cultural terms. However, they have only been incorporated in a form in which they complement each other. *Wabi*, the search for elegance in simple things, *sabi*, the return to the original, and *yugen*, the secret depth in every concrete appearance of the moment, are the highest Japanese Shinto values and have also deeply penetrated Buddhism. Shinto's this-worldly enjoyment of life, the turning of attention to transitoriness and suffering in Buddhism, and the disciplining of these feelings in a strictly arranged social organization modeled on Confucianism created a unique synthesis. Matsubara Hisako explains this admirably in a poem that all Japanese children for the past thousand years have memorized, because it contains all the syllables of the Japanese language and thus belongs to the most elementary level of preschool instruction without the religious content being immediately obvious:[2]

iro ha nihohe to	Color is a breath
chirinuru wo	blooms and comes to nothing
wakayo tare so	what remains of this world
tsune naramu	today my path leads me further away
uyi no okayama	through the thicket of a short life
kehu koyete	I free myself
asaki yumemishi	from vapid dreams
ehi mo sesu.	and satiation.

The answer to the question of what might remain of the world is thus not simply "nothing." Much more, it is hinted that a way through life's individual experiences will be shown, a path that frees one from "vapid dreams" and promises "satiation."

Already the structures of the Chinese and Japanese languages with their common system of writing are a reason why East Asian Buddhism has a very different character, compared to Indian Buddhism with its precise and abstract epistemological analyses. The language juxtaposes concrete images and feelings without establishing their complex relationships clearly.[3] Buddhist-Christian dialogue is

---

[2] H. Matsubara, *Blick aus Mandelaugen: Ost-westliche Miniaturen* (Hamburg: Knaus, 1980), 180ff.

[3] H. Nakamura, *Ways of Thinking of Eastern Peoples* (Honolulu: University of Hawaii Press, 1964); see also H. Waldenfels, *Absolutes Nichts: Zur Grundlegung des Dialogs zwischen Buddhismus und Christentum* (Freiburg: Herder, 1976), 41f.

influenced by this fact as well as by the Shinto-Buddhist unitary experience of nature and a transpersonal experience of reality that is derived from it.

FIRST POLITICAL REACTIONS TO CHRISTIANITY IN THE MID-SIXTEENTH CENTURY

Christian missionary work began in 1549 with the Spanish Jesuit Francis Xavier. From the beginning it was combined with a confrontational field of political interest. In the fifteenth and sixteenth centuries an immense civil war raged in Japan, in which all the different Buddhist sects (especially the Nichiren and Tendai schools) were embroiled. The distinguished Japanese historian of religion Anesaki Masaharu is of the opinion that "religious leaders were stamped with the martial spirit and corresponding usage of this era, and they joined their religious ambitions with the struggle for power."[4] Christianity appeared to many war-plagued Samurai and princes, and also to exploited farmers, as an alternative, especially since its connections to the European powers at first appeared to be advantageous. The military dictator Nobunaga Oda (1534-82) wanted to check the political influence of the great Buddhist monasteries, because they stood in the way of his efforts to create an organized central authority. For this reason he encouraged Christianity, although he himself was not a Christian. Because along with Christian influence technology, especially military technology, came to Japan, this policy was especially promising. Christian success was astonishing: c. 1578, some twenty years after Xavier's arrival, there were about 30,000 converts to Christianity, principally on Kyushu; c. 1605 there were 750,000 (or 4 percent of Japan's population).[5] Not only political encouragement led to this success, but also the religious impotence of Buddhism at this time, corrupted as it was by power and formalized Confucian ethics; there was also a longing for renewal through a novelty that was accepted as truth.[6]

At first the Buddhists did not react at all, because in the earliest mission period they mistook the Christian groups for a new Buddhist sect.[7] The following dictator, Toyotomi Hideyoshi (1536-98), who came to power in 1582, adapted his political stance toward Christianity to the political circumstances. The power struggles among the numerous feudal lords also plunged the Buddhist monasteries into dependence and shifting political loyalties. Some of the monks even took up arms to protect themselves from encroachments and also often took part in the altercations between the princes. Hideyoshi thus at first continued his benevolent policies toward Christians, in order to strengthen his own central power.

---

[4] M. Anesaki, *History of Japanese Religion* (Rutland/Tokyo: Charles Tuttle, 1963; 1st ed. 1930), 229.

[5] Ibid., 244.

[6] Ibid., 241.

[7] The reasons are, as we already saw in the chapter on China, the celibate lifestyle of the monks, the focus of piety on the other world, the veneration of the Virgin Mary (which appeared similar to the cult of the Buddhist Kannon—the bodhisattva of compassion, Avalokitesvara, reinterpreted as a female form), and so on (see Yoshiyuki Nitta, "Die antichristlichen Schriften in Japan im 17. Jahrhunder," in *Religion und Philosophie in Ostasien: Festschrift für H. Steininger*, ed. G. Naundorf, et al. [Würzburg, 1985], 334).

This soon changed, as he began to fear that Christianity could place his own power and Japan's unity (which he wanted to advance) in question. There were two reasons for this: the fear of foreign influence, and the internal conflicts of the Christians.

In 1592 Spanish Franciscans came from the Philippines to Japan. They concerned themselves diplomatically with Spanish interests and in missionary matters they competed with the Portuguese Jesuits. When in a famous incident in 1596 Spanish seamen invoked Spain's territorial and military power, Hideyoshi suspected the Spaniards of having expansionist plans. This led on 5 February 1597 to the first great persecution: in Nagasaki twenty-six Christians were publicly crucified. After 1602 Augustinians and Dominicans came, and later Dutch and English merchants, each European nation warning the Japanese rulers of the economic and military interests of its rivals. It became clear that these European colonial interests were very closely linked to the missions, so Hideyoshi rejected his earlier alliance and declared himself in favor of a strengthening of Buddhism. From this time until the end of the Tokugawa period, Buddhism was perceived as the "national religion" of Japan.[8] Hideyoshi summarized the anti-Christian stand in four arguments:

1. Christianity is alien to Japanese sensibilities.

2. The missionaries violate holy places.

3. Belief is a private matter that ought not be used by foreign powers for political purposes.

4. Under the cloak of religion, Christians are aspiring to imperial territorial benefits (in 1580 the Christian convert Prince Omura had granted the region around Nagasaki to the church).[9]

Then the Tokugawa family (1603-1867/68) came to power. The Tokugawas wanted to unify Japan by centralizing power and exerting total control over all aspects of life. The persecution of Christians rose to incredible proportions, especially in 1627-34. As had already been the case with Hideyoshi, though, religious matters were not the decisive issue. Instead, everything that stood in the way of the dictatorship's control was persecuted (including Nichiren Buddhism).[10] In 1614 Ieyasu outlawed Christianity, in agreement with the increasing opposition to Christians in Buddhist circles. After the peasant rebellions of Shimabara, caused by social distress and substantially supported by Christians, in 1637 the government took the step of a massive separation of Japan from the outside world.

Christianity was now perceived as alien and internally rent by controversy, although the Jesuit theologians around Francis Xavier had made notable adaptations of Christian concepts to Buddhist ideas and concepts and had also incorporated

---

[8] M. Anesaki, 246ff.

[9] Hideyoshi's letter to the Jesuit G. Coelho of 1587 (see Y. Nitta, 335).

[10] The Nichiren Buddhists did not want to subject themselves to the military dictators and thus preached their own political Buddhism. They were persecuted in 1579 by Oda Nobunaga, in 1586 by Toyotomi Hideyoshi, and in 1608 by Ieyasu. It is clear from this that the religious policy of Hideyoshi and the Tokugawas was not primarily oriented toward *religious* questions.

Japanese ritual forms—for example, using elements of the tea ceremony in cel-
ebrations of the eucharist.[11] Xavier himself, to be sure, backed off from too direct
an identification of the Christian God with Buddhist concepts. But the principle
remained intact: "on the one hand consciously and deliberately to use originally
Buddhist expressions that were familiar to the Japanese, and on the other hand to
rebut Buddhist teaching and thus attest to the correctness of Christianity,"[12] as for
example in the *Nijugokajo*, a catechism written in 1555. A clear theological
conceptualization as well as a true notion of dialogue were lacking, and so agreement on important questions was impossible. For example, God (Latin *deus*) was
also expressed in Japanese with the word *daisu*, and Christian baptismal names
were distinguished according to Portuguese and Spanish pronunciation, as if this
were a matter of different "paths to salvation"![13]

But still the Buddhists did not deploy a philosophical polemic against Christianity, especially since they knew hardly anything about the foreign religion.
Only when the Jesuit Fukan Fabian converted to Buddhism did the situation
change. In 1620 he wrote a polemical treatise, *Ha daisu* (Against the Christian
god), that for the next 250 years supplied the arguments for anti-Christian polemic. In 1605 Fabian had laid out a defense of the Christian concept of God in
Myotei mondo (Conversation between Myoshu and Yutei); now he simply turned
the arguments on their head. The earlier treatise argued above all that Buddhist
meditation on nothingness or emptiness must lead to spiritual inactivity or de-
rangement (an argument still beloved today in evangelical circles). However,
Fukan Fabian decided later that belief in a personal God could not answer the
question of evil.

After the Shimabara uprising, the anti-Christian polemic became more aggressive. In 1642 Suzuki Shosan took up Fabian's arguments and added two of
his own: First, if the Christian God as creator and omniscient universal ruler of
history were good, he would not have revealed himself in only *one* place in history (and that in the West), leaving the other peoples unredeemed. This must
mean that he had not known that other peoples would be redeemed by other
divinities. But if this is the case, he would not be all-knowing. Second, Christian
belief in miracles is primitive and proves nothing. In Japan even "foxes and bad-
gers" (an allusion to Shinto *kami* [divinities]) perform miracles.

This enmity toward Christianity did not change during the entire Tokugawa
period (1603-1867/68). On the contrary, especially in its first decades it was
Buddhism that was thoroughly encouraged, each Japanese family being required
to declare its membership in a Buddhist temple—a step taken mostly from the
political grounds of separating the people from foreign influence and to encourage the accepted method of government and surveillance. Besides this, the country was hermetically sealed off, and small Christian groups survived only in hid-
ing. In the short period of open encounter between Japanese culture and

---

[11] In regard to the relationship between the tea ceremony and the eucharist a reversed
or many-sided influence is also possible.

[12] Y. Nitta, 332.

[13] M. Anesaki, 248.

Christianity there was a lively exchange—a Christian influence even on the tea ceremony appears to have taken place.[14] This suggests that perhaps Christianity might in time have undergone a process of "Japanization" similar to what Buddhism had experienced a millennium before,[15] if only the Christians had been able to accept the validity of non-Christian religions and if the connection the Japanese made between Christianity and European colonialism had not hindered all possibility of a true encounter between the religions.

THE POLITICAL SITUATION AT THE END OF THE NINETEENTH CENTURY

There is a similarity between China, where the "closed door" was broken down in the mid-nineteenth century by British gunboats (the Opium War), and the opening of the "closed land" of the Tokugawa period by Commodore Perry's ships (1853-54). However, Japan never had to suffer the national humiliation that China endured. Japan indeed lost certain territorial rights when the government permitted the establishment of foreign settlements in its port cities. Japanese nationalists also feared that the "mixed residence" granted to foreigners and missionaries would spread to the interior of the country. As before, in the second half of the nineteenth century the Christian missions were regarded as the helpers and agents of Western imperialism. Japan had the horrible example of China before its eyes, and there was xenophobia in Japan as well as China. Still, with the modernization and economic-technological opening to the West of the Meiji reform of 1868 there also came a cultural opening. This promised a more favorable climate for Buddhist-Christian encounter in Japan. Nevertheless, it was marked by bitter conflict.[16]

Without a doubt the Asian peoples perceive Christian mission and imperialism as inextricably linked. But is this really entirely true? The goals of the missionaries were doubtless in most cases not identical to the goals and interests of the states from which they came. The missions could be in complete conflict with the politics of the colonizers they encountered (an example from Indian history is the attempt the British East India Company made to repudiate the missionaries). Even though, corresponding to the spirit of the age, gospel and culture were deeply engaged with one another, few missionaries failed to grasp the difference between the kingdom of God and the kingdoms of this world. But from the perspective of those who were being colonized and evangelized, these

---

[14] T. Immoos, 63.

[15] It cannot remain unmentioned that at the beginning of the national restoration in the Meiji era (after 1868)—and then in the context of the reaction against European influence—there was a major effort to encourage Shintoism as the Japanese national religion and to denigrate Buddhism as "foreign religion." The motto was spread: *baibutsu kishaku* (Away with Buddha, destruction of the texts). To show themselves as nationalistic, young Buddhists attacked "Western Christianity," for example in the group S*ei-kyo-sha* (Politics and Religion). See M. Anesaki, 360ff.

[16] N. Thelle, *Buddhism and Christianity in Japan: From Conflict to Dialogue, 1854-1899* (Honolulu: University of Hawaii Press, 1987).

two kingdoms stood in a public and unholy alliance. There were indeed memories of the peaceful mission methods of the Jesuits Francis Xavier in Japan and Matteo Ricci in China. However, in both countries people were acquainted with the bloody entry of the Spaniards into the Philippines (second half of the sixteenth century), an invasion that was even more uncompromising than their conquest of South America. The closing of Japan at the beginning of the Tokugawa period (the policy of *sakoku*) was the consequence. And this political decision was carried out with police-state inflexibility for centuries.

As in China, in the final analysis the enmity toward Christians in Japan until the late nineteenth century was especially grounded on the reproach that with their foreign belief the Christians wanted to undermine the national identity and weaken Japan. The wounds on both sides were by no means healed, and dialogue is difficult if it goes beyond courtesies and wants to progress to honorable settlement of historical issues.

At this point, however, Japan's history has some significant differences from China's in regard to encounter with the West. These are of overarching significance for the contemporary encounter between the cultures. Most important is the fact that, after bloody battles, Chinese territory was conquered by Europe's colonial powers, while Japan was opened up especially for trade purposes by a New World power (the United States) without a war. The European churches were more closely linked to their states than was the case in America, so that the American churches were at first politically more disinterested. In the nineteenth century Europe's economy had reached the end of its possible quantitative growth, and thus Europeans aggressively sought sources of raw materials and markets. It was for these reasons that in China the connection of evangelization by the church and colonization by the state had been so close. Nineteenth-century America, on the contrary, had just discovered its western regions, settling them and expanding to the Pacific. America's economy did not yet have the world in its sights. Besides this, church and state were constitutionally divided, and the numerous American churches tended to be decentralized and democratically organized.

Consequently, the American missions that constructed their first bastions in Japan distanced themselves both from politics and from economic machinations as they were known in the Old World. Remembering its own war of independence and its own colonial past, the United States did not regard itself as a colonial power, although de facto it joined itself to the European powers and reached out over the Pacific in 1853-54, when Perry's fleet sailed into the Bay of Tokyo. However, American policy was firmly against letting Japan suffer the same fate that had befallen China.

In this sense Europe's confrontation with China in the nineteenth century was different from America's encounter with Japan. At first, Europe was deeply impressed by China's size, riches, and unknown cultural and political might. Since the eighteenth century, European intellectuals had dreamed a myth of China that was nourished more by their own longings than by contact with the real China. Compared to this the Japanese were only an island people with a limited market and scant natural resources. But once the door to China had been broken down, the earlier fascination with China gave way to Eurocentrism and the claim to world rule on the basis of belief in Europe's cultural superiority—an attitude that persists to the present. Then in the beginning of the twentieth century, after the Boxer Rebellion, people also developed the bogeyman of the "yellow peril," in part to divert attention from the crisis in their own civilization.

However, unlike the turn of tide from fascination with China in the nineteenth century to its opposite, the destruction of Japan's policy of national seclusion did not mean that this country lost its exotic charms. America's view of Japan was not shaped by the European erudition that had studied classical Chinese culture (James Legge), but by a literary romantic transfiguration of contemporary Japan (Lafcadio Hearn). One can also see this American trend later in Pearl S. Buck's novel *The Good Earth*, published in 1931.

The American Protestant missionaries who came to Japan in the late nineteenth century were very different from their European counterparts who had established themselves in China in the middle years of the century. The latter were in general influenced by Pietism and were critical of culture. The Americans, on the contrary, brought an optimistic evolutionism with them and wished to present America's "civil religion" to the rest of the world. Most missionaries shared this concept of political evolutionism, and the "superiority" of Western technologies was often felt to be a proof of Christianity's truth. In this context the influence of Unitarian intellectuals on the journals that were read in educated Japanese circles is surprising. Unlike the Protestant missions in China, which had aimed their conversion efforts toward the masses, the missions in Japan were able to convert many people from the Samurai class. While in China the training of native pastors only began at a late stage, Japan very quickly had its own pastors, who already propounded a native Japanese theology in the last decades of the nineteenth century! China, for its part, had to wait until the 1920s for a similar development, and the Chinese Christian theologians never reached the status of somebody like Uchimura Kanzo, who in 1891 had courageously refused to venerate an edict with the emperor's signature (the emperor was regarded as divine).

The Protestant missionaries in Japan perceived the "Buddhist clergy"—as did their counterparts in China—as corrupt, ignorant, and of dubious morality. These are similar accusations to those the Protestant Reformation made against the clergy of Europe, and they also differ little from the charges the reformed Meiji Buddhists made against the traditional Buddhist temple hierarchies. The charge has some foundation but is connected more generally to the fundamental change in religion and society in this period. Someone who visited *honganji* (the chief temple of the Jodo-Shin school) in Kyoto would be blinded by the wealth of the *monshu* (the leader of the school) and the power of the higher clergy, the polished rituals, and the material well-being—in short, the pomp of a "high church." In contrast to this, the simple priests *(boshi)* in the countryside pursued their modest daily and rather worldly routines. So it is no surprise that the Puritans, who led a simple, strict, and God-fearing life and were always ready to evangelize, found the high Buddhist officeholders pompous and corrupt, while condemning the lower ranks as too uneducated.

In Christian as well as reform Buddhist complaints we can see a shift in religious sensibility. The less reflective, obvious faith, linked to worldly comforts, vanished to the degree that it had become a part of the certainties and structures of the feudal order. The Buddhist priests were responsible above all for ritual, and were only secondarily concerned with morality. The priests in the country-side were by no means completely ignorant: the priest was literate and usually the best-educated and most widely traveled man in the village. As a national educational system developed in Japan, however, the priest came to be relegated to an inferior position. In the eyes of the missionaries, who saw the village priest as their main Japanese opponent, he seemed narrow-minded and ignorant when measured by their own standard of understanding and knowledge of the ways of the world. In this period, however, not only the monk but everyone in Japan was ignorant of modern Western-style knowledge and lacked a correspondingly en-lightened piety. Thus it follows that Christianity as such was not more open to the world than Buddhism, but rather in Japan after 1854 two steps of social de-velopment collided with one another. Christianity had already entered the social dislocations of an industrial society, which only now stood before Buddhism.

Perhaps nothing can demonstrate this transformation more clearly than the question of the advantages of Christian compassion, because nineteenth-century Buddhists recognized, not without jealousy, Christianity's success in this realm. From India to Japan, Asian people had come to know Christian institutions of compassion, from soup kitchens to famine relief, from free education to free medical services, and more. These selfless signs of Christian love of neighbor had filled the Buddhists with shame. But as institutions, these works were for the most part new, the product of European developments in the nineteenth century. They were the Christian-humanist answer to the new social and economical prob-lems that faced the wretched urban population of Europe in the wake of the Industrial Revolution. This new urban proletariat had been created by the Protes-tant-influenced societies of Europe and America in a fashion that was completely unfamiliar to preindustrial Asia. Only gradually did Japan become acquainted with such socioeconomic changes, and began to react to them. It is not true, however, that Buddhism had no habit of compassion. Centuries before Constantine, Asoka had constructed charitable institutions in India. Still, these Buddhist institutions were always linked to imperial, feudal, or rural orders. They were not created to care for the uprooted urban population that soon grew to monumental proportions in the area around Japanese harbors after 1864. Chris-tian sects that had come into being in a similar environment of social dislocation in the industrial cities had had to learn their lessons quickly and in the hard way. The institutionally organized forms of Christian compassion had become neces-sary in an all too uncompassionate era.

This was one of the reasons for the creation and rapid growth of new religious movements in Japan from the end of the nineteenth century until World War II.[17] They were the Japanese response to the uprooting of great strata of the popula-tion as a consequence of urbanization.

---

[17] Soka Gakkai, Rissho Kosei-kai, PL-Kyodan, and others could reach the people through programs of economic compassion and thus established a place in the urban middle and lower classes.

While the Chinese *samgha* was not open to encounter with Christianity and only entered into discussions through T'ai-hsü's efforts after the revolution of 1911-12, it is astonishing that Japanese Buddhism already had entered into dialogue with Christianity in the late nineteenth century. This relatively quick adaptation to altered circumstances shows that the supposedly pompous, corrupt, and ignorant Buddhist clergy of Japan could hardly have been so completely untouched by reality that they could not mobilize themselves.

As was the case in Francis Xavier's time, it was again the Confucians and Shintoists who first reacted directly to the propagation of Christianity and accepted it. The number of Buddhist temples in the Edo period (1603-1867/68) had grown, thanks to the governmental regulation that every family had to belong to a Buddhist temple *(tera-uke, danka)*. On the one hand this made it easier to collect taxes, while on the other hand it strengthened the community of the living and the ancestors within the feudal order and provided a material basis for the temple priesthood.[18] Thus, conversions to Christianity undermined the economic basis of the Buddhist priests. The Confucians and Shintoists did not have this problem and so were more open to discussions with Christians, although the Confucians were not traditionally interested in questions about a transcendental salvation in either China or in Japan. Instead, Confucians engaged in dialogue with Christians (and Buddhists) mostly about the usefulness of religion in general, which for them was questionable. After 1868 Shinto, however, was much more strongly encouraged by the state, to the point of its establishment as the state religion, especially to give a new legitimacy to the empire and to nationalist patriotism. This signified a removal of power from Buddhism, which suddenly in this respect found itself again on the side of Christianity. Also, the national reforms after 1945 (in the context of the division of Shinto from the state and Japan's democratization by the Americans) led to a further loss of power and dispossession of the Buddhist temples. This led to self-reflection and new formulations in Buddhism.[19]

One must consider all of these issues in order to understand the modern dialogue in Japan between Buddhists and Christians. This is philosophically productive but often highly abstract. In this way, perhaps sometimes the current dialogue thrusts aside the real problems: the encounter of Buddhism and Christianity in Japan was and is not only a meeting of religions, but also a cultural and political confrontation that especially in the nineteenth century influenced the character of Japan's new orientation toward the West.

Immediately after 1854 Christianity for the Buddhists was an unloved gatecrasher, while Christians believed that they could ignore Buddhism as antiquated and certainly destined for extinction. By the end of the nineteenth century, though, the situation appeared differently. Buddhism had shown itself to be vigorous, had by no means foundered, and constituted a challenge to the Christians. The Buddhists for their part had to reorient themselves in a modern industrialized society. For them, this made conversation with Christians more desirable, since

---

[18] M. Eder, *Geschichte der japanischen Religion*, vol. 2 (Nagoya, 1978), 161f.

[19] N. Thelle, 248.

the latter had more experience of this sort of situation. So now they met at the same level, each side believing that in the end it would be able to defeat the other.

THE ENCOUNTER OF BUDDHISM WITH EUROPEAN SCIENCE

The realization that Mahayana Buddhism could not have been founded by the Buddha himself had led in mid-eighteenth-century Japan with Tominaga Nakamoto (1715-46) to discussions and a tendency to demythologize.[20]

The Buddhists, however, saw their faith discredited by the new Western world view. Before this time Buddhists had disputed with Neo-Confucians over the credibility and sense of sacred geography (the mythical Mount Sumeru as axis of the world, around which all the continents are grouped). In this case, though, neither side had had the empirical knowledge that would have made polemics against the other side possible. Now, however, the missionaries used the new scientific knowledge against Japanese-Buddhist concepts. For example, they could attest in terms of scientific geography that Amida's Pure Land could not lie in the West. Still, the Buddhists learned quickly. In the 1880s the Buddhist apologists, as in Sri Lanka, used scientific rationalism to formulate arguments against Christianity. It was popular to take up the opposition between Copernicus and the Bible's geocentric view of the world. But the Buddhists also learned that even Galileo Galilei could not really shake the Christian faith. In other words, at a certain level knowledge and belief could completely diverge. But if this was the case, then it was just as true for Buddhist belief. From this developed an enlightened Buddhist modernism that questioned the authenticity of Mahayana, instead going back to the historical Buddha. In the process it created modern Japanese academic Buddhology.

So now the Jodo Buddhists (Buddhists of the Pure Land or Amida Buddhists) were in a position to demythologize the Sumeru cosmology, while they could still hold to their belief in Amida. The Buddhist modernists used historical criticism in controversies with other sects as well as against the Christian menace. They appropriated the new scientific interest in the "real world" and pushed for a greater emphasis on the individual consciousness and conscience in place of unthinking ritual. Since they also sought for criteria for a new ethical code, they also criticized the traditional Buddhist priesthood. But the Buddhists, like the Christians, were not yet in a position to link old local organizations with new cosmopolitan structures. As a result, the various schools or sects still remain rigidly divided from one another today.

The 1870s and 1880s, in brief, created the following starting points for dialogue: (1) The Christians in general held onto their stereotypes about the moral and intellectual inferiority of Buddhism. However, they recognized that Buddhism represented a real power with which it was necessary to deal in order to

---

[20] Michael Pye has given us special material on this issue. See K. Mizuno, "Looking at the Sutras," *Dharma World* 8 (8 February 1981): 40-42; N. Tominaga, *Emerging from Meditation* (*Shutsujo kogo*, 1745), trans. M. Pye (Honolulu: University of Hawaii Press, 1990).

make progress in the mission field. (2) The Buddhists had become acquainted with historical and critical research on the New Testament and had extracted from this new arguments against the church. Buddhists valued and accepted Jesus but rejected the missionizing church. In this way it was possible to make alliances with Unitarians and other Christian liberals against church-based Christianity. At the same time, Buddhist liberal circles sought, through historical inquiries, to create a renewed and enlightened form of Buddhism.[21]

THE FIRST DIALOGUE OF 1896

After the conflicts and confusion of the Chinese-Japanese war of 1894-95, liberal intellectuals looked to the Christian and Buddhist camps for a basis for a new social consensus.[22] These reformers, who wanted the opening to the West to advance in cultural matters as well, had had the wind in their faces since the 1880s. This headwind became ever stronger, because although technological and industrial development progressed, conservative consciousness of the past that focused on "Japanese values" wanted to check cultural and social foreign influence.

The World Parliament of Religions held in Chicago in 1893 also made a deep impression on Japan. Shaku Soen, head of the Rinzai Zen school and abbot of the famed Enkakuji in Kamakura, proposed an interreligious conference. Its purpose was to discuss the question about Japan's future religion posed by the newspaper *Nihon Shukyo*, which was the most important meeting point between East and West in the country. The conservatives on both sides replied to the Christian Unitarians with their quest for a "sympathy between the religions" with the argument that a "synthesis" of religions would only water them down and eventually make them superfluous. The tendency of this meeting, held in the villa of Viscount Matsudaira in Tokyo on 26 September 1896, was to avoid controversial questions of doctrine in favor of seeking the common ground in the identity of Christian love and Buddhist compassion, as Shaku Soen formulated it. Unlike the bitter antagonism between the two religions in the preceding decades, now discussion produced three new viewpoints that could serve as a basis for the Buddhist-Christian dialogue that began here. First, a new *Christian patriotism* emerged that went hand in hand with the call for a Japanization of Christianity and promised loyalty to state and emperor, so all religions might join under the banner of *nationalism*. Second, Christian accomplishments in the social realm were recognized. While Buddhism might contribute significantly in philosophy and psychology, Christianity has accomplished useful things in practical charitable work. Now the religions must work together, in order to solve urgent *social* problems jointly. And third, religions must join together in a *common front against atheism and materialism,* especially because the alliance between Buddhism and Western atheism against Christianity had recoiled against Buddhism.

All three aspects are still important in dialogue today, at least subliminally. Still, in 1896 the participants remained at the level of generalities and courtesies.

---

[21] N. Thelle, 249.

[22] On the following issue, see N. Thelle, 225ff.

The thorny problem of the rivalry of both religions in mission was indeed raised, but to the present it really has not been discussed, except somewhat in engagement between Rissho Kosei-kai and Christianity (see "Joint Community Dialogue" below).

A second conference in 1897 did not attract nearly as much attention as the first, even though John Henry Barrows (general secretary of the World Parliament of Religions in Chicago) had been invited. In Chicago he had expressed the hope that all religions would finally find fulfillment in Christ, which the Buddhist partners naturally protested. Still, this expressed accurately the goal of many Japanese Christians, just as most Buddhists hoped for an assimilation of Christianity into Buddhism. There were also others who argued for a religion of the future that would be different from the contemporary established religions, unifying the best elements of all of them. The visions for the future differed from one another and were unclear. But precisely this circumstance made possible the acceptance of new Buddhist-Christian cooperation in wider circles on the basis of both religions, because each hoped to further its own interests.

Although this first trial at dialogue never made it past the first steps, it became the model for the dialogue movement of the twentieth century. Besides this, it had shown that religions that had hitherto bitterly fought each other could at least talk together, as long as Christianity was now recognized as native Japanese. From the efforts for dialogue and search for the essence of the religions came an impulse for historic-critical research and comparative religious studies. These tendencies crystallized in Japan with Anesaki Masaharu (1873-1949) in Buddhist-Christian dialogue.

THE DIALOGUE SITUATION AT THE END OF THE NINETEENTH CENTURY

When one analyzes the content of the Buddhist-Christian debates at the end of the nineteenth century, it is astonishing to discover that the same *dogmatic problems* are relevant both now and then.

On the *Buddhist side* the problems were and are:
• Why should a good God create a world of suffering?
• Why did God let Adam sin?
• Why did God establish enmity between humans and animals?
• Why should one worship a creator God who (like Brahma) apparently still has desires and thus is not free of *samsara*?

On the *Christian side* the questions were and are:
• Why and how can someone live in such an amoral and impersonal universe?
• How can one be happy without a benevolent creator?
• Why this belief in previous lives and reincarnation?
• Why the fixation on suffering instead of on sin?

Up to the present, such fundamental differences in understanding reality, nature, and human determination have divided Buddhists and Christians into two world views. These problems are hardly solvable unless one goes beyond the narrow boundaries of this sort of presupposition. The dialogue in the nineteenth century tended to remain stuck on the comparison of two different cosmological systems. Participants could not yet (or only in small part) push forward to more abstract levels of reflection to a "theo-ontology" and the "atheo-deconstruction" that appears to dominate recent discussions and dialogue. What will prove to be more fruitful in the end is not yet clear. Certainly it is impossible to ignore the primary language of the sutras and the Bible (the myths and tales) or to pass over the exegesis of the sastras or dogmas. Dialogue must be built up from bedrock— in other words, it must take account of the levels of both language and tradition.

The dialogues at the end of the century set the standard for succeeding development. The Norwegian theologian and missionary to Japan Notto Thelle differentiates between three levels in Japan's Buddhist-Christian dialogue, which since then have made their mark:[23]

Dialogue between institutions. At this level, dialogue has political connotations and especially in the Russian-Japanese war of 1904-5 was concerned with harmony under national protection. The pacifism of some Christians and socialists like Uchimura Kanzo could scarcely find an audience. Instead, it was believed that politics, religion, and national education should work together to give spiritual strength to emperor and empire, as a national conference of religions formulated the issue in 1912. After World War II and especially in recent times, however, Buddhist and Christian institutions have also joined in opposition to the government. This situation arose because in 1969 the government introduced a draft law to nationalize the Yasukani shrine, in which since 1978 war criminals had been enshrined along with other war dead as heroes or "apotheosed souls" *(kami)*, so that all Japanese were obligated to venerate them. The controversy escalated when on 15 August 1985 the Japanese prime minister paid an official visit to the shrine on the fortieth anniversary of Japan's capitulation. Christians and Buddhists protested together, none as vehemently as the Protestant Christians.[24]

Anti-establishment dialogue. A Buddhist monk and professor from Tokyo, Watanabe Kaikyoku, called upon the Basel congress for religious history in 1904 to unite Buddhism and Christianity into a single religion of the future, since both religions rest on a common foundation. The Japanese were called to transform this dream into reality.[25] Although such a voice was isolated, the proposal still shows a change in Japanese opinion. For example, the political dialogue attitude behind such a program shows Japanese pride and desire to make a special mark on worldwide political development.

At the beginning of the century reformed Buddhist movements also made common cause with Christian socialists in national politics. Together they criticized

---

[23] Ibid., 250ff.

[24] A newer and readily available collection of some documents can be found in *Brennpunkte in Kirche und Theologie Japans*, ed. Y. Terazono and H. E. Hamer (Neukirchen, 1988), 97ff.

[25] H. de Lubac, *La rencontre du bouddhisme et de l'occident* (Paris: Aubier, 1952), 238.

the close cooperation between religious leaders and the government, and especially their support for the government's program of militaristic patriotism. D. T.
Suzuki, the student of Shaku Soen and Zen philosopher, criticized the government for its 1901 ban of the Social Democratic Party. Also from the ranks of
these reformed Buddhists and Christian socialists came opposition to the gov-
ernment-sponsored conference of religions in 1912, mentioned above. Thelle
gave as his opinion: "The relationship between Buddhist socialism and social
Christianity in these years must still be researched, but there were obviously
direct contacts as well as ideological nearness."[26] The reform Buddhists saw the
Pure Land of Amida Buddha not only as a spiritual state, but as a social reality to
be striven for (which admittedly was not new; this was the belief of the White
Lotus sects of twelfth-century China and Japanese Nichiren Buddhism since the
thirteenth century). On the Christian side it was especially the Quakers who,
with their undogmatic, noninstitutional, and praxis- and peace-oriented Christianity, nourished on silent meditation, decisively kicked off the dialogue movement in the 1960s. The conclusion to derive social and political consequences
from Buddhist inspirations and thus cooperate with Christians reached as far as
Hisamatsu's F.A.S. Party, which was founded during the Second World War in
the context of the Kyoto school and is still active today.

Dialogue on a spiritual basis. In the last decade of the nineteenth century
there already were leading Buddhists who also became Unitarians and vice versa.
The Unitarian principles of free use of reason on religious questions and the
moral development of the individual as well as society as the core of religion did
not fail to attract enlightened Buddhists. The Unitarians themselves believed that
they stood intellectually close to Buddhism. And some Buddhists accepted monotheism, which they considered not so much in the Christian sense as corresponding to the "modern spirit."[27] Men like Ouchi Seiran, Nakanishi Ushio, Hirai Kinzo,
Saji Jitsunen, and others lived on the border between Buddhism and Unitarian
Christianity. The Christian Yoshida Seitaro had at that time already undertaken a
three-year Zen praxis; another pastor, Katayama Yukichi, pleaded for a "Zen
Christianity." Other groups wanted to combine Buddhism and Christianity spiritually, especially Nishida Tenko (1872-1968), who in 1928 founded the *Ittoen*
(Garden of Light) society to further this goal.[28] This spiritual question, in which
the individual heart is the location of an ongoing dialogue between the two religions, became known worldwide especially thanks to Hugo Makibi Enomiya-
Lassalle (1898-1990). In Japan he had several predecessors and found numerous
successors. Dialogue in meditative silence, seeking spiritual experience beyond
words and teaching, is then perhaps also "the most characteristic expression"
(Thelle) of Buddhist-Christian dialogue in Japan.

---

[26] N. Thelle, 253.

[27] Ibid., 185ff.

[28] The opportunity presented itself when Nishida Tenko and his disciples were given
land in Yamashina, near Kyoto (see N. Thelle, 254f.). For details on this group, see H.
Thomsen, *The New Religions of Japan* (Tokyo: Charles E. Tuttle, 1963).

THE CONTEMPORARY DIALOGUE

Recent dialogue bears the stamp of postwar circumstances, in which Japan reacted ambivalently toward the West. With a mostly suppressed war guilt and as an ever more self-conscious economic rival, Japan at least in part is gradually accepting joint responsibility for world peace. We can trace five different strands of dialogue, which admittedly also overlap one another:

1. Dialogue in the *Zen praxis*, which is especially connected with four names: the Jesuit Hugo M. Enomiya-Lassalle, the Dominican Oshida Shigeto (b. 1922), the Jesuit Kadowaki Kakichi (b. 1926), and the Buddhist Zen master Yamada Koun (1907-1989), who educated an entire generation of Christian Zen teachers.

2. The religious-philosophical approach initiated by D. T. Suzuki and the *Kyoto school*. This dialogue approach is strongly oriented toward Zen in conferences and publications as in practical matters.

3. The practical and engaged *community solidarity dialogue*, led by Rissho Kosei-kai and other groups. The goal is the promotion of peace and harmony between the religions as well as joint social engagement in the world's crisis areas.

4. Dialogue in *dialogue centers* created by Christian churches (or religious orders). Through translations, colloquia, research projects, and personal encounters they seek to include the entire new religious scene in Japan and learn to understand it.

5. The *Japanese Society for Buddhist-Christian Studies (Tozai Shukyo Koryu Gakkai),* which has been in continual operation since 1982. This group carries on and develops dialogue in the Kyoto school, enjoys a high international reputation, and reacts to Buddhist-Christian dialogue in America.

DIALOGUE IN THE ZEN PRAXIS

For decades Christians, Buddhists, and atheists, both Japanese and foreigners, have lived the dialogue between Zen and Christianity (with daily celebration of the mass) in one-week *seshins* at the Zen center *Shinmeikutsu* near Tokyo, founded by Lassalle. At the same time, the Dominican Oshida founded an ashram-style community in the Japanese mountains near Takamori. Its members live in the simplest Zen style, cultivate their own fields, and are joined together by *zazen* practice, Christian prayer, and daily love of neighbor. Oshida, "a Christian heart in a Buddhist psyche"[29] *(Abhishiktananda)*, does not theorize but instead lives the dialogue in prophetic radicalism. Kadowaki, on the other hand, a Jesuit and professor of philosophy of religion at Sophia University and Zen master in the Rinzai tradition, has become known through books in which he seeks to bring

---

[29] According to Swami Abhishiktananda, from an oral relation by Odette Baumer-Despeigne (Frauenfeld, Switzerland).

the *physicality* of Zen into harmony with the spiritual *word* of God.[30] Kadowaki outlines a theology of the *way*. For him, the way is the overcoming of all dualities as fixed positions. Above all, his concern is with the overcoming of the "I," which as "lumps of self-imprisonment"[31] attain awakening to the self. This awakening, he argues, shows itself in the deeds of Jesus, which are overly provided with *personal* qualities.[32] The "charm of the way" lies in the fact that in practice one is already and always moved by the activity of the way,[33] which in return corresponds to the encircling love of God.

To this context also belongs the worldwide circle of Christian Zen students. Since the 1970s they have been educated in San-un Zendo around Yamada Koun Roshi (1907-89) in Kamakura and have come from Christian Zen masters such as Enomiya-Lassalle in Japan, Willigis Jäger in Germany, Ruben Habito in America, and A. M. A. Samy in India. Yamada in his praxis transcended the differences between the religions, as well as between layperson and monk, secular and spiritual. His dialogue was based on the experienced intensive teacher-student relationship.

ZEN-ORIENTED RELIGIOUS-PHILOSOPHICAL DIALOGUE: SUZUKI DAISETSU

Suzuki Daisetsu Teitaro (1870-1966) was without a doubt one of the most influential transmitters of Japanese Mahayana Buddhism to the West. He decisively influenced Buddhist-Christian dialogue by means of numerous writings, direct encounters with Christians (such as Thomas Merton) and psychotherapists (Erich Fromm), and through his activity as a teacher in America.[34] In c. 1907 Suzuki believed he recognized the Buddha and Jesus as kindred spirits who had attacked the religious institutions of their time and had blazed a path for a message of love and confidence in the inner voice. To that extent, for Suzuki, the two founders are closely related. In dialogue, he argued, one must consider the essence and bring the positive sides of each religion to the fore. Then, in c. 1957, Suzuki discovered Meister Eckhart and Christian mysticism. He reproached ecclesiastical Christianity especially for its dualism, which he believed makes human freedom impossible and is thus answerable for modern atheism and nihilism (Nietzsche). Here he agreed with Nishitani Keiji. Because, however, Zen desires complete freedom, including freedom from a binding concept of God, Suzuki in his later years avoided the expression *mysticism* when he spoke of Zen. In a famous conversation with the Christian missiologue Hendrik Kraemer in 1960, Suzuki condemned dualism but also Christian teaching about judgment and the

---

[30] K. Kadowaki, *Zen und die Bibel* (Salzburg, 1980); Kadowaki, *Erleuchtung auf dem Weg: Zur Theologie des Weges* (Munich: Kösel, 1993).

[31] Kadowaki, *Erleuchtung*, 114.

[32] Ibid., 283.

[33] Ibid., 115.

[34] It is not possible to assess his work in detail here. See J. Spae, *Buddhist-Christian Empathy* (Tokyo: Oriens Institute for Religious Research, 1980), 175ff., and the literature cited there.

Christian understanding of love of enemies. From the standpoint of Shin and Zen Buddhism there is no enemy, because in the final analysis there is no duality of I and you—in other words, no Other. Love, he argued, is total, and is not just limited to participation in the Other, a stand that marked him off from Tillich.[35] Above all, however, Suzuki disliked the Christian symbol of the cross. As he repeatedly thematized, beginning with his book *Mysticism: Christian and Buddhist*, he sees in the cross a symbol of gruesomeness and inhumanity, not of solidarity. For him, the cross is the high point of the dualistically-thinking "I" in the West, which must come to such a horrible death because it was falsely constructed in the first place. He also stressed another criticism Buddhism has made against Christianity: that Christ, having gained heaven, stays there and enjoys communion with God, while humans in the world continue to suffer. The Buddhist bodhisattva, on the other hand, returns to the world to free all living things from suffering.

Christian dualism and the theistic concept of God that appears to deny human freedom were the problems that especially concerned Suzuki in his exchanges with Christianity. They are also the most important dialogue themes of the Kyoto school.

THE KYOTO SCHOOL

In Kyoto, one of the most important centers of Japanese Zen and Jodo Buddhism, for nearly a century Japanese philosophers have concerned themselves with European philosophy and Christianity. They have concentrated especially, through this confrontation, on the philosophical reformulation of Zen Buddhism, thus reacting to the questions posed by modern atheism and nihilism from a Buddhist standpoint. In their religious exploration they especially have paid attention to Hegel, Kirkegaard, Nietzsche, Heidegger, and, to some extent, more recent Christian theology. The most important thinkers of this school are here presented in brief.[36]

Nishida Kitaro

The founder of the so-called Kyoto school was Nishida Kitaro (1870-1945). His important book *Beyond the Good* (*Zen no kenkyu*, 1911)[37] draws upon William James's categories of the psychology of religion. Nishida searches for a "pure experience" (*junsuikeiken*), in which intellectual intuition may be characterized as manifestation of unity in the development of consciousness. By this means it only gradually becomes clear that he is dealing with the mystical experience of

---

[35] Ibid., 177.

[36] We cannot present here all the important personalities of the Kyoto school (Nishida, Tanabe, Nishitani, Takeuchi, Hisamatsu, Abe, Ueda). Instead, we have selected some based on their significance for *current* dialogue in *Japan*. For an introduction to the philosophy of the Kyoto school with extensive bibliography, see R. Ohashi, ed., *Die Philosophie der Kyoto-Schule: texte und Einführung* (Freiburg/Munich: Karl Alber, 1990).

[37] Nishida Kitaro, *Über das Gute* (Frankfurt a. M.: Insel, 1989).

Zen or the unity in belief of Jodo Buddhism (Nishida came from a Jodo-shinshu family).[38] In his later phase, despite the use of Western categories with his "logic of the place," Nishida developed an intellectual structure that attempts to break out of the epistemological and metaphysical dualism imposed by European philosophy. This effort placed him, at the beginning of the twentieth century, on the side of those Japanese intellectuals who wanted to develop a particularly Japanese identity in philosophy. This goal was developed and misused by nationalists during the Second World War, although Nishida openly fought against this misuse of his philosophy. For Nishida, as in all East Asian Buddhism, the influence of the *Yogacara* school is clear. Emptiness is identified as the basis of all the consciousness resting in it, knowing no more distinction of self and thus finally the only reality. Thus the place *(basho)*, the origin, foundation, and development structure of multiplicity, lies in its unity. (This "place" is thus in a certain sense less comparable to the Greek *topos* than to *arche*.) The dualistic confrontation of reality reaches fulfillment as negation, and inasmuch as this negativity is again emptied out, the *place comes to pass*. To express this concept, Nishida used the image of a sphere with an infinite diameter, the center of which is thus everywhere and which, since it has no transcendent basis outside itself, mirrors itself in itself. The image is reminiscent of Nicholas of Cusa's unending circle.[39] The "place" is the dynamic occurrence of expression in many and impression in the one, in other words dynamic emptiness. The "pure experience" as experience of the unity of consciousness in itself is for Nishida the self as the *absolute nothing*.

Thus, Buddhist nothingness is not a "something," toward which we can direct attention, but a transparent "space" that links the attention to the concrete forms of life, so that they appear *in their fundamental unity*.[40] The absolute nothing is thus the basis for love and a life of turning toward all beings, because the individual "I" enters entirely into the Other, giving itself up completely.

In this issue the Kyoto school already indicated the fundamental theme of later Buddhist-Christian dialogue. Nishida himself cites Francis of Assisi's "Canticle of

---

[38] For a short but very enlightening introduction to Nishida and the other philosophers, see H. Waldenfels, 48ff.; see also F. Buri, *Der Buddha-Christus als der Herr des wahren Selbst* (Bern/Stuttgart, 1982), 53, 80 (we cannot discuss here Buri's problematic portrayal and dialogue method in regard to Nishitani; on this issue see T. Vetter, "Buddhismus und Christentum. Zum buddhistischen Hintergrund von K. Nishitanis Dialektik (I) und zu F. Buris Vorschlag zum christlich-buddhistischen Dialog (II)," *ZMR* 1 [1987]: 1-24). For further introduction to the Kyoto school, see T. Unno, ed., *The Religious Philosophy of Nishitani Keiji* (Berkeley, Calif.: Asian Humanities Press, 1989); S. Heine, "Postwar Issues in Japanese Buddhism," in *Religious Issues and Interreligious Dialogues*, ed. C. Wei-hsun Fu and G. E. Spiegler (New York, 1989) 249ff.; R. Ohashi, ed., *Die Philosophie der Kyoto-Schule: Texte und Einführung* (Freiburg/Munich: Alber, 1990); D. W. Mitchell, *Spirituality and Emptiness* (New York: Paulist Press, 1991), 10ff.; and especially Nishitani Keiji's reflections on his teacher Nishida from the year 1950, in K. Nishitani, *Nishida Kitaro* (Berkeley and Los Angeles: University of California Press, English translation 1991).

[39] D. W. Mitchell, 12.

[40] We have taken elements of this formulation from D. W. Mitchell, 25.

Brother Sun," interpreting it as a statement that, for Francis, sun, moon, and stars were symbols of God (in other words, that there was a certain difference between them). Nishida responded to this with the argument that all things have the same root and same being as the self; in Christian terminology this is God. He bases this and other arguments in the context of his teaching about God's self-emptying (kenosis), which here appears for the first time in dialogue. The context of this assertion of Nishida's is an examination of the death of the self. For him, this death, not anticipatory but existential and not-objectively experienced, signifies encounter with the absolute, because the self-conscious I-duality unifies and thus in self-contradiction becomes identical. The same is true of the absolute: in order to be absolute, it must stand in opposition to an other, and therefore God creates and is immediately in the "place" that in itself realizes the unity of oneness and differentiation. Nishida already mentions the trinitarian structure of this thought.[41]

Tanabe Hajime

Tanabe Hajime (1885-1962), who was allied with Nishida from 1911 on and later became his successor and critic at Kyoto University, opposes the "logic of place" with a "logic of species" in his *Philosophy as Metanoetics* (1944). This is a program of direct self-determination through absolute mediation. Nishida was influenced by Zen, Tanabe by Pure Land Buddhism. Therefore Tanabe does not stress unity but *difference*. Metanoia *(zange)* is for him the transformative alteration of consciousness effected by the "other power" *(tariki)* of Amida's grace. Tanabe's statements are filled with autobiographical shock—his work mirrors his sense of hopelessness and suffering at the experience and guilt of the war.[42] The submission of self to the "other power" comforts the individual, and from this comfort awaken spiritual peace and thankfulness. For Tanabe, the resolution of the contradiction between *be* and *ought* in the human condition (that is, in historical reality) is not to be found in the individual will through penetration of the absolute nothing. Instead, it is the mediation through these in the context of human "other power." The nothingness of Zen for him must be penetrated by self-sacrificial love. Tanabe invokes Shinran, the founder of Japanese Jodo-Shin (Amida) Buddhism, but his method of mediation is instead Hegelian. Tanabe knows that his thought is near to the Judeo-Christian prophetic tradition. Also, like other philosophers of the Kyoto school, he comes to grips with Martin Heidegger.

Tanabe challenges Heidegger's philosophy on the idea of freedom. For Tanabe, "being unto death" is too limited, perhaps also because he is at home with Kierkegaard's radicalism and dialectic theology. True freedom for Tanabe develops from the encounter with the ever-present and indeed greater nothingness of the absolute nothing. For only the absolute nothing can guarantee *gensho*, a return in love to the *samsara* world. But this freedom does not come from humans

---

[41] The corresponding citations are laid out in F. Buri, 77ff.

[42] See H. Tanabe, *Philosophy as Metanoetics* (Berkeley and Los Angeles: University of California Press, 1986), 2ff.

themselves, argues Tanabe, for they cannot free themselves from the web of past *karma*. Freedom blooms much more from the metanoetic recognition of the futility of the "I" or self. It will be opened up by the "other power" through Amida's grace, which revokes the past and directs life toward the future. That means that the self must die its own death in order to be awakened in the communal life of human society (logic of the species). Thus Tanabe has transformed Heidegger's concept of time, according to which the time modes were constructed following one another as an existential horizon of future-past-present. Tanabe reconciles the opposition of past (the "being," blind *karma*) and future (the "ought," Pure Land) in the present, which by its own power creates from unity *(itten)* the person *(ki)* and the power of objective *dharma (ho)* in consciousness of freedom of belief.

Shinran had described this unity as "the natural path of *dharma*" *(jinen honi)*, but unlike Shinran and the later Jodo-shinshu sects Tanabe never fully trusted the "other power." Instead, he preserved a dialectical tension between personal power *(jiriki)* and other power *(tariki)*. In this way Tanabe charted a middle course between the extremes, in which the unity of wisdom, action, and belief is similar, for example, to the approach that the Tendai and Kegon tradition (the doctrine of the reciprocal penetration of antitheses, including the time modes) had always maintained.

The debate between Nishida and Tanabe is as informative about the new orientation of Buddhist religious philosophy as it is about Buddhist-Christian dialogue. First, the issue can be understood as a contribution to the Buddhist paradox of what it means that *nirvana* and *samsara* are identical *(soku)*. The problem is posed existentially in Zen as the question of original enlightenment *(hongaku)*, which dwells within every being. Three features of the relationship between *nirvana* and *samsara* repeatedly resurface: (1) only *nirvana* is real; *samsara* is illusion; (2) there are two realities that melt into one; and (3) there is only a single non-duality between the two, and only a blinded consciousness sees it as two.

The first position represents the monistic misunderstanding and risks a relative nihilism, because the world too easily disappears from view. The second position operates dualistically and reaches unity only secondarily. The third position is the best attested in the Buddhist tradition, because it maintains the dialectical tension and remains non-dualistic—*samsara* does not lose its reality and the bodhisattva can really engage in the world. From Nishida to Nishitani this thought can be expressed thus: this side is *(samsara)*, without ceasing to be this side, directly within the other side *(nirvana)*.

Second, however, Tanabe differs from Nishida in his determination of the balance between personal power and other power, in other words, in the determination of the bodhisattva vow. For him, the metanoetic power to change consciousness can only come from outside. For this reason he also distrusted Hegel's belief in self-purifying power and instead perceived in the autonomous reason the power of self-destruction. His dialectic of mediation can be expressed as "personal power is other power," without his identification of both powers or leading them back to one another. For salvation the human needs Amida, and Amida, in order to bring about salvation, needs the human—but the relationship is not symmetrical (or "reversible," as it is called in the discussion with Takizawa).

To summarize briefly, among the Kyoto philosophers Nishida is the uncompromising *hongaku* thinker (original enlightenment) in the spirit of Zen, while Tanabe introduces the element of *shigaku* (enlightenment acquired at a particular moment) into the *hongaku* formula, because he regards Nishida's view as lacking in ethical accountability: in view of real history it is urgently necessary to recognize the reality of evil. This dialectic of *hongaku* and *shigaku* has been a fundamental problem in the Zen school at least since the time of Dogen (1200-1253)!

Nishitani Keiji

Nishitani Keiji (1900-1990) proceeds from an analysis of the different forms of Western nihilism (especially that of Nietzsche). In his judgment these all had to develop upon a foundation of Christian dualistic thought and have thus brought the chasm between subject and object to the fore in modern science. While Tanabe's philosophy reacted to war guilt and made the problem of freedom—in opposition to Heidegger—into a central theme, Nishitani Keiji wrestles with pre-war nihilism. Thus he also responds to Heidegger, whom he criticizes for the remnants of ontological substantialization in his thought, which cannot comprehend the concept of the absolute nothing. Nishitani believes that the disavowal of teleology through science must necessarily come to an end in European nihilism. Because of this belief he would like to surmount this problem by means of a corresponding interpretation of Zen.[43] His interest is thus thoroughly existential-religious.[44] He seeks from this position to erect a Buddhist-Christian dialogue alternative to the exclusively scientific-technological approach that has been dominant,[45] which he (like Heidegger) regards as destructive. For him, the key to this alternative is the Zen Buddhist understanding of the absolute nothing *(zettai-mu)*.

In his 1950 study of Nishida's philosophy,[46] Nishitani bemoans the loss of the "inner life" in the modern quest for "objective certainty." According to Nishitani, the "inner life" was still alive in medieval European spirituality. This view of the past separates Nishitani from Heidegger. Both do indeed criticize modern psychology and sociology, but Nishitani elaborates with the argument that in medieval society all human beings were equal before God. This belief is supposed to have had a psychically and socially stabilizing effect. In the nineteenth century, however, Marx demanded this equality also on earth, while Freud developed "technologies" for the dissection of the soul, from which humans in the second half of the twentieth century could hardly expect salvation any longer. However, the belief that psychology can heal the "inner life" and sociology can solve social and moral problems is still barely contested. In this uncritical attitude toward the social sciences Nishitani sees the greatest threat to philosophy. Nishida's

---

[43] K. Nishitani, "Science and Zen," *The Eastern Buddhist*, NS 1 (1965/66): 79-108.

[44] H. Waldenfels, 68f.

[45] J. v. Bragt, "Religion and Science in Nishitani Keiji," *Zen Buddhism Today: Annual Report of the Kyoto Zen Symposium* 5 (November 1987) (Kyoto: Kyoto Seminar for Religious Philosophy, 1987), 161-74.

[46] See K. Nishitani, *Nishida Kitaro.*

quest for the good, which is manifest in pure experience, is according to Nishitani an attempt to rediscover the "inner life" that has been lost in the modern era, inasmuch as the self and the transcendent would be united. To this degree the title of one of his greatest works—*Shukyo-towa-nanika* (What is religion?), 1961—is the fundamental question for his own thought. His criticism of Nishida arises because Nishida in his concentration on "pure experience" neglected the less pure experiences of the everyday self—again analogous to Heidegger's critique of Husserl's *epoché*.

Nishitani, like Tanabe, understands the realization of absolute nothingness as a conversion experience. Nishitani, using Zen terminology, calls it the great death (the disappearance of the ego). This, however, should not be understood only at the individual level; for him, it has social relevance in the Japanese postwar situation with the issue of political morality. In this sense Nishitani would like to demythologize the cross of Christ, in order to bring Christianity to itself through Buddhist experience. This experience consists of a breakthrough by means of the great doubt, which in the subject-object dichotomy focuses itself on the subject and thus leads to great awakening. Upon the backdrop of Nishida's philosophy and the claim of the German idealistic tradition to surmount the Cartesian tension, Nishitani once again turns the double negation of absolute nothingness against the Christian creator God, who remains external to the subject. This is because, for Nishitani, the fundamental contradiction in Christianity is that freedom from the ego can only be attained in total dependence on God (and his will), which however makes freedom from egocentrism impossible. Human beings remain in conflict, uncertain and unfree, because they must repeatedly ascertain their own self-interest. Paul's famous statement in Galatians 2:2—"It is no longer I who live, but Christ who lives in me"—raises the problem of *who* speaks in this statement: Paul, Christ, or Christ-Paul? The non-dualism inherent in Christianity must still be brought to light.

Nishitani cannot accept the beliefs of contemporary Christianity, but he is also well aware of Buddhism's weakness. Therefore, using Buddhism as a starting point, he would like to bring both religions to a new orientation in dialogue. That is why he can describe himself dialectically as a "having become Buddhist" and "becoming Christian."[47]

Hisamatsu Shin'ichi

Hisamatsu Shin'ichi (1889-1981),[48] more than the philosophers already discussed, is *first* a Zen master and *then* a philosopher. He was born into a very pious Shin Buddhist family, but lost the "medieval" belief under the pressure of modern scientific doubt. Under the influence of Nishida's philosophy he developed after his *satori* experience a "philosophy of awakening," in which he breaks

---

[47] Cited in H. Waldenfels, 84.

[48] See S. Hisamatsu, "Memories of My Academic Life," *The Eastern Buddhist* 8/1-2 (1975): 12ff.; M. Abe, "Hisamatsu's Philosophy of Awakening," *The Eastern Buddhist* 14/1 (1981): 26-42.

through the boundaries of rationality to a *life* of the formless self, which expresses itself in all forms of human existence. Insofar as the true self can be known objectively to itself, there is knowledge itself and the possibility of a *philosophy* on the foundation of the absolute subjectivity of the self. For Hisamatsu, this is the absolute truth of reason in contrast to the merely relative truth of rationality. In other words, autonomous reason cannot be truly autonomous, because it must always remain uncertain and thus cannot resolve the absolute antinomy of life and death or good and evil. If the autonomous reason, for example, chooses life in contrast to death, life thus remains always threatened, which leads to an unregulated and endless quest for certainty. The human being ought rather to die the great death through the great doubt of self-opposition of the autonomous reason, in order to recognize that he or she will not die but rather every moment actualize the dynamism of life-and-death. Thus death is vanquished in the awakening to the formless self.

The starting point for Hisamatsu's philosophy, as for Nishitani's, is an existential-religious concern, namely, the freeing of the doubting ego. This liberation for Hisamatsu also means liberation from the egoism of nationality, race, and religion. From it is born openness to "brotherly love for all humanity." Although Hisamatsu criticizes Christian theism for its failure to transcend the absolute antinomy of good and evil, he sees in the Christian notion of God's self-sacrificial love the form of love that could correspond to the subjectivity of the formless self in Zen.

For Hisamatsu, religion changes real history by transcending it. In his view, however, religion does not transcend history in the sense that it leaves it behind. Instead, Hisamatsu's formulation of a "supra-historical" inclusion of time means that the formless self is the fundamental subject of time; that is, it constitutes *all* historical moments in time. Thus a new, non-ego-based action in history is possible from the spiritual stand of awakening. Hisamatsu wished to transform this into reality in his F.A.S. Society.

Ueda Shizuteru

Ueda Shizuteru (b. 1926), Nishitani's successor as professor of philosophy of religion at Kyoto, especially enriched the dialogue with his studies of Meister Eckhart.[49] More generally he is engaged in the "mystical renaissance" that has occurred in Christianity since the 1960s, and which has again rescued Buddhist-Christian dialogue from the unproductivity of simple opposition of conceptual antinomies (theism-atheism, and so on). In 1948 Nishitani had published his book *Kami to Zettai-mu* (God and Absolute Nothingness), upon which Ueda built. Ueda sees significant similarities between Eckhart and Zen, as well as a deep difference.

---

[49] For example: S. Ueda, *Die Gottesgeburt in der Seele und der Durchbruch zur Gottheit: Die mystische Anthropologie Meister Eckharts und ihre Konfrontation mit der Mystik des Zen* (Gütersloh: Gütersloher Verlagshaus, 1965); idem, "Die Bewegung nach oben und die Bewegung nach unten: Zen-Buddhismus im Vergleich mit Meister Eckhart," *Eranos* 50 (1981): 223-73.

Eckhart speaks first of humans' return to their original state of being through "self-release" and "solitude"; second of bareness, that is, the qualitylessness, formlessness, and imagelessness of this foundation; and third of the return to a daily life from this base. In these he is similar to Zen. He differs as well. Against the background of trinitarian doctrine Eckhart understands God's birth in the soul as analogous to the eternal procession of the Son from the Father. The divine occurrence of salvation thus reaches each person directly and without intermediary. (To this point Zen and Eckhart are in agreement.) When, however, the soul would enter into the trinitarian divine life, it seeks, according to Eckhart, to be more incorporated in God, the "nothingness" that Eckhart describes as the purity of *God's being*. Thus, according to Ueda, Eckhart remains imprisoned in the idea of substance. In Zen, to the contrary, the nothing is the ever "de-substantializing" movement; that is, the human is not only divided from all in order to be in God but is also divided from separation itself. Thus for Ueda, Zen is more radical, even though perfection in Zen, as with Eckhart, consists of a "return to the marketplace" or in "rising from the union with God." Eckhart in his famous exegesis of the tale of Mary and Martha expressed it thus: not Mary but Martha reached the higher spiritual perfection, because she is and remains fully with the lord *in the midst of her work*.

ZEN BUDDHIST-CHRISTIAN COLLOQUIA

Thanks to Quaker initiative, since 1967 there have been annual four- to six-day consultations in Japan among Zen masters, Buddhist philosophers, and Christian theologians. The Friends World Committee for Consultation (FWCC) of the Quakers had called for agreement between religions as a response to the Second World War's genocide. They did this invoking the British historian Arnold Toynbee and his famous comment that future generations would especially remember the twentieth century for the beginning of interpenetration between Buddhism and Christianity, and that a solution to contemporary world problems would only be possible through a mutual reorientation of religions. In this way it was hoped that in Japan the personal path of belief as well as the social responsibility of individuals and religious communities could be thematized.

The first meeting, held 27 March to 1 April 1967, was financed by the Quakers; all later meetings were paid for by the groups involved and the individual participants themselves. Among those invited were the German-Japanese Jesuit Heinrich Dumoulin, Hisamatsu Shin'ichi, and Yamada Mumon Roshi. The proceedings of the first ten colloquia (1967-76) were at first published in Japanese as a special issue of *The Mahayana Zen Buddhism* (no. 627). They evoked such a strong response that an English edition was also published.[50] Some of the participants (Yagi Seiichi, Honda Masaaki, Abe Masao, Heinrich Dumoulin, and others) have remained the backbone of Buddhist-Christian dialogue in Japan. An account of their work follows below. Some, most notably Yagi, have a broad

---

[50] Irie Yukio, ed., *A Zen-Christian Pilgrimage: The Fruits of Ten Annual Colloquia in Japan 1967-1976* (Hong Kong, 1981).

influence thanks to popular writings with a large Japanese readership. One can trace the growing friendships among the disputants, as well as the progress in understanding and the moderation they showed in the balancing of attainments. We wish to call attention to several important points of these colloquia:

Zen as the foundation of all religions. The Zen master Shibayama Zenkei distinguishes between *Zen* as an expression for pure religious experience separate from specific historical context and *Zen Buddhism*. In pure experience—the reader will recall Nishida's early work—there can be no differences between religions;[51] in all cases, humans return to a source of all religious viewpoints. The individual schools and religions are only necessary as guides along the path. Interestingly, Shibayama argues, using the example of the possibility of conscientious objection to war in America (unfortunately still lacking in Japan), that the development of religiously motivated conscience against generally accepted norms can be a step toward spiritual awakening! This must be an issue in the context of Buddhist-Christian dialogue.

The fundamental difference between inability to reverse (Christianity) and ability to reverse (Zen) the relationship between humans and the absolute. This problem repeatedly recurs in the work of Hisamatsu, Abe, Yagi, Takizawa, and others. What is involved here? According to Abe,[52] in Christianity the concept of God is not reversible because of the belief in humans' personal dependence. In other words, the primary movement is from God to humans, while humans on their own cannot reach God. Zen, on the contrary, is based on the idea of complete reversibility, the reciprocal dependence or "reciprocal immanence" of relative and absolute, between the concrete human and the formless self. In Christianity this irreversibility means (though not inevitably) that God is objectified, since it is God's call that sets the norms that make human freedom possible. Zen, however, aspires to freedom from every normalcy, and indeed aims toward spontaneous self-showing of concrete reality here and now. In other words, would it mean the same thing if a Buddhist said that he *becomes* entirely Buddha, and a Christian said that she *will be* entirely God? The problem remains debated. Abe himself is of the opinion that a norm based on the word of a personal God cannot really be grasped by Zen Buddhism. Thus the question comes up of whether it can be transmitted, if Zen has a universal claim and a universal responsibility toward all beings. Incidentally, Amida Buddhism also stands on the side of irreversibility, because it is only Amida who saves from sin.[53]

But the problem reaches still more deeply for Abe. Behind the Christian unrenounceable divine norm lurks unobjectifiable evil, because it is not integrated into the concept of God.[54] Only the complete reversibility of the relationship between God and human can deal with evil in such a way that it is not

---

[51] Ibid., 10.

[52] Ibid., 36ff.

[53] Ibid., 41.

[54] God as good and evil is foreign to Abe. That there can also be an ambivalence about God, according to which "evil" lies in Godself, is only a marginal issue in the Judeo-Christian concept of God.

suppressed, by acting as a new starting point (never as an accomplished goal, which would mean anarchic over-elevation of the ego!).

Thus far the argument has often been repeated, and it can appear that there is an insurmountable obstacle between Zen and Christianity. This opposition could, however, possibly be overcome with the following consideration: the formless self (or God) is the basis, source, and spontaneous impulse for every self-realization. The possible significance of this is clear in a conversation between Hisamatsu and the Christian theologian Yagi Seiichi, reported by the latter.[55] Hisamatsu is supposed to have translated *mu* as "*the* nothingness," wanting in that way to give expression to his Buddhist atheism, which accepts no transcendence beyond the self. When Yagi on another occasion made him consider whether *awakening* as pure immediacy of enlightenment could not be distinguished from the *becoming conscious* of awakening, so that awakening would make itself as it were the object of perception, Hisamatsu agreed. But then the other-being of the transcendent would be on the ladder of reflection—we would have an immediate non-duality to present, which however always appears in consciousness as a modified duality between God and human, and can never be resolved. Precisely this issue is the starting point for Yagi's later theology, as we will show.

Self-criticism of the religions. Several participants in the dialogue, especially the Zen master Akizuki Ryomin, complain about the self-righteous attitude of their own religion. Akizuki directly opposes Abe on the issue of reversibility. He does so because he sees in this concept the basis for a self-righteous and proud attitude in many Zen Buddhists, who would, if left unchecked, upset the precarious actual state of Buddhism in Japan.[56] For Akizuki, the strength of Zen indeed lies in the continuing consciousness "of trans-individual individuals," that is, in *unity* with the Buddha nature, but often "personal enlightenment" is too swiftly identified with "original enlightenment." To understand Zen as a religion of "personal powers," argues Akizuki elsewhere,[57] is a serious error or a linguistic misunderstanding. For just as a newborn baby is in every circumstance reliant on the help and love of the mother and others, so no human can live entirely self-sufficiently, not to speak of reaching enlightenment. For Akizuki, Zen awakening is the experience of the "great," to which life owes itself. Christianity's clear distinction between God and human is a strength, because from this basic attitude it is possible to accept the imperfection of all perception and each life situation. Thus among Christians, for Akizuki, there is more readiness to learn and openness to dialogue than in Buddhism. This, by the way, also agrees with Zen master Dogen's insight that the realization of *dharma*, as he experienced it, can only appear completely to one who is not yet fully awakened.

At this point it would be useful to ask what practical difference these differing viewpoints make for the praxis of each. We suggest that both positions can be understood as dynamic poles in an elliptical motion, in which the existential realization of original awakening never comes to rest, but original awakening is

[55] I. Yukio, 112ff.

[56] Ibid., 48ff.

[57] Akizuki Ryomin, "Christian-Buddhist Dialogue," *Inter-Religio* 14 (fall 1988): 47.

never given except at times in spontaneous awakening. "Objectification" (and irreversibility) would be the extreme result of a constantly ongoing process.

JOINT COMMUNITY DIALOGUE

Only two examples of this very substantial dialogue form will be given here.

Rissho Kosei-kai

Rissho Kosei-kai (RKK), founded in 1938 by Niwano Nikkyo (b. 1906), is a Buddhist lay organization constructed on the foundation of Nichiren Buddhism,[58] which sees in the Lotus sutra the source of all revelation and truth.[59] It is one of the new religious movements in Japan that promise a new home for the urbanized population that has been uprooted from its home temples. A witness of its success in this goal is its meteoric rise in a few decades (today there are about six million members). It sprang from the Reiyukai movement with its tradition of charismatic healing and corresponding this-worldly interpretation of Buddhism. Niwano does not understand the concept of *karma* individualistically, as it was in early Buddhism. Instead, he believes that *karma* is rooted in the community, so that in the end the *samgha* will include all of humanity. Peace, harmony, and balanced compassion should take the place of the traditional forms of socialization (which in the case of the extended family have collapsed), and in this regard there are also no boundaries between religions. Dialogue between religions is necessary for the sake of world peace and spiritual harmony. And so, just as the confession of faults and penance in the personal association of members with each other and in "group discussions for spiritual care" *(hoza)* plays a role, so too must Japan meditate on its role in the Second World War and recognize the suffering that Japan brought to other peoples. The Rissho Kosei-kai is one of the few groups in Japan that assert this publicly, and since 1948 it has borne the religious and economic consequences. This attitude appeared first in the attempt to join together different Nichiren groups, then in the joint foundation of *Shinshu-ren* (League of Japanese religions), established in 1951, whose president in 1969 was Niwano). Finally, Rissho Kosei-kai helped found and finance the World Conference of Religions for Peace (WCRP), whose first meeting in Kyoto in 1970 was substantially organized and financed by the RKK. The RKK supports its own department for dialogue with other religions, has published a dialogue periodical—*Dharma World*—since 1974, and also organizes a student and teacher

---

[58] Nichiren (1222-82) founded his own school of Japanese Buddhism on the basis of a political-"eschatological" interpretation of the Lotus sutra. It criticized all the other schools, as well as the political regime, and inspired exclusivist reform efforts.

[59] The most recent survey of the movement's history and character is A. Nehring, *Rissho Kosei-kai* (Erlangen: Verlag der Ev.-Luth. Mission, 1992); see also K. J. Dale, *Circle of Harmony: A Case Study in Popular Japanese Buddhism* (Tokyo: Seibunsha, 1975); R. Italiaander, *Eine Religion für den Frieden: Die Rissho Kosei-kai* (Erlangen: Verlag der Ev.-Luth. Mission, 1973).

exchange with Christian institutions. Niwano Nikkyo took part in the Second Vatican Council, in the prayer meeting of religions at Assisi, and in other interreligious encounters. The movement also maintains intensive contact with the Christian spiritual renewal movement Focolare in Italy, founded in 1943 by Chiara Lubich (b. 1920).[60] In Japan itself, the RKK does not have many contacts with Christian churches; its effort at dialogue is mostly limited to the international conference culture. Nevertheless, the RKK also supports development projects and peace projects along with international organizations. Recently, however, it has been establishing contacts with congregations and other religious groups in Japan. It has begun to sponsor "dialogue councils" that seek to work on practical questions such as education of the young, drug problems, the power of the media, medical ethics, the suppression of dying and death in Japanese society, and so on. It is astonishing how similar the dialogue themes are, on the basis of corresponding experiences, in Europe and America, ranging from the joint prayer meeting to the Gulf War![61] Japanese Christians often regard Rissho Kosei-kai with distrust because of its success; it missionizes in Japan and has still not satisfactorily clarified its position on the proper relationship between active mission and interreligious dialogue.

The Albert Schweitzer Temple in Tamana[62]

A relic of Schweitzer's hair, earlier possessed by the Japanese Protestant Albert Schweitzer Association, was given to Furukawa Tairyu Roshi in April 1969 after the death of the association's president, Mukai Tadashi. The reason for the gift was that Tairyu had since 1961 fought tirelessly against the death sentences of two men whom he knew were innocent. (One was executed; the other's sentence was commuted to life imprisonment and then overthrown in 1989.) Zen master Tairyu and his wife converted a *ryokan* (Japanese hotel) they owned in the Kumamoto district of Tamana into a Buddhist temple, in which the hair relic is now venerated as sacred, and which bears the name Albert Schweitzer (Schweitzer-ji). The Catholic theologian Honda Masaaki in 1978 brought Zen master Tairyu together with Brother Franco Sottocornola of the Xavieran Missionary Fathers, who established a Catholic house for prayer and encounter (Seimeizan Katorikku betsu-in) on the grounds of the Buddhist Schweitzer Temple in 1987. This was a unique event, that a religious institutionally defined body (a Catholic prayer center) should become part of a body with a different legal definition (a Buddhist temple). Seimeizan, the temple of universal life, combines Christian prayer, *zazen*,

---

[60] On this issue, see D. W. Mitchell, 158ff.

[61] There is an interesting report in A. H. Kroehler, "Religious Dialogue at the Grassroots Level," *Japanese Religions* 18/1 (January 1993): 76-87.

[62] This information comes from a report that Honda Masaaki gave at the International Buddhism-Christianity Conference, Berkeley, 1987 (unpublished conference papers, library of the Graduate Theological Union, Berkeley, California). See also R. Corless, "Seimeizan: A Living Buddhist-Christian Dialogue," *Buddhist-Christian Studies* 12 (1992): 233-40. Corless speaks of a "combined call of an Italian Christian and a Japanese Buddhist to transcend nationality in planetary awareness" (239).

and celebration of the eucharist in its liturgy. The house has become a center for interreligious dialogue (Tozai Shukyo Koryu Center), whose directors have included a Muslim. Christians meet with Buddhists and get to know the practice of *zazen* and *nembutsu*,[63] while Buddhists come to learn about the prayer life of the small Christian community. The Schweitzer Temple and the dialogue center both engage in social work, for example when a living and rehabilitation center for disabled children was built in China. This is in concord with Furukawa's own life experience; in the course of his activism for those condemned to death for political reasons, he had become sensitive to the bitter suffering of the Chinese, which had been caused by Japanese aggression. He is an engaged Buddhist, who emphasizes the role of the laity and who preaches against Japanese nationalism from a sense of Buddhist political responsibility. But that is not all. Since 1988 he has led pilgrimages to Nanking to keep alive the remembrance of the massacre of 1937 and the Japanese invasion of China. The Christian-Buddhist dialogue center is also planning a *Muslim betsu-in* and, if possible, houses of other religions.

THE CHRISTIAN DIALOGUE CENTERS

The Dialogue Center of the National Christian Council in Kyoto

The oldest dialogue center in Japan is the Center for the Study of Japanese Religion, founded in Kyoto in 1959 by the Protestant National Christian Council (NCC). From 1965 to 1985 it was led by Doi Masatoshi (1907-88).[64] His basic approach to dialogue was that only a final reality can be binding for any human being. Since each person only has a relative and faulty perception of truth, however, this must mean that other people can have similarly significant experiences in totally different fashions.[65] In this spirit the center for decades has organized public lectures, seminars, interreligious conferences, and study projects. An interreligious study group meets monthly to work on Buddhist texts; seminars for pastors and missionaries are held at Buddhist and Shinto centers, Buddhist universities, and in Zen monasteries. Invitations to pastors to take part in Zen meditations are also part of the regular activity of the center. But above all, since 1959 the center has published the journal *Japanese Religions* bi-annually in English, and the Japanese journal *Deai* (Encounter) since 1966.

The journal *Japanese Religions* began in 1959 with an exposition that, within Japan and without the direct participation of Christians, struggled with a new interpretation of traditional Japanese religion in the modern world. It is concerned with religion and magic, and attempts to free Buddhism from mistaken belief in magical practices. According to this view, recitation of the Buddha name

---

[63] *Zazen* is the sitting meditation in Zen style; *nembutsu* is the adoring invocation of the Buddha name in Pure Land Buddhism.

[64] See F. Spier, "'Dialogue Is between Fully Committed Persons': A Portrait of Doi Masatoshi," *Japanese Religions* 13/4 (1985): 3-15.

[65] M. Doi, *Man's Search for Meaning through Interfaith Dialogue* (Tokyo: Kyobunkwan, 1976), 131.

(nembutsu) is an expression of personal belief and not a magical formula with a utilitarian purpose, intended to satisfy certain specific worldly wishes, as many Japanese have falsely thought.[66]

For years the Norwegian missionary Notto Thelle worked as assistant director of the center. With the China missionary Karl Ludwig Reichelt as his model, Thelle wanted to appropriate Buddhist wisdom in order to preach Christianity more effectively. His own summary after sixteen years in Japan is this: "I was cast back to the condition of a pilgrim who approached Buddhism with fear and trembling. I wandered in a universe that was much bigger than I had been able to imagine in my apologist dreams."[67] Now he wished to integrate not just intellectual doubt but also Buddhist wisdom into his own Christian belief in a reformulation of Christianity. For him, the unity of intellectual understanding, spiritual deepening, and human friendship is the essence of his dialogue experiences. In this way the dark elements of encounter with other religions—hypocrisy, power struggles, and so forth—which occur in Buddhism as much as in Christianity, may not be overlooked. The ever newly constructed personal witness to the partner in dialogue would become an inner process of transformation, joining firm commitment to the Christian homeland to absolute openness, spiritual quest, and frequently spiritual transformation.[68]

That, so it appears to us, is authentic dialogue. Thelle also, however, bemoans the isolation in which Japanese Christians usually live—without true contact and neighborliness in regard to Japan's religious context, but instead with an identity transplanted from the West.

Oriens Institute in Tokyo

In 1964 the Belgian Catholic missionary Joseph Spae (b. 1913) founded in Tokyo the Oriens Institute for Religious Research, which publishes the *Japan Missionary Bulletin* and which has contributed to dialogue, especially through Spae's own activities. For Spae, dialogue is *mutual* conversion of the partners *to each other* through sharing and empathy, through which both would be drawn to the transcendent; and the sharing of both traditions as far as possible.[69] Spae sees dialogue in Japan in the context of the whole society's break-up and shift in values. He believes there is a quest for subjectivity, activity, and realism that springs from the fatalism of the Buddhist pattern of cause and effect. Besides this, especially young people search for a sense of "belonging" that will not be satisfied in the vertical hierarchical structures of Japanese society,[70] but much more in an "emotional democracy" that extends on a horizontal level between people, a democracy to which Christianity must contribute. Turned around, the Japanese search for the beautiful and the balance of intuition and authority can

---

[66] A. Bloom, "Is the Nembutsu Magic?" *Japanese Religions* 1/3 (1959): 31ff.

[67] N. Thelle, "Reflections on Dialogue as a Spiritual Pilgrimage: On Theological Addresses," *Japanese Religions* 13/4 (1985): 18.

[68] Ibid., 20.

[69] J. Spae, 63.

[70] Ibid., 13ff.

give much to a Christianity that is mostly fixated on "the last things." The new religions like Tenrikyo and Perfect Liberty, for Spae, have already adopted the Christian notion of a personal God, only in a changed form—God as "parent." In many of these movements this-worldliness and optimism are linked to a Japanese consciousness of being a chosen people on the basis of transcendent spiritually experienced strength, which attests to the powerful fermentation process in Japanese religious consciousness. Even Pure Land Buddhism with its personal veneration of the Buddha and humorous-tolerant tales of sacred popular heroes *(myokonin)* is supposed to be a Buddhist parallel to the praise of spiritual poverty and simplicity in the gospels.[71] Dialogue may not be limited to philosophical abstractions, argues Spae, but must include these popular traditions if it wishes to be relevant for Japanese society. Especially in the poetry of Akutagawa Ryunosuke (1892-1927) there are parables that must be worked out in dialogue. A good example is the tale *The Death of a Christian*. In this story a woman accuses a man of being the father of her child, because he has not returned her love. When a fire breaks out in the city, he rescues the child at the cost of his own life, despite all the humiliation he has suffered. The people regard him as a martyr, indeed as Christ come again.

Interestingly, there is a Buddhist parallel to this story that Spae does not mention. It is told of the Zen master Hakuin (1686-1769): A girl imputed the paternity of her son to him. He reacted tranquilly, saying only, "So?" And he brought up the child, while people wagged their fingers at him. When the girl was filled with remorse and told the truth, Hakuin returned the child, saying only, "So?"

Do the two stories represent the difference between suffering, self-sacrificial love and tranquil, dispassionate compassion? And if this were the case, do the attitudes of Christianity or Buddhism conform to either tale?

Spae adds an important observation to his insistence that dialogue above all ought to be at the level of stories told among the people: Japan's strikingly non-dualistic basic attitude in philosophy and life praxis is not a consequence of Buddhist education, but was already established in the linguistic structure of the Japanese language itself.[72] The Western oppositions of body and spirit, death and life, immanence and transcendence, and so on, are *polarities* for the Japanese, which assimilate to one another on a higher level or in the process of lived praxis. This, according to Spae, is the reason for Japanese caution toward final dogmatic statements about the absolute. Also, the Japanese cannot understand a "historical fundamentalism"[73] that regards historical truths as absolute and does not recognize a deeper transchronological significance that can be grasped intuitively.

Besides this, argues Spae, the character of spoken communication is completely different in Japan than in Europe or America. In Japan, language especially serves a feeling of community; it does not define, but designates feelings.[74]

---

[71] Ibid., 29.

[72] Ibid., 70, as also H. Nakamura and H. Waldenfels before.

[73] J. Spae, 43.

[74] See the very instructive article "Skepsis bei Wörtern," in *Blick aus Mandelaugen*, ed. H. Matsubara, 54ff.

People chatter gladly and much (in everyday life there is by no means a "cult of stillness") in order to produce moods; but there is silence in the face of things that are essential. The unclear expression ensures that communication is not broken off and that the community will be furthered. An opinion is consequently not an individually reached clear standpoint that is demarcated from other opinions, but the result of a process of finding consensus. Some thoughts (deviating from the group) are carefully guarded, so as not to endanger the community. The reason for Japanese reserve toward definitions of beliefs is thus not only an epistemologically founded distrust of every concept (of God or the absolute)—understandable in Mahayana Buddhism since Nagarjuna—but the *different social function of language* in Japan. Christian-Buddhist dialogue will have to work out a hermeneutics that considers the different functions of languages in different cultures.

Institute of Oriental Religions in Tokyo

In 1969 the Jesuit Heinrich Dumoulin (1905-95) founded the Institute of Oriental Religions at Sophia University in Tokyo. Besides the founder, this institute has especially given a platform to the Jesuits Kadowaki Kakichi, William Johnston,[75] and Hugo M. Enomiya-Lassalle, important advocates of Zen Buddhist-Christian dialogue. Symposia, scholarly exchange, and scientific work are the main efforts here, rather than dialogue as such. Therefore we can content ourselves here with a brief reference to the institute. Heinrich Dumoulin's contribution to dialogue, because of his translation and commentary work with Zen texts (*Mumonkan* and others) and his monumental history of Zen Buddhism, can scarcely be exaggerated.[76]

Nanzan Institute in Nagoya

The Christian Nanzan Institute for Religion and Culture in Nagoya, founded in 1975, functions similarly. Its decades-long director Jan van Bragt (b. 1928) engaged in dialogue with the Kyoto school and especially with Nishitani Keiji. Van Bragt in recent years, however, has also committed himself to dialogue with Pure Land Buddhism. Other intellectual trailblazers are the translation of Tanabe Hajime's main works by the American James Heisig (the current director of the institute), the ongoing "Nanzan Studies in Asian Religions," and the *Japanese Journal of Religious Studies* (since 1975), which the Buddhist-Christian dialogue worldwide must take into account. Besides this, a *Bulletin* is published annually, reporting on academic activities and Buddhist-Christian dialogue (especially in Japan).

Tozai Shukyo Koryu Gakkai

The Tozai Shukyo Koryu Gakkai (Japan Society for Buddhist-Christian Studies, JSBCS) has been in continual operation since 1983. When David Chappell

---

[75] The American William Johnston has become known worldwide especially through his book *The Still Point: Reflections on Zen and Christian Mysticism* (New York: Fordham University Press, 1970).

[76] See also the discussion of his contribution to the problem of "person" in "Personality and Person" (in chap. 5 herein).

of the University of Hawaii inaugurated the East-West religions project with its first international conference, East-West Religions in Encounter (1980), world-wide Buddhist-Christian dialogue entered a new phase, with a shift of the balance toward America. Stimulated by the Hawaii conference, the Protestant Christian Doi Masatoshi invited his two theological colleagues Honda Masaaki (Catholic, b. 1929) and Yagi Seiichi (Protestant, b. 1932) to found a scholarly society for Buddhist-Christian dialogue in Japan. The first meeting took place in Kyoto, 26-28 July 1982. About twenty Lutheran and Catholic theologians attended, as well as Zen and Pure Land philosophers and Buddhologists. Since that time there have been meetings annually. The society is indeed better organized than its American counterpart; at meetings, there is a keynote address with commentaries, and the entire discussion is published by the Zen master Akizuki Ryomin as a special issue of *Daijo Zen* (Mahayana Zen Buddhism). In 1991 the society had about sixty members, and future participation will be held to that level.

Two general themes run through the society's discussions. First, Nishitani, Abe, and others repeatedly refer to the argument that Christians and Buddhists should join together to combat secularization and the modern world's obsession with material goods. For them, who all come from the Kyoto school, the reciprocal understanding of Christians and Buddhists is possible on the basis of mystical experiences—which are indeed not identical in the two religions, but still attest to the same direction toward transcendence of self. And second, dialogue is difficult, if not impossible, if religions appear as institutions with definite ideologies and identity or power interests. Religion in this sense should be supplanted in favor of interreligious communication. To reach this goal, it is necessary to search for the spiritual core of religion, that is, for the praxis of "revelation" and "awakening."

BASIC PROBLEMS

We now wish to consider three basic problems in Buddhist-Christian dialogue, which for years have been discussed in the dialogue centers we have mentioned, and which also influence dialogue outside of Japan:

1. the question of the reversibility (Zen) or irreversibility (Pure Land Buddhism, Christianity) of the relationship between God (the absolute) and humanity;

2. the specifics of Christian dialogue with Pure Land Buddhism, which appears to be so similar to Christianity; and

3. the most recent Zen Buddhist-Christian discussion of God's kenosis.[77]

THE PROBLEM OF THE IRREVERSIBILITY OF THE RELATIONSHIP BETWEEN HUMANS AND GOD

The Kyoto school first raised this issue in debate, and the most important Christian reactions to it have come from Takizawa Katsumi (1906-84) and Yagi

---

[77] Concerning the following reports, see S. Yagi, "Bericht über Tozai Shukyo Koryu Gakkai," *Dialog der Religionen* 1 (1993): 93-100.

Seiichi (b. 1932).[78] A second phase of the discussion was influenced by the Zen master Hisamatsu Shin'ichi (1889-1980), a philosopher of religion and student of Nishida, who became Paul Tillich's partner in discussion. Hisamatsu represented a Buddhist atheism. For him, an objectively conceived God in the Christian or Amida Buddhist mold must be an illusion or a mental projection. As long as the object "God" is *imagined*, the final depth of awakening has not been reached, because the formless, which encompasses and contains all, is always present as the absolute *subject*. This criticism of Hisamatsu's is connected to the debate, described above, about irreversibility versus reversibility in the relationship of God and human that Abe initiated.

Takizawa Katsumi

Takizawa Katsumi (1909-84) was a student of Nishida who had been sent by his teacher to study with Karl Barth in Europe. Under Barth's influence Takizawa became a Lutheran Christian. While abroad he also encountered Martin Heidegger, Rudolf Bultmann, and Helmut Gollwitzer. It is important to note that his interest in Buddhist-Christian dialogue was not at all merely academic or theological. During the Second World War he had studied Karl Marx as well as Japanese authors (especially Soseki Natsume). In the late 1960s he took the side of the students in the violent student revolts that broke out in Japan, seeking to force a reform of the university system. This led to his retreat as professor to Kyushu University, which he founded in an open letter.[79]

Takizawa responded to Hisamatsu's atheism and his Zen-conforming adherence to the total reversibility of the relationship between the Buddha (the formless self) and the human being. In his book *Buddhism and Christianity—A Conflict with Hisamatsu* (1960),[80] he interprets Hisamatsu as a religious atheist and accepts his critique of pantheism, idealism, and dialectical materialism against the background of the "Eastern nothingness." Takizawa differentiates between God's primary contact with humans and the secondary contact. He also calls the primary contact the "Ur-fact Immanuel"—God with us. This ur-fact lies at the root of every human unconditionally and directly, in other words is indwelling. However, not all people are awakened to the ur-fact. When, though, it occurs that a person awakens to God's primary contact with humans, religious life is accomplished. This occurrence—the *awakening* to the primary contact or the actualization itself—Takizawa calls the secondary contact of God with the human. According to Takizawa, the relationship between the primary and secondary contacts should be designated as "indivisible-not-identical-irreversible" because the historical Jesus Christ is none other than God Immanuel in humanity (ur-fact). Thus, Jesus Christ is not simply identical with God, but the *realization* of God in history.

---

[78] See Yagi's own depiction of his debate with Takizawa in A. Dohi, T. Sato, S. Yagi, and M. Odagaki, *Theologiegeschichte der Dritten Welt* (Japan/Munich: Chr. Kaiser, 1991), 141ff.

[79] *Takizawa Katsumi: His Life and Thought* (Japanese) (Tokyo: Shinkyo Shuppansha, 1986), 228ff.

[80] K. Takizawa, *Bukkyo to Kirisutokyo* (Kyoto: Hozokan, 1960; German translation 1964).

In just this way the relationship between God and human in the primary contact is also determined: *indivisible*, because God is always with the human (ur-fact Immanuel); *not identical*, because God does not become the human being (and vice versa); *irreversible* because in the history of salvation God in Christ becomes a human being, and not the reverse. For Takizawa, God has absolute primacy in all—for this reason the relationship between God and human is strongly irreversible. According to Takizawa, Buddhism as well as Christianity is a religion founded upon the primary contact, in whatever specific form it might conceive of the secondary contact.

It is upon this theology that Takizawa bases dialogue between Buddhism and Christianity. One must add that here Takizawa thoroughly identifies himself with the well-known thought system of natural theology, which is not unusual for Catholic and liberal Protestant theologians. In the circle of Karl Barth's dialectical theology,[81] however (which remains very influential in Japanese Protestantism up to the present), it caused scandal. Takizawa, to be sure, wants to attribute his understanding of the secondary contact, which is indivisible from the primary contact, to the late thought of Barth himself.[82]

In his 1960 study Takizawa thus criticizes Hisamatsu's philosophy of religion on this basis. Zen atheism, for Takizawa, belongs in the category of the primary contact—so Hisamatsu too stands in this reality. Because, however, Zen does not make a clear distinction between the primary and secondary contact, Zen awakening (which, however, depends upon concrete conditions) must become excessively the measure of all things, which is an inadmissible absolutization of relative appearances. The Zen unity of absolute and relative, for Takazawa, is an unacceptable mix of the founder with the founded. The god whom Hisamatsu denies, he argues, is a metaphysical construction that has nothing to do with the dynamic God of love.

Takizawa, however, valued the fact that Hisamatsu speaks not only of the absolute formless, but of the formless *self*. This self of the absolute formless can rightly criticize Western subjectivity and individualism and could open the way for a trans-individual personalism, which, however, Hisamatsu has not done. Perhaps, though, this perspective can indeed be recognized in Hisamatsu's thought, in his view—unlike Nishida—that Zen can put the socioeconomic problems of the present in their proper relationship, a belief that was put into concrete form when he founded the F.A.S. Society.

Takizawa followed Barth in his critique of the anthropocentrism of liberal thought and agreed here with Hisamatsu's critique of Western nihilism. He could not, however, share Hisamatsu's concept of humankind when, under the influence of Zen

---

[81] Dialectical theology was developed by Barth after 1919. It proclaimed the radical division of God and world (God as the "entirely other") or gospel and culture. With this, every point of connection between the gospel and human religious or cultural endeavors was called into question.

[82] See especially Barth's *Die Menschlichkeit Gottes* (1956). On the theology of the late Barth and his dialogical claims, see M. v. Brück, *Möglichkeiten und Grenzen einer Theologie der Religionen*, 45ff.

awakening, it implied sinlessness and an already-accomplished victory over death. For him, *irreversibility* is a guarantee against hubris. Takizawa follows Hisamatsu as far as the structure of the modern self that is known to itself as self, which is only possible on the basis of the formless self, which is thought of in Buddhism as *dharmata* (being-*dharma*) or *dharmakaya* (absolute *dharma*—body of the Buddha). Because for Hisamatsu this is shown in the substancelessness of all appearances (also human ones), emptiness *(sunyata)*, the not-self of *dharmata* (for Takizawa the transcendent or the first person of the Trinity), Hisamatsu here comes close to what Takizawa himself calls the primary contact. However, Hisamatsu (according to Takizawa) does not know the secondary contact, which reaches full realization in Christ. Thence Hisamatsu's assertion that the transcending of sin and death can only transcend their *form* but not the substance, in other words, only the concept of sin, but not the reality, a view that was already the error of *idealism*.

On the other side, Takizawa also criticizes traditional Christianity. He believes it ignores the difference between God and human in Jesus' person, although otherwise this difference is obvious. For Takizawa, Jesus is a human being who so completely embodied the secondary contact that he became the standard for all humanity. That means that the primary contact, unconditionally applied to all people, cannot have first come through Jesus and in Jesus, a stand that relativizes Christianity's claim to absoluteness.

Takizawa's position of "irreversibility" drew a critique from Abe Masao, a student of Hisamatsu and Buddhist leader in the discussion of kenosis. In the final analysis, in Buddhism the principle of reversibility triumphs. A person who speaks of irreversibility still clings to something conceptually acknowledged. For Abe, this is a sign that one is not yet entirely free of "differentiating thought," in other words, from the illusion that differences are absolute or of dualism. As in Buddhism in general, for Abe ego and self are a unity that shuts out duality or ontological gradations.

For Akizuki Ryomin, on the contrary,[83] a former student of D. T. Suzuki and now himself a Zen master and teacher, individuality (ego) and super-individuality (the self) are neither one nor two. But insofar as they can be spoken of as two, a definite hierarchy of the two can be adopted, although it is to be sure—as Yagi Seiichi interprets it—more functional than substantial.

Akizuki agrees with Takizawa's differentiation of primary and secondary contact and compares this with Zen's distinction between original *(hongaku)* and acquired *(shigaku)* enlightenment. Takizawa had indeed regarded God and human being as two different substances, and had thus adhered to the idea of structural irreversibility (in contrast to Yagi's functional distinction), which is not conceivable in Buddhism. Because Buddhist thought is atheistic, *all* beings are Buddhas or can awaken to Buddha-ness. That is why Buddhism speaks of

---

[83] R. Akizuki, "Inseparability, Non-Identifiability and Irreversibility: A View from the Perspective of Zen-Buddhism for a Buddhist-Christian Dialogue," lecture at the International Buddhist-Christian Conference, Berkeley, 1987 (unpublished conference papers, library of the Graduate Theological Union, Berkeley, California).

reversibility on principle, which—in a typical Zen paradox—also means that there is no difference between the subjective self and the true self. Akizuki believes that Takizawa in a "both—as well as" dialectic *(soku-hi)* wanted to present the triad of "indivisible—not-identical—irreversible." However, he did not carry further this interesting possibility for interpreting the work of Takizawa.

Yagi Seiichi

Yagi Seiichi (b. 1932 in Yokohama) is one of the most influential and most original Christian theologians in Japan. With his dialogical theology, however, the for the most part conservative Protestant churches barely accept him. He grew up in the circle of the Not-Church movement *(Mu kyokai)* and became a Christian under the influence of Kierkegaard and Uchimura Kanzo (1861-1930). His study in Germany led him into historical-critical research. Then in 1958 in Ulm he met Wilhelm Gundert, the translator of the Zen classic *Hekiganroku* (Chinese *Bi-Yän-Lu*). At the readings of this translation, and especially of the famous saying "open expanse—nothing of holiness," which is put in Bodhidharma's mouth, Yagi had a spontaneous Zen enlightenment experience, sparked by the sight of an ordinary tree. Zen master Akizuki Ryomin comments that Yagi was awakened from the perception of things through the dark glass of concept to a direct perception of *this* tree; that is, he had overcome the projection of categories by the perceiving subject, which thus makes the perceived into an object.[84]

Yagi's theology is an attempt to grasp the significance of this experience in the context of his very personal Jesus-centered piety upon the background of New Testamental hermeneutics.

Toward this goal, Yagi is in general agreement with Takizawa. However, he disagrees with him on one major point. The problem of reversibility versus irreversibility was already discussed in the book *Buddhism and Christianity: An Invitation to Discussion with Takizawa* (1981), which Abe, Akizuki, Honda, and Yagi worked on together.[85] This work did not resolve the problem, though, so the Japan Society for Buddhist-Christian Studies has repeatedly returned to it. The difference between Takizawa's and Yagi's views falls into two significant categories: First, Yagi would like to make the relationship between primary and secondary contact clearer. Second, he goes beyond Takizawa in his reinterpretation of Galatians 2:19-20 (a key text in dialogue with the Kyoto school). Paul's statement is: "For I through the law died to the law, that I might live to God. I have been crucified with Christ; it is no longer I who live, but Christ who lives in me." Yagi comments that the "I" or ego has died and was newly called to life in Christ (2 Cor 5:17). What now lives is no longer an independent subject, because "Christ in me" is his foundation. This, however, is the true subject of the believer, what Yagi calls "the self" in contrast to "ego" and compares to the "true human

[84] R. Akizuki, "Christian-Buddhist Dialogue," *Inter-Religio* 14 (fall 1988): 42.

[85] S. Yagi, *Bukkyo to Kirisutokyo—Takizawa Katsumi tono taiwa o motomete* (Tokyo: San'ichi shobo, 1981).

being of no position" (the super-individual) in Zen Buddhism. It is obvious in Galatians 2:20 that ego and self are both one and two, of which the self has primacy. Unlike Takizawa, Yagi searches for the point of departure for his thought in "direct experience." He draws upon Nishida's work, but describes the circumstances more precisely in the context of his dialogue with experienced Zen masters.[86]

Yagi does not just understand "Christ in me" at an individual level, but as a collective quantity. For him, "Christ" is entirely in every Christian (Rom 8: 9-11) but is equally present in the church as his body (2 Cor 12). In this sense a part is equal to the whole, and Christ's body, which consists of many parts, constitutes a unity, indeed a single person, corresponding to 2 Corinthians 12:12, where the church is equated to Christ. Thus, to Yagi, Christ is not only the true subject of the individual believer, but also faces him in the midst of the Church, so that the believer can enter into a personal relationship with Christ without having to make him into an "illusionary" and "mythical" object. This can be easily overlooked by the Buddhist, who for the most part does not think in collective-historical categories.

Yagi argues further that with Jesus the substantial-absolutizing ego has completely disappeared, inasmuch as he accepted humankind and his fate without differentiation and unquestioningly (Mt 5:48). In this way he was able to bring the active rule of God into historical reality through himself, which nevertheless came to pass of its own power *(automaté)* (Mk 4:28). In this sense Yagi compares Jesus' word and deed with the basic position of Zen.

Yagi has conceived the unity of the divine and the human in the self christologically in the doctrine of two natures. In partial opposition to Takizawa, Yagi says that the self will indeed be activated in primary contact through the secondary contact. In a certain sense this can be compared to the distinction between original enlightenment *(hongaku)* and acquired enlightenment *(shigaku)* in Zen.[87] Until the point of actualization, the primary contact would have been unreal, because the self-showing or revelation of the "self" is the "awakening" itself. To that extent, the self is a gift and not a possession. Expressed otherwise, the incarnation of the immanent logos (Jesus) must be distinguished from the transcendent logos (the eternal Christ). But for Yagi the primary contact or presence of the transcendent logos is actualized *universally* (unlike Takizawa's view). In Yagi's interpretation, the new being did not first come into the world with Jesus, but Jesus was the first fully actualized Christ. While for Takizawa, too, the appearance of Christ is decisive for the actualization of "Immanuel," for Yagi *all* humans have the Buddha nature or the "Christ-in-us," and the form the actualization takes can be very different in the historical record. Thus far, one might say that Yagi thinks through what Tillich had already indicated after his visit to Japan—that the one God as the foundation of being is the center of all religions, which will be actualized in belief, that is, in the conquest of the ego by the

---

[86] S. Yagi, *Theologiegeschichte der Dritten Welt*, 149f.

[87] In Zen the paradox must be expressed more precisely: *hongaku* is primary in relation to *shigaku*, for we become enlightened because we are already enlightened; but thus the two are reversible, insofar as *shigaku is* nothing other than *hongaku*.

transcendent subject. For Yagi, it follows from this that a Christian, for whom Christ as "new being" has become the center of life, is distinguished only conceptually from a Shin Buddhist, for whom Amida's original vow has become the center of the reborn self.

Yagi supports this thesis with his understanding of the "direct experience," in which the true structure of reality shows itself as a "melting together of differences" (front structure). His example is the wall between two rooms. They belong on the one hand to one room, on the other hand to the other; respectively belonging to one, each is the *front* of the other and vice versa.[88] Yagi links to this model a critique of language, which on the one side reveals "the thing as it is," but on the other side also veils it, inasmuch as people read their concepts into the objects and mistake the concept they have projected for the essence of the thing. Yagi expanded these thoughts in his program of philosophy of religion as hermeneutic, which we cannot discuss here.

This designation of relationship between direct experience and language is corroborated by Yagi Seiichi's student Yagi Yoichi. The latter created a philosophy of language on the basis of religious experience (direct experience). Proceeding from Ferdinand de Saussure's concept of the sign, he shows that the ordering and grouping of things to be experienced is not merely assumed but was first constructed linguistically. That means that the sign would have a certainty that would create an epistemical order in the chaos of reality. This is the case when we read various constellations into the starry sky and connect certain stars with one another or divide them from others, so that we can localize and identify structures. What we designate as things or events are thus not *facta*, but *facta dicta*. This becomes intuitively clear in the "unmediated experience" that has a directness going beyond any verbalization and thus brings the linguistic certainty of our everyday "experience" to light. Such a direct experience is the Zen experience.[89]

Honda Masaaki

Honda Masaaki, a Catholic philosopher of religion from Kita-kyushu, took the Buddhist *soku* logic (both—as well as) as the point of departure for dialogue and the reformulation of Christian theology. Beginning with the concept of emptiness *(sunyata)* and origin in mutual dependence *(pratityasamutpada)*, he defines this logic as the coincidence of opposites *(mujun-teki sosoku)*. Honda believes that this is not an exclusively Buddhist mode of thought, but rather a fundamental insight that occurs, if not in all religions, then at least also in Christianity (for example, in the thought of Nicholas of Cusa). For Honda, *soku* does

---

[88] On this issue, see the graphs in S. Yagi, *Die Front-Struktur als Brücke vom buddhistischen zum christlichen Denken* (Munich: Chr. Kaiser, 1988).

[89] We cannot investigate here the problem of direct (mystical) experience and its interpretation, which is connected and indeed possibly constitutes every possible experience (see M. v. Brück, "Mystische Erfahrung, religiöse Tradition und die Wahrheitsfrage," in *Horizontüberschreitung: Die pluralistische Theologie der Religionen*, ed. R. Bernhardt (Gütersloh: Gütersloher Verlagshaus, 1991), 81ff.

not mean either that two things are united into one (dualism) or that two things outwardly appear to be different while they are really one in essence (essentialistic monism). In either case unity would proceed from difference and thus create a still more subtle dualism. Instead, *soku* is the relationship of the coincidence of opposites, in which neither is lost in the other—in the way that a well is not water, but the two cannot exist separately from one another. In this way the so-called absolute (Honda prefers the term "trans-relative") and the relative coincide; that is, they are *soku*. All abstract one-sided positions of division *or* unity must be overcome, because being one with the other is *soku*. In this system the world is not one *or* many, not subject *or* object, and so on, but is formed by the relationship of "duality in unity," "unity in duality," and so forth. (Yagi Seiichi had expressed this with his concept of the front structure.) For Honda, the trans-relative must now construct itself through absolute self-negation of itself as relative. That, for Honda, is kenotic (self-emptying) love, which finds expression as creation. Honda compares the transcendence of the concrete place or projection in an objectified image of God (which he believes can be found in all religions and is linked to human perception) to the act of seeing: Waves of moonlight meet the eye's retina, but the image seen does not originate either outside or on the retina but rather in the vision center of the brain. This, however, immediately objectifies the image—we *believe* we *see* the moon "outside." In similar fashion, for Honda, the immanence *soku* (both—as well as) understands God's transcendence. While Honda wants to substantiate the *reversibility* in the relationship with God by means of this argument, the *soku*-based irreversibility he postulates is more weakly argued, as the American theologian Paul Knitter has commented.[90]

Honda makes it clear that his *soku* logic does not deny the existence of individuality, because in the Buddhist tenet of mutual dependence (because A is B, and vice versa), attention links not only to the structure of mutual dependence, but also to A and B themselves, which to be sure cannot exist independently of each other. The two statements "God and our self are in a relationship of interdependence and mutual inhabitance (reversibility)" and "God is the independent reality and precedes creation (irreversibility)" are for Honda two moments in our consciousness that together constitute the coincidence of opposites (*soku* relationship) in the same act of belief. In the first aspect (reversibility) we would perceive God's trans-relative transcendence in every moment, and indeed in the concrete place that would be created by the second aspect (irreversibility).

Honda here apparently means something similar to Takizawa's distinction between the first and second contacts of God with humans. Yagi Seiichi in general agreed with Honda at the JSBCS conference in 1988, although Yagi regards the relationship between self and ego as relatively irreversible and sees the unity of divine and human in the self ("Christ in me").[91]

---

[90] Honda first examined "The Logic of Soku" at the Buddhist-Christian Conference, Berkeley, 1987 (unpublished conference papers, library of the Graduate Theological Union, Berkeley), which also include Paul Knitter's response. Honda presented his thesis again at the seventh congress of the JSBCS in Kyoto, 1988.

[91] S. Yagi, "Bericht über Tozai Shukyo Koryu Gakkai 1982-1991," *Dialog der Religionen* 3/1 (1993): 93ff.

Preliminary Results

God and human being—an irreversible relationship or not? The question is fundamental in Buddhist-Christian dialogue. It is mostly handled in a highly abstract fashion but contains within it the question of human potential: Do human beings have an open future? Are they masters of their fate? Are they anchored on a dependable foundation, even if all human certainties have proved brittle? Are human beings alone answerable for dealing with the crises of our time? Could this religious question take on social and political relevance?

The question of the reversibility or irreversibility of relationship with God cannot be answered with a simple yes or no, because the starting points for posing the question differ so widely. Far beyond Japan, the problem also played a great role at the Buddhist-Christian Conference held at Berkeley in 1987. There, indeed, the Harvard theologian Gordon Kaufman objected that the problem was discussed too intellectually and abstractly.[92] The modern person, he argued, experiences things differently from someone at the time of Buddhism's and Christianity's origins, and one must proceed from that point. The search for something irreversible, for Kaufman, describes the turn toward a final foundation of all things and is thus substantial or "foundational" thought, while the model of reversibility corresponds instead to a holistic thought structure. Both, for him, are metaphors with historical roots and cannot make absolute claims. While on the one hand the search for the dependability of a final foundation is necessary, on the other hand holistic thought opens an unlimited horizon.

This measured-out balance shows admirably what possibilities can be opened up by Buddhist-Christian dialogue when it grows beyond the exchange of "standpoints." And indeed, open horizons built upon an ultimate foundation are the best fruit of dialogue.

DIALOGUE WITH PURE LAND BUDDHISM

Since Karl Barth took up discussion with Amida Buddhism in 1939 in *Church Dogmatics*, Christian dialogue with Jodo Buddhism has had a special standing, even though Barth only accorded it the status of a "somewhat primitively understood Christian Protestantism."[93] Since Barth, Emil Brunner and others have pointed out amazing similarities between the doctrines of grace taught by Shinran (1173-1262, the founder of Jodo Shin Buddhism) and Luther. Since the end of the nineteenth century, however, Amida Buddhism in Japan (especially the Jodo Shin school itself) has had to defend itself against the criticism levied by historically questioning new Buddhology that Jodo Shin is not true Buddhism. This criticism argues that Amida Buddhism, with its doctrine of salvation by an "other power" *(tariki)*, is in direct opposition to the original Buddhist emphasis on salvation through "personal power" *(jiriki)*. Phenomenologically, Amida Buddhism

[92] G. Kaufman, "Holism and Foundationalism—Buddhism and Christianity," Buddhist-Christian Conference, Berkeley, 1987 (unpublished conference papers, library of the Graduate Theological Union, Berkeley).

[93] K. Barth, *Kirchliche Dogmatik* I/2, 5th ed. (Zürich, 1960), 375.

stands close to Christianity. For this reason, Jodo Buddhists enter only hesitantly into dialogue with Christians and instead try to create a clear demarcation between the two religions in order to preserve their Buddhist identity. Between the internal Buddhist critique from Zen and the danger of absorption by Christians they are anxious to emphasize the unique characteristics of this Buddhist tradition, which in Japan has more adherents than any other.

The controversy about whether Jodo Shinshu conforms to the mainstream of Mahayana Buddhism (anchored as it is in the doctrine of *sunyata*) is not new. Dogen (1200-53) and Shinran (1173-1262), who were contemporaries, made arguments corresponding to the modern ones. Most recently D. T. Suzuki, for example, defended the "orthodoxy" of Amida Buddhism. Jan van Bragt has organized and published the arguments in years of encounters and studies.[94] One should note, argues van Bragt, that there is an important difference between the Chinese and Japanese Pure Land traditions, so that some interpretations are not adequate.[95] All depends on how the relationship between *karma* and grace, the "objectivity of Amida Buddha," and the relationship between Amida and the human being is determined. On this point there is a controversy within the Jodo Shin school, but philosophical reflection remains remarkably undeveloped and mostly assumes the classical "Mahayana dogma" of emptiness, formlessness, and impersonality, even when this leads to contradictions with Shinran's *religious impulse*, essential to the doctrine of grace.[96]

Popular belief in Japan doubtless understands Amida being a personal reality vis-à-vis humankind, who exists outside of the human "I." Philosophically, Amida must be identified as a projection of consciousness.

Van Bragt now argues that the contradiction between the two perceptions does not need to be understood as either-or. After all, every religious tradition is pluralistic within itself and contains contradictions that cannot be resolved by use of logic, so *logically* there remains a creative tension that can be very fruitful *religiously*. Jodo Shinshu in this sense would be a truly "cumulative tradition" (Wilfred C. Smith). Even if Christianity and Jodo Shinshu are very similar in regard to the religious impulse of the experience of grace, Amida Buddhism still remains philosophically at home in Buddhism and thus foreign to Christianity. Neither reduction to Christian faith experience nor reduction to the Buddhist logic of origin in mutual dependence and emptiness is consistent with the phenomenon of Jodo Buddhism. In dialogue, however—and this is true of all Buddhist-Christian dialogue—at least as much attention must be given to the living belief of ordinary people as to philosophical systematization. Amida Buddhism has already

---

[94] J. v. Bragt, "Buddhism-Jodo Shinshu-Christianity: Does Jodo Shinshu Form a Bridge between Buddhism and Christianity?" *Japanese Religions* 18/1 (January 1993): 47-75.

[95] Von Bragt criticizes, for example, Henri de Lubac, *La rencontre du bouddhisme et de l'occident* (Paris: Aubier, 1952).

[96] Unno Taitetsu has also argued that the *sunyata* doctrine cannot simply be taken as the "essence" of Mahayana Buddhism (see R. Habito and T. Unno, "Forging New Horizons of Religious Awareness: Two Reviews of Buddhist-Christian Dialogue," *Buddhist-Christian Studies* 10 [1990]: 246).

actualized a good deal of this approach in itself, and for this reason is a bridge ready for others engaged in dialogue to use.

Van Bragt isolates three basic questions: (1) Amida's grace vis-à-vis awakening to wisdom; (2) grace vis-à-vis *karma*; and (3) the "objective" existence of Amida Buddha as a redeemer god and the Buddhist philosophy of consciousness.

While in traditional philosophical Buddhism compassion *(karuna)* is regarded as inferior to wisdom *(prajna)* and the former limited in individual and spiritual importance, this relationship appears to be reversed in Amida Buddhism.[97] Because here the believer is not saved by a "principle" but through Amida's original vow, a natural consequence is the personalization of the saved. Remarkably, this has not been thematized in Jodo Shinshu theology. Of course Christian theology also ornaments the ontological-static assertion about God's unchanging perfect being with the dynamic language of love.

We can add that philosophical wordplay in both traditions tends toward abstractions, on the Christian side with the dynamic of love expressed in the symbol of the Trinity, on the Buddhist side in the *unity* of *prajna* and *karuna* or in the doctrine of *trikaya* (the Buddha-*dharma* becomes *comprehensible* as a historically active teacher through a stepwise "revelation" to humanity). The *religious primary language*, indeed, out of which belief lives, relates tales of personal love that can be entered into sensually. So this primary language arouses the *emotional* aspect of *faith*, while *cognitive* secondary abstractions provide the conceptual *confirmation*. This distinction appears in both Christianity and Buddhism, and when making comparisons it is necessary to consider which level each side is on.

Van Bragt rightly judges that a strictly individual understanding of *karma* collides with Amida Buddhism's grace-filled breaking in "other power." Such an individual understanding of *karma* is however not compulsory in Mahayana, in view of the mutual interpenetration of all phenomena. In Pure Land, argues van Bragt, *karma* would be interpreted on the one side as a description of the human condition, namely human sinfulness, and on the other side as an aspect of the anticipated efficacious grace of Amida. Amida's earlier vow, to want to save all people, itself creates a karmic field in which all *karma* that individuals have amassed is reordered. The interplay between these two fields *is* the past *karma*. This is comprehensible in the language of classical Mahayana understanding of causality as well as in the Christian concept of human historical authenticity.[98]

Christian faith lives from the I-thou relationship to God. The devotional texts of Amida Buddhism appear to express a similar relationship to God. Indeed, D. T. Suzuki has already emphasized that in the folk poetry of someone like Saichi, who is in the ranks of the *myokonin* (holy folk heroes), the *unity* of Amida and the believer is unmistakably expressed.[99]

---

[97] Van Bragt shows elsewhere that the lack of socially liberating impulses in Japanese Buddhism also has roots in history (see J. v. Bragt, "Liberative Elements in Pure Land Buddhism," *Inter-Religio* 18 [fall, 1990]: 44-69).

[98] See M. v. Brück, *Einheit der Wirklichkeit*, 2d ed. (Munich: Chr. Kaiser, 1987), 88ff.

[99] Suzuki translates Saichi: "I exchange work with Amida:/I worship him who in turn deigns to worship me—/This is the way I exchange work with him" (*Mysticism Christian and Buddhist* [1957] [London: Unwin, 1979], 125).

But we must add that the sinful person can only *absolutely* trust in the saving Amida if Amida is *unending* and *absolute*. In the language of Soya Ryojin, which van Bragt cites, this close relationship or penetration means: "The Tathagatha is my self, but I am not the Tathagatha," or "I am not he, but he is I."[100] This is not a simple expression of identity but an identity in nonidentity, which triumphs over the dualism of identity and nonidentity (*fuichi funi*; not one, not two). This, however, is equally the language of Zen and might reflect the already-mentioned debate about the irreversibility or reversibility of the relationship with God. The self-in-unity-with-Amida would be a "self beyond the I" in which the opposition of immanence and transcendence would be raised into a relationship of overflowing into one another. Buddhist non-dualism (also Vedic and Christian-trinitarian[101]) deals with a dynamic of transcendence of opposites, not with a static-monistic identity. But then what Jodo Buddhism speaks of is no different from Zen awakening. In this view, this single issue simply appears in two different modes of expression.

Christiane Langer-Kaneko in a 1986 study worked out these connections. For Shinran, she argues, belief is less a substantial gift that one receives from outside than it is the "action of Amida Buddha's true and real heart in human hearts"—in Christian language a mystical indwelling of Christ.[102] The believer, for Langer-Kaneko, is not the subject, nor is Amida the object of belief. Instead, the adoring calling upon the Buddha *(Namo-Amida-Butsu)* is the "dynamic reality" of what is done, which encompasses all and everything.[103] Outside of the human heart there would be no Buddha. Thus it is significant that Jodo Shin Buddhism may not be interpreted in the Christian categories of I-you-other, as Hans Küng has pointed out.[104] Langer-Kaneko cites here the Jodo Shin Buddhist Bando Shojun, who attempts to translate Jodo belief into Christian terminology. "The reality that the old self is dead and a new self will be born, that this everyday 'I' is entirely dead and the true 'I' will be born again, in other words the reality of being dead to the old Adam and living in Christ, so that the cross of the self is also its resurrection—this is the 'birth of the other side,' this is 'Namu-Amida-Butsu.'"[105]

---

[100] J. v. Bragt, "Liberative Elements," 44ff.

[101] M. v. Brück, especially 243ff.

[102] C. Langer-Kaneko, *Das Reine Land: Zur Begegnung von Amida-Buddhismus und Christentum* (Leiden: Brill, 1986), especially 134ff.

[103] J. Cobb, "Can a Buddhist Be a Christian, Too?" *Japanese Religions* 11/2-3 (1980): 35-55, emphasizes that Amida's *vows* are the basis of belief, that is, not a human state of consciousness. Only in this way can salvation be absolutely certain. Amida is not subordinated to the absolute *dharmakaya* (the fully transcendent body of the Buddha), but a *form* of it; that is, in Christian trinitarian categories, he is thought of modalistically rather than subordinatistically.

[104] H. Küng, "Foreword," in Y. Takeuchi, *The Heart of Buddhism* (New York: Crossroad, 1983), xi. The dissertation cited by C. Langer-Kaneko was written under Küng's direction.

[105] S. Bando, "Jesus Christus und Amida: Zu K. Barths Verständnis des Buddhismus vom Reinen Land," in *Gott in Japan*, ed. U. Luz and S. Yagi (Munich, 1973), 79.

Perry Schmidt-Leukel in 1992 worked out Shinran's position in relationship to Christianity with great clarity.[106] For him, Amida is the point of intersection of two movements: the manifestation of the formless in the form, and the recognition of the formless through the form. Thus it is a movement "from above to below" and "from below to above,"[107] as also appears in Christology. The acquisition of the enlightenment reality, which hitherto was to be expected through Amida, occurs in "natural spontaneity" *(jinen)*. It is the natural, which comes to pass without its own effort, the other power *(tariki)*. In this interpretation, Shinran's position would be as little "salvation through grace" in the Christian sense as the early Buddhist position of "self-salvation" is. In both cases this is for the same reason, on account of Buddhism's special understanding of "self," because liberation cannot be a "deed" of the "I," which does not exist as such.[108] According to Schmidt-Leukel, the "salvation" is much more similar to a "change in status, which must be seen as a passively befalling exchange of personality." "'Jinan' is the 'other power' where this no longer stands in contrast to 'personal power,' but is the end of all 'personal power,' which reveals the *only* (i.e., not dualistic) reality of holy occurrence, where the spirit becomes the Buddha, or recognizes *that it is Buddha*."[109] In other words, Schmidt-Leukel believes that Shinran did not proclaim a new path, but wrestled to express the suitable *spiritual stance* that is necessary for an earnest journey along *a* Buddhist path.

Buddhist-Christian dialogue in Japan has also promoted discussion between different Buddhist traditions. Thus at the second annual meeting of the Japan Society for Buddhist-Christian Studies (1983) there was a dialogue between Jodo Shin and Zen Buddhism in which the evenly handled problematic was extended. The Jodo Buddhist religious philosopher Hoshino Genpo developed a counter-argument to Hisamatsu's critique of the position of Jodo Buddhism. For Hoshino, Jodo Buddhist belief is reached throughout the depth of the formless self in Hisamatsu's sense, which can already be discerned with Shinran himself. Shinran is supposed to have become conscious thanks to his enlightenment, and already in his lifetime believed in the Pure Land. This is a contrast to current Jodo Shin belief, according to which the believing person will only be born in the Pure Land after his death, in order to reach enlightenment there. Shinran's experience of belief *(shinjin)*, as the Shin Buddhist Kenneth K. Tanaka explains elsewhere, is a recognition of union with the entire universe, on account of which for Shinran the individual fate after death became a matter of less importance.[110] But Shinran is supposed to have come to know Zen in the last depth, and built an indivisible unity of the formless self and the ego. Since Shinran, however, sharply defined the crass difference between ego and formless self on account of human sinfulness, for him there is also a radical difference between Amida Buddha and humankind.

---

[106] P. Schmidt-Leukel, 605-54.

[107] Ibid., 611.

[108] Ibid., 621.

[109] Ibid., 622.

[110] K. P. Kramer and K. K. Tanaka, "A Dialogue with Jodo-Shinshu," *Buddhist-Christian Studies* 10 (1990): 181.

RESULTS AND PROSPECTS

RESULTS

• Although Buddhist-Christian relations are encumbered by history, especially because since the sixteenth century Christianity has been regarded as foreign to "Japanese values" and as a political threat, today that issue is outweighed by a tendency to make a *common front* against atheism and materialism.

• Neither Christian communities nor Buddhist institutions have yet engaged deeply in dialogue, except for a few exceptions and courtesy visits. However, in terms of philosophical and spiritual dialogue, no place in Asia has been as active as Japan. Zen philosophy presents itself in the Kyoto school as the religious answer to European nihilism and existentialism. The Zen praxis includes the churches (more outside of Japan than within) and contributes substantially to a renewal of meditation and the mystical traditions in Christianity.

• Philosophically-theologically the dialogue circles around the question of the irreversibility or reversibility of the relationship between human and God. The Japanese *soku* logic as a relationship of coincidence of opposites, where no aspect is merged into the other, but one coincides with the other, appears currently as the most-discussed solution to the problem.

• Pure Land Buddhism, too, does not describe the duality of God and human in its teaching about the faith. Instead, it presents the dynamic reality of awakening or new birth to the true self or to the real human, what in Christianity is expressed in the symbol of the resurrection. Belief is Amida's working in the human heart, which appears to correspond to the Pauline "Christ in us."

• The religious praxis in each religion, and also in interreligious dialogue, ought to distinguish between the *religious primary language* out of which the faith lives and that tells the story of personal love (which is entered into emotionally and is often paradoxical), and the *cognitive secondary language*, which seeks conceptual *confirmation* in order to situate religious experience in the full context of the intellectual and social occupations of human life. Both languages are necessary, and they must be recognized as such in dialogue. They must also be clearly distinguished, however, because otherwise misunderstandings would be inevitable.

• The Buddhist lay organization Rissho Kosei-kai is engaged in practical dialogue about international peace efforts. This readiness for dialogue is linked to the theological insight in the catastrophic consequences of the isolationist nationalism that Japan roused in the war. Reflection on the question of guilt leads here, as on the Christian side, to interreligious cooperation.

PROSPECTS

• The questions raised by the breakdown of tradition in modern industrial societies are completely comparable in Japan and Europe/America. While, however, in Japan this crisis has led to a reformulation of *Zen philosophy* in dialogue with nineteenth-century German philosophy, *Zen praxis* has spread in Europe and America, increasingly including Christian circles. The debate in Japan shows that Zen cannot be separated from Buddhism without more ado; the exchange will thus bring further change to religious-philosophical thought. One can already see this change in the fact that Christians speak much less of God as the "entirely other" (God's transcendence) but rather in dialogue link themselves to the Christian traditions that speak of "God in the world" (God's immanence). This tendency is likely to become stronger.

• The future of dialogue in Japan will largely depend upon whether it proves possible to join philosophical debate to the questions of practical religious lifestyle that face countless people with the modernization in industrial society; loss of roots, individualization, and loss of identity are phenomena that cause uncertainty especially to the younger generation in Japan, too. The quest for absolute values, human communication, and spiritual certainty must therefore find a much more solid consideration in interreligious dialogue than hitherto. Only then will it be possible to see whether the encounter of Buddhism and Christianity in Japan can offer solutions to the concrete questions about the future and fears about identity that present themselves to people in the modern industrial societies. These solutions might also be significant in Europe and America.

5

Germany

In Germany, encounter with Buddhism was founded upon a fascination with the foreign philosophy that appeared to be so much more rational than Christianity. Intellectuals converted to Buddhism, not without a significant and wished-for departure from their Christian background.[1] Later it was especially the meditation schools of Buddhism that advanced triumphantly. Rational Western thought wanted to expand its sights through the meditative intuition of the East. But does this marriage of meditative East and rational West really work? And what will become of Europe's identity, if apparently alien psychic and spiritual attitudes should fundamentally alter Western spiritual certainty? What are the perspectives for human self-perception and the further development of what is Christian in Europe? Is Buddhism in Germany just a passing fad, or will it make the Christian Western tradition fragment and bring it to an end? Or are there signs of a synthesis, whose range cannot yet be seen, but whose outline one can perhaps already trace?

The development of German Buddhism and the subsequent dialogue with Christianity can be divided into three phases: the exposition of Buddhist sources; the meditation movements; and the clothing of Buddhism in a European form.[2]

EXPOSITION OF THE SOURCES

The work of translation into German as well as the fascination of some intellectuals with joining various Buddhist monastic orders in Asia can to an important degree be traced back to Arthur Schopenhauer and the reading of his works.[3]

---

[1] This is not the place to treat in detail the history of German Buddhism or the social and spiritual structure of the approximately eighty thousand Buddhists. See H. Hecker, *Chronik des Buddhismus in Deutschland*, 3d ed. (Stuttgart: Deutsche Buddhistische Union, 1985); K.-J. Notz, *Der Buddhismus in Deutschland in seinen Selbstdarstellungen* (Frankfurt a. M./Bern: P. Lang, 1984); V. Zotz, "Zur Rezeption, Interpretation und Kritik des Buddhismus im Deutschen Sprachraum vom Fin de Siècle bis 1930," dissertation, University of Vienna, 1986; M. Baumann, *Buddhisten in Deutschland. Geschichte und Gemeinschaften* (Marburg: Diagonal Verlag, 1993).

[2] M. Glashoff, "Afterword," in H. Hecker, *Chronik des Buddhismus*, 3d ed., 119f.

[3] H. Hecker, 12, 17.

Before Schopenhauer, Buddhism was scarcely known. Hegel was aware that it was something different from Hinduism but had no detailed knowledge about the individual philosophical schools. Indeed, Schopenhauer too could not clearly distinguish between Buddhism and the Hindu Vedanta philosophy.[4] Schopenhauer believed he could see a great similarity between Buddhism and Christianity in the radical world rejection and pessimistic anthropology of both religions. Nietzsche adopted this judgment, but then in contrast to Schopenhauer used it as a basis to attack Buddhism as well as Christianity and to oppose the "will to power" to every supposed renunciation of the will in both "nihilistic" religions.[5] It is important to take this intellectual historical constellation into account, because nineteenth-century religious criticism, especially Nietzsche's because of a frustration with Christianity that was also projected onto Buddhism, was mostly leveled against both religions together. The verdict that Buddhism is pessimistic and world-denying stuck and still today in part obstructs proper understanding of the religion.[6]

In the 1880s the Viennese intellectual Karl Eugen Neumann (1865-1915) and Paul Carus (1852-1919)[7] reached Buddhism through Schopenhauer. Neumann, who came from the Jewish tradition, in 1892 published the first anthology of sayings of the Buddha in a German translation. After that, he obtained direct knowledge of the spiritual world and environment of Buddhism by traveling to India and Ceylon in 1894. Neumann lived in great poverty as a private intellectual, like many who came after him, setting himself to the translation of Buddhist texts; the German universities in this period—unlike their counterparts in England—had little interest in making sources linguistically accessible.[8] Shortly

---

[4] The Vedanta is the philosophy that goes back to the Upanishads; it recognizes the existence of an unchanging core (*atman*) behind the physical-psychic appearance of human beings, which is identical to the absolute primal basis of the world (*brahman*). On Schopenhauer and the influence of Buddhism on German philosophers and poets in the nineteenth and twentieth centuries, see Zotz, "Zur Rezeption"; H. v. Glasenapp, *Das Indienbild deutscher Denker* (Stuttgart: Koehler, 1960); G. R. Welbon, *The Buddhist Nirvana and Its Western Interpreters* (Chicago: University of Chicago Press, 1968); W. Halbfass, *India and Europe* (Albany, N.Y.: SUNY Press, 1988). See also E. Benz, "Buddhismus in der westlichen Welt," in *Buddhismus der Gegenwart*, ed. H. Dumoulin (Freiburg: Herder, 1970): 198.

[5] E. Benz.

[6] We will only mention Albert Schweitzer here as an example of this attitude, whose judgment had great influence on German Protestantism. He did indeed admire the reform-oriented human effort of the Buddha (and saw parallels to Luther), as well as his high ethical standard. However, Schweitzer believed that he could only identify world negation in original Buddhism. Thus later developments in Japanese Mahayana (e.g., with Shinran) were fundamental reorientations, because people could no longer bear the Buddha's atheism and pessimism (see A. Schweitzer, *Die Weltanschauung der indischen Denker. Mystic und Ethik* [1935], cited from the edition in *Ausgewählte Werke*, 5 vols. [Berlin: Union, 1971], 2:508ff.; see also H. de Lubac, *La rencontre du bouddhisme et de l'occident* [Paris: Aubier, 1952], 253).

[7] For Carus, see chapter 6.

[8] H. Hecker, 13f.

before this time, in 1888, Friedrich Zimmermann (1851-1917), a mathematician and engineer who converted from Judaism to Buddhism, had published a "Buddhist Catechism." This work was ground-breaking for a broad academically educated middle class in Germany.[9] In 1903 Karl Seidenstücker (1876-1936) founded the Buddhist Mission Union of Germany in Leipzig. From October 1903 to March 1904 Seidenstücker held a series of public lectures about Buddhism, in which he presented Buddhism as "transcendental idealism" and set himself as an "apologetic propagandist" against the misunderstanding of Buddhism as nihilistic by Christian theologians and critics.[10] The name of the union was programmatic and controversial, because numerous Buddhists did not want to be associated with Christian "missionary strategies." So in 1906 the organization was renamed as the Buddhist Society for Germany. In 1905 the first journal was published that significantly reflected this name change *(The Buddhist, Buddhist Lookout, Mahabodhi Journal)*.[11] The society dissolved in 1911. In the same year, however, Seidenstücker published his anthology of texts from the shorter collection of the Buddha's teaching *(Pali-Buddhism in Translation)*. Its second edition (1923) found a wide readership. In the meantime, in 1909 the Berlin physician Paul Dahlke (1865-1928), Seidenstücker, Markgraf, and others founded the German Pali Society. This group was dedicated to publishing parts of the *Anguttara-Nikaya*. Very quickly, however, tensions arose between a monastic and Theravada-oriented current (Markgraf) and a group focused on a Buddhism for the laity based on Mahayana ideals (Seidenstücker). This led to the collapse of the society in 1913.[12] During the first two decades of the century many small Buddhist societies were founded. They did not last long, with the exception of the Buddhist League for Germany, founded in 1921 by the lawyer Georg Grimm (1868-1945) and Karl Seidenstücker in Munich. In Christian circles it was known as the "aristocratic religion," because it presented Buddhist teaching as a "highly developed intelligence."[13] Grimm's masterpiece, *Die Lehre des Buddha, die Religion der Vernunft* (The Buddha's teaching, the religion of reason) was published in 1915 by Piper in Munich and found a wide readership. Originally Grimm had studied theology and had only transferred to the field of law because of deep doubts about theology and the church.[14] His understanding of Buddhism as a rational system deepened over the years, and so he reached a "religious disposition" grasp

---

[9] M. Baumann, "Buddhismusrezeption in Deutschland—Kontinuität und Wandel," *Buddhistische Monatsblätter* 37/2 (1991): 55ff.

[10] The announcement of this series is apparently the oldest Buddhist leaflet in the German language (1903). A facsimile was kindly made available to us by Friedrich Fenzl of Salzburg, head of the Austrian branch of the Buddhist society Jodo Shin Europa.

[11] H. Hecker, 41. Hecker has assembled a bibliography of Buddhist periodicals in Germany, which appeared divided regionally and were often soon reprinted elsewhere, in H. Bechert, *Buddhismus, Staat und Gesellschaft in den Ländern des Theravada-Buddhismus*, vol. 3 (Wiesbaden: Harrassowitz, 1973), 325-32.

[12] H. Hecker, 41f.

[13] M. Baumann, "Buddhismusrezeption in Deutschland—Kontinuität und Wandel," 56.

[14] H. Hecker, 64.

of Buddhism.[15] Thus he gave the fifteenth edition of his book in 1957 the subtitle "The Religion of Reason and of Meditation." The emphasis on *meditation* also, as we will see, corresponded to the spirit of the age. In contrast, Paul Dahlke further championed the empirical and rationalistic direction within German Buddhism. Tensions constantly emerged between the two tendencies.[16] Dahlke had become more closely acquainted with Buddhism in Ceylon in 1900, and had converted predominantly for rational-intellectual reasons. In 1924 he founded the Buddhist House in Berlin-Frohnau. He also translated texts from the Pali canon and wrote about Buddhism from the perspective of European analytical thought. The Nazis in 1942 forbade the Buddhist meetings in Frohnau (as elsewhere in Germany), and in 1957 the house was transferred to Ceylonese ownership. In the 1970s and 1980s it again became a newly strengthened center for the growing number of Buddhists in Berlin and also opened itself to Mahayana Buddhists.

After 1945, Buddhism in Germany experienced many new foundations of base groups and centers. The German branch of the Mahabodhi Society merged in 1952 with the Buddhist League for Germany, which however remained distant from the already existing larger German centers. More successful was the German Buddhist Society, which was founded in 1955 by joint action of the Munich, Hamburg, and Berlin groups. From this organization in 1958 came the German Buddhist Union, which acted as an umbrella organization for the many individual groups. This left the regional centers great independence but at the same time encouraged joint efforts. Only organizations were admitted to membership, rather than individuals, and the individual teaching traditions were not touched. In 1985 the Buddhist Religion Society in Germany was constituted in Hamburg as a public corporation. However, because of differences between German and ethnic Vietnamese Buddhists, as well as because of the legal form (which was typical of Christian churches but alien to Buddhism), it soon collapsed.

There are several reasons for the fragmentation of the Buddhist movement in Germany. First, from the beginning the centers came into existence due to the initiative of individual founders, whose sphere of action was only regional. Second, Buddhism was understood as an alternative to organized institutional Christianity. Since it focused on individual personality and spiritual schooling, every institutionalization was regarded with suspicion. Third, the founders had become acquainted with Buddhism in a variety of ways; they followed different traditions or masters—the obvious difference between Theravada and Mahayana is only the commonest division. Only after the Second World War was it generally recognized that Mahayana texts were scarcely known and, when they were, were mostly misinterpreted as "un-Buddhist." Fourth, people projected greatly varying expectations on Buddhism, which mostly stemmed from the quest for a rationally based religion and the rejection of Christianity.

---

[15] Ibid., 52.

[16] The old controversy between the "old Buddhists" around Grimm and a "new Buddhism" around Dahlke concerns understanding of the doctrine of *anatta* (see M. Baumann, "Buddhismusrezeption in Deutschland—Kontinuität und Wandel," 56).

Renewal of Christianity through Buddhism?

In 1955 Hellmut von Schweinitz reacted against the division from Christianity that Paul Dahlke and Georg Grimm had emphasized, in his treatise *Buddhismus und Christentum* (Buddhism and Christianity), which surprisingly is almost completely forgotten today.[17] Von Schweinitz in this work presented one of the more general Christian answers to Buddhism in Germany. It was not inspired by polemic but by a spirit of dialogical understanding. He welcomed the arrival of Buddhism in Germany and joined to it a hope for a renewal of Christianity. Many of his suggestions only bore fruit in later dialogue. We will consider von Schweinitz's forty-year career in detail because in retrospect it is possible to discern in his ideas basic tendencies in the Buddhist-Christian encounter in Germany whose consequences may well reach into the future.

Inspired by the works of the Marburg theologian and scholar of religion Friedrich Heiler (1892-1967), von Schweinitz attempted a comparison of Buddhism and Christianity. In this work he assumed historical interdependencies that are for the most part no longer accepted. In the development of the religions, however, in their hierarchies and institutions, in Buddhology and Christology, he rightly sees many structural parallels. Thus, for example, he extols Asoka's state as a democracy in spirit for which nothing comparable can be found in Christian history. He also points out parallels in the biographies of the founders of the two religions and in miracles tales. However, the author is entirely silent about the great differences between early Buddhism and early Christianity in literary-critical, contextual, religious-sociological, and actual terms. So, for example, the Buddha's entry into Kapilavastu and Jesus' entry into Jerusalem have nothing to do with each other either typologically or phenomenologically, which von Schweinitz appears not to have realized. Still, he pointed out other important differences with astonishing accuracy. These include the sociological background of the two founders, the relationship between God's grace and individual efforts, the position of the founders (Christ as the way, the Buddha as guide along the way). Above all, their attitude toward suffering differs widely: Jesus transformed suffering through his death on the cross; the Buddha "fled" from it through the renunciation of *all* emotions, that is, he had to refuse to let in both hate *and* love (42ff.).

Although modern scholars are able to differentiate more precisely, von Schweinitz's remarks very early hit an important nerve in Buddhist-Christian dialogue. He did not argue polemically but felt that Christianity would be transformed by encounter with Buddhism and vice versa. He spoke of a "fulfilled and unfulfilled Buddhism in Christianity" and of a "fulfilled and unfulfilled Christianity in Buddhism" (45ff.)

Von Schweinitz also dismissed Dahlke's and Grimm's rejection of Christianity that used the arguments of Buddhist atheism. He argued that the Buddha's atheism cannot at all be compared with modern European atheism. The Buddha was not godless but only rejected the personal anthropomorphic concept of God;

---

[17] H. v. Schweinitz, *Buddhismus und Christenum* (Munich/Basel: Ernst Reinhardt Verlag, 1955). Page references in text are from this work.

he did this not to disavow God but from awe in the face of God's inexpressible greatness. Similar to a Meister Eckhart or Angelus Silesius, says von Schweinitz, the Buddha wished to emphasize the undefinability of God. In this way he stands "perhaps closer to the living idea of God than does the anthropomorphic image of God that so many Christians make" (47).

We can agree with von Schweinitz but must also point out that many Buddhists in the villages of Sri Lanka, Burma, Thailand, China, Korea, and Japan also have an anthropomorphic image of the deified Buddha. What is involved here is not the difference between Christianity and Buddhism, but between popular and epistemologically reflected religion. If one does not pay attention to this difference, again and again we will find a comparison of apples and oranges. The "silence of the Buddha" in regard to the question of God can be used in dialogue as an important indication of the necessary perception that every image of God is pervaded by human projections. We believe that von Schweinitz was also right when he wrote: "Only when we have rediscovered the silent, unplumbed-sublime foundation of being can we see the light shine out from the beginning-less world origin, which appeared as the creative life principle that we call Christ" (47).

Von Schweinitz believes in the sense of the theologically beloved fulfillment theory—that what began with the Buddha reached fullness in Jesus Christ. He champions the theory of a gradual spiritual development that is readable in the activation of the *chakras* as spiritual energy centers along the spinal column (which is decisive for all India) (58ff.). Three important steps within this development are enlightenment, transfiguration, and transformation. While both Gautama Sakyamuni and Jesus attained enlightenment and transfiguration (there are corresponding reports of both), it remained for Christ alone to bring to completion the step of transformation in cross and resurrection. In his transformed resurrection body is the *atman* reality,[18] through which the suffering of the world could be transformed and healed. Thus for von Schweinitz, Christ completes what the Buddha had begun. "Christianity is fulfilled Buddhism. But this fulfillment lies still in the earth's further future. The resurrection morning of humankind is still a distant dream" (60).

This means that the beginning of this transformation into reality, already provided in Christ alone, has for a long time not been present in the church. According to von Schweinitz, with the first Easter "high powers streamed into being" that the Buddha could not know, so that finally he had no choice but to reject the world of appearances. In Christ, though, no aspect of reality will be cast off, but instead everything will be transformed—including the church, as the author hopes. However, Christians must first awaken to this wisdom, by turning again to their long and often mocked mystical tradition. As von Schweinitz argues: "In mysticism Buddhism and Christianity encounter one another. Here there is much more common ground than dissimilarity between the two, even if starting point and goal are different" (62). Besides this, von Schweinitz recommends taking belief

---

[18] By *atman* von Schweinitz does not mean the philosophical category of *atman* as an ultimate unchangeable base in humans (in contrast to the Buddhist non-*atman*) in the strict sense, but the dimension of transcendental fulfillment of the human being more generally.

in reincarnation seriously, because in the face of the often unwanted completion of the individual life it can fulfill people with calm and worldly wisdom. For many Christians belief has become a "comfortable resting pillow," but the "hankering after eternal rest, while one leaves the between-worlds and between-times to evil" is, says von Schweinitz, a totally unchristian attitude. Although, indeed, some Christians believe that it is not them but the Buddha who "hankers after the life to come, without engaging in this world."

No, he argues: Christianity needs, much more, new powers of perception, a new "spiritual organ" (63) in order to recognize Christ. Buddhism as a religion of perception is to be found *within* Christianity—the "unfulfilled Buddhism in Christianity." On this issue von Schweinitz is not only referring to theological knowledge but above all to Buddhist meditation praxis. Buddhism, Hinduism, and Christianity, for von Schweinitz, are at one in the expectation of the coming of a divine lord, even if the Asian religions have not yet realized that he is already come in the form of Jesus, and the *avatara* ideal of Hindu Vishnuism as well as the Buddhist Maitreya myth have already been fulfilled. But for the Christians, hope for the future is also, as expectation of Christ's second coming, a *promise*. Von Schweinitz leaves it an open question whether he thinks of a second coming of Christ in the spirit of one who through meditation experience and transformation of life makes the "Christ in us" living, or as a concrete historical return. In either case, a de facto fulfillment of Buddhism and Christianity can be seen in mutual learning, if only the Christians do not ignore the call to inner experience through meditation that Buddhism offers. "Here the way is paved for an ecumenicism beside which contemporary Christianity would grow pale, a new catholicism, which would spread the concept of catholicism world-wide" (72).

In the 1950s such words were unusual. They proved to be prophetic, even if some of von Schweinitz's judgments on individual points have not stood up to the judgment of modern religious studies. Also, as we know today, the theory of fulfillment is problematic theologically, since there is a danger that people might understand Buddhism in Christian terms and seek to overcome the reality of religious pluralism with cultural imperialism. Still, one can find almost all the important dialogue themes of the 1980s and 1990s brought up in von Schweinitz's work. Admittedly he raises these issues in the hope of awakening a renewed Christianity in Germany, based upon mystical spirituality, in the face of what many contemporaries regard as two-dimensional religious experience. Precisely this motive is also typical of the Christian reaction to the Buddhist meditation movement in Germany.

MEDITATION MOVEMENTS

The conversion of some prominent Germans to Buddhist monasticism and the spread of their books as well as their direct teaching of Buddhist meditation to countless students has greatly encouraged the growth of Buddhism in Germany. For the first time people have come into direct contact with authentic Buddhist experience. In comparison to England and America, it is noteworthy of the German situation that the influence of Buddhist meditation practices has penetrated deeply into the church and—especially in the Roman Catholic Church—has to some extent been encouraged by religious orders and churches. Thus it makes sense to discuss the development of the Buddhist meditation movement in some detail; it is already an aspect of the history of Buddhist-Christian dialogue in Germany.

THE GREAT TRANSMITTERS

For the early phase of the meditation movement (until approximately 1960) three names are prominent: the German-born Nyanatiloka, Nyanaponika, and Lama Anagarika Govinda. All three were outstanding personalities, competent meditation masters, and productive scholars. For this reason their influence reached far beyond Buddhist circles to the midst of the church and theology, and they had an influence on contemporary German spirituality that can scarcely be overstated.

Nyanatiloka[19] (Anton Gueth, 1878-1957) first became acquainted with Buddhism through Schopenhauer. He then came into direct contact with Buddhism in Colombo in 1903 during the course of a concert tour (he was a violinist). He gave up his bourgeois life, went to Burma to study with an English monk there, and was himself consecrated as a Buddhist monk *(bhikkhu)* in 1904. In 1905 his first translations appeared. He accepted students, mostly from Europe, which soon led to the wish to found a monastery in Europe. Attempts to do so in Switzerland in 1908 and 1910 came to nothing, however. In 1911 he founded the Island Hermitage in southern Ceylon. In 1914 he wanted to go to Tibet as a missionary for Theravada Buddhism, but his travel plans fell through. During the First World War he was interned in Australia and finally reached China. After periods in Germany, Japan (lecturer on Pali at Taisho University), and Siam he returned in 1926 to his Ceylonese hermitage. During World War II he was interned in Dehra Dun (India), where he met with Nyanaponika, Lama Govinda, Heinrich Harrer, and others. He died in 1957 as a citizen of Ceylon, after he had taken part in the Sixth Buddhist Council in Rangun (1954-56). Besides editing texts,[20] Nyanatiloka was most notable for his ordination of European monks and as a meditation instructor. His hermitage was the first great pilgrimage goal of Western youth in Asia.

---

[19] H. Hecker, 17ff.

[20] Only a few of the most important text editions can be named: *Anguttara-Nikaya: Die Reden des Buddha aus der "Angereihten Sammlung"* (Leipzig: Max Altmann, 1907; new edition Cologne: Du Mont Schauberg, 1969); *Buddhaghosa: Visuddhimagga oder der Weg zur Reinheit*, 2d ed. (Constance: Christiani, 1952); *Milinda-Panha. Die Fragen des Milinda: Ein historischer Roman* (Breslau, 1914; new edition *Milindapanha: Die Fragen des Königs Milinda,* ed. Nyanaponika (Interlaken, 1985)); *Tripitaka: Das Wort des Buddha* (Munich, 1921); *Tripitaka, Suttapitaka: Der Weg zur Erlösung: In den Worten der buddhistischen Urschriften* (Constance: Christiani, 1956); *Dhammapada und Kommentar* (by Buddhaghosa) (Uttenbühl: Jhana Verlag, 1992).

Nyanaponika (Siegmund Feniger, 1901-94) came from a Jewish family. He converted to Buddhism through the intellectual study of classical Buddhist texts. After his conversion he was engaged (motivated by his Buddhist beliefs) from 1933 to 1936 in the Central Committee of Jews for Social Improvement and Help in Berlin. After he emigrated, Nyanaponika lived with Nyanatiloka from the time of his novitiate in 1936 (consecration as *bhikkhu* in 1937) until 1952, when he opened his own forest hermitage near Kandy in the mountains of Ceylon/ Sri Lanka. From 1968 on he returned occasionally to Germany to lead meditation courses. Besides his text editions (especially a new edition of Nyanatiloka's *Anguttara-Nikaya*[21]), Nyanaponika is mostly known for his writings about the meditation of attentiveness.[22] These works provided the foundation for meditation in many Christian as well as Buddhist circles and meditation centers. In Erich Fromm's opinion, there is "no other book about Buddhism like his 'spiritual training through attentiveness' that presents with such clarity the essential thought of this new 'atheistic religion' that is so paradoxical for Europeans."[23] Fromm adds that in his opinion Nyanaponika is one of the few authentic voices among a hubbub of false gurus.

Lama Anagarika Govinda[24] (Ernst Lothar Hoffmann, 1898-1985) published his first book on Buddhism in 1920 after studying philosophy, art history, and archeology, and joined several Buddhist unions. In 1928 he went to Ceylon to live at Nyanatiloka's hermitage. In the same year Lama Govinda founded a Buddhist missionary society (International Buddhist Union) with Buddhist-ecumenical intentions. To further this organization he traveled to Burma with Nyanatiloka in 1930, where at the advice of his friend Anagarika Dharmapala he left the monastic order so that he could be free for ecumenical missionary work. On a similar mission he attended a Buddhist conference in Darjeeling (northern India) in 1931. There he became acquainted with Tibetan Buddhism in the old monastery of Ghoom, and was initiated into the Tibetan *kagyüpa* tradition by a geshe[25] of the Tomo monastery in Tibet, who was visiting Ghoom at the time. Until his death in 1936 this teacher was the decisive influence on Govinda's career. In 1933 Anagarika Govinda at the All-India Buddhist Conference in Darjeeling founded the order Arya Maitreya Mandala, inspired by his teacher. After the Second World War this group began to expand worldwide, reaching Germany in 1952. He proclaimed and lived in this order a Buddhism that transcended the differences between schools (and indeed all of Mahayana as a teaching system) and that was

---

[21] Freiburg i. Br.: Aurum, 1984.

[22] Nyanaponika, *Geistestraining durch Achtsamkeit: Die buddhistische Satipatthana-Methode* (Constance; Christiani, 1950; 3d. ed. 1984).

[23] E. Fromm, "Die Bedeutung von Nyanaponika Mahathera für die westliche Welt," *Bodhi Baum* 1 (3 September 1976): 88f. Also in Erich Fromm, *Gesamtausgabe*, vol. 6, *Religion*, ed. R. Funk (Stuttgart: DVA, 1980): 359-61.

[24] H. Hecker, 93ff.

[25] Geshe is the highest academic-philosophic level in Tibet. However, not every geshe is the abbot of a monastery and/or a well-known meditation master, as was the case with Lama Govinda's teacher.

oriented toward the problems of the modern world. Several journeys through Tibet deepened Lama Govinda's understanding of this culture. In 1957 his famous book *Grundlagen tibetischer Mystik* (Principles of Tibetan mysticism) appeared. Its publication made the spiritual world of Tibetan Buddhism known, not just to Germany but to the West in general. The book is admittedly deep and not easy to read, so that Govinda only gained a worldwide popularity with the 1969 publication of his account of his travels through Tibet, *Der Weg der weißen Wolken* (The path of the white clouds). In this work, besides his own experiences Govinda included and expanded some of the fantastic experiences of Alexandra David-Neel (1868-1969).[26] Govinda lived until 1978 at the Kasar-Devi Ashram near Almora in Indian Kumaon-Himalaya, which had been founded by William Y. Evans-Wentz (1878-1965). Acting with his wife Li Gotami, who as an artist expanded his studies, Govinda offered hundreds of religious seekers lodging and instruction. When he moved to Mill Valley near San Francisco in 1978 for reasons of health, Govinda worked with the San Francisco Zen Center and with his open house and correspondence remained the spiritual father of countless people around the world. In his last years, encouraged by Teilhard de Chardin and Jean Gebser, Govinda approached an ideal of wisdom transcending all religions and was himself the embodiment of a meditative-active life in the postmodern age. He was as interested in dialogue with Christian partners as in a spiritual and moral renewal in the technocratic world.[27]

As general secretary of the International Buddhist University in the 1920s Govinda had composed a treatise, *Why I Am a Buddhist*, which was disseminated by the Mahabodhi Society.[28] In this work he defends his conversion to Buddhism as the reasonable step of a rationally thinking European who could no longer accept the supernatural creed of Christianity. He argues that the Buddha never claimed to be above humanity; he taught nothing that went against natural law and also invited rational criticism of Buddhist assertions. For Govinda, every philosophical interpretation is relative in Buddhism, which frees the religion from intolerance and narrow-mindedness. This allows to Buddhism a tolerance in regard to other religions that should be exemplary and through the law of reason should mark an ethical summit.

To this point Govinda's argument about spiritual standing corresponds to that of people like Seidenstücker, Grimm, Dahlke, and others. But then Govinda adds a new issue to the discussion: Buddhism does indeed have many similarities to Christianity; however, its ethical system does not end with humankind but instead includes *all* living things. He points out how the unity of all living beings is

---

[26] See her books: *Heilige und Hexer: Glaube und Aberglaube im Lande des Lamaismus*, 3d ed. (Leipzig: Brockhaus, 1936; French translation 1929); *Wanderer mit dem Wind (Journal de Voyage 1904-17)* (Wiesbaden: Brockhaus, 1979).

[27] For his interreligious and ecumenical views, see "The World View of a Mahayana Buddhist," *ReVision* (fall, 1977); and A. Govinda, *Buddhistische Reflexionen: Wege der Befreiung ohne Verleugnung der eigenen Wurzeln. Die Bedeutung von Lehre und Methoden des Buddhismus für westliche Menschen* (Munich: O. W. Barth, 1983).

[28] A. Govinda, *Why I Am a Buddhist,* 2d ed. (Sarnath: Mahabodhi Society, 1958).

much clearer than in Christianity, and he regards this as a necessary expansion for every cultivated Western consciousness, if the "restlessness" of the European-American consciousness is to be healed. Govinda cites the life-philosopher and biologist Hans Driesch (1867-1941), who also proposed the Buddhist-taught unity of humans, animals, and plants as the essence of a modern philosophy.[29] *Dharma* (the insight into the world proclaimed by the Buddha) is universal, because it mirrors back the cosmic order. A rationally examinable ethics can thus only be based in Buddhism, because Buddhism does not acknowledge a creator God. For how can humans be answerable for their mistakes if they were created so flawed by a creator? The Buddhist idea of *karma*, for Govinda, unites demands for justice and self-determination, inasmuch as each person gathers the fruit of his or her own actions and, through insight into the psychological mechanisms and the meditation praxis from which they emerge, can continually improve. Thus the worth of each individual is grounded in Buddhist rationality. As the most modern (or better, ageless) religion, Buddhism is indeed necessary for the solution of modern problems.[30]

Govinda does not expect that all the world will or ought to become Buddhist. However, just as mathematics as a timeless science always accompanies human intellectual life, so Buddhism as a timeless human science will never be imagined away from humanity.

Zen and Tibetan Meditation

Currently in Germany the meditation methods of Zen Buddhism and Tibetan Buddhism have spread substantially.

Zen became known in Germany as early as 1923, thanks to an article by theologian and scholar of religion Rudolf Otto (1869-1937), who was especially struck by Zen's irrationality and paradox in light of his theory of the numinous.[31] This work prepared the ground for the collaboration of Zen master Ohasama Shuei with August Faust and the philosopher Eugen Herrigel in the reading of European philosophy. Ohasama and Faust in 1925 published the important book *Zen— Der lebendige Buddismus in Japan* (Zen—the living Buddhism in Japan), with an introduction by Rudolf Otto.[32] This book, like the first translations of D. T. Suzuki's works (*The Great Liberation*, 1939; *Zen and Japanese Culture*, 1941), attracted little attention. A breakthrough was only reached in 1948 when the philosopher Eugen Herrigel, who had spent five years in Japan learning Zen practice and the connected art of archery, published his book *Zen in der Kunst des Bogenschießens* (Zen and the art of archery). Herrigel's work became the most widely disseminated Buddhist book in the German-speaking world. The

---

[29] Ibid., 3.

[30] Ibid., 10f.

[31] R. Otto, "Über Zazen als Extrem des numinosen Irrationalen," in *Aufsätze das Numinose betreffend* (Stuttgart/Gotha: Verlag Friedrich Andreas Perthes, 1923), 119-32.

[32] S. Ohasama and A. Faust, *Zen—Der lebendige Buddhismus in Japan*, 2d ed. (Darmstadt: WBG, 1968).

clear and sparse language, but especially the authenticity that comes from the author's own practice, makes the work unique. Countless Germans were won to the practices of Zen by Herrigel. Among them was Gerta Ital, who wrote and published later about her own experiences in Japanese monasteries.[33] Since then the number of personal reports and philosophical studies available from nearly every paperback publisher under the category of religion and esoteric studies has swollen to hundreds of thousands, and many people have been stimulated by these works to begin their own Zen praxis.

Another important transmitter of Buddhism to Germany was Wilhelm Gundert (1880-1971). He was a significant philosopher who grasped the spirit of Zen as few others have and translated it into the thought structure of the German language. His main work was the translation of the Zen classic *Bi-yän-lu* (Japanese *Hekiganroku*) with commentary,[34] which today is still studied by all Zen practitioners. In the examples, metaphors, and rhetorical combats of this text Zen comes alive, and Gundert's agreeable translation loses none of this living quality, but rather enhances it. Educated in the spirit of Swabian Protestantism, Gundert went to Japan as a missionary and discovered that his Christianity began to change under the powerful influence of Japanese religions, especially Zen. Gundert remained a Christian but wrote in retrospect that he had to free himself from many points of accepted dogma, "and this liberation appeared, from the earlier standpoint, almost like apostasy." However, he believed it had led him "to see the unfathomable secret of God, of which the Bible speaks, in a new light."[35] In this light, Buddhism and Christianity touch one another intrinsically. For Gundert both religions are a retreat from the personal world, although Christianity in the end leads to affirmation and Buddhism to a certain resignation.[36] At least, he argues, one must see that both religions repeatedly aim to transcend all possible oppositions, but each speaks of this process with different metaphors: Buddhism in the *spatial* metaphor of emptiness *(sunyata,* Japanese *ku)*, Christianity in the *temporal* metaphor of eternity (Greek *aion)*. In both metaphors the main point is to overcome the ephemeral, material, and contrary in an experience that already here and now illuminates the complete otherness of "divine reality." Buddhism does this in negative language, while Christianity is colored more positively, inasmuch as "eternity" can be imagined positively. This does indeed conceal the danger that eternity might be imagined only as an extended time, while the eternal (as Paul says in 2 Cor. 4:18) is imperceptible and unimaginable.[37] Gundert leaves it at this suggestion; the comparison of the metaphors of emptiness and eternity have not yet been taken up again in Buddhist-Christian dialogue, to the

---

[33] G. Ital, *Der Meister, die Mönche und ich im Zen-buddhistischen Kloster* (Weilheim: O. W. Barth, 1972).

[34] W. Gundert, *Bi-yän-lu: Meister Yüan-wus Niederschrift von der Smaragdenen Felswand, verdeutscht und erläutert,* 3 vols. (Munich: Hanser, 1960-73).

[35] W. Gundert, "Zur übertragung des Bi-yän-lu ins Deutsche," in *Bi-yän-lu,* ed. W. Gundert, vol. 3 (Munich: Hanser, 1973), 109ff. First published in Japanese in *koza Zen,* vol. 8, *Gendai to Zen,* ed. K. Nishitani (Tokyo, 1968), 305-20.

[36] Ibid., 122.

[37] Ibid., 121f.

best of our knowledge. So Gundert finds on the one hand a deep inner relationship between Buddhism and Christianity, but on the other hand finds a difference in their mode of expression and in their attitude toward the world.

Above all, though, it was the Jesuit Hugo Makibi Enomiya-Lassalle (1898-1990) who made Zen known in Germany. He inspired Zen circles and co-founded Zen centers. (These included the ecumenical Christian Exercitium Humanum in Tholey/Saar, later refounded as the Ecumenical Center for Meditation and Encounter in the "Neumühle" near Mettlach/Saar, and the Franciscan Meditation Center in Dietfurt/Altmühltal.) At some of these centers Lassalle held ongoing sesshins (Zen training courses). There are both Buddhist and Christian teachers, and since the late 1980s students of Lassalle who have remained Christian have also taught at Buddhist centers (for example, at the Buddhist house in Allgäu). Lassalle himself was first invited to give a course at the Buddhist meditation center House of Silence (in Roseburg near Hamburg, founded 1962) in 1969—and, since he was a Christian, "not without the opposition of orthodox Buddhists."[38] In the 1960s Lassalle had to fight Catholic opposition to his integration of Zen into Christianity. That changed in the late 1960s and 1970s as the Catholic church rediscovered mysticism. In the 1980s, it was finally possible for someone like Franz Cardinal Hengsbach to express the judgment: "Father Lassalle is convincing to me as a human, a priest, and a Jesuit. He has opened up a path to inner life for many people in East and West. God alone knows the full extent of his work."[39] One can see that in the last four decades the Catholic church has carried out a clearly visible process of gradual opening toward Buddhism and its meditation!

Thanks to participants in Lassalle's courses, both Christian-ecumenical and Buddhist-Christian meditation centers have appeared. A good example is the Ecumenical Neighborhood at Christchurch, Hamburg.[40] Various Catholic monasteries today practice Zen as an accepted meditation method. On the Lutheran side, too, Zen praxis was promoted in the late 1960s by the Fraternity of St. Michael in both West and East Germany. Here, too, the stimulus came from Lassalle. Since then, almost every larger city has developed ecumenical Zen circles. Benedictine Willigis Jäger (b. 1925), a student of Yamada Koun Roshi and also finally introduced to Zen by Lassalle, is also a recognized Zen master with numerous students. He holds ongoing sessions in St. Benedict House, Würzburg. The Japanese-educated Lutheran pastor Gundula Mayer, who studied with both Lassalle and Yamada Roshi, offers Zen courses for the evangelical Lutheran state church in Hannover. Also, the Loccum working group for meditation draws together Lutheran theologians who teach Zen and other missionary methods. Since 1986 there have been regular offerings on Zen theory and practice for students in all fields at the universities of Tübingen, Regensburg, and Munich. These activities, too, can be traced to Lassalle's influence. On the Buddhist side,

---

[38] H. Hecker, 109.

[39] H. M. Enomiya-Lassalle, *Das Glück im eigenen Herzen finden*, ed. C. Eschricht, (N.F. Weitz: 1993), book cover.

[40] See H. Hecker, 110.

one should note, there is also protest against such tendencies. Some fear Christian absorption and a watering down of Buddhist identity and the purity of Zen.[41]

Zen has also spread in Germany by other means, especially through Karlfried Graf Dürckheim (1896-1988) and his existential-therapeutic encounter center in Rütte/Schwarzwald. There, in conjunction with the gestalt psychology of Maria Hippius (b. 1909) a new spiritual movement was created that came to influence the development of humanistic and transpersonal psychology in Germany (founding of the German Transpersonal Society in 1986). Dürckheim, like Lassalle, came to the conviction, in face of the misery of both world wars, that European culture must return to its spiritual roots. For this, he believes, the development of a meditative consciousness, such as can be learned in Buddhism, is necessary.

Zen philosophy also entered German philosophical discussion through the colloquium held in May 1958 on the theme "Art and Thought." This colloquium, sponsored jointly by the renowned Zen master and philosopher Hisamatsu Shin i'chi and Martin Heidegger, met at the University of Freiburg. The dialogue between Christian theology and the Kyoto-school philosopher Nishitani Keiji was especially furthered in Germany by the works of Hans Waldenfels (*Absolutes Nichts* [Absolute nothingness], 1976) and the translation by D. Fisher-Barnicol of Nishitani's masterpiece *What Is Religion?* in 1982. With his work Waldenfels anticipated many issues that in the American discussion would first be worked out in the second half of the 1980s about the (ontological) self-emptying of God (kenosis).[42] In the 1980s, Christian theology (Hans Küng, Jürgen Moltmann, Wolfhart Pannenberg) was influenced by these works. Compared to this influence, the discussion with the Kyoto philosopher Tanabe Hajime has not yet aroused the interest it should.[43]

Tibetan Buddhism, as mentioned above, first gained a foothold in Germany thanks to Lama Anagarika Govinda and his order Arya Maitreya Mandala. But it is especially through Tibetan exiles that more and more new centers in Germany (and in Switzerland and Austria) have been founded since the 1970s. The monastic Tibet Institute in Rikon (Switzerland) was the first, in 1968. In 1977 the Hamburg Tibetan Center was founded under the direction of Geshe Thubten Ngawang; it has come to offer a large-scale and demanding correspondence course on Buddhism. In 1994 the third seven-year course began. Since 1984 it has also held regular dialogue seminars, working jointly with the Study Society

---

[41] R. Meyer, "Christen und buddhistische Praktiken," *Lotusblätter* 3 (1944): 67f.

[42] See especially J. B. Cobb and C. Ives, eds., *The Emptying God: A Buddhist-Jewish-Christian Conversation* (Maryknoll, N.Y.: Orbis Books, 1990), which had its origin in a lecture by Masao Abe at the International Buddhist-Christian Conference in Hawaii, 1984, and the discussion that followed it.

[43] The exception is J. Laube, *Dialektik der absoluten Vermittlung: Hajime Tanabes Religionsphilosophie als Beitrag zum "Wettstreit der Liebe" zwischen Buddhismus und Christentum* (Freiburg: Herder, 1984). See also Fritz Buri, *Der Buddha-Christus als Herr des wahren Selbst* (Bern/Stuttgart: Haupt, 1982), which could transmit the philosophy of the Kyoto school only to insider circles in the German-speaking lands.

for Interreligious Dialogue of the Lutheran theology school at the University of Hamburg. From the beginning this has also included the Hamburg Islamic Center, and since 1991 Jewish groups have also taken part. The seminar themes range from the analysis of spiritual paths (1985) to the question "who are saints?" (1992) and to the theme "education in the religions" (1993).[44] The Aryatara Institute was founded in Jägerndorf (Bavaria) in 1980. When Rangjung Dorje (1923-81), the sixteenth karmapa (the leader of the Tibetan Karma-Kagyu order)[45] visited Germany in 1974 and 1977, new kagyu centers appeared throughout Germany (most notable is the Kamalashila Institute in Wachendorff near Bonn). Lama Loden Dagyab Rinpoche was especially open to dialogue. He teaches at the University of Bonn, leads the Tibetan center Chödzong near Nürnberg, and is co-editor of the periodical *Dialog der Religionen* (Dialogue between religions), which has been published since 1991 by the Lutheran Kaiser-Verlag/Gütersloher Verlagshaus.

Not only Tibetan Buddhism but Theravada, too, found a home in Germany as part of Nyanaponika's heritage. The Jew Ayya Khema (b. 1923, Berlin) studied with Nyanaponika in Sri Lanka from 1979. She founded a hermitage for nuns there and also established a Buddha house in Allgäu, to which in 1994 she added a center in Munich. In 1996 a monastery was founded in Allgäu, to be conducted in Buddhist fashion, but kept interreligiously ecumenical. Through publications as well as radio and television appearances Ayya Khema has been able to win a large following.

At the end of the 1980s there were approximately 120 Buddhist centers or societies in Germany, many of which provide lodging for a small monastic community, the members of which provide a focus point for the laypeople of the area to gather around them in a more or less intensive form.

The process of Buddhist development in Germany can be characterized as follows: although Buddhism until the 1920s was a phenomenon that appealed to members of the middle class who felt distanced from Christianity, since the 1960s students, members of alternative groups from the 1968 movement, and also Christians with religious socialization of various strengths have joined in. They have not necessarily formally converted to Buddhism but have selectively integrated some Buddhist aspects (especially meditation) into their own religious observance. Continually since then meditation and study courses have been offered in all the centers, and house-circles have been initiated to further deepen meditation work. The dialogue between formerly Christian formal converts to Buddhism with Christian groups or theologians has for the most part developed only weakly—for these Buddhists especially are mostly concerned with the search for their own new identity and old negative experiences with the churches stand in the way of unprejudiced encounter.[46] Thus the dialogue often concentrates on Buddhists from Asian countries who visit or live in Germany.

---

[44] *Tibet und Buddhismus* 6/21/2 (1992): 49, and 7/25/2 (1993): 45.

[45] The main directions or orders are: Nyingma, Sakya, Kagyu, and Geluk.

[46] See K. Bitter, *Konversionen zum tibetischen Buddhismus: eine Analyse religiöser Biographien* (Göttingen: E. Oberdieck, 1988).

EUROPEAN BUDDHISM

In recent times more and more Buddhists have consciously concerned themselves with adapting the Buddhist movement to European realities. Martin Steinke (1882-1966) expressly tried to further this goal. In 1922 he founded a "community about Buddha" in Berlin, and in 1933 in China was consecrated as a monk of the Pure Land school.[47] Lama Anagarika Govinda wanted to give his order Arya Maitreya Mandala a contemporary (and thus also European) identity that moved beyond the purely Asian form of Buddhism. Gerhard Szczesny's 1976 book, *Ein Buddha für das Abendland* (A Buddha for the West), adopted his ideas; Szczesny's work met with approval in Buddhist circles.[48] Thus the Berlin banker Max Glashoff wrote in 1978 in the name of the German Buddhist Union: "The duty of the eighties will be to find a form that will allow Buddhism to play a helpful role in the West. What Europeans need above all is a surmounting of material superficiality, which is the greatest hindrance to an acceptance of Buddhism and bringing it to fruition among us."[49]

In the founding call of the Buddhist Religion Society in Germany, Karl Schmied (president of the German Buddhist Union) wrote in 1984: "We are called to enrich the Buddha's teaching as a living world religion that has significance for our age and region in creative forms with new aspects and facets, without detracting from its fundamentals and timeless truths. This will come to pass in the first line through praxis, training, and testing of the teaching in the realities of daily life as well as in an open, intensive exchange of experiences."[50] Schmied understands by this also the intensification of the "constructive, unbiased conversation" with the churches.[51]

The Buddhist Religion Society in Germany (Buddhistische Religionsgemeinschaft in Deutschland—BRG) was finally founded in Hamburg on 7 September 1985. To satisfy the requirements of a public corporation and to unite all Buddhists in Germany under a single umbrella organization, the BRG adopted a general creed, stating that besides the refuge to the *three jewels* (Buddha, *dharma*, and *samgha*), and trust in the *four noble truths*, there is also a duty to fashion a personal transformation of life in accordance with the *five fundamental moral commandments* (1) not to kill or injure, (2) not to take what is not given, (3) not to engage in any unhallowed sexual relationships, (4) not to lie or speak profanely, and (5) not to dull the consciousness with intoxicating substances. Besides these rules, the creed will be propagated for the sake of the *unity of all Buddhists*.

At the founding convention it was again proclaimed as a duty to acclimatize Buddhism in Germany so that it might correspond to the specific demands of the

---

[47] H. Hecker, 52ff.

[48] W. Karwath, recension of G. Szczesny, "Ein Buddha für das Abendland," *Bodhi Baum* 1/4 (1976): 200f.

[49] M. Glashoff, 119.

[50] K. Schmied, "Afterword," in H. Hecker, *Chronik des Buddhismus in Deutschland,* 3d ed., 121.

[51] Ibid., 122.

time, but remain "true to its own foundation without self-assertiveness after a prize." A separate secretariat for dialogue between Buddhism and Christianity was established under the direction of Geshe Thubten Ngawang (director of the Hamburg Tibetan Center). There are several reasons why the BRG was not able to maintain itself as an institution, as pointed out above. Still, it succeeded in strengthening interest in dialogue with Christian partners and in the quest to live a European Buddhism. For the encouragement of a European Buddhism, the congress Unity in Multiplicity marked a temporary plateau. This meeting of the European Buddhist Union was held in Berlin in September 1992, attracting more than two thousand participants. As features of a *European* Buddhism, the following were named:[52]

• the equal significance of laypeople and monks (and nuns),
• the equality of women,
• consciousness of Sakyamuni Buddha's original teaching as separate from cultural specifics that Buddhism has adopted in different Asian lands,
• strengthened social and political engagement in the sense of the bodhisattva ideal.

This agenda shows how close Buddhist goals are to corresponding Christian programs for the renewal of Christianity.

BUDDHIST-CHRISTIAN ENCOUNTER

In 1965 the Japanese philosopher of religion Ueda Shizuteru produced a study comparing Meister Eckhart and Zen Buddhism.[53] In this way he continued the tradition begun by Rudolf Otto of dialogue in the comparative representation of the mystics.[54] Ueda characterizes Eckhart's thought as "infinity mysticism with a theistic substructure."[55] In this way, argues Ueda, Eckhart differs fundamentally from Zen—despite so many perplexing parallels. In Zen, there is nothing to add to the Nothingness that rejects and penetrates everything. "What Meister Eckhart means with his concept of the One, Zen Buddhism applies beyond the One,"[56] that is, in Nothingness, which is not *beyond* every number, even an all-inclusive one, but constitutes their essence. Nothingness, for Ueda, is not in silence (as opposed to "word") but "also beyond human silence."[57] While Eckhart refers to the godhood behind God, for Ueda, Zen points to the pure "thus-ness" of flowers, mountains, or the fall of a leaf in autumn. Can Christianity follow here, asks Ueda?

---

[52] See the report in *Publik Forum* 21 (6 November 1992): 26.

[53] S. Ueda, *Die GottesGeburt in der Seele und der Durchbruch zur Gottheit* (Gütersloh, 1965).

[54] R. Otto, "Introduction," in Ohasama and Faust, *Zen—Der lebendige Buddhismus in Japan* (1925); idem, *West-Östliche Mystik* (1926), the latter work a comparison of Eckhart and the Hindu philosopher Sankara.

[55] S. Ueda, 143.

[56] Ibid., 149f.

[57] Ibid., 151.

A book written in 1968 shows how strongly the new Buddhist-Christian dialogue in the 1960s was still marked with prejudice. This work, by G. Siegmund,[58] had significant influence on the Christian circles as they formed their opinion of Buddhism. The essential assertion of this book is the old claim that Buddhism disavows history, while Christianity is established on a basis of historical liberation: while Jesus was directed totally toward the future, the argument runs, Buddhism faces backward and desires to tear down the present "in order to submerge again in the beginning." This, according to Siegmund, comes from the fact that the Buddha lived in a "very peaceful and spiritually exhausted age," and that the "tendency toward flight from the world" is supposed to be typical of Indians in general. Thus they are supposed to have longed to escape the agitation of history from a sense of disgust at life.[59]

It was not new to portray Asian meditative practice as a sort of infantile regression, but still this view has very little to do with the real Buddhism of history. It has been hard to surmount this sort of prejudice even for noted intellectuals and Christians who approach Buddhism with open sympathy and who want to integrate some elements into Christianity. One can see this problem in the writings of Heinrich Dumoulin (1905-95) and Hugo M. Enomiya-Lassalle from the 1960s. We mention this not for the sake of cheap criticism but because the Buddhist-Christian discussion in Germany in the 1960s is especially instructive; fascination with Buddhism on the one hand and old Christian missionary-apologetic interests on the other produced an ambivalent field for interpretation. In changed form it is still necessary to reckon with the effects today. This can teach us an important point: the *caution* necessary in the interreligious process of understanding.

ZEN PRACTICE AND THEOLOGICAL REFLECTION

In 1966 two important books appeared, written by two German Jesuits living in Japan—Heinrich Dumoulin and Hugo M. Enomiya-Lassalle. They helped bring Buddhist-Christian dialogue to wide circles, especially within German Catholicism.

Heinrich Dumoulin called his first great work on the theme of dialogue *Östliche Meditation und christliche Mystik* (Eastern meditation and Christian mysticism).[60] His method is phenomenologically descriptive as well as structurally comparative and theologically judging. He reports first on an audience that Pope John XXIII granted to thirty Japanese Buddhists on 18 November 1962: Belief in the Buddha and belief in God, said the pope, rest on a common foundation. Thus, all religious people should work together for the well-being of humanity (35). Dumoulin then goes on to lay out his own theological basis for dialogue: he sees in every individual human conscience the "entry-way for miraculous grace." The

---

[58] G. Siegmund, *Buddhismus und Christentum* (Frankfurt: Knecht, 1968), 262.

[59] Ibid., 262f.

[60] H. Dumoulin, *Östliche Meditation und christliche Mystik* (Freiburg: Alber, 1966). Page references in text are from this work.

conscience *first* perceives a duty to heed natural law, and *second* its own dependence on divine being. Non-Christians, too, perceive divine being and necessary morality in their own fashion. Both aspects, for Dumoulin, provide the foundation for dialogue. The Second Vatican Council satisfactorily solved the question of the salvation of non-Christians, inasmuch as it underscored that God's plan of salvation is for *all* of humanity.

Dumoulin distinguished three steps in Buddhist-Christian encounter. *First* comes recognition of "striking similarities in the outward appearances" of both religions. These, however, evaporate as soon as perception reaches deeper to a *second step*, at which "fundamental differences in motivation" can be discerned. But then in a *third step* "convergences" can be traced, especially between Zen and Christianity, because, according to Dumoulin, "all true non-Christian spirituality invokes advent-filled longing for fulfillment in Christ" (259).

Dumoulin knows that the law of *karma* and belief in reincarnation are unrelinquishable basic principles of the Buddhist spiritual world. Both, however, appear "strange and improbable" to Western thought, he says (261). This is a judgment that must be revised today, because since Dumoulin wrote many Europeans have come to believe in reincarnation and the concept of *karma* is no longer a foreign word. To be sure, Dumoulin in the 1960s was still repeating old stereotypes while interpreting the concept of *karma*. For example, on the one hand he speaks of *karma* theory as "destroying" the essence of the human as person and his personal value (262f.) by preserving no free will (264), while on the other hand he admires and accepts Buddhism's unremitting admonition to penance. As he says, "The Buddhist who stands under the law of *karma* feels himself duty-bound and qualified for customary actions"; he develops a "first-rate ethics" (262). Flagrant contradictions of this sort stem from insufficient interpretation of the doctrine of *karma*. Further, to presume a "convergence with the Christian" where the Buddhist practices the virtue of selflessness in such a way that he neglects "the metaphysical content of the teaching of "not I" (276) distorts the historical-philosophical context in a far from trivial manner, because it is precisely the not-I teaching that motivates Buddhists to the practice of selflessness. Dumoulin believes that Zen Buddhism, in its adherence to Mahayana philosophy, is imprisoned in a monistic-pantheistic metaphysics. This, for Dumoulin, is a mark of the "advent position of non-Christian religions," which "possess truths and values only in a fragmentary fashion and mixed with errors" (42). This is because the "monistic metaphysics destroys the anthropological principles of the human social ethic" (275). What, however, this "monism" consists of, how it appears differently in the different Mahayana Buddhist schools and must therefore be distinguished carefully, Dumoulin does not explain. He points out the alleged monistic deficit of Buddhism in contrast to Christian personalism. In this he still proceeds without break from the theory of fulfillment, according to which the longings and presentiments of other religions would be fulfilled in Christianity—if only Christianity would stop presenting itself in such an exclusively Western guise (47). This could not only open up a new perspective for the acculturation of the gospel to Asia, but Christianity itself ought to receive enriching answers in encounter with Buddhism (45). To be sure, in the early 1960s Dumoulin was emphatically against the Christian polemic that Buddhism is an attempt at human self-extinction in favor of the Zen teaching that the "original religious tension between freedom and grace" is common to both Christianity and Buddhism (42). For Dumoulin, to portray Buddhism as a religion of self-annihilation comes from a grossly over-simplified observation. On this point he cites with approval the notes of a Zen practitioner, who in the midst of the exertion of meditation on Kannon, the bodhisattva of compassion (regarded in East Asia as female), in his humble flight to Kannon received even more power of concentration for meditation: *jiriki* (own power) and *tariki* (other power) did not designate types of religion, but a dialectical tension in the religious experience of *each* religion (42).

Under the theme of "Christian values" Dumoulin in his early writings sees Christian meditation as superior in the final analysis to Buddhism, because here it becomes clear that the spirit is more important than the technique, which, he argues, is often overlooked in Buddhism (220). The "authentic spirit of meditation," for Dumoulin, is nowhere "more magnificently realized" than in Christianity. Such generalizations appear strange today, but they show how difficult it is even for a Buddhist scholar of world renown to assess the other religion without prejudice, when at the same time he has a missionary agenda. In his last great work on Buddhist spirituality (1995) Dumoulin openly leaves such valuations behind. He acknowledges in Buddhism a "striving for transcendence" that also differs in "Buddha veneration and devotion,"[61] which through self-renunciation (the kenotic way of being) in the attitude of "sympathetic empathy or selfless love"[62] may come to the goal of the bodhisattva idea. And, "like the Christian for holiness, the Buddhist strives for the bodhisattva character. In both cases, the criterion is selfless love."[63] Dumoulin ends his work with the comment that this religion can lead "to mystical heights" and to "authentic religious experience."[64]

Hugo M. Enomiya-Lassalle, in contrast, wrote *Zen Buddhism* (1966)[65] from the perspective of his own Zen experience. He does not remain silent about his conviction that this experience has deepened his Catholic faith. In Zen he finds above all that the significance of the body for the spiritual life is taken seriously, an issue that the Western churches for a long time had culpably neglected (406).

He explains the great similarities between the mystical experiences of Christians and non-Christians theologically with the statement that "God also works in the soul of the non-Christian" (408). He is less interested in a philosophical exposition of Buddhism than in Zen praxis. Lassalle presents his arguments upon a Buddhist backdrop that is not yet differentiated, but for him still needs "to be rightly transformed in the Christian sense" (412). For him, this means especially the rejection of the doctrine of emptiness *(sunyata)*. Still, he adds that a Zen enlightenment experience must also be tested in the light of Buddhist philosophy. What that means for the Christian, however, has not yet been thought through in this book (413).

---

[61] H. Dumoulin, *Spiritualität des Buddhismus: Einheit in lebendiger Vielfalt* (Mainz: Grünewald, 1995), 250.

[62] Ibid., 252.

[63] Ibid., 253.

[64] Ibid.

[65] Hugo M. Enomiya-Lassalle, *Zen-Buddhismus* (Cologne: Bachem, 1966). Page references in text are from this work.

Lassalle sees another difference between the two religions in the fact that for a Christian the enlightenment experience cannot be the only way to salvation, which is clearly the case in Buddhism (413). In these early works of Lassalle's the real encounter of the spiritual worlds of Buddhism and Christianity have not yet been sufficiently ventured or reflected upon.

PERSONALITY AND IMPERSONALITY

This is a fundamental problem in discussion with Buddhism. Heinrich Dumoulin repeatedly dealt with it, and here also occasionally demonstrates one-sided Christian assumptions that hinder proper understanding of this theme in Buddhism. Religion, Dumoulin judges, signifies a polar relationship between God and human, and in complete unification with God the human being, in the Christian view, does not lose the "personal being" he has received as a gift from God.[66] This doubtless holds true for Christianity, but to reach the conclusion from this point that Buddhism is inferior on account of its supposed impersonality is very problematic. On the one hand, Dumoulin says that "Eastern thought" (by which he means Japanese Zen Buddhism) is existence thought and affects the human in his "uniqueness, concreteness, and wholeness" so that through "self-realization" the sense of humanness will be achieved: "all Eastern paths have as their goal making the human whole and holy."[67] But how does this sentence relate to the other statement, that in Zen Buddhism "no personal worth" is due to the individual person?[68] Is becoming whole and holy even conceivable without the individual person in the process coming to know his eternal significance? Has not the Buddhist, when he has actualized the Buddha nature in this one-time human form that is himself, integrated the personal and the transpersonal?

The problem of personality and impersonality is especially complex in Buddhist-Christian dialogue. In Buddhism the issue of *anatta* is conditioned by its philosophical ambiance. Thus the history of Buddhist philosophy can by no means be restricted to simple reduction to the issue of impersonality, especially since it must first be clarified what is meant by *personality* in the first place. Here, however, we have to deal with subtle differences within Christianity as well as opposing histories of concepts. Dumoulin, too, does not differentiate clearly between person and individual.[69] It is clear that we need an intercultural hermeneutic of the concept of person before we can make any theological judgments.

INTENSIVE DIALOGUE WITH THE KYOTO SCHOOL

In 1976 the Catholic theologian Hans Waldenfels published a basic presentation of Nishitani Keiji's philosophy and a dialogical confrontation with this thinker from the Kyoto school.[70] His book *Absolutes Nichts* (Absolute nothingness) has

---

[66] H. Dumoulin, *Östliche Meditation und christliche Mystik*, 222.

[67] Ibid., 279.

[68] Ibid., 275.

[69] Ibid.

[70] H. Waldenfels, *Absolutes Nichts: Zur Grundlegung des Dialogs zwischen Buddhismus und Christentum* (Freiburg: Herder, 1976).

remained to the present one of the most important contributions to the process of philosophical clarification between Buddhism and Christianity in the German-speaking world. In this work Waldenfels describes the dialogue situation soberly: In the cause of mutual understanding, he says, we still stand at the beginning. Japanese Christians, and also Europeans, have still hardly understood Buddhism, he argues, when they have taken notice of it at all. So to begin, the dialogue partners must learn to listen. In dialogue it is not the situation that one wins over the other, but that the partners "selflessly. . . let the truth of things as they are come to light."[71] For him, dialogue can lead to mutual transformation, to reach to the depths of each religion. This can be seen in Waldenfels's treatment of the Christian faith in connection to Nishitani's philosophy.

Waldenfels here marks out three problem areas for dialogue: mysticism and Zen, God and absolute nothingness, and Jesus Christ and the doctrine of kenosis.

It is a long-argued question whether Zen (or Buddhism in general) can be described appropriately with the Christian category of mysticism. The negative language of Buddhism certainly has a different background from that which stands behind the Christian negative (apophatic) way of speaking about God, namely, a principle of the unification of all dualism. Criticism of Waldenfels's book on this issue was thus also loud on the Buddhist side. Buddhists were especially concerned with Waldenfels's understanding of not-self *(anatta)* and the consequences in Buddhism for valuation of the world and history. Their main point was that one must not only recognize the this-worldly character of Zen, but its radical this-worldliness.[72]

For Nishitani the question of person, non-self, individuality, and history is central. Waldenfels makes it clear that the Buddhist partners had not understood the trinitarian and relational concept of person in Christianity. Instead, they had used a modern, individualistically defined concept of the autonomous "I" as their starting point, which however does not accurately represent the classical Christian understanding of the person. For these reasons Buddhist-Christian dialogue, points out Waldenfels, still has important work to do simply to *understand* the partners in this central question.[73]

To be sure, it is also necessary to ask who is engaging in dialogue with whom. Is there *a* Buddhism or *a* Christianity? Are not the intellectual postulates so diverse even within a religion, whether from confessional particularity or philosophical approach as well as the different social past of the partners, that dialogue can only be understanding between individuals or schools, but can never be between "the religions" as a whole?[74]

---

[71] Ibid., 155.

[72] F. Cook, "Encounter with Nothing-at-all: Reflections on Hans Waldenfels' Absolute Nothingness," *Buddhist-Christian Studies* 2 (1982): 136-44.

[73] The theme of the trinitarian concept of person in relation to the non-substantial "concept of person" in Mahayana Buddhism has been treated many times. A few examples are J. P. Keenan, *The Meaning of Christ: A Mahayana Theology* (1989); M. v. Brück, "Shunyata and the Christian Trinity," in *Buddhist Emptiness and Christian Trinity*, ed. R. Corless and P. Knitter (1990); D. W. Mitchell, *Spirituality and Emptiness* (1991).

[74] F. Cook, 142.

We believe that this objection must be taken seriously, but it cannot be raised to the level of an absolute. After all, there are general spiritual structures in the religions that come to light especially in dialogue, as long as that dialogue takes care to use language consistently. Waldenfels at any rate describes the background of his dialogue partner Nishitani at the beginning of his book: his thought is marked by a "weak sense for the problems of the modern world, as they appear in a highly industrialized Asian country."[75] This could be an important point of reference for similar problems among the Christian dialogue partners.

Nishitani's thought could without a doubt be of extraordinary significance for the encounter between Buddhism and Christianity, and generally for the understanding of Japan in Europe and vice versa. Hans Waldenfels gave the impetus to pursue this study. But theological discussion in German-speaking lands has not yet taken up the invitation, with the exception of Fritz Buri, Heinrich Ott, and Hans Küng (all of whom are Swiss).

RELIGIOUS-HISTORICAL COMPARISONS

In 1978 Gustav Mensching's (1901-78) book *Buddha und Christus* (The Buddha and Christ) appeared. This is a fundamental religious studies investigation that had influence in Germany, not least because its conclusions were also taken up in Hans Küng's 1984 *Christentum und Weltreligionen* (Christianity and world religions) and thus were more widely disseminated. Mensching is skeptical about how ready the church is for dialogue. In his opinion the Christian churches will not be so ready to give up their claim to absoluteness (based on sole possession of the truth that leads to salvation). One can see as evidence of this, he argues, that the churches have distanced themselves so much from the historical Jesus and the original gospel, where it did not support claims to power.[76] Doubtless interreligious dialogue is also concerned with the issue of truth, but this is not identical to dogmatically formulated rightness (242). Mensching in this context cites the saying of the Indian poet Rabindranath Tagore (1861-1941): "Can not the different religions let their different light shine for the different worlds of souls that need it?"

Methodologically, Mensching's stance is not new, but it is laid out with greater precision and is thus extraordinarily helpful. Mensching would like to join the Christian faith standpoint to the historical-critical methods of "objective portrayal" of both religions (12f.). As starting point and first issue for comparison he uses the historicity of the two founding figures Jesus and Gautama. So he does not start with dogmatic systems but instead attempts to uncover commonalities and differences between Buddhism and Christianity from the point of view of social and intellectual history.

The common ground of the two founders, for Mensching, is that
• they were wandering preachers.

---

[75] H. Waldenfels, *Absolutes Nichts*, 13.

[76] G. Mensching, *Buddha und Christus* (Stuttgart: DVA, 1978), 235. Page references in text are from this work.

• their primary social environment (the family) had almost no understanding of their mission, and the guardians of the existing religious tradition also opposed them.

• they gathered groups of disciples around themselves in similar concentric circles (76ff.).

The differences are just as obvious:

• Gautama's social milieu (noble) is not comparable to Jesus' environment (artisan).

• With Gautama, the emphasis was on a way of disappearance from earth; with Jesus, it was on personal relationship with God.

• Gautama's followers were prosperous and gave up material things from this privileged position, while Jesus' disciples were poor.

Mensching sees Gautama primarily as *mystic* and Jesus as *prophetic reformer*. Correspondingly different are the deaths of the two founders: Jesus dies, condemned by the religiously and politically powerful, on the cross; Gautama smilingly enters *nirvana*.

Whether or not these descriptions are accurate in particulars, it is important that Mensching does not deduce dogmatic differences from them but instead points to psychologically and socially different lives that need not be mutually exclusive. This is because they correspond to different human situations that, since they are historically conditioned, cannot be taken as absolutes. Mensching in this sense pleads for a Christianity that is tolerant and liberal about content, that does not set itself off educationally, even when it covers its own positions in different ways, but instead proves itself to be a socially useful movement in political life (267ff.). In face of the materialism of modern societies, against which (along with its corollaries of senselessness and superficiality) Mensching appeals for the integration of essential values, both Buddhist and Christian, into life, so that dialogue could become the common quest for authenticity. Mensching at the end of his book refers approvingly to Hans Waldenfels, who ended *Absolute Nothingness* with the following sentences:

> Since the Buddha's enlightenment, for Buddhism enlightenment has been the measure of all things. The Buddhist is a person who strives for self-realization in his life, and knows that he cannot win without radical disengagement. The true enlightenment, however, calls him back in an engagement of empathy and compassion.
>
> Since Christ's death on the cross, for the Christian love has been the boundless measure of his conduct. The Christian is a person who strives for self-realization, in which he is consumed in radical engagement for others. The true love knows itself to be propelled by enlightenment through Christ's spirit.
>
> Enlightenment, which radiates love, and love, which is enlightened and stirring, depend upon one another. But here it must be asked: do they encounter one another in the new communication of depth, where in poverty, death, and absolute nothingness the true self first arises, rather than in the

smile of the enlightened Buddha and the suffering countenance of the crucified Jesus? (277)

This is a synoptic presentation of both religions, with which we too wish to
agree without reservation, especially since in the realm of praxis of Buddhist-
Christian meditation and living community since then it has in many ways proven
to be true.

In the same year that Mensching's *Buddha and Christ* appeared (1978),
Heinrich Dumoulin again declared himself in his book *Begegnung mit dem
Buddhismus* (Encounter with Buddhism), which aimed to be both an introduction to Buddhism and a presentation of the dialogue fields of Buddhism and
Christianity. "Book-learning without inner understanding is not enough," the
author comments,[77] presenting again the point that he sees mysticism as the most
fruitful field for encounter between the religions (21). This, admittedly, is contested on phenomenological grounds, because a religion is certainly more than
its mystical traditions. Dumoulin does not, however, limit the perspective at all.
Instead he presents the historical development of the Buddhist systems so that
the corresponding or contradicting Christian developments can be pointed out
clearly. In the final chapters, the issue of the personal and the person in historical
perspective is again central. Now, however, it is presented substantially differently than in the 1960s.

Dumoulin recommends looking at Buddhism in regard to the personal from a
cosmic, historical, and mystical perspective. In this way, there is no doubt that
Buddhism rejects the concept of person for the "final validity," because it is anthropomorphic (134). But does it follow that Buddhism thinks in a way that
approaches or is before the personal? Dumoulin is now more cautious in his
judgment. He draws upon Karlfried Graf Dürckheim and the Hindu scholar and
former Swiss ambassador to India J. A. Cuttat, both of whom appeared to speak
of a "fore-personal structure" that would be open for the personal. This can also
be seen in the works of modern Buddhist authors like Nishitani Keiji, Abe Masao,
and the Thai monk Buddhadasa.

Dumoulin argues in regard to the cosmic perspective of the personal that the
historic Buddha is "de-personalized" in *dharma*, especially in Mahayana (117).
He comes to the conclusion that in Buddhism cosmic universalism and personality are not mutually exclusive, which he also believes to be true of a Christian
perspective, as one can demonstrate in connection with Teilhard de Chardin.
Teilhard found the "personal applied in all of reality" (120). Recent years have
shown that Buddhism and Christianity can discuss this issue more deeply. This is
especially true when the questions have been taken up in Buddhist-Christian
conversation of a change in the understanding and signifying of reality in the
natural sciences. Dumoulin believes that to blame Buddhism for the sublimation
of the historical into the cosmic is a Western misunderstanding of Buddhism.

---

[77] H. Dumoulin, *Begegnung mit dem Buddhismus* (Freiburg: Herder, 1978; new edition 1982), 13. Page references in text are from this work.

On the question of sense of history, however, thinkers are as divided as before. It will not be possible to progress on this issue until the question is posed fundamentally, allowing for changing approaches in different areas and times in both Buddhist and Christian thought. To date, this has only come to pass in a fragmentary fashion. Without such a clarification, however, it is impossible to say what a mystical experience of unity means, which in another time might pass as normal human understanding. It can better be expressed in the categories of synchronicity or entirety of time. The usual understanding (daily consciousness), though, lies at the root of our concept of the historical and the personal. Whether mysticism can be accentuated as more personal or more apersonal is a secondary issue to this. It is not contested that reality appears in authentic mystical experience. It must, however, be thematized, since, in Buddhist-Christian dialogue, it can as little be treated as an "in itself" as it can in normal chronological experience of "before" and "after."[78] At times, it appears, positions will be set against each other with a pre-Kantian naiveté and treated as categories of different cultural thought types, so that certainly it will give way to the perception-theoretical problem.[79]

ARE THE CHRISTIAN AND BUDDHIST DOCTRINES OF JUSTIFICATION DIFFERENT FROM ONE ANOTHER?

In 1979 Takizawa Katsumi published "'Justification' in Buddhism and Christianity."[80] It roused great interest because it brought the theme of justification doctrine, central to German Protestant discussion, into Buddhist-Christian dialogue in a sharply formulated form. For this reason we wish to discuss this article briefly, expanding on the comments about Takizawa in the chapter on Japan. Since 1965 Takizawa had taught repeatedly at German universities. His experience in Germany shows, he states soberly, that basically Buddhists and Christians have been totally uninterested in one another, despite the demand for dialogue and understanding. Takizawa believes that for the Protestant theologians in the tradition of Karl Barth the "name of Jesus Christ" is the only decisive factor—so what could Buddhists have to say that would be of interest, since for them the decisive name sounds completely different?

---

[78] Cf. M. v. Brück, "Wo endet Zeit? Erfahrungen zeitloser Gleichzeitigkeit in der Mystik der Weltreligionen," in *Was ist Zeit?*, ed. K. Weis (Munich: DTV, 1995), 207-62.

[79] In the discussion of historical materials the question can perhaps be posed in a new way, if one does not discuss the differing basic model of reality (e.g., in the *Prajnaparamita* literature and in the *Avatamsaka sutra*) as linear representations but as paradigms. In this way, in the first case, reduction to the concept of emptiness (*sunyata*) describes the interrelational character of the temporal structure, so that the individual appears as *relative*, but *real*. At the same time in the sense of the cosmic One the *personal rather disappears* in the *Avatamsaka sutra* and the later Hua Yen philosophy of totality of the whole. Possibly what is involved here is a model of experience that also agrees to various Christian developments and in that case has brought forth different experiences of the personal, which as such are however neither specifically "Buddhist" nor "Christian."

[80] K. Takizawa, "'Rechtfertigung' im Buddhismus und Christentum," *EvTh* 39 (1979): 182-95. Page references in text are from this work.

To such christological reflections Takizawa, however, argues in opposition that the bearer of this one name "who in and for himself exists *for all of us*, recommends from his own original stand to relax the grip with which we claim him for ourselves in this name, indeed, to open the hand" (195). Is there not then a "factual-essential correspondence between the things that *Hozo-Amida* and *Jesus Christ* express about the relationship between God and human and about human justification"? (194). Hozo-Amida, Takizawa argues, stands completely for justification by grace alone. This is because the Buddha nature that transcends the "I" is embodied in him, which is superior to any human act of will and makes possible the Buddhist path of salvation. The human's belief is for Takizawa the answer to Amida's vow of loyalty, which however cannot be thought of as outside of or distant from the human, but is originally and causally always with him, without indeed coinciding with the human "I." The awakening to "the truth of the Buddha nature" is the moment at which Gautama Sakyamuni actualized and completed this Amida reality in himself. One must indeed grasp that Amida is not a historical figure, but for us in the history of his activities is always interrelated to the historical Buddha. The reason for awakening to truth can be nothing other than the still-buried true self of the human, which negates every usual "I," and inasmuch as this is "nothing other than the original, eternally present, boundless, compassionate Buddha" (185).

The Buddha's awakening as well as that of every believer to the Buddha nature is thus for Takizawa the action of the ur-fact that every person "was one with the true original Buddha" (185) in his ("I"-transcending) being already before awakening. The "Buddha-becoming" would thus not be a temporal process of change, but a *becoming aware of the real*. Amida's power is, for Takizawa, a completely other designation to the empirical human being, but is the human's true designation, which is always already active.

The history of Jesus Christ is for Takizawa an exact correspondence to this structure. He comprehends this within the Barthian concept of the "ur-fact Immanuel." In Jesus, God and human are in fact one, but at the same time unmixably different from one another (192). Jesus' obedience to God is thus not the effort of the corporeal "I," but comes from the true God, who is eternally present to the human being. And thus Takizawa distinguishes between the eternal Christ, who is contemporary with all of humanity, and the "symbolic" historical Jesus of Nazareth, who lived at a particular time and is only recognized in a limited religious tradition. God's unlimited grace is thus the essence of the eternal Christ, the "ur-fact Immanuel," while the answering belief can be taken as the corporeal representation itself.

Thus it follows for Takizawa: "'Justification by God's grace alone' in its strong original sense and 'justification by faith alone' cannot be divided from one another, but are not simply identical" (194). The first leads logically to the second; otherwise people would fall into a "vulgar religiosity" that represents a self-seeking magical invocation of the name or a similar level of belief as human works under the law, against which Barth himself fought so vehemently. If this is so, the reality of Christ must be greater and more comprehensive than the Jesus of Nazareth who is proclaimed in the church. This should be the christological starting point for dialogue with other religions.

In "Reflections on the Universal Foundation of Buddhism and Christianity" (1980)[81] Takizawa returned to these thoughts and demonstrated that they describe not only the structure of the Pure Land school but also the basic structure of Zen Buddhism, even if it is expressed there in other terms. As he says, for Zen master Dogen (1200-1253) the question of "original enlightenment" was central, and it was only on the basis of this precondition that acquired enlightenment was possible for him. Dogen did indeed reject the idea of a pure "otherworldly" outer power, because an "other power" of this sort would be injurious to humans: it would conceal the true transcendent life power within the human being, which is totally independent of the everyday "I-self." Dogen, according to Takizawa, wanted to allow all people to return to their true home that is common to all, where the eternal self, totally transcending the "I," would be completely at one with every person. From the point of view of the "I" this self is the "wholly other."

Takizawa asks, Isn't there the same problem in Christianity? He says yes, there is, and adds:

> Whether one has clarity or not in this issue is much more important in daily life than the nominal religious affiliation of the person concerned, since this affiliation is dependent on each person's contingent historical encounter. . . . We must know that the one living truth that there and then appeared as Jesus broke down the fence a long time ago, indeed throughout eternity, not only between Jews and gentiles, but also between Christians and non-Christians.[82]

Thus argues Takizawa, who with this theological foundation of Buddhist-Christian dialogue has provoked notice in Germany (although hardly at all in the conservative churches of Japan). Perhaps this interest is precisely because Takizawa worked out the implications of Karl Barth's thought, who had opened his eyes to the "ur-fact Immanuel" in the first place. Before this, for the most part, Barth's theology had been interpreted and understood completely differently in its missionary-theological implications, in which it was also misunderstood.[83]

NEW PARTNERS—NEW METHODS IN DIALOGUE

In 1979 the Catholic Academy in Bavaria (Munich) organized a congress on the occasion of the visit of a group of Japanese monks to Germany that reached a new height in theoretical reflection on dialogue as well as in relation to practical interest in meditation.[84] Two themes ran through the discussion: (1) the issue of person, and (2) the problem of language in Buddhist-Christian dialogue. Demonstrations of the Japanese arts of calligraphy *(shodo)*, fencing *(kendo)*, and archery *(kyudo)* during the congress illustrated Heinrich Dumoulin's comment that

---

[81] K. Takizawa, *Reflexionen über die universale Grundlage von Buddhismus und Christentum* (Frankfurt, 1980), 53f.

[82] Ibid., 64.

[83] For a theologically open signification of Barth's theology, see also M. v. Brück, *Möglichkeiten und Grenzen einer Theologie der Religionen.*

[84] The lectures and a report are printed in H. Waldenfels, ed., *Begegnung mit dem Zen-Buddhismus* (Düsseldorf: Patmos, 1980).

in Japan *personality* is by no means underdeveloped or underexpressed. It is different only in other ways and cannot be understood merely through analysis of philosophical concepts. The calligraphic page of a Zen master or Buddhist portraiture is a signature, highly individual and unique. But this uniqueness opens up transparency into the ineffable that surpasses every individual concrete expression.[85]

Hans Waldenfels inquired into the language of both religions and the language of dialogue. Because silence too contains an understanding that is always joined with significance, he argued, language also remains the central problem in dialogue with Zen. Christianity's word become flesh can be interpreted as the individual concretization of the divine language event.[86] In Zen, language has a referring character, like the finger that points at the moon—the "object" is thus beyond the individual concrete expression. This would also mean that the individuated picture—like the finger—would also only be provisional, because the pointing finger is not the moon.

We must supplement these comments about language in dialogue with Zen, because Waldenfels's and Dumoulin's 1979 analysis does not include the deeper content of Zen experience and its linguistic expression. For in Zen it is the case that every concrete thing, the gesture, the linguistic expression, the unique person, *is also at the same time* the absolute. That to which the finger refers is at the same time the finger itself. The absolute is nowhere other than in the penetrating experience of the authentic here and now. In order to will this concrete "all form," the absolute must be grasped as "absolute nothingness"; otherwise it would be *something* and could only appear outside of a given concrete object—a "bad absoluteness" (or "bad infinity," in Hegel's sense). If that is so, is it then also impossible to grasp Christ's personality as the concrete true self of the infinite God? Would this logos of God then not be the absolute self-transmission in concrete name and occurrence? Admittedly language is then no longer only the descriptive logos, but the event opening itself up in hymn.

At the congress itself Waldenfels already gave a suggestion in this direction: silence and praise touch upon one another as opening up of the *presence*,[87] he says, and whether one calls this presence God or not is a secondary issue. Of primary interest is the praise that not only sings all of creation, but whose reality *is* the one and all of creation.

This congress was a milestone for Buddhist-Christian dialogue in Germany. This is in part because it also concerned itself with the Zen praxis of many Christians. Since Hugo M. Enomiya-Lassalle began creating Zen centers in Germany, the question has been left hanging whether it is possible to practice Zen without getting involved in the Buddhist background of this praxis. The answer made by this congress (in our opinion rightly) was that Buddhist meditation methods ought not be adopted unless the practitioners accept Buddhism's spiritual claim and its otherness, because the practice of Zen is *not* separable from Buddhism. Thus dialogue cannot reject conceptual clarification.

---

[85] Ibid., 20.

[86] Ibid., 11f., 62ff.

[87] Ibid., 12.

In agreement with this recommendation, so it appears, since the beginning of the 1980s events have tumbled over each other in Germany: forums, congresses, and publications on our theme are now too widespread to ignore. This demonstrates a fermentation process that has not yet come to an end. Therefore we will only briefly characterize the most important events. These mostly fall close to one another but are not formally linked.

Certainly the Japanese-German philosophers' colloquium must be named. In three conversations in 1981 and 1982 (Bad Homburg, Munich, Kyoto) philosophers examined the theme of "all unity" in both thought systems and traditions.[88] The theme of "all unity" has since Nishida been a "beginning of orientation of Japanese philosophy on the German tradition." Nishida and his successors (Kyoto school) could have connected themselves to Hegel and Schelling, the latter of whom was inspired by Schlegel's Sanskrit studies, so that the circle would now be complete. Characteristically, the collected articles of the Japanese-German philosophers' colloquium appeared, because of their nearness to Hegel's philosophy, in the publications of the International Hegel Union. The collection refers to European history of philosophy from Parmenides through Plotinus and Nicholas of Cusa to Hegel and compares it to Chinese-Japanese thought since Fa-tsang. The Japanese philosopher Tsujimura Koichi formulated this most precisely:[89] Plotinus in common with the entire West understood the One as foundation, cause, and above all principle, which could first be experienced in ecstasy. In the East, on the contrary, the Buddhist concept of *pratityasamutpada* (Japanese *engi*) points to a fundamental interrelationship, an original connection, in which every appearance *is* also every other. The One is thus not a principle in this case, but the relationship of each one to this "all." History thus should not be considered the secondary unfolding of a principle, but the original relation of each one to all.

Ueda Shizuteru carries this thought further:[90] If the One is understood as differentiated from the many, a fundamental opposition arises that begets in turn all further tensions (idealism against materialism, theism against atheism or nihilism, etc.) as Western history testifies. Thus one should ask in Zen: "What is the source of the One?"[91] Ueda provides the answer that the One can be traced back to a level beyond duality, where no substantial fixing is possible and the One is the same as nothingness and multiplicity. The collected volume from the conference demonstrates impressively that individual Christian thinkers (for example, Nicholas of Cusa) could also think in this way.

In 1982 a series of dialogue lectures took place at the University of Tübingen, which had as their theme, along with Islam and Hinduism, also Buddhism and its

---

[88] D. Henrich, ed., "Foreword," in *All-Einheit. Wege eines Gedankens in Ost und West* (Stuttgart: Klett-Cotta, 1985).

[89] K. Tsujimura, "Zur Differenz der All-Einheit im Westen und Osten," in D. Henrich, ed., 23ff.

[90] S. Ueda, "Vorüberlegungen zum Problem der All-Einheit im Zen-Buddhismus," in D. Henrich, ed., 136ff.

[91] Ibid., 137.

future in dialogue with Christianity. Hans Küng gave there the "Christian answers" to the characterization of Buddhism presented by Heinz Bechert. It is noteworthy that here for the first time things were not organized either all lumped together or dogmatically graded or only oriented on individual themes, but instead both religions were compared in their entire historical-paradigmatic formation and coordinated with one another. This dialogue series reached a wide public in the form of a book entitled *Christentum und Weltreligionen* (Christianity and world religions)[92] and since then has not only influenced Buddhist-Christian dialogue in Germany but has brought broad popular classes in general into the debate for the first time.

First, the historical Gautama and the historical Jesus were compared to one another, for which Hans Küng had recourse to Mensching's typology. Differences between the authoritative founders were not dogmatically played against each other but were viewed in their historical context. This made possible an unbiased evaluation of the phenomenon. This approach was significant, for example, on the question "*nirvana* or eternal life?"[93] Fortunately Küng does not attempt, like many Christian theologians before him, to answer this question as a matter of either/or. Instead, he first shows how much understanding of *nirvana* varies within Buddhism itself. Second, he comments that the Christian concept of eternal life is also unclear among Christians and can be presented in very different ways. At any rate, "eternal life," argues Küng, is "a condition that can only be experienced, not comprehended in our thought and descriptive categories." And this is also true of *nirvana*. So with both statements, one is not dealing with dogmatic fixable concepts but with symbols, the understanding of which always remains a challenge. This can perhaps be resolved at a deeper level in dialogue than in a situation without the critical corrective of the at-first-strange tradition.

On the other hand, Küng also makes it clear that Buddhism's apersonal interpretation of reality is just as inadequate as Christian anthropomorphic personalism. Küng therefore pleads for a transpersonal concept of final reality (of God, of *nirvana*, of the Buddha nature, etc.), that transcends the polarity of personal and apersonal and at the same time integrates them.[94]

Certainly, with these general bridging statements about the history of both cultures certain details remain unmentioned. Küng's complete paradigm analysis—seen by Bechert as methodical rather than critical, because for the sake of comparison he only wishes to relate the original forms of the religions to one another—can, however, provide clear evidence that there have been developments within each religion that were not accidental but followed an inner logic. These developments in turn have not produced a pure history of ideas but instead should be seen as ideas and symbols in their social-historical context.

This also applies to the process of interreligious dialogue. It more and more understands and changes the classical developed religions, and the cultures that

---

[92] H. Küng, et al., *Christentum und Weltreligionen* (Munich: Piper, 1984).
[93] Ibid., 462ff.
[94] Ibid., 552ff.

are indivisibly bound to them. Thus, in a collection of essays by Hans Waldenfels that appeared in 1982 with the suggestive title *Faszination des Buddhismus* (Fascination with Buddhism),[95] the discussion with the Kyoto school is not continued. Instead, the author approaches Buddhism as a means of inquiry into Western civilization in general. Buddhism's admonition to understand the "kenotic" as the basis of true communication would help Christianity look back on its own roots, and on the other hand could call Buddhism to responsibility to the "liberation praxis in the area of history."[96] Besides all analytical investigations on the problem of the personal, of language, of the relationship between prayer and meditation, of the question of suffering and tolerance in Buddhist-Christian dialogue, Waldenfels also finally speaks of the *religious alternative* that plays an increasing role in German Buddhism, too. As he presents it:

> In the case of Buddhism, however, individual fascination and the power of transmission meet with the offer of an alternative to a Christianity that no longer appears to offer a convincing way of life to many people in its sphere of influence. Indeed, in its ecclesiastical form, it appears today rather to stand in the way of the great ideals of its own origin.[97]

Thus the core of encounter with Buddhism receives more than a mention in Germany. It should be emphasized that at this point dialogue reaches far beyond academic interest. For example, the number of books and films about Buddhism, especially Buddhist meditation, has risen constantly. Especially psychological interpretations of the Buddhist path of meditation have become ever more popular with the help of Jungian psychology or in the realm of transpersonal psychology,[98] while theological discussion has now reached the Lutheran academy as well as the Catholic. Whether this will in fact lead to understanding and the West's coming to perceive Eastern ways of thought in their individuality and otherness remains to be seen. The voice of Jan van Bragt should certainly be heard in this context. In 1985 in the Dumoulin festschrift he wrote in regard to the question of whether Europe had struggled through to recognition of the pluralistic structure of equally valued races and cultures: "From my point of view it appears that this is certainly not true when seen from the East. On the contrary, Europe appears almost incredibly (according to Edward Conze) provincial, self-centered, self-indulgent, focused on itself."[99] This judgment especially applies to theology, not only what concerns accepted wisdom about each other's religions, but also what touches theological methodology. In Buddhism a unity of philosophy and

---

[95] H. Waldenfels, *Faszination des Buddhismus: Zum christlich-buddhistischen Dialog* (Mainz: Grünewald, 1982).

[96] Ibid., 10.

[97] Ibid., 174.

[98] See, for example, the collected volume edited by E. Zundel and B. Fittkau, *Spirituelle Wege und Transpersonale Psychotherapie* (Paderborn: Junfermann, 1989).

[99] J. v. Bragt, "Begegnung von Ost und West: Buddhismus und Christentum," in *Fernöstliche Weisheit und christlicher Glaube*, ed. H. Waldenfels and T. Immoos (Mainz: Grünewald, 1985), 269.

religion, logic and religious experience face us, which for the most part is not yet taken seriously enough in Buddhist-Christian dialogue.[100]

But how can Buddhism's foreignness be respected and understanding still be possible? Is there perhaps a starting point that would be so universal that it could serve as a basis for comparison and conversation for both religions, so that one could be certain that in dialogue the participants are really talking about the same thing?

ANTHROPOLOGY AS A BASIS FOR DISCUSSING THE RELIGIONS?

Human beings in relationship with God and the world must be the starting point of interreligious discussion, even if not necessarily the cardinal point, Hans Waldenfels suggested in 1983.[101] Thus he gave food for thought that the question of God in the final analysis may not be a question of reflection, speculation, or language form but an issue of experience "of life and death."[102] Focused on Hinduism but also applicable for the formula of "fascination with Buddhism," he spoke of the urgency of existential dialogue, in which the philosophical debate could only have a subsidiary, if also hermeneutically important, function:

> But it is precisely where the conviction is dominant that the One exists and works in all and behind all that will be in the consciousness of many believers, but also in the teachings of certain religious groups that the names and images of God are interchangeable today. One reflects that already today there is a possibility of religious dual and multiple membership. Thus the signs of an interreligious "intercommunion" appear everywhere on the horizon—and that in a time at which this question still awaits a convincing interconfessional solution.[103]

The Lutheran theologian Wolfhart Pannenberg also wished to take anthropology as the starting point for dialogue, although with a different focus from that of Waldenfels, because both religions inquire into subjectivity or the self, and the question is answered in different ways.[104] For Pannenberg, this is Paul's question—Who might the inner person be before and after conversion? (Rom 7:22). Also because, according to Luther, the subject itself is changed by belief, and it

---

[100] Ibid., 277.

[101] H. Waldenfels, "Gott-Mensch-Welt: Zum Angelpunkt des interreligiösen Gesprächs aus christlicher Sicht," in *Christliche Grundlagen des Dialogs mit den Weltreligionen*, ed. W. Strolz and H. Waldenfels (Göttingen: Vandenhoeck & Ruprecht, 1986), 84, which argues that the Christian-Buddhist dialogue should concentrate on anthropology. A newer collection of articles by H. Waldenfels under the title *An der Grenze des Denkbaren: Meditation—Ost und West* (Munich: Kösel, 1988) collects especially his articles from the 1970s, without including his more recent ideas. The American discussion of Buddhist-Christian dialogue as well as religio-sociological studies remain uncollected.

[102] H. Waldenfels, *An der Grenze des Denkbaren*, 37.

[103] Ibid.

[104] W. Pannenberg, *Christliche Spiritualität* (Göttingen: Vandenhoeck, 1986), 84.

is not just a quality being restored that it used to have, belief can be experienced as a "becoming moved," as an "experience of spiritual ecstasy that spreads itself out over us."[105] And this, then, is the true human identity, which was imprisoned and is now freed. To overcome the self-assertiveness of the empirical "I" is at the heart of Buddhist praxis as well as Lutheran theology, argues Pannenberg, and the death of the human "I," in Buddhism as in Christianity, will be the radical condition of salvation. The true form of the human being can only appear when the everyday "I" is negated.

For Pannenberg, the anthropological question is thus essentially theological. That means, however, that the starting point of dialogue cannot be the supposedly universal and culture-surmounting human experiences like love, creativity, suffering, or death. This is because, argues Pannenberg, every such experience is always already given its significance at the level of a specific religion.

Pannenberg, then, sees Buddhist and Lutheran-Christian spirituality in deep agreement with his fixing of true human identity in the "liberation from 'I.'" But what then is the essential difference between the two religions? Does it lie in their determination of the relationship between God and world—sharp division between God and world in Christianity versus complete unity of the absolute and secular reality in Buddhism? Pannenberg warns that caution is necessary. In Christianity, too, it is not possible to speak objectively of God, and God's kingdom is at the same time both transcendent and immanent. Also christologically a dualistic intellectual model is not permissible, and not only because Christ's unification of divine and human natures was declared (and the formula of the Council of Chalcedon is only one of several possibilities), but because, for example, for Luther, Christ points the way for every Christian who is called to "conformity with Christ." The "unity in diversity" that is necessary here reaches completion in the idea of the Trinity.[106]

What, then, is the difference between Buddhists and Christians? According to Pannenberg, it is only the *contemporary certainty of salvation* that, according to Christian belief, can only be attained within the church, because the church is the sole source of the sacraments.[107] However, we would like to object that this is an abstracting contention that does not necessarily result from Pannenberg's two basic premises, the reality of salvation in the religions and the trinitarian idea. For if in the religions God's salvation is present and the criterion for gaining it is Christian love of neighbor, then a perception of salvation must also be possible outside of Christianity, because the cognitive and ethical aspects of truth cannot be divided from one another in Christianity. If, however, there is valid perception of God that—to speak in Christian fashion—is indebted to God himself, then

---

[105] Ibid., 88.

[106] Ibid., 80ff. See also idem, "Auf der Suche nach dem wahren Selbst," in *Erlösung in Christentum und Buddhismus*, ed. A. Bsteh (Mödling, 1982), 128-46. For Luther, see M. v. Brück, *Einheit der Wirklichkeit* (Munich, 1986), chap. 7.

[107] W. Pannenberg, "Religion und Religionen: Theologische Erwägungen zu den Prinzipien eines Dialogues mit den Weltreligionen," in *Dialog aus der Mitte christlicher Theologie*, ed. A. Bsteh (Mödling, 1987), 189.

thus for non-Christians too a *final level* opens that makes possible the *certainty of salvation*. To be sure, the religions speak of this reality in different ways. Still, Buddhists and Christians are also in the deepest agreement on the issue of certainty of salvation, and there is no foundation in Christian theological terms for the pre-eminence of Christianity—at least not using the arguments presented by Pannenberg.

THE PROBLEM OF LANGUAGE

We have already referred to this issue several times. In dialogue between Buddhism and Christianity the problem of language arises with particular clarity. It cannot be solved by the remark that the essential can in any case only be experienced in silence. The difference is evident: Christianity speaks of creator, creation, a human selfhood, a colorfully painted fulfillment in God's kingdom, and so forth, while Buddhism employs a negative form of language and for the most part rejects all these metaphors. Both religions develop a "suffering for the transcendence of the absolute,"[108] but each in a different form. Christianity employs the agapeic *language of love*, and Buddhism the gnostic *language of conviction*,[109] with which, however, each aspect can contain that of the other in itself.

What does this mean for mutual understanding? Catholic Christian and scholar of literature Walter Strolz made an important remark on this subject in 1986: even if what each means never exhausts itself in language, still a "trust in language" is important, which initiates in silence. As he says: "So far can one comprehend the essence of language that that which is not said cannot be grasped or explained, which brings us closer to the *origin of language*, encompassing being and nothingness, life and death."[110] Language for Strolz knows an "overlapping depth of meaning"[111] in which the human situation comes to linguistic expression in such a way that the religions can and must encounter one another despite all differences. In Buddhism as in Christianity the human being is prone to change, so the language of religion is also prone to change. Indeed, it *must* change, if what is in Christian meaning is to be brought to validity in a linguistically meaningful way for the Buddhists. The linguistic change in Christianity that Strolz recommends concerns above all the far-flung dualistic symbolism and conceptualization that possibly was always inappropriate, that creator and creation could never be divided, even if they are not identical.[112] On the other hand, Buddhism also has something to learn. It must ask itself whether in light of the current spiritual situation "the Buddhist lack of differentiation can be the basis and guiding star for responsible transmission.[113] Strolz cites in this regard the Kyoto school philosopher Ueda Shizuteru, who has shown that, in face of the

---

[108] Ibid., 195.

[109] This formulation influenced Aloysius Pieris; in the Greek Bible *gnosis* is salvific perception and *agape* is taking part in the self-giving love of God.

[110] W. Strolz, *Heilswege der Weltreligionen*, vol. 2 (Herder: Freiburg, 1986), 27, cf. 210.

[111] Ibid., 158.

[112] Ibid., 56.

[113] Ibid., 199.

technological-dominating thought in Japan, Buddhist teaching can all too quickly transform into a "destructive lack of differentiation" and ambiguity of values, which is directly contrary to Buddhist ideals.[114]

Methodologically significant are these remarks of Strolz (which go back to the interreligious encounters of the Oratio Dominica Institute of the Herder Press in Freiburg, which Strolz led for years) that the Christian-Buddhist conversation about philosophical insights cannot take place in a no-man's land or in a spiritual climate of the past. It is the industrial technological society that expects answers from both religions in appropriate linguistic form. That is the challenge to dialogue.

This challenge was taken up in a dialogue conversation in November 1984 with the theme "Human Responsibility for a Livable World in Christianity, Hinduism, and Buddhism." It was organized and published by the Oratio Dominica Institute under the direction of Walter Strolz and with the participation of the philosopher of religion Raimon Panikkar, the Kyoto philosopher Ueda Shizuteru, the Basel theologian Heinrich Ott, and others. Besides explaining the different positions in the history of each religion, the editors come to the conclusion that "the connecting point between the sacred and profane, the timeless and the temporal, the otherworldly and this-worldly may not be overlooked. Somehow the final result is connected to the preliminary."[115] How this connection is understood, what it consists of in particulars, and how it can motivate both individual and societal dealings is contested not just in interreligious dialogue, but also intra-religiously. That is, *within* each of the religions there are significant *differences* in *social*, *ethical*, and *political* positions that cannot be pushed to one side in future Buddhist-Christian dialogue.

But the theologically based engagement with other religions also still varies greatly in the Christian churches. We would like to draw attention to two recently published official church documents, one from the Catholic position and one from the Lutheran position.

"Dialogue and Proclamation"

A text published in 1991 by the Papal Council for Interreligious Dialogue entitled "Dialogue and Proclamation"[116] carries the tendency to engage with other religions further, in a way already characterized by the Second Vatican Council.[117] The text says unmistakably:

---

[114] S. Ueda, "Sein-Nichts-Weltveratwortung im Zen-Buddhismus," in *Die Verantwortung des Menschen für eine bewohnbare Welt im Christentum, Hinduismus und Buddhismus,* ed. R. Panikkar and W. Strolz (Freiburg: Herder, 1985), 37-58.

[115] R. Panikkar and W. Strolz, eds., 7.

[116] "Dialogue and Proclamation," in *Origins*, CNS Documentary Service, vol. 21/8 (July 4, 1991): 122-35. See P. Schmidt-Leukel, "Der schwierige Weg vom Gegeneinander zum Miteinander der Religionen. Neue Dokumenta zur theologischen Grundlegung des interreligiösen Dialogs," *Una Sancta* 47/1 (1992): 54-77.

[117] For an overarching analysis of the dialogue documents of the Council, see J. Zehner, *Der notwendige Dialog: Die Weltreligionen in katholischer und evangelischer Sicht* (Gütersloh: Gütersloher Verlagshaus, 1992), 19-64.

• *Other religions are valid paths to salvation.* This is true, the document argues, because God created all human beings in his image and planned only *one* history of salvation for all humanity, so the church and other religious organizations find themselves on a common pilgrimage to a completion that is still forthcoming for all.

• Not all that calls itself religious is good, and *for Christians, the only standard* by which to differentiate between salutary and unsalutary *is the values of the gospel*. When others follow these values in their lives, they implicitly follow God's healing will, which manifested itself in Jesus Christ, even if their praxis is founded on another basis.

• Even though all of truth is manifest in Jesus Christ, it does not follow that the Christian is in full possession of the truth. *The search for truth*, purification, and steps toward a genuine way of life are much more *a never-ending process* in which the religions in dialogue must learn from one another.

This theological inclusivity of the Papal Council makes the point that in the final analysis Christian proclamation is a gift of God to all peoples. It also makes mutual criticism possible, which in dialogical fulfillment can lead to a deepening of the understanding of truth by all who take part. Proclamation here is no longer mission in the classical sense of converting others to one's own standpoint and incorporating them into one's own institution, but mutual respect and critical solidarity, in which each brings its own standards into dialogue.

"Religions, Religiosity, and Christian Belief"

The German Lutheran Church's study "Religions, Religiosity, and Christian Belief," written in 1991, presents a very different basic stand toward other religions.[118] This study on the one hand approves of German Protestantism's desire for theological interreligious dialogue. On the other hand, however, it is expressed through an "ambiguity and unclarity of many formulations,"[119] because it would like to engage in dialogue but in principle cannot surmount the exclusive Christian claim to salvation: (a) It is impossible to say whether other religions convey salvation or not; thus (b) other religions are again degraded to objects of Christian evangelization.[120] In this it becomes clear that the desire in interreligious practice is to pray *for* rather than *with* others.[121] (c) If, however, *communicatio in*

---

[118] *Religionen, Religiosität und christlicher Glaube: Eine Studie,* published by the leaders of the Arnoldshainer conference and the church directorship of the United Evangelical-Lutheran Church of Germany from the offices of the Arnoldshainer conference and the Lutheran Church office, Hannover (Gütersloh: Gütersloher Verlagshaus, 1991).

[119] P. Schmidt-Leukel, "Der schwierige Weg," 61.

[120] Although it means on one side that religions should not be the objects of mission, on the other side a theological foundation for this is lacking, as Schmidt-Leukel rightly points out ("Der schwierige Weg," 67). For if I as a Christian am not certain that the Other is saved, I must missionize out of love.

[121] This attitude toward interreligious prayer was underscored by the Lutheran Church in Bayern, despite substantially different judgments by the three Lutheran theological faculties in Bavaria (in *Nachrichten der Ev.-Luth. Kirche in Bayern* 46, no. 23/24 [1991]: 478). The theological evaluation by the faculties are themselves printed on 455-58.

sacris is denied, interreligious "cohabitation"[122] of people of different beliefs is reduced to a secularly understood sense of fellow humanity. This might suffice for a post-Enlightenment European, but never for a Buddhist, Hindu, or Muslim. With this a European thought pattern would again be forced on the other religions, which would make dialogue more difficult or impossible.

The study approaches Buddhism with a Christian theological bias. This comes to expression, for example, in the scandalous division it makes between Buddhism and Tibetan Buddhism, which is denigrated as "lamaism."[123] Here, unfortunately, too little can be seen of the decades-long debate that brought noticeable results in Buddhist-Christian dialogue in Germany, as we have presented above.

HERMENEUTICS

As significant as the exertions in Buddhist-Christian dialogue have been in recent decades, it has not yet proven possible to agree upon a single hermeneutic method. In other words, the question of how and under what circumstances understanding is possible for the other without being understood too strongly and one-sidedly through one's own judgments or prejudices has still not been resolved in a satisfying way. On this issue a new milestone has been erected by the monumental work of the Munich Catholic theologian Perry Schmidt-Leukel, *Den Löwen brüllen hören* (1992). This work is of significance not only for Buddhist-Christian dialogue in Germany but for interreligious dialogue worldwide.

The author demonstrates that earlier comparisons of Buddhism and Christianity have mostly been marked by the transference of Christian thought categories onto Buddhism (sometimes totally consciously for apologetic purposes, but often also unconsciously). The result has been that not only a part of the pair being compared but also the *standard* for comparison has been defined in a Christian manner. This has often led to a distorted understanding of Buddhism.[124] For example, in comparing God and *nirvana* or soul and *anatta*, scholars have proceeded from a beginning in which they imagine the two as of equivalent importance, which is not the case. Besides this, in past dialogue Buddhism and Christianity have mostly been handled in a generalizing fashion, while in reality individual epochs and lines of tradition have given rise to very different forms of each religion. The correspondences or differences, he argues, can only be established from examining the complete texture of each tradition. However, because of historical superimpositions and dislocations this is such a complex undertaking that one must at least begin with a relatively simple and uncontested starting point. This starting point, argues Schmidt-Leukel, can be found in *basic human experiences* that appear in all cultures (however differently they relate with one another). While Buddhism proceeds from the *experience of transitoriness*, it is the *experience of personal relationship* that stands at the center of the Judeo-Christian experience. All further differences in emphasis of specific theoretical

---

[122] The expression was coined by the Heidelberg theologian Theo Sundermeier, a co-author of the study.

[123] See the recension of the study by R. Ficker in *Dialog der Religionen* 2 (1991): 222.

[124] P. Schmidt-Leukel, *Den Löwen brüllen hören,* 50.

or ethical aspects in Buddhism and Christianity can be traced back to this difference. This argument is not unlike the experiential and linguistic model of the two religions presented by Aloysius Pieris, which is based on the difference between *gnostic* and *agapeic* approaches.

Schmidt-Leukel does indeed know that these basic experiences are also linguistic as soon as they become known to individuals. Languages, however, rest upon cultural traditions that are specific to each case. There is no such thing as a consciously perceived "unsignified experience."[125] So, too, Buddhist experience of transitoriness and its significance is entirely embedded in much older specifically Indian mythical fundamental structures and the categories that proceed from that source, as is condensed in the concept of *karma* and time *(kala)*. The situation is similar for the Judeo-Christian tradition of experience of personal relationship. These basic human experiences are transmitted historically. Thus they cannot form a starting point that would be independent from each's linguistic or religious tradition without pre-assumptions and still be generally insightful. But at least the basic experiences of death, transitoriness, love, and so on form a field of human commonality from which understanding of the Other becomes more easily possible than if one begins with abstract concepts like God, Buddha nature, and so forth. Still, the basic experiences are not ahistorical events.

For this reason, we would like to propose, the hermeneutic criteria can first be found in the *contemporary* and *topical* dialogue process between Buddhists and Christians; it is not to be found in assuming something beyond the accepted grounds of the religions. Much more, both partners carry on dialogue on the background of their own traditions and with connections to it. The Buddhist-Christian dialogue hitherto has demonstrated impressively that in this method each conceptualization appears in tentativeness and relativity, although it refers to a final standard. Both partners learn from one another in this conversation—and let themselves mutually "transform" (J. Cobb)—as much for understanding of their own tradition as for interreligious hermeneutics.

RESULTS AND PROSPECTS

RESULTS

• The Buddhist-Christian dialogue in Germany is gaining in density and depth. However, few established theologians yet regard it as vital for Christianity's self-consciousness in the modern world. The churches have not yet sufficiently recognized that the plurality of religions in modern pluralistic societies will fundamentally change their classical approach to other religions. The most important dialogue themes in Germany (God's personality and impersonality, language and

---

[125] This is a similar problem to unsignified, and thus independent of language, mystical experiences. See M. v. Brück, "Mystische Erfahrung, religiöse Tradition und die Wahrheitsfrage," 81ff.

silence, justification and "self-redemption," meditation and dogma, dialogical hermeneutics) in the 1970s anticipated much of the content that would mark the better-publicized and institutionally better-supported American discussion since the 1980s (American Academy of Religion, Society for Buddhist-Christian Studies).

• While during the 1920s it was predominantly Protestant theologians who were engaged in dialogue (Otto, Mensching, Heiler [who became a Catholic], and later Tillich), since the Second Vatican Council the weight of dialogue has lain on the Catholic side. Up to the present, German Protestantism has lacked a clear, affirmative statement on the reality of salvation in other religions.

• Practical dialogue is by no means limited to libraries and academic conferences. Instead, increasingly it also appears at the level of *meditation praxis*, which in Germany is offered by ever more centers, both Buddhist and Christian. A certain "double residence" in Christianity and Buddhism is no longer a rarity for many engaged Christians; a certain synthesis of elements from both religions distinguishes this practice. It is, however, too early to discern whether this could lead in the future to an amalgamation of the two religions in Germany. The theoretical reflection of those who have experienced this synthesis has not yet been in the foreground, but it is necessary if contemporary praxis is to be linked to its own history and tradition.

PROSPECTS

• The assumption that *the* East is meditative while *the* West represents rationality has proven to be too simplistic. The history of *both* traditions is—with different emphases—marked by *both* aspects of human experience. In Germany there is a longing to bring rational, technological society into balance with the help of a wholeness-focused, meditative lifestyle, without turning its back on the social realities of life. In other words, few become (Buddhist) monks or nuns, but many integrate meditative consciousness training into their daily lives. It goes without saying that this will deeply change the traditional forms of Christian-signified experience of the world. Whether this will lead to an identity break within Christian history cannot be foretold.

• The dialogue situation in Germany is especially characterized by the fact that even in ecclesiastical circles and religious orders, more or less "church-approved" Buddhist meditation is practiced. The de facto penetration of the church with Buddhist thought and Buddhist praxis has made more progress than theological reflection.

• This also shows itself in the fact that laypeople from both religions want to encounter one another without bias and bring forward their own traditions in an effort to find answers to contemporary questions. Thus since the Lutheran Church congress in Frankfurt (1987) Buddhists have regularly taken part in work groups at successive congresses or have presented themselves in their own integrated programs. At the Munich church congress in 1993 a joint Christian-Buddhist morning meditation and a dialogue arrangement took place with the XIV Dalai

Lama and the German philosopher Carl-Friedrich von Weizsäcker on the theme "Peace—Justification—Protection of Creation," which was the preliminary— and in Lutheran circles contested—high point of this encounter. Lutheran and Catholic academies have invited more and more Buddhist teachers to thematically organized conferences and to meditation seminars, and this cooperation may gain even more intensity in the future.

6

United States of America

In this chapter we wish to ask why the United States of America has become the showplace of Buddhist-Christian dialogue in the world today. The reasons lie in American history and current processes of change in American society that in other ways also include Europe (multicultural society). But does the multireligious situation in the United States mean that dialogue has had influence on political discourse? In the modern pluralistic industrial societies the future of traditional religious values in general is in question: Can religions or interreligious dialogue contribute something to the search for meaning, community, and peaceful conflict resolution? What degree of institutionalization has dialogue in the United States reached, and what are its essential themes?[1]

THE DIALOGUE SITUATION

Since about 1980 the center of Buddhist-Christian dialogue has shifted from Theravada Buddhist Sri Lanka to Christian-shaped America. Especially middle-class American Christians are involved, who enter dialogue with American Buddhists of the same social class. Principally this has taken the form of an extremely interesting *academic discussion* of the relationships between Buddhism and Christianity, which has its roots in America's intellectual history in the nineteenth century. At the second International Buddhist-Christian Conference, held under the auspices of the University of Hawaii in 1984, the Cobb-Abe Group (named after its founders, the Protestant theologian John Cobb and the Kyoto school philosopher Abe Masao) was founded for theological exchange with the philosophical Kyoto school. Since that time this dialogue group has arranged a large number of events. Besides this impetus for dialogue, the majority of Western academic Buddhologists work in the United States. Among them, Berkeley is the seat of the International Association of Buddhist Studies, which also publishes a journal. The Hawaii International Buddhist-Christian Conferences began

---

[1] In this chapter we will discuss more the framework for dialogue and less the detailed content of the argumention on individual themes, because this discussion between Buddhism and Christianity in the United States has so strongly dominated the current international debate that it requires separate systematic treatment elsewhere.

in Honolulu in 1980. They were organized by David Chappell, then professor of Chinese religions at the University of Hawaii. Chappell began editing the journal *Buddhist-Christian Studies* in 1981. Since 1987 this journal has been published by the Society for Buddhist-Christian Studies. In recent years it has taken a leading role in worldwide dialogue.[2]

Unlike Asia (especially Sri Lanka), where dialogue takes place between religious groups and has great political significance, in America it takes place between individuals. The numerous Christian religious groups in the United States, especially the conservative evangelical churches, have hardly been involved at all.

THE ONE-HUNDREDTH ANNIVERSARY OF THE CHICAGO WORLD PARLIAMENT OF RELIGIONS, 1993

The Chicago World Parliament of Religions in 1893 was a great event in America's religious history. It also marks the beginning of Buddhist-Christian dialogue in the United States. The one-hundredth anniversary of this memorable occasion was celebrated in 1993 in an event that drew seven thousand participants from around the world. The centenary parliament throws a floodlight on the contemporary dialogue situation in America. It is especially clear that the religious demographic structure of America itself has fully changed—in the greater Chicago area today there are more Hindus than Episcopalians, more Buddhists than Hindus, and more Muslims than Jews. In 1893 the Americans for the first time met representatives of the Asian religions; in 1993 Asian religions groups from Chicago organized the reception for the many foreign visitors.

The 1993 parliament was not as well attended by conservative Christians as the one a hundred years before. This is probably connected to the fact that the interreligious dialogue movement, which especially since World War II has also played a public role in America, has broken away from its roots. At any event, this anniversary conference was not officially organized by either the major Protestant churches or the Catholic church. The reason for this was that the World Council of Churches, like the Vatican, at first hesitated to take part at all in the fall 1993 event. Finally, the centenary conference was called together by a local council under the leadership of the president of the McCormick Theological Seminary of Chicago. The money came from various organizations and private donors. Religious leaders of various traditions acted as "presidents of the parliament," including the fourteenth Dalai Lama and the Syrian Orthodox bishop of Delhi, Paulos Mar Gregorios. This is not the way the interreligious dialogues that are planned by the World Council of Churches or the Vatican are initiated. For

---

[2] Naturally it is no coincidence that it was Hawaii that provided the starting point for this sort of intensive Buddhist-Christian encounter. In Hawaii, ethnic Buddhists (Japanese and Chinese) have lived side by side with Christian Americans of European descent since the second half of the nineteenth century. On the island of Maui alone (population 80,000) there are approximately 250 religious groupings, of which many have an Asian-Buddhist background (see W. Kreisel, *Die ethnischen Gruppen der Hawaii-Inseln* [Wiesbaden: Steiner, 1984]).

them, the dialogue among representatives of the meeting religious hierarchies ought to be "official." The Chicago conference, like the first World Parliament of Religions in 1893, had exactly the opposite features—organized by laypeople, governed by committees, carried out by volunteers, it demonstrated how very different groups and individuals could commit themselves to contribute to peace in the world and among its religions. The most important result of the meeting was the "Declaration of World Ethics" of 4 September 1993, initiated and largely formulated by the Christian theologian Hans Küng. In this document the attending religious leaders solemnly pledged to make conscious and to make into reality the common foundation of unshifting ethical directions that already exist in the religions, based on the "fundamental unity of the human family."

Most dialogues in the United States are carried out by laypeople and mostly draw attention outside of the regular ecclesiastical institutions. They are motivated by an enthusiasm that is still lacking in the traditional church organizations in regard to this issue.

When we speak of lay dominance in this and other dialogue meetings, that does not mean that the participants were not educated or that the clergy was closed out. Among the participants in the centenary World Parliament of Religions were priests, monks, and nuns. American academics are naturally also engaged in these dialogues. This is not new within American religious history. For a long time intellectual liberals have operated as moderators of such exchanges "outside of the church."

If, as we will show, the professors and students of religious studies in American colleges and universities have played the greatest role in American interreligious dialogue, we must seek the reasons for this in a wider context. We can best show this by turning once again to the first great Buddhist-Christian conversation in America—the first World Parliament of Religions in Chicago in 1893. The epoch-making significance of this event, however, makes sense only in light of American religious history in the eighteenth and nineteenth centuries. Therefore we will now discuss this background briefly, as far as it is necessary to understand the beginning of interreligious dialogue in the last decade of the nineteenth century.

HISTORICAL BACKGROUND

PECULIARITIES OF RELIGIOUS SOCIALIZATION IN AMERICA

If one considers the religious history of America in the eighteenth and nineteenth centuries, it is astonishing that this of all lands should have become the showplace of Buddhist-Christian dialogue in the twentieth century. The Calvinistic Puritans considered New England, their new home, to be their new Jerusalem.[3] They regarded themselves as the elect and felt that they must maintain a

---

[3] The first group of Pilgrims from England arrived on the coast of Massachusetts on the Mayflower in 1620.

strictly regimented and pure societal life to maintain their position as God's chosen people. Thus, mixing with outsiders or indeed with natives was prohibited. The Catholic Spaniards in Louisiana and elsewhere, who still regarded Spain as their homeland (and thus perhaps for that reason had greater reserve about their cultural identity), could acculturate themselves more easily. They married into the American Indian communities and converted the natives with such great industry that we still find their "missions" all along the California coast (e.g., Santa Barbara, Santa Clara). The Puritans were more stand-offish in this regard.[4]

This situation changed in the first half of the eighteenth century as cities grew and trade became more important.[5] The smoothly flowing socioeconomic model of a formerly strictly organized society solidified into a pronounced "providential order." The first great Protestant Awakening movement was an answer to this social change: people wanted to halt the falling away from "true piety." This movement passed right through the classical confessional dividing lines throughout the country and included various theologians. Similarly to German Pietism and English Methodism, the First Great Awakening had an emotional impact and set the stage for experience of spiritual rebirth, which was supposed to bring about or express an unmediated relationship with God. Such emotional outbursts were regarded with suspicion by the traditional Puritans—they focused on a patient and disciplined interior life.

Jonathan Edwards (1703-58) was a significant figure in this movement. Although the emphasis on an entirely *personal relationship* with God in the awakened circles dissolved the community ideal of the Puritans, this First Awakening movement, as the first really self-standing American religious movement, led at least indirectly to the development of American national feeling, linking together individualism, independence from the state-church systems of Europe, and economic expansion into the "New World." This in turn was one of the preconditions for the American Revolution. The Declaration of Independence invoked the "deity" (not the Christian God); the Constitution, the most secular document of its age, did not even mention this "deity" a single time. The only direct reference to religion is found in Article 6 of the Constitution, which formulates negatively that *no* religious test may be required as qualification for holding public office. At the beginning of the first amendment (that is, the Bill of Rights), the principle of strict division of church and state was established: Congress will pass no law that shows partiality to any religion or that would hinder the free practice of religion.

In Europe the seventeenth-century religious wars between Catholics and Protestants had led to a compromise that signified the tolerance of different Christian

---

[4] There were indeed a few exceptions. The Protestants at first began to missionize the native Americans in fine style, when the government brought them onto reservations. The conversion of African slaves, on the contrary, followed a different course; they lived so close to their masters that the purification of the pagan practices appeared as Christian duty and social necessity.

[5] On the following, cf. P. W. Williams, *America's Religions: Traditions and Cultures* (New York: Macmillan, 1990), 127f.

belief systems: *cuius regio eius religio*—each ruler should decide the confession of his land. But religious tolerance in the personal sense, in which people can choose their own religion on their own responsibility and based on a personal conception of God, first became real in the American colonies, first in Rhode Island, then in Pennsylvania (home of the Quakers). In the new United States religion was privatized, in part because there was no consensus about which religion the state ought to support officially. More important, however, was another reason. The representatives of both sides—the confessions and the states—feared that either the state might be corrupted by religious influences or the churches by state surveillance. The liberal Deist Thomas Jefferson (1743-1826) and the Enlightenment Anglican James Madison (1751-1836) thus took care that the separation of church and state could not be revoked.[6] In this way, religious tolerance developed into an *individual right to freedom of religion*.

The current interreligious dialogue is based on these principles of American history, although the founding fathers could not have foreseen this development. At that time America was predominantly Protestant. Thus, for example, school prayer was perceived as completely natural, since, after all, all the students were Christians. There were few Jews or Catholics, and both minorities were completely integrated into American society; this remained the case until the recent past. Besides this, Jews and Catholics prayed to the same God as the Protestant majority. Hindus, Buddhists, and Muslims were not a factor, because America was not a colonial power and not involved in the cultural repercussions linked to colonialism, as was the case with countries like England. In London the inhabitants included British subjects from non-Christian cultures, whereas in New York in the late nineteenth century the only demographic groups that had come together were from the Old World.

But in the middle of the nineteenth century America experienced an unparalleled economic expansion. In a shorter time than seemed possible, hundreds became enormously rich, but hundreds of thousands were impoverished and settled in the slums of the major cities. The mid-nineteenth century saw the opening-up of the continent by a railroad network and the expansion of America's merchant marine on the high seas (one calls to mind the rise of the industrial giant Cornelius Vanderbilt, 1794-1877). In addition, the California Gold Rush, the related industrialization of the West Coast, and the opening of the Pacific (especially to Japan) followed in short order. In short, America saw the unbounded subordination of all values for the sake of material profit. The whole phenomenon naturally provoked reactions. Among American intellectuals a climate arose that created a nature romanticism, praising a noncivilized lifestyle in face of this rapidly progressing urbanization and industrialization. In this context, non-European/American cultures came under regard. This development encouraged interest in Asian religions; to see the process, one need only consider the importance of the American essayist Ralph Waldo Emerson (1803-82). Emerson and his friend Henry

---

[6] Thomas Jefferson was the third president of the United States from 1801 to 1809 and the author of the Declaration of Independence; James Madison was his successor as president (1809-17) and brought about the composition of the Bill of Rights.

David Thoreau (1817-62) were leading figures of the New England Transcendentalists. They became familiar with Hindu, Buddhist, and Taoist texts through the earliest translations, and were two of the first thinkers to understand the difference between Buddhism and Hinduism. Emerson's representations of nature and the natural life were linked, for example, to Taoist and Buddhist views.[7]

The Transcendentalists were under the influence of "transcendental" thought, which reached America from Germany by way of England. It was inspired by German Romanticism. At the heart of the movement is the conviction that there is a sense of a deeper, purer original truth that lies hidden behind all the appearances of reality but is present everywhere in nature. This truth, they believed, is accessible to human beings, if only we can surmount the limitations of culture (family, institutions, even organized religion).

Emerson and his group did not limit themselves only to ideas but in 1844 undertook an experiment in communal life in accordance with their ideals—the Brook Farm. It was anti-urban and anti-materialistic in its orientation but only survived a few years. Henry David Thoreau then retreated to Walden Pond, in order to live entirely in nature. Emerson's and Thoreau's experiments with an alternative lifestyle influenced no less a figure than Mahatma Gandhi.[8] Their influence can also be traced in the United States right up to the current alternative-culture scene. Emerson quarreled with Thoreau over the question of whether such a lifestyle would permit engagement in daily political life; Emerson thought it should, while Thoreau regarded a full retreat from the world as essential.

This short-lived cultural movement of the Transcendentalists left an extraordinarily lasting literary and intellectual heritage. Their ideas were spread by the journal *Dial* and later through the literary journal *North American Review* (founded in 1815), as well as through Emerson's lecture circuits to universities and churches. Transcendentalism influenced academics and intellectuals in Boston and Cambridge and taught an optimistic gospel of human growth and social progress. In retrospect it is possible to say that this movement created the intellectual avant-garde of America in its time.

It is no coincidence that Emerson was a Unitarian. Unitarianism is a Christian tradition that goes back to anti-trinitarian "free spirits" of the Reformation era, like Michael Servetus (1511-53) in Geneva and the Italian Socinians in the sixteenth century. They owe less to the ideas of the reformers than to humanism and Renaissance philosophy. The movement began in Italy, spread to Poland (where it was persecuted by the forces of the Counter Reformation), thence reached Holland and England, and appeared in the New World shortly after the American Revolution. Enlightenment Unitarians like Joseph Priestley (1733-1804) combined study of natural science and theology. They disavowed the Trinity and preached that there is only one God. For them, Jesus was an inspired and important human being but not God. Theologically, this movement is liberal, intellectual, and humanistic, but not secular. Because they were persecuted in their homeland, the

---

[7] See H. Welsh, *Taoism: The Parting of the Way* (Boston: Beacon, 1957).

[8] Gandhi knew both through their writings (see M. Chatterjee, *Gewaltfrei widerstehen: Gandhis religiöses Denken* [Gütersloh: Gütersloher Verlagshaus/Chr. Kaiser, 1994]).

Unitarians immigrated to America. Once in the New World they developed in a new direction that had its start with events during the Great Awakening movement after 1740. The Awakening had caused a schism within the Congregationalists (who had come out of Puritanism)—into the "New Lights" (the circle around the already-mentioned Jonathan Edwards) and the "Old Lights" (based in Boston). The latter criticized the awakened "enthusiastic" preaching of the former group and developed an American form of Unitarianism. What this meant was that they turned against the Calvinistic view of a fearsome God above and a fallen humanity below. Instead of human fear of possible damnation because of their sin, these new Unitarians preached God's inward gifts and human capacity for good.[9]

The Unitarians clustered in the cities and found adherents especially among the educated. The country people of this time were attracted by another movement, that of the Universalists. They, too, rejected the Calvinist doctrine of predestination (according to which salvation will only come to those chosen by God) and believed that in the end all humankind would be saved (including also the "pagans").[10] In their churches one can see religious symbols that originate in the various world religions. Quite naturally, interreligious dialogue results from this belief, since it rests on the conviction that *one* God is present behind all religions, who wishes the salvation, enlightenment, and liberation of all people.

The American Unitarian Association was founded in 1825. The Unitarians had mostly spiritualized the views of the thinkers of the Scottish Enlightenment as well as the Common Sense philosophy of authors like David Hume, according to whose philosophy the sense organs transmit valid perceptions. This liberal spiritual current first won entry to Harvard University and finally took over its spiritual leadership. From this heritage grew the modern Divinity School of this famous university.[11]

During the great economic and social changes in America in the late eighteenth century there appeared a Second Great Awakening movement (c. 1790-1830). At this time, as great masses migrated westward, many new religious and quasi-religious movements arose, which today would be described with expressions like *perennial philosophy*,[12] *harmonialism*, or *occultism*. From the Mormons to the Swedenborgians, from Victorian spiritualism to Christian Science, from Mesmerism to pragmatic research on the varieties of religious experience (as with William James), the young America discovered new paths to religious self-realization and the synoptic presentation of "health, wealth, and metaphysics,"

---

[9] The break between the Unitarians and the Congregationalists in 1785 did not concern this revision of the doctrine of predestination but the doctrine of the Trinity.

[10] This group united with the Unitarians in 1961 and now bears the name Unitarian Universalists.

[11] In the twentieth century Unitarianism, with its emphasis on ethics, moved still closer to humanism, and became independent from theology or indeed from belief in God (see Williams, 204-9).

[12] The eternally same philosophy as foundation of all schools of thought and religious traditions in the various cultures.

which the traditional churches had been unable to oppose. From this movement there are direct connections to the New Thought movement of the 1890s and the success-oriented "positive thinking" of the 1920s.[13] From there it was only a step to the New Age movement of our time.[14]

In 1893, America had spread to the west coast of the continent and had created contacts over the Pacific as far as Japan. Those who looked beyond the horizon of the Old World and the Christian tradition felt themselves drawn to Eastern mysticism, as it was popularized with much success in America by the newly founded Theosophical Society. Victorian spiritualism and theosophy appear naive and inaccurate from the modern perspective, in ways that affected their knowledge of the "real" East. In their time, however, these movements were pioneering efforts. They were catalysts for Western intellectuals to come to know the "Orient."

In the mid-nineteenth century Buddhism was still little-known in America. For example, Emerson in 1845 still regarded the Bhagavadgita as a "very important Buddhist book."[15] However, the Buddha was already compared to Jesus, Muhammad, Zoroaster, and Confucius as a great figure of religious history. Thoreau had indeed translated into English and published passages from Eugène Burnouf's (1801-1852) French translation of the Lotus sutra, but in general Buddhism received less attention at first than Islam and Confucianism (67). It was only in 1860 that Buddhism finally reached public awareness. Even then, dependent on European historians (including Burnouf himself), Buddhist *nirvana* was interpreted as absolute negation and American scholars turned away with horror from this "passive and world-denying philosophy of life" (68). The American-Victorian quaternity of theism-individualism-activism-optimism, which was at least the creed of the urbanized Protestant middle class, made heavy weather with reports about Buddhism. In their negative valuation of Buddhism there were hardly any differences between the major Protestant confessions and the conservative Unitarians. Buddhism, as Pastor Edward Hungerford (1829-1911, from Menden, Connecticut) said in an article in *The New Englander* in 1874, is neither a religion nor a philosophy, but pure pessimism, which could not possibly have any future (78). Oddly, Hungerford and many others could not explain how such a religion could have spread over all Asia in a short time and could have brought about great cultural accomplishments.

Some interpreters regarded the Buddha as a moralist and social reformer of India's corrupt caste system. For this reason American authors showed him respect, for example, the China missionary Rosewall H. Graves (1833-1912) and

---

[13] See Norman Vincent Peale's bestseller, *The Power of Positive Thinking* (1952).

[14] P. W. Williams, 307-19.

[15] T. A. Tweed, "The Seeming Anomaly of Buddhist Negation: American Encounters with Buddhist Distinctiveness 1858-1877," *Harvard Theological Review* 83/1 (1990): 66. The material is further unfolded in T. A. Tweed, *The American Encounter with Buddhism, 1844-1912: Victorian Culture and the Limits of Dissent* (Bloomington, Ind.: Indiana University Press, 1992). Page references in text are to the first-named article.

many others (71, 81). Within the Buddha himself they made a distinction between a negative philosophy and an admirable morality. Indeed, Buddhism was elevated to the status of a supposed "Indian Protestantism."

The Unitarian circles were also hard on Buddhism. James F. Clarke (1810-88), a prominent Unitarian and probably the first academic in the United States to teach comparative religious studies, perceived Buddhism as "quietist" and separated from the world, although doing good was still a part of the religion. He was only able to bear Buddhism in general inasmuch as he read a belief in God and the immortality of the soul into Buddhist texts (84).

Only gradually did a more positive image of Buddhism become established among the liberal Unitarians, Transcendentalists, and the Free Religious Association. An author from this circle indeed regarded Buddhism as the most superior religion.[16] Charles D. Mills (1821-1900) wrote the first survey book to appear in America about Buddhism in 1876. He solved the old problem of "world rejection" by attributing to the Buddha himself the affirmative and world-forming element of the religion, and the negation and emotional cooling to later Buddhist philosophers (84).

By approximately 1870 the opinion about Buddhism had finally changed. In 1872 the social reformer and free religious thinker Thomas W. Higginson in a speech praised the Buddha especially for his tolerance. Higginson was deeply moved by the "beauty and deep insight" of the classical Buddhist *Dhammapada*, with which he had become acquainted in Max Müller's translation (87). Higginson championed an inclusive theological position. Following this trend, in the 1870s Buddhist *nirvana* was interpreted ever more as a condition of blessedness (89). Also, by that time people had come to study Buddhism more precisely, even though the sources were still not sufficiently known.

There were liberal currents among the intellectuals, especially the Unitarians, that opened up toward other religions and came to agreement with them. For the major Protestant churches or American Catholicism, though, non-Christian religions were only "paganism." That, in brief, is the religious and social historical background to the calling of the World Parliament of Religions in Chicago.

A PARLIAMENT AHEAD OF ITS TIME

The World Parliament of Religions came together in Chicago in 1893 in conjunction with the World's Fair held on the occasion of the four-hundredth anniversary of Columbus's discovery of America. It was an event that was far ahead of its time. The meeting religions, with their formerly more or less absolute claims of validity, gathered with equal powers in a religiously democratic "parliament"— and that at a time when there were still very few Hindus, Buddhists, Muslims, or Taoists in America. At that time, when the average American knew only of Christianity and regarded its claim to truth as self-evident and mostly also plausible,

---

[16] On this issue, see C. T. Jackson, *The Oriental Religions and American Thought* (Westport, Conn.: Greenwood, 1981), 103ff., cited by Tweed, 83.

the idea of organizing a meeting with other religions in Chicago, at which all would be equal participants, was a provocation. Correspondingly, the organizers had to come to terms with sharp criticism from various churches.

At the same time, though, the parliament received support from numerous American intellectuals and businessmen. The idea of a conference of religions in conjunction with the World's Fair first came from the lawyer Charles C. Bonney, a Swedenborgian, who was appointed president of the parliament by a Chicago committee of businessmen, pastors, and educators. He named the Presbyterian pastor and theology professor John Henry Barrows (1847-1907) as secretary; Barrows, in fact, for the most part organized the parliament. In his proposal for the parliament and in his greeting address Barrows invoked the belief that in the final analysis *one* God stands behind all religions, a statement that not only revealed his liberal theological position but also ignorance that, for example, the Buddhists could not agree to this declaration. Barrows himself saw in this event "the morning star of the twentieth century," which would radiate the spirit of love, bury the sharp antagonism between religions, and promote understanding among the religions.[17]

In 1893 the Buddhists Shaku Soen (1859-1919) from Japan and Anagarika Dharmapala from Ceylon did not oppose theism as the religious basis of the parliament. The Hindu monk Swami Vivekananda, too, saw no difficulty in identifying the Vedanta philosophy of one *brahman* with the one God of liberal Christians, or understanding Jesus (and Muhammad) as avatar (incarnation) of the *one* deity, because "it is *a* light, which radiates in different colors."[18]

The theosophy that flourished in England and the United States supported the parliament. The German-born Indologist Max Müller (1823-1900), whose career was in England, had sent a welcoming address from Oxford that combined suitable texts from the scriptures of the different religions.

The Buddhists were well represented. Their main spokesmen were the layman Anagarika Dharmapala from Ceylon and the monk and Zen master Shaku Soen from Japan, whose journey to America had been made possible by the Theosophists. Besides these, another representative of Pure Land Buddhism was present. Dharmapala spoke about the fundamental commandments of Buddhism; Shaku Soen gave a presentation on the law of cause and effect in Buddhism.[19] Reading his lectures today, it seems remarkable that the Buddhist made no direct criticism of theism—and thus of the entire ideology of the parliament. Shaku Soen's personal secretary, Suzuki Daisetsu, reserved such a critique for later.

The parliament was not only ahead of its time because in 1893 there were still no aspirations toward an interreligious ecumenicism, but also because there were still no sociological grounds for holding such a meeting, especially in America. At this time hardly any Asians lived in America. There were, to be sure, about

---

[17] H. Barrows, "Words of Welcome," in *The Dawn of Religious Pluralism: Voices from the World's Parliament of Religions 1893*, ed. R. H. Seager (LaSalle, Ill.: Open Court, 1993), 23ff.

[18] R. H. Seager, 430f.

[19] The lectures are printed in ibid., 406ff.

300,000 Chinese who had been brought to America to build the intercontinental railroad. But in 1882 Congress had passed a law that withheld citizenship and the right to own land from the Chinese, so that by 1920 the number of Chinese in America had sunk to approsimately 61,000. Consistent with this attitude, in 1893 there was no spokesman for Taoism. The Confucians, however, were represented by the Korean trade mission in Washington.

America was, according to its own self-understanding, for the most part white and Protestant. The Columbus exhibition was a trade fair that was organized in conjunction with the anniversary of Columbus's "discovery" of the New World. In his opening address Barrows named in a single phrase Jesus, the light of the world, "and the Christian America, which owes so much to Columbus, Luther, the pilgrim fathers, and John Wesley."[20] In 1893 it still had not occurred to anyone that this discovery of America had another side—the annihilation of the native cultures and entire peoples! In the final analysis, the "New World" was only new to the Europeans; it had long been populated by old cultures. But at the time the level of consciousness was very different; at the parliament the native Americans were not represented at all. There were also no invitations to representatives of African religions. Islam was represented, and Catholicism was handled as a separate religion from Protestantism; the "black churches" were represented separately.

In the white Protestant America of that time there was therefore no political necessity to convene a parliament of world religions in Chicago. It was called together out of pure idealism.

The parliament itself had a great resonance in the Chicago press and forged links among intellectuals that would endure for a long time. Reactions and counter-reactions released a series of aftereffects and a web of discussion such as America had never seen before. After the parliament Dharmapala, Shaku Soen, and others traveled through the United States, introducing Americans to Buddhism and founding the first Buddhist societies.[21] Barrows was supported by the publisher E. G. Hegeler (Open Court Publishing) in his plan to publish all the documents of the parliament. And he was the father-in-law of Paul Carus (1832-1919), the German philosopher and author who had taken part in the world parliament as secretary. Later Hegeler issued an invitation to Suzuki Daisetsu, who for twelve years (1897-1909) worked with the Open Court Press in LaSalle, Illinois, undertook lecture tours, and made Zen Buddhism popular in America. But America's

---

[20] In ibid., 25.

[21] For a more detailed portrayal of the development of Buddhism in America see C. S. Prebish, *American Buddhism* (North Scituate, Mass.: Duxbury Press, 1979); R. Fields, *How the Swans Came to the Lake: A Narrative History of Buddhism in America* (Boulder: Shambhala, 1981); T. A. Tweed, *The American Encounter with Buddhism*. On the history of Zen in the United States, see Samu Sunim, "A Brief History of Zen Buddhism in North America," in *Zen Buddhism in North America* (Toronto: The Zen Lotus Society, 1986). On the intellectual influence of Buddhism in America, see K. K. Inada and N. P. Jacobson, eds., *Buddhism and American Thinkers* (Albany, N.Y.: SUNY, 1984); C. H. Libby and P. W. Williams, eds., *The Encyclopaedia of American Religious Experience* (New York, 1988).

connections to Japan were much more encompassing and so significant for the development of Buddhist-Christian dialogue in America that we must deal with them in a special section.

THE JAPANESE CONNECTIONS

Japan was viewed very differently than China by people in America (and Europe). The island empire had from the beginning attracted aesthetic admiration. Lafcadio Hearn's (1850-1904) reports about Japan and especially his book about Japanese *ryokans* (countryside hotels), which told his readers about Buddhist and Shinto pilgrimages, stimulated an entire generation of fascination with Japan. Hearn was searching for a "pure spiritual home," where "life's whirlwinds are calmed and absolute truth can be found." Similarly, when John La Farge (1835-1910) and Henry Adams were asked in 1886 about the goal of their shared journey to Japan, La Farge answered that they were "searching for nirvana."[22]

In Europe the French Impressionists had discovered Japanese art. In America the painter James Whistler (1834-1903) asked a wealthy friend to endow a collection of Eastern art; this became the basis of the famous Freer Museum in the National Museum in Washington.

Japan's significance for America's encounter with Buddhism finally reached a high point with the activities of the Zen interpreter Suzuki Daisetsu (1870-1966). Suzuki's writings, especially his three-volume *Essays in Zen-Buddhism* (1927-1934), inspired a worldwide readership to the study and praxis of Zen. Suzuki himself, however, already by this time had a long history of encounter with America behind him.

We have mentioned that Suzuki Daisetsu had accompanied Shaku Soen to the World Parliament of Religions in 1893 as the Zen master's student and secretary. Shaku Soen, who agreed completely with the spirit of the Meiji era (Japan after 1868) and who as a reaction to Japan's modernization had already long before Suzuki interpreted Buddhism as a *universal* faith, was invited again to San Francisco in 1905-6.[23] He had founded the first Zen societies in America there in 1893, which had visibly grown since that time. Then he sent three of his students to America to further consolidate Zen Buddhism on the West Coast. Besides Suzuki, there were Senzaki Nyogen (1876-1958) (whose student Robert Aitken [b. 1917] founded the Diamond Sangha in Hawaii), and Shaku Shokatsu, who had Sasaki Sokeian (1882-1945) as a student. Sasaki's American wife, Ruth Fuller-Sasaki, had a substantial influence on the development of American Buddhism. After the war, her house in Japan became a meeting point for the great generation of scholars who researched Zen Buddhism—Yanagida Seizan, Heinrich Dumoulin, Philip Yampolsky, and others. These intellectuals have for decades put their mark on academic Zen studies in America.

---

[22] We draw the evidence from J. Kitagawa, "Western Interpreters of Japan," in *On Understanding Japanese Religion,* 289 n.13, which cites Arthur E. Christy, ed., *The Asian Legacy and American Life* (New York, 1942), 43.

[23] See J. E. Ketelaar, *Of Heretics and Martyrs in Meiji Japan: Buddhism and Its Persecution* (Princeton, N.J.: Princeton University Press, 1990).

All of the Zen centers that can be traced back to Shaku Soen are indebted to the Japanese Rinzai school of Zen. Soto Zen (in part combined with Rinzai) first came to America after the Second World War, thanks to three students of the famous Zen master Harada Sogaku (1870-1961): Maezumi Taizan (1931-95), Yasutani Hakuun (1885-1973), and Philip Kapleau (b. 1912). The pure Soto tradition made a home in America in 1959 through the work of Suzuki Shunryu (1904-71). A somewhat anglified form of the Zen tradition made its entry at Mount Shasta in California with the abbess Jiyu Kennett Roshi (1924-96), who had formerly been an organist in the Anglican church. Rinzai Zen blossomed under the direction of Sasaki Joshu (b. 1907) at Mount Baldy in California. All of these Zen lines founded numerous centers throughout North America after World War II and especially since the 1980s. Above all, they have educated American-born Zen masters. The number of centers and sub-centers can scarcely be calculated. (Besides these Japanese lines, there are many Korean ones.)

America's connections to Japanese Buddhism during the 1920s and 1930s were not limited to the foundation of Zen centers in the United States. The universities, too, pledged academic exchange, of which the best evidence is the first conference of philosophers from East and West, held in Hawaii in 1939.[24] All of these connections between America and Japan are important evidence of the cultural relations between the two countries in general, and especially for Buddhist-Christian dialogue.

AMERICA AFTER WORLD WAR II

Japan had been the privileged partner for American interest in Buddhism, but the Theravada tradition had also become known. Henry Clark Warren (1854-99), the co-founder of the *Harvard Oriental Series*, had first learned Sanskrit but had then concentrated on the Pali texts of Theravada Buddhism. His widely disseminated book *Buddhism in Translation* first appeared at Harvard in 1896.

The World Parliament of Religions in 1893 was the starting point for a growing interest in comparative studies of religions. The Foreign Mission Board of the United States and Canada had already in 1904 recommended that all seminaries offer courses in comparative religious studies.[25] The church seminaries did begin to warm to this idea, but the secular liberal arts colleges in America were still more enthusiastic.

Viewed historically, however, the study of Buddhism in America developed late in comparison to the countries of Europe. Europe had the older Anglo-German and Franco-Belgian schools, as Edward Conze calls them. Even Russia, which had no Buddhist colonies, developed Buddhist studies in the Leningrad school earlier than the United States. Sanskrit studies and Indology did indeed appear early—at Harvard, Henry Clark Warren had organized them, and the Hindu

---

[24] J. Kitagawa, "Buddhism in America with Special Reference to Zen," *Japanese Religions* 5 (1967), 32-57.

[25] J. Kitagawa, "Western Interpreters of Japan," 318f.; see also 318 n.19, which contains an indication of his importance in the history of religious studies as an academic discipline in America.

Swami Vivekananda had attracted more interest in 1893 than the Buddhists. Only Japanese Buddhism could be studied relatively early, as part of Japanese studies. Today, in contrast, nowhere in the world is Buddhism so much studied in the academic realm as in America. The Japanese historian of religion Anesaki Masaharu (1873-1949) taught as early as 1910 at Harvard. However, the first comprehensive Buddhism program was not established until 1981, at the University of Wisconsin, under the leadership of Richard Robinson. In all of this, it can be seen that the balance of interest had shifted from Theravada to Mahayana Buddhism. The text editions of the German-British intellectual Edward Conze (1904-79) played a vital role in this shift.

The wisdom literature of Mahayana Buddhism, especially the Prajnaparamita sutras, were edited, translated, and made available to the European and American readership by Edward Conze.[26] Conze had been inspired to study Mahayana's wisdom texts through an encounter with Suzuki in London. Conze thereby put the reading of Buddhism, up until then almost exclusively rationalistic, in question. He played an essential role in discovering the mystical and meditative dimension of Buddhism, as it appears in the wisdom literature of Mahayana. Indian scholar of Buddhism T. R. V. Murti followed him in this endeavor.[27] If today Nagarjuna's Madhyamika philosophy, especially the philosophy of emptiness *(sunyata)*, has become an important starting point for Buddhist-Christian dialogue, this interpretation of Mahayana Buddhism was essentially laid out by Conze, Murti, and others.

Suzuki's "intuitive" interpretation of Zen[28] drew significantly on philologically and historically oriented academic studies of Buddhism.[29] Therefore his influence reached especially to educated circles, although outside of the academic world in the strict sense. Suzuki's books and articles changed countless people's attitude toward life; these people were also motivated by him to undertake the academic study of religions, especially Buddhism.

This development first appeared after the war, when Suzuki himself had returned and lived in Japanese Kamakura. He again had a direct influence on the development of Buddhism in America, though, when in 1950, at the age of eighty, he set out on a journey around the world. On this trip he visited the United States, where he taught, wrote, and gave lectures for eight years. His appearances are said to have been "triumphal," and this characterization is doubtless correct.[30]

---

[26] Edward Conze was a German Buddhist who was mostly active in England and had a great influence on the development of understanding of Mahayana in America (see his autobiography, Edward Conze, *The Memoirs of a Modern Gnostic* [Sherborne: Samizdat]; *Life and Letters* [1979]; *Politics, People and Places* [1979]).

[27] T. R. V. Murti, *The Central Philosophy of Buddhism* (London: Allen & Unwin, 1955).

[28] J. Kitawaga, "Western Interpreters of Japan," 321, 323.

[29] Suzuki's solid academic textual analyses and historical works on Zen are written in Japanese and not accessible to the English-speaking reader.

[30] J. Kitagawa, "Western Interpreters of Japan," 323. The audience at his lecture at Columbia University also included the Zen master Philip Kapleau.

The literary exchange between the Chinese philologue Hu Shih and Suzuki came at the initial kindling of Zen studies in America. This debate appeared in an early issue of the journal *Philosophy East and West*, published in Hawaii.[31] On one side was Hu Shih, who argued that historical and textual-philological studies could uncover the underlying truth of texts beyond the facts. On the other side, Suzuki doubted that one could understand the deeper sense of a religious text only through textual criticism without inner sympathy with the text's contents. It finally became the mission and contribution of the Japanese Zen researcher Yanagida Seizan and his American students to clarify this controversy.[32]

It is impossible to write about Suzuki's influence without mentioning Alan Watts (1915-73), who popularized Suzuki's philosophy and propagated it as a "lifestyle."[33] Watts was an Englishman who met Suzuki in London before he left England (before the war broke out). Watts lived first in New York and was then a campus pastor in a college in the Midwest. There he wanted to incorporate Zen into his work, which his ecclesiastical superiors would not permit. As a result, Watts left the pastorate. He finally came to San Francisco, where he spoke about Zen on a radio program. Although Alan Watts belonged to the middle class and was regarded as bourgeois, Zen reached the young generation of the 1950s from this forum. The "beat generation" of protest against the American dream of affluence in the 1960s took up this inspiration, including the poets Allen Ginsberg (b. 1926), Jack Kerouac (1922-69), and Gary Snyder (b. 1930). Snyder even went to Japan to study Zen, a course followed by many young adults. These poets represented an intellectual movement that celebrated the immanence of inspiration in daily life and throughout the world, as Zen teaches.

The "beat Zen" generation protested against the enticements of the American dream, the material culture, and the Puritan work ethic, without being politically active. Only in the 1960s was a new social-political dynamic created. The Zen of the 1950s had no interest at all in Buddhist-Christian dialogue, in part because it was a totally negative reaction to "Christian values." The beat generation of the 1950s despised the narrow-minded conformity and complacence of the middle class. But as a counterculture it was only weakly organized, because members wished to avoid any sort of institutionalization. In the economic boom of the 1960s this movement transformed itself into a wide-ranging protest against American consumerist values in general, attracting a wide range of social classes. In conjunction with the protest against the Vietnam War, in which many Christians also took part, the counterculture transformed itself into a political counter-movement, propagating an alternative lifestyle and experimenting with new sorts of communal life.

The Asian lifestyle, or what people thought was the Asian lifestyle, fascinated many disillusioned young people from the middle classes. Japan especially was

---

[31] *Philosophy East and West,* vol. 3 (Honolulu University Press, 1953).

[32] Recently Bernard Faure has reinterpreted and expanded the entire history of Zen studies in *The Rhetoric of Immediacy: A Cultural Critique of Chan/Zen Buddhism* (Princeton, N.J.: Princeton University Press, 1991).

[33] D. Stuart and A. Watts (Radnor, Pa.: Chilton Book Comp. 1978), esp. 26f.

"romanticized," because a special relationship also existed with this land in political terms after the war. Postwar Japan was occupied by the Americans, and
the U.S. government issued many grants for studies of all sorts in Japan. Although it was not an American colony, Japan became something of an "Asian home"
for many Americans who lived in Asia. At the time, so it appears, a new generation
looked toward America (Japan was Americanized), and on the other side a generation of Americans gazed with fascination at a rapidly vanishing "old Japan."

AMERICA IN THE 1960s

During the 1960s so many traditional values in America were overthrown that
the debate continues even to the present what the consequences were for society.
Some see that decade as the final ruin of American values and the collapse of
European civilization. It was the time of the Civil Rights movement and the
social and political emergence of the formerly completely marginalized black
population. It was the time when college courses on "great books of Western
civilization" came to be supplemented with courses on "great books of the East,"
and the voices of women and ethnic minorities were also introduced.[34] The sexual
revolution drove a wedge between young people and the older generation that
had lived during the Great Depression of the 1930s—many of them puritans who
by hard work had survived hard times. The members of this older generation had
sacrificed themselves to defend Europe against Hitler, had won, and had returned
as heroes. During the Cold War they had defended freedom in Korea and Vietnam. But on the other side now stood the "baby boomers," who had been born
after the war and had never known the privations of the Depression.

These children of affluence scoffed at wealth and took a stand against American imperialism and America's role in the Third World. They also turned to non-
Christian religions and liberalism, defended leftist politics and civil rights, and/
or refused the draft for the Vietnam War. All this ripped a chasm in American
society that is still not bridged.

Looking back, the sociologist Robert N. Bellah points out that the youth of
the 1960s were indeed on a true search for social engagement, community, and
new values. At the same time, however, they had an excess of "utilitarian individualism" that, he argues, destroyed the texture of family life and the social
community.[35] This individualism later produced the egocentric "me generation"
of the 1970s, with all its vindication of material greed. This was in turn elevated
to the level of a social standard in the Reagan administration of the 1980s.

---

[34] The discussion continues today. When in 1988 students at Stanford University demanded a change of the core curriculum (Plato, Aristotle, Kant, etc.), on the grounds that
reading of Western texts is inherently discriminatory against African Americans and other
minorities, and the university agreed to include Asian and Latin American texts as required reading, the issue grew to a national debate (see D. D'Souza, "The Victims' Revolution," *The Atlantic Monthly* 3 [1991]: 52ff.).

[35] See R. N. Bellah, *Habits of the Heart: Individualism and Commitment in American
Life* (Berkeley and Los Angeles: University of California Press, 1985).

NEW DEVELOPMENTS IN MULTICULTURALISM

Buddhist-Christian dialogue must thus be seen in the larger context of America's social collapse. In addition to the factors named above, four further aspects play an important role for the development of this dialogue:

1. the Second Vatican Council and the liberalization of Catholicism;
2. the decision of the Supreme Court to abolish school prayer in 1962;
3. changes in American Buddhism; and
4. the development of religious studies departments in universities and colleges.

LIBERALIZATION OF CATHOLICISM

Until the Second Vatican Council (1962-65), liberal Catholic traditions were suppressed as part of Rome's policy of "anti-modernism." A consequence of this stance was that Catholics were significantly under-represented in America's liberal universities and colleges. Historical prejudices against the "backward" Catholics had created a distance between Protestants and Catholics, especially in academia. This changed at the latest during World War II, which brought America's Catholics and Protestants closer. They had fought side by side against Hitler or in Japan. And when the soldiers returned from the war, a law for reintegration of war veterans (the G.I. Bill) played a strong role in opening colleges and universities for veterans, so that substantially more Catholics enrolled in public universities than ever before. In the 1950s the farming population also dwindled rapidly, and the cities with their cosmopolitan cultural imprint absorbed diverse religious groups. Through this and other developments American Catholics more and more entered the mainstream of Protestant America. They, too, now took to religious freedom and oriented themselves on individualism, as the Protestants had always done. In the 1960s the Catholics were visibly politically active in the Civil Rights movement and the Antiwar movement. For example, Daniel and Philip Berrigan occupied the American press for months. One was a Jesuit, the other a Josephine priest; they were incarcerated for a time because they had burned their draft orders in Boston and Baltimore.

The growing acceptance of Catholics by the Protestant majority can also be seen in John F. Kennedy's election as president in 1960. This would have been unthinkable a generation before, because the Kennedys come from the Irish-Catholic tradition. Now, however, Protestants and Catholics were divided among themselves: liberal Protestants, together with liberal Catholics, voted for Kennedy; conservatives of both confessions were in favor of Richard Nixon. Politics, rather than religion, now divided the populace into different camps. There had never before been such a shift in votership. This, however, meant that from now on Protestants and Catholics were unified or divided on general issues, for example, the anti-abortion campaign. This division into liberal and conservative (moralistic fundamentalists), cutting straight through the old confessional divides, still characterizes America's political situation today.[36]

The Second Vatican Council contributed greatly to the liberalization of American Catholicism. Instead of studying only in traditional educational institutions (for example, Jesuits took care only to study at Jesuit universities, and so on), priests, candidates for the priesthood, and former priests now also attended the formerly taboo Protestant seminaries. Instead of striving only for degrees at ecclesiastical seminaries, they now worked toward master's or doctorate degrees at departments of religious studies in the public universities. They were allowed to practice Zen meditation and took part in interreligious dialogue. They learned and taught Eastern religions with greater freedom than ever before. The ever-growing independence of American Catholics since that time is well known.

Catholic women, too, could now take part in the feminist movement and began the struggle for offices in the church.[37] They studied at colleges and received academic degrees in theology, even though the priesthood is still denied them today. From the pens of these women academics came some of the best-qualified scientific critiques of the ecclesiastical hierarchy of the 1980s. One need only think of Rosemary Radford Ruether, who teaches at the Garrett-Evangelical Theological Seminary, Northwestern University, and is also engaged in Buddhist-Christian dialogue.

THE 1962 SUPREME COURT DECISION ON SCHOOL PRAYER

Liberalism, whether religious or secular, was and is a strong voice in American educational institutions. The liberal lawyers and judges of the American Civil Liberties Union took action to see that church and state remained separate in public universities. The 1960s in general were a victory for liberalism. This state of affairs lasted until 1970, when a new conservative evangelical movement, the Moral Majority, mobilized against "secular humanism," attempting also to repress it in education.

The abolition of school prayer by the Supreme Court in 1962 was a precedent-setting decision, because through this decision schools were still further secularized. The decision also meant that religion and theism (Jewish-Christian-Muslim belief in God) were no longer simply equated to one another—the court had taken seriously the religious groups that do not believe in a God (Buddhism). And the same court decision ruled that academic study of religions does not impinge on the principle of division of church and state. This set loose a boom in religious studies programs at colleges and universities after 1964, which in turn had great influence on Buddhist-Christian dialogue. We will go on to analyze the university religious studies programs, which made a new interreligious

---

[36] See P. W. Williams, "America's Religions, Vatican II, and the End of the Catholic Ghetto," in C. H. Libby and P. W. Williams, eds., *The Encyclopaedia of American Religious Experience* (New York, 1988), 374-81.

[37] P. W. Williams, *America's Religions*, 108.

ecumenicism possible that was driven by an academically educated laity. First, however, we must consider the change of Buddhism itself in America.

CHANGES IN AMERICAN BUDDHISM

Two factors play a role in this context: the Americanization of Buddhism, and a new immigration from Asia. Liberalized immigration laws after World War II had opened the door for waves of immigrants from Asia.

As the youth of the 1960s began to question American values, Christianity and indeed every institutionalized form of religion was caught in the crossfire of criticism. The "psychedelic generation" took consciousness-expanding drugs, and Zen and Tibetan Buddhism were also introduced as "consciousness-widening" in a similar fashion. Zen, as we have seen, had already put down roots in the 1950s; now it blossomed outside of the universities as part of a counterculture. This new movement was no longer connected to Zen's original socialization forms in Asia, and accordingly Zen itself changed.

The Americanization of Zen took place in yet another way—through the universities. Especially because of the critical research into Zen's history and sources by Yanagida Seizan, Heinrich Dumoulin, and Philip Yampolsky, Zen in the United States became an academic subject, which it had never been in Japan. Tibetan Buddhism was first introduced in the United States after many Tibetan lamas had fled to America in the wake of the Chinese invasion of Tibet in 1950 and Lhasa's unsuccessful revolt in 1959. Tibetology began to establish itself at universities on a new basis (with Tibetan scholars and Tibetan teaching methods) and reached an unparalleled flourishing. The Tibetan tradition, which in Tibet itself was only transmitted in the monasteries, was "secularized" in America, and formerly secret initiations were exactly described and analyzed in academic dissertations. That changed Tibetan Buddhism in America very much, and these changes reached back to the lamas and their existing lines of tradition that continued to exist in America.

Early American scholars of Buddhism had come mostly from the ranks of the missionaries. The Protestant pastor Winston King is a good example of this phenomenon. As a missionary in Burma, King (b. 1907) was introduced to attentiveness training *(sati)* and wrote books on the subject that reached a wide audience in America.[38] Another example is Donald Swearer, who introduced the Thai Buddhist reformer Buddhadasa to America. Swearer's book *Dialogue: The Key to Understanding Other Religions* (1977) had a deep influence on dialogue in America.[39]

---

[38] For a presentation of King's and Swearer's positions, see P. Schmidt-Leukel, *Den Löwen brüllen hören*, 172-84 and 203-12. See also William Pieris, *The Western Contribution to Buddhism* (Delhi: Motilal Barnarsidass, 1973). Pieris's book is a compendium, a "who's who" in Buddhist studies.

[39] D. Swearer, *Dialogue: The Key to Understanding Other Religions* (Philadelphia: Westminster Press, 1977); see also Swearer, *Buddhism in Transition* (Philadelphia: Westerminster Press, 1970); and his book *The Dhammic Socialism of Bhikkhu Buddhadasa* (Bangkok: Thai Interreligious Committee for Development, 1986).

Since the 1970s and 1980s, however, a new generation of American Buddhist scholars have gained positions in the universities. Often they are themselves practicing Buddhists, which creates a completely new situation.

America came into contact with Vietnamese Buddhism through the Vietnam War (1959-75). Most important in this development is Thich Nhat Hanh, the Vietnamese Zen monk and peace poet, who was active in America for many years. Still, Vietnamese studies could only really be established in the universities after the war.[40] The many Vietnamese immigrants are cared for by monks from their homeland, and most have kept their native ethnic folk religion. They are also not engaged in dialogue, in large part because most of these monks cannot speak English. The group around Thich Nhat Hanh is the exception in this regard, one that, to be sure, has a great influence on the formulation of a politically engaged American Buddhism.

Japan's "new religions," such as Soka Gakkai and Rissho Kosei-kai, are also well represented in the United States. At first their membership was limited to Americans of Japanese descent, but missionary efforts were soon successful. For example, Soka Gakkai has a temple and a radio station in Los Angeles and has been able to win over many African Americans from southern California. Still, no group except Rissho Kosei-kai has been actively engaged in Buddhist-Christian dialogue.

The Buddhists in America are a combination of two very different groups. On the one hand are the ethnic Buddhists, who are immigrants from Asia and for the most part remain loyal to their religion; on the other hand are formerly Christian Americans who have converted to Buddhism, who are looking for an American Buddhist identity, and who thus want to separate Buddhism from its Asian cultural roots. There is an intensive controversy about the relationship between beliefs and this change. A very important factor in this controversy is the Buddhist feminist movement. This movement has developed the same spiritual independence in regard to Buddhist (male-dominated) institutions that Christian women have developed toward Christian (male-dominated) institutions. Many American women Buddhists were and are unwilling to accept the traditional patriarchal structure of the Buddhist *samgha*. They play an important role in Buddhist-Christian dialogue, and their close ties to leading Christian feminists add networking community work to the agenda. Rita Gross[41] is certainly one of the most active academics in this process.

These developments have made the American cultural and religious melting pot even more complex. Still, despite all ethnic and racial tensions, the United States is much more positive toward multireligiousness and multiculturalism than other countries, for example, Europe, which is still deeply permeated with

---

[40] The government financed studies of Southeast Asia's political culture, such as Donald E. Smith, *Religion and Politics in Burma* (Princeton, N.J.: Princeton University Press, 1965).

[41] See her book *Buddhism after Patriarchy* (Albany, N.Y.: SUNY, 1993), and also her contributions in discussions in Buddhist-Christian dialogue; see especially the journal *Dialogue*, NS, 19-20 (Colombo, 1992/93).

Christian or post-Christian attitudes. In the United States religious pluralism has become the obvious foundation for every sort of liberal Christian theology. And it is the universities where such theology has found a home and continues to flourish.

RELIGIOUS STUDIES PROGRAMS AT THE UNIVERSITIES

Religious studies programs are an expression of the liberal heritage. Various institutions have built up different programs. Private colleges, too, which have close ties to the churches, have introduced religious studies, and even most traditional seminaries have a general religious studies program. Although these programs are often one-sided (for example, often only one of the Asian religions is taught), the mere fact that non-Christian religions are represented is a sign of an irreversible change. At a time when classical family structures are collapsing and it is no longer taken for granted that the family will pass on religious values to the next generation, colleges with their free offering of information about different religions are often the place where young Americans first become acquainted with religious questions and possible answers. Whether one wants it so or not, religious studies programs, which according to the basic understanding of the discipline ought not "preach," also make it possible for students to make a choice in religion.

Although the discipline of religious studies or comparative religious studies has also been introduced at universities in Europe, Japan, England, and Canada, it does not there play an equally important role to religious studies in the American liberal education. In Europe it is still a highly specialized field and in many cases is still closely linked to the theology faculties. In Japan, too, it is a very specialized discipline that offers no substitute for individual personal belief— scholarly views have no influence on the religious praxis of scholars.

In America, on the contrary, this discipline is not very sharply defined, the faculties are diverse, and often the program has no common methodological focus. Thus, religious studies frequently teaches about the "wisdom of the world religions." The professors themselves often combine personal belief and corresponding praxis with academic activity. Thus it is a liberal-humanistic education in the broadest sense. Still, since study of the phenomenon of religion is not the same thing as theology, and there is a difference between descriptive and normative methods (or teaching and preaching), it is the assumption that "insider" and "outsider," or subjective and objective perspectives, can be fully divided from one another. In the current debate, however, this has become questionable. Religion is so essential to humankind that neither the human nor the religion as such can be completely objectified. Existence is not a "thing" and religious studies is not impersonal natural science. This does not mean that the ideal of the greatest possible objectivity should not be upheld—objectivity is the ultimate foundation of science. But the personalities of academic teachers have indeed changed. The days are past, at least in America, of someone like Étienne Lamotte (b. 1903), who as a Catholic could combine his subtle studies of Abhidharma and excellent translations of Mahayana sutras with extremely existential and religious non-interest. For him, Buddhism was indeed rational and good but not true and vital. Very many American intellectuals and students "engage" themselves existentially in what they study. Critics of religious studies programs lay their finger exactly on this point, because they fear a new confusion between state and religion, even when the religion involved is not necessarily Christian. Those answerable for such programs also see this connection, but they welcome the link because it serves the cause of moralistic education.

The University of Chicago was one of the first to introduce a program of history of religion within its Divinity School.[42] Jerald C. Bauer, general editor of the series *Essays in Divinity*, which opened with a volume entitled *The History of Religions* (edited by J. Kitagawa, Chicago, 1967), writes in his foreword that history of religions should be a distinct field among the subjects necessary to a theological education. He closes with the comment that the theologian Paul Tillich, whose last article is included in the volume,[43] so determined the future of Christian theology that it was newly imagined in the context of dialogue with other religions, through which the field of history of religion has acquired new significance.

Dialogue with other religions can and must contribute to Christian self-awareness. This premise, which many American theologians since Tillich have taken as self-evident, explains the interest of American theology in dialogue. This is also the inner reason why Buddhist-Christian dialogue in America is almost exclusively a concern of academia.

At Harvard an institute is active, now called the Center for the Study of World Religion,[44] whose program in comparative religious studies was inspired by scholar of religion Wilfred Cantwell Smith (b. 1916). It is permeated throughout by the belief that interreligious dialogue (Smith prefers the term *colloquia*) should contribute to religious self-awareness as well as to Christian theology. In this way religious studies is a precondition to academically responsible dialogue. He argues that a hermeneutically conscious scholar of religions cannot ignore the personal belief of believers, and a good theologian cannot ignore the religious traditions of the world. Smith interprets objectivity in religious studies as the need to evaluate in accordance with the method of the object that is being described. In the study of religion it is necessary to learn to speak from the perspective of a believer, one who "recognizes the truth." Thus belief is not "holding for truth what has no foundation," but the "recognition of the real."[45]

---

[42] By the way, the ideals of the 1893 World Parliament of Religions appear also to have influenced Caroline Haskell, who financed the religious studies Haskell lectures at the University of Chicago beginning in 1895 (Barrows gave the first lecture) and who also endowed a separate Barrows lecturership.

[43] P. Tillich, "Die Bedeutung der Religionsgeschichte für den Systematischen Theologen," in *Werk und Wirken Paul Tillichs* (Stuttgart: Ev. Verlagswerk, 1967), 187-203.

[44] Wilfred Cantwell Smith took care that *religion* should appear in the singular rather than the plural, because he proceeds from the belief in *one* religion that appears in different forms.

[45] Smith laid this out successively in his books: *The Meaning and End of Religion* (1963); *Questions of Religious Truth* (1967); *Religious Diversity* (1976); *Belief and History* (1977); *Faith and Belief* (1979); *Towards a World Theology* (1981). See also A. Grünschloß, *Religionswissenschaft als Welt-Theologie: Wilfred Cantwell Smiths interreligiöse Hermeneutik* (Göttingen: Vandenhoeck & Ruprecht, 1994).

The belief that university academic studies have little to do with interreligious dialogue between Buddhists and Christians is contradicted by the American experience. The reproach that academics do not really represent a "community of the faithful" is certainly accurate. But this "non-community" is certainly not lacking in existential devotion. For every intellectual must be dedicated to the truth. Vice versa, the lack of religious community ties in America is not necessarily linked to the status of a scholar of religion. There are many prominent intellectuals who are also believers, and some who understand themselves as combined scholars of religion and theologians. Anyone who works in a hermeneutically conscious fashion knows that judgment is always limited by the suppositions with which one enters the "object" of the interest. As long as these assumptions are made visible and reflected upon, as long as it is clearly recognized how and why a given state of mind has been created, open academic dispute will not be hindered by the religious views of a scholar. On the contrary. The problem is rather that the religious studies departments at American universities suffer from an isolation of the various subjects that makes interdisciplinary methodological debates only rarely possible. Perhaps it is for this reason that conferences and seminars promoting interreligious dialogue are so attractive, because at such meetings it is easier to break down this sort of barrier than in the usual routine of academic research and teaching.

Within the current religious studies programs there are only few professorships that have been directly dedicated to Buddhist-Christian comparison or dialogue.[46] Specialization in a specific religion and a limited region (geographically, historically, phenomenologically) still remains the academic norm. Positions in comparative religion, which are directly based on comparison and which encourage doctoral candidates to work specifically with two religions, are still the exception. Because of specialization and the basic knowledge of the material that is necessary, comparisons of religions are quickly viewed with distrust as superficial. The universities and colleges attempt to solve this problem in different ways. At Harvard, for example, it is a requirement that students study two traditions; Chicago works instead with a focus on overarching theory and method; at Stanford the method has become established of looking for thematic parallels between the religions; Temple University perhaps produces the most religious-philosophical comparative works.

The hiring practices of universities reflect this trend. Typically a university seeks a professor with an area of specialty who can also teach general introductory courses. But because most religious studies programs have only one or two positions in Asian religions, programs will often choose a scholar of Buddhism, since Buddhism is the religion that historically has included all of Asia. (India, Tibet, China, and Japan are also represented in departments of "area studies," which often include specialists in Confucianism, Taoism, Hinduism, and Japanese religions, who are then at the service of religious studies programs.)

In many cases, intellectuals who deal with Buddhism or Hinduism work (especially in smaller universities) in a department that is still very much dominated

---

[46] W. E. Mills, ed., *Directory of Departments and Programs of Religious Studies in North America* (Macon, Ga.: Council of Societies for the Study of Religion, 1991).

by Judeo-Christian themes. The result is that scholars of Buddhism, if they are not totally alienated from Christianity, enter into a businesslike conversation with the biblical traditions. Considering this background, it is natural that there is a desire for thematic collaboration (mostly at the personal level rather than motivated by professional or administrative decisions), which promotes Christian-Buddhist dialogue.

Still, we must go into even greater detail to illuminate why the university religious studies programs have so strongly encouraged Buddhist-Christian dialogue at the academic level. Besides the factors already mentioned, there are at least three underlying causes, of which two are typical of the West and one is specifically American: modern Western interest in religion; the selective perception of "religion"; and the attempt to understand religious studies as a culture-framing science.

Modern Western Interest in Religion

First we must bear in mind that modern Western interest in Buddhism, including this book, is entirely "modern and Western." The reproach of "orientalism" (the term implies that Islam was and is no longer regarded through the lens of European imperialism) can in part be transposed to the study of Buddhism.

Suzuki's portrayal of Zen for his Western audience and readership can be described as "reverse orientalism" (B. Faure). It is "reversed" in the sense that Suzuki wished to create a counterbalance to the denigration of Buddhism that the missionaries had established. He agreed in this with the quest of many Western intellectuals from Richard Wagner to Hermann Hesse, and gave a response to their romantic imagining of "Eastern wisdom." This transfigured view had a very strong influence on the West's view of India, Tibet, China, and Japan.[47] The East served as a blank screen onto which Westerners could project a critique of their own culture as they tried to surmount the rationalism of the Enlightenment. In consequence, people accepted Hinduism and Buddhism as religions of "mysticism" or "wisdom" without concerning themselves with the social and political realities of these religions.

We discussed in chapter 2 how, on the contrary, a totally different communication model between Christianity and Buddhism developed in Ceylon. There, it was not "reverse orientalism," but a Buddhist national awakening. It was promoted by the American Colonel Henry S. Olcott and the Sinhalese Dharmapala, in order to overcome British colonial power. As a result, Theravada was interpreted as the only purely rational and thus superior religion. Gananath Obeyesekere named this development "Protestant Buddhism."[48]

---

[47] On this theme, see also W. Halbfass, *India and Europe: An Essay in Understanding* (Albany, N.Y.: SUNY, 1988), especially 69ff.; and M. v. Brück, *Religion und Politik im Tibetischen Buddhismus* (Munich: Kösel, 1999).

[48] G. Obeyesekere, F. Reynolds, and B. S. Smith, eds., *The Two Wheels of Dhamma: Essays on the Theravada Tradition in India and Ceylon,* The American Academy of Religion. Studies in Religion, Monograph Series no. 3 (Chambersbury, Pa., 1972), 58-78. The concept of "Protestant Buddhism" has been adopted by Richard Gombrich in his book *Theravada Buddhism.*

Whether it was an issue of orientalism (which looked down on everything non-Western), or reverse orientalism (which romanticized everything non-Western), or rationalist Protestant orientalism (which wanted to uncover the same—or superior—rationality in other cultures as in the West), in every case the dominant interpretations of other religions were stamped with corresponding intellectual prejudices in both the nineteenth and twentieth century. Common to these intellectual suppositions is that they regard Buddhism as the religion that had dominated the East in a similar fashion to Christianity in the West. So both were established at one or the other end of the same spectrum of human intellect: Buddhism as the *rational* religion and Christianity as the *supra-rational* religion. Buddhist-Christian dialogue is still not completely free of these assumptions.

The Selective Perception of "Religion"

This perception of Buddhism rests upon a selective perception of what "religion" is. It focuses above all on *dharma*, that is, the realm (so people believe) of ideas. From the Eastern traditions that appeal to *readers* in the West (with emphasis on the word *reader*), this became the most important object of interest, one that could be included without further ado in conceptual systems and ideas. Buddhism appears to be consistent with it; Vedanta and Taoism are other examples. It is much more difficult to speak of Hinduism without taking caste into account, or of Confucianism without discussing the family. But there is the assumption that it is possible to philosophize about Buddhism, Vedanta, Taoism, or Zen without having to consider all this "cultural baggage." In other words, this philosophy of dialogue is built around religious truths or rational truths.

The assumption that religion is identical to religious truths and that religious truths can be expressed in theological statements is by no means so central in all forms of Buddhism and Christianity as it is in Christian Orthodoxy, or in some Buddhist schools.[49] If, however, people believe they can find the "core" of religion especially in its writings, the study of other religions consists above all in the collection and interpretation of texts—whether they be the Bible, the sacred books of the East, or the sutra canon. This view of religion, doubtless encouraged by European Protestantism, defined the way Europeans since the nineteenth century have studied religions, and it is this attitude that has made possible the great translation projects. The invention and rapid spread of the printing press (in Europe itself a consequence of Protestantism) meant that modern people learned about other religions by reading about them. This is an important means of access to religion (and, considering the transmission of Buddhism from India to China, by no means new), but it is not the only means.

In recent times there has been an overabundance of editions of texts and a multiplication of words. Still more, writings are being displaced by pictures that are transmitted especially by television. This has begun yet another revolution in the mode of human global communication. It is still too early to see how this will

---

[49] In Buddhism the great significance of precepts is emphasized for example in Theravada or in the Tibetan Gelukpa school, but not in Zen.

change the picture of the world, including religions, especially through the development of multimedia. The presumption that through television formerly disembodied ideas would be given flesh again through pictures has not proven to be the case, as far as can be seen. Attention has rather diminished because of the mass of images. Now that modern telecommunication has created a partially global world culture that has dazzled us at home, wherever home might be, we learn about other cultures and religions without even having to pick up a book or leave the couch. Even if we are supposed to be able to experience a "virtual reality" stereophonically on the screen in the near future and will be able to choose between the animal spirit world of the native Americans and Tibetan tantric rituals at the push of a button, we have lost the innocence of the imagination. Original cultures saw the world through their individual active imagination or spirituality. Television, on the contrary, has a *standardized* image for everyone, which irons out and simplifies the complex historical singularity of an event (including religious ones). Besides this, the world to which we return, after our excursion to the global village, is completely standardized commercially.

And even if academic work on the traditional literary sources of religions still knows how to hold at bay this standardized image-world of the media, preconceptions enter everyday consciousness thanks to the *media-made* world. The dynamic of interreligious dialogue is thoroughly permeated by this.

The Attempt to Understand Religious Studies as a Culture-Framing Science

The alliance of Unitarian liberalism with theosophical orientalists at the parliament of 1893 was decisive for the opening of universities to the world religions. After World War II this tradition joined with the far-reaching changes in American society that also affected universities, especially since a university education was now accessible to a much broader sector of the population than before.

The liberals believed that a general college education would transform the provincially oriented Americans into cosmopolitans. And to some extent this did come to pass. With the Vietnam War college students were politicized, which had a direct influence on the perception of (Vietnamese) Buddhism. The conflicts that followed in churches and seminaries were aggravating. Religious studies programs, too, were politicized in the process.

Buddhism had long been entwined in the political fate of Vietnam and Tibet, and corresponding impulses from Asia reached as far as the American peace marches and the feminist movement. This political dimension distinguished Buddhist-Christian dialogue after the 1960s from the interests of the beat generation in consciousness-broadening and a certain interreligious academic conference culture.

The religious studies programs, on one hand, were supposed to make allowances for the social changes in America, and especially give academic representation to the great number of people in America who practiced non-Christian religions. On the other hand, it was hoped that the introduction of "religion" in colleges and universities would lead to necessary discussion about values and create a moral consensus in American society. Religious studies was supposed to be a sort of framing science that would provide a framework within which to understand the individual cultures within America and provide a common ground for discussion on issues of values. These had no other place in multicultural America but urgently needed to be addressed.

But the hope that religious studies could provide such a framework has not been fulfilled. The individual disciplines have decayed into more or less autonomous areas. The reasons for this are academic specialization on one side and differing political interests on the other. The ideal of a university community made up of seekers after truth does not correspond to reality. Also, the required courses on the "great books of humankind" and general lectures have changed little. Still, as we saw, these courses led to an argument that is important for America's future: It revolves around multiculturalism on one side and on the other side fear of losing America's (Western) identity in the face of ethnic claims by different cultures and religions. Not only do these questions still exist at universities and colleges, coming out of the multicultural synthesis of professors and students, but the academic world also has the subject competence necessary to investigate these questions. This can also be seen in interreligious dialogue conferences.

Therefore the professors from university religious studies departments and theological seminaries will probably continue to play the dominant role in American Buddhist-Christian dialogue in the future. This has had an impact on the style of dialogue: its institutionalization has very much cooled off the once-fiery discussions between the different camps. This older type of discussion has moved to the nonacademic environment of New Age bookstores or metaphysical circles of the urban middle class, and occasionally also to new cults and sects. Such groups continue tendencies that were daily occurrences in earlier American history. Indeed, it is too early to tell what influence this scene might still come to have on Buddhist-Christian dialogue.

THE INTERNATIONAL DIALOGUE CONFERENCES
AND THE SOCIETY FOR BUDDHIST-CHRISTIAN STUDIES

In 1980 the East-West Project was called into life under the leadership of Professors David Chappell and George Tanabe from the department of religious studies at the University of Hawaii. This project also organized the first International Buddhist-Christian Conference in Hawaii. About fifty scholars from around the world met to discuss the theme "East-West Religions in Encounter: Buddhist-Christian Renewal and the Future of Humanity." The program included historical and phenomenological comparisons of the two religions as well as mutual suggestions for a further development of social ethics. Interesting links were formed at the meeting, so that there was an agreement to create the periodical *Buddhist-Christian Studies*, edited by David Chappell. Also, the Japanese sister organization of the East-West Religions Project was founded under Doi

Masatoshi's leadership in Kyoto.[50] Shortly afterward a permanent theological encounter group began work under the leadership of the Christian John Cobb and the Zen Buddhist Abe Masao (the Cobb-Abe Group).

Invitations were also issued to a second International Buddhist-Christian Conference in Hawaii in 1984. It was organized under the theme "Paradigm Change in Buddhism and Christianity." Two main speakers at this conference were the Christian theologian Hans Küng and the Japanese Indologist Nakamura Hajime. The latter analyzed the change in the basic paradigms of Buddhism and Christianity (following Thomas Kuhn's theory of scientific revolutions) in the history of both religions and worked out parallel processes. This method provoked a flood of publications, with interesting insight on details of all areas of the history of Christianity and Buddhism.[51]

About 150 scholars and believers from both religions took part in this second Hawaii conference. At the meeting there was also protest from the ranks of the historians of Buddhism against schematization into paradigms, because textual analysis and historical wealth of data were opposed to such a method.

The third International Buddhist-Christian Conference was held in Berkeley, California, in 1987. Eight hundred participants, mostly from the United States, Canada, and Japan, but also from Europe, Sri Lanka, and India, discussed the theme "Buddhism and Christianity: Toward the Human Future."[52] This conference enjoyed an enormous success, including the meeting of nuns, monks, priests, and lay practitioners of both religions to exchange their experiences. As a result, the participants agreed to found a Society for Buddhist-Christian Studies. Since then, this society has been responsible for the periodical *Buddhist-Christian Studies* (founded in 1980). It also publishes a newsletter, supports studies in the field of Buddhist-Christian dialogue, promotes coordinating meetings at the local level around the world, and meets yearly in conjunction with the annual meeting of the American Academy of Religion.

The society, acting jointly with the Boston Theological Institute and the Boston University School of Theology, arranged the fourth International Buddhist-Christian Conference in July/August 1992 with the theme "Buddhism, Christianity, and Global Healing."[53] Most of the participants came from America; South, Southeast, and East Asia; as well as Europe. The conference showed that Buddhism and Christianity are no longer identifiable in terms of their geographical and cultural homelands. The Canadian theologian John Berthrong remarks anecdotally: "An amazing experience in every major Buddhist-Christian dialogue is

---

[50] See the section "Dialogue Center of the National Christian Council in Kyoto" in chap. 4 herein.

[51] Several contributions can be found in various issues of *Buddhist-Christian Studies*. The majority of documents, however, are in the conference materials in the library of the Graduate Theological Union in Berkeley.

[52] The materials may be found in the library of the Graduate Theological Union, Berkeley, California.

[53] An introductory report: J. Berthrong, "Reflections on the Fourth Buddhist-Christian Conference," *Buddhist-Christian Studies* 13 (1993): 135-45.

the wonderment on the face of a person asking an Asian participant about the Buddhist tradition, only to discover that this Asian is a Christian, but a North American of European descent is ready to answer the question from a Buddhist perspective." Dialogue has thus grown far beyond the possible borders of ethnic association. (In Canada, according to the last census, Buddhists are the fastest-growing religious group.)

These major conferences have created their own social and theological field for Buddhist-Christian interaction. In this context the confessional differences on both sides vanish. Both sides learn from each other and adopt concepts that appear useful for their own arguments or for the answer of both traditions to the questions of the age. In the process Buddhists show themselves to be influenced by Christian social activism and Christian theological subtlety in their defense of belief in God. The Christians are especially fascinated by Buddhist meditation praxis and the Buddhist psychology of meditative consciousness. Joint meditation groups or meditation houses, at which both Buddhist and Christian meditation practices are taught, are no longer a rarity. Some participants declared that they were Buddhists as well as Christians. And fear of syncretism is fading—at least in the circle of these academics.

The conferences also show that not only classical themes like suffering, God and *nirvana*, tradition and intuition, and so on, have been considered. Instead, the main stress has lain especially on comparative social ethics, art, holistic medicine, feminism, healing, compassion, and wisdom. The theme of founding a new environmental ethics based on Buddhist and Christian principles has provoked dialogue activities worldwide. Participants from Canada and Thailand reported at the Boston meeting about joint projects with regard to immigration policies and an ethically responsible tourism.

But specialized philosophical dialogue also goes further. In America the process philosophy of Alfred North Whitehead (1861-1947) particularly serves as a foundation for dialogue with the Buddhist concept of *pratityasamutpada* (origination in mutual dependence). This can also be connected to Charles Sanders Peirce (1839-1914), who in the last decade of the nineteenth century conceptualized the self not as substance but as ongoing new event of creative self-creation.[54] Whitehead touches upon basic Buddhist principles in his process thinking,[55] especially insight into the non-substantiality of all appearances. John Cobb's process

---

[54] See C. Hartshorne, "Toward a Buddhist-Christian Religion," in *Buddhism and American Thinkers*, ed. K. Inada and J. P. Jacobson (Albany, N.Y.: SUNY, 1984), 2ff.

[55] It is difficult to say how much Whitehead knew about Buddhism. He did indeed see that dialogue between Buddhism and Christianity could open up an essentially new self-understanding of both religions. As he said, "Buddhism and Christianity have their origin in two inspired moments of history: in the life of the Buddha and the life of Christ. Buddha gave his teaching in order to enlighten the world; Christ gave his life. It is up to the Christian to recognize that teaching clearly. In the final analysis, the most valuable part of the Buddha's teaching is perhaps its interpretation of his life" (A. N. Whitehead, *Religion in the Making* [Cleveland: World Publishing, 1926]). We thank P. Schmidt-Leukel for this reference.

theology also plays a prominent role in this context, as we will show in the next section. We cannot detail the immense richness of lectures, comparisons, philosophical stimulations, and practical recommendations that take place at these conferences. As an example, though, we will briefly sketch out the course and results of the International Buddhist-Christian Conference held in Berkeley in 1987.

THE BERKELEY BUDDHIST-CHRISTIAN CONFERENCE, 1987

Never before were so many theologians, philosophers, and meditation teachers engaged in Buddhist-Christian dialogue gathered together, and never before did conference themes range so widely.

The Classical Philosophical Themes

The philosophical themes differed little from the classical dialogue themes. They included the Buddhist teaching on causality and belief in creation, the nothingness of Zen and the Christian concept of God, the Pure Land tradition and Christian doctrine of grace, and so on. Individual thinkers of the past were compared, as well as concepts of belief, grace, causality, time, and space that run through both traditions. The comparisons are so complex and the traditions so branched-out on individual points that it is difficult to find a common thread in the various lectures and discussions. The only theme that ran through all the sessions was the final surmounting of the false judgment that Buddhism is interested only in pure salvation of self, while Christianity teaches the salvation of others. For in both religions an arrival from outside is experienced in the salvation and enlightenment experience, which determines the life of the individual believer.

Theologian John Keenan (Middlebury College) presented here for the first time his "Mahayana theology," that is, a comparison of the Mahayana Buddhist *Yogacara* philosophy (a widespread idealistic consciousness analysis) with Christian theology. He interprets the Christian faith in Buddhist categories, so that Jesus is not understood as substantial but as an empty mirror of the Father. Jesus, who is in perpetual communication with the absolute truth (Buddhist *paramartha satya*), expresses this as conventional truth (Buddhist *samvrti satya*). Jesus thus "empties" the misuse of religion for egotistic manipulation of reality (magic), and the politics of confrontation, that is, use of force between humans.

Jan van Bragt, a Belgian Catholic priest (S.V.D.) who lives in Japan and is an active dialogue partner with the Kyoto school, presented a retrospective view of the dialogue between Japanese Shin Buddhism and Christianity, in which he himself is engaged.[56] He warns against equating Shinran's psychology of belief to Luther's doctrine of faith *(sola fide)* and ignoring the philosophical differences. He argues that it is also impossible to reduce Shinran's teaching to individual Buddhist assertions; one should instead study teaching and religious praxis in their interdependence. In the Meiji era (1868-1912) the proponents of Pure Land Buddhism disavowed too great similarities with Christianity in order to

---

[56] See the section entitled "Dialogue with Pure Land Buddhism" in chap. 4 herein.

preserve their own identity. Just as Christians sometimes want to reinterpret Shinran as a Japanese Luther, Suzuki Daisetsu[57] nearly made him into a Zen master. Van Bragt argued that this is harmful to understanding, as Nishitani Keiji also believed.

Buddhists of Asian Background and Newly Converted American Buddhists

The Berkeley conference had still another aspect that is significant for the religio-sociological processes in America: for the first time at such a dialogue meeting the American Buddhists of ethnic Asian background also met with the Buddhist guests from Asia. These encounters were an important part of the conference. The foreign delegations, whose members spoke little English, enriched the conference especially through rituals for peace and the well-being of humanity. Although language proved to be an obstacle, the rites joined participants together. The ethnic-Buddhist groups in America also do not base their identity upon individual belief or unifying ideas but on solidarity of their members and a common lifestyle, which is imprinted with the rites and festivals of the Buddhist calendar. The membership structure (as family units or marked by language or ethnicity) makes it difficult to have contact with outside individuals from the academic realm. It is a function of these religious communities to preserve ethnic identity, so that intra-Buddhist or interreligious ecumenicism is not really part of their agenda. The ethnic groups in America admittedly fear loss of their identity, because the younger generation is separating itself from old models of conduct, a process that is mostly conditioned by social or economic mobility. They have only limited contact with other religious bodies. The American situation (with its strict division of religion and state) appears to sharpen these conditions, which also exist in England or Canada. But in England and Canada the state or communities themselves organize interreligious conferences, in order to disarm ethnic tensions; in America this is not possible. Thus it also becomes the task of Christian-Buddhist dialogue to encourage the integration of religious groups into the multicultural community.

It is certainly no coincidence that very shortly after the Berkeley conference in July 1987 another meeting was organized. This was the Conference on World Buddhism in North America, held in Ann Arbor, Michigan. It was organized by various Buddhist groups and scholars of Buddhism at the universities. The delegates were concerned to surmount tensions within Buddhism, including the tensions between ethnic Buddhists and the new American converts, as well as the tensions among the various schools of Buddhism.

The participants formulated a common Buddhist statement that took account of the common Buddhist "confessions" of the past, which above all included the "four noble truths" and the "five fundamental virtues."[58] In this endeavor the

---

[57] D. T. Suzuki, *Amida: Der Buddha der Liebe* (Bern/Munich/Vienna: O. W. Barth, 1974).

[58] The common confession of the Buddhist Religion Society in Germany has a very similar content, which was already formulated and adopted in 1985 (see chap. 5 herein).

"common platform, to which all Buddhists can agree" of the Buddhist Congress in Adyar, Madras, from January 1891 served as inspiration. This statement had been initiated by Colonel H. S. Olcott (1832-1907). Other sources were the "twelve principles of Buddhism" set out by Christmas Humphreys (1901-83, president of the Buddhist Society in London), as well as the "six points of connection between Mahayana and Theravada," formulated by G. P. Malalasekera in 1947 before the All Ceylon Buddhist Congress.

Several of the organizers of the 1987 conference were previously acquainted from Buddhist-Christian dialogue conferences. They had learned in that context that for dialogue with Christianity it is necessary to formulate a statement about the essential content of Buddhism, to which all the Buddhist traditions could agree. Thus the Buddhist-Christian dialogue efforts in America have stimulated new quests for intra-Buddhist ecumenicism.

Dialogue between ethnic Buddhists and American historians of Buddhism remains difficult, however, as the 1987 conference in Berkeley also showed. The former are mostly uneducated historically, because the faith is transmitted through participation in rituals. The latter, on the contrary, are oriented toward history and ideas, which are not necessarily linked to ritual praxis or a regular community life. An important exception is the Tibetan Buddhist groups in relation to Tibetology. The entire field of Tibetan Buddhism studies in the United States and to some extent also in Europe was initiated by lamas and rinpoches.[59] Most of them live in monastic-style communities and can thus unite teaching and ritual, theory and praxis.

Dialogue concerning Pressing Contemporary Issues

The Buddhist-Christian conference in Berkeley by no means only concerned itself with the classical philosophical dialogue themes. The working groups were much more dominated by liberation theology, feminism, and deep ecology. These issues were discussed from the perspective of a dialogue-based Buddhist-Christian spirituality. The conference was marked above all by a great interest in spiritual exchange.

Zen master Yamada Koun (1907-89) from Kamakura was himself present. He trained many Catholics from Europe and North America to become Zen masters. Common meditations and an analysis of Zen-Christian contemplation and Buddhist awareness traditions *(sati)* punctuated the conversations. Monasticism was discussed as a communal form that overlaps the religions, and a worldwide Buddhist-Christian contact group for spiritual exchange of monks and nuns

---

[59] *Lama* is the Tibetan term for any spiritual teacher who gives instruction in Buddhist philosophy and meditation praxis. *Rinpoche* is a title of honor ("more precious") that not all lamas attain. One must distinguish these from the monk (*gelong*) who is not (or not yet) a lama. *Geshe*, on the contrary, is an academic title, which is awarded after rigorous examinations, comparable to the Western academic Ph.D. Not every lama is a geshe.

was constituted. This group spreads information about Christian-Buddhist meditation groups and encourages reflection about them.[60]

The Hermeneutics of "Skillful Means"

The 1987 Berkeley conference also took significant interest in *hermeneutical questions*. Many discussions revolved around the Buddhist concept of *upaya*, that is, the "skillful means" that served the Buddha in order to be able to bring all beings the liberating message each in a way corresponding to its previous understanding. Roger Corless, professor of Buddhism and comparative religious studies at Duke University, showed in his lecture "The Hermeneutics of Polemics" how the terms "*Hinayana*" (lesser vehicle) and "*Old* Testament" (devaluing "lesser" and "old") came into being. The labels were often not applied against true Hinayana Buddhists or true Jews, but rather expressed identity demarcations that were useful to their own group. They were intended to say whom one ought *not* follow. In other words, this is an issue of invention or *construction of traditions*.[61] This process occurred in both Buddhism and Christianity.

Whether the self-understanding of a religion (in the principle of interpretation) can be employed for understanding another religion presents itself as a methodologically important question. Several participants in discussion explained that the principle of *upaya* must be applied to the understanding level of the other. Just as the Buddha preached despite his original hesitation at expressing his inexpressible message in words, religious self-understanding can only be demanded from those standing outside making use of comparisons and metaphors in fragmentary fashion.

José Cabezon, a Tibetologist of Mexican descent (one of the few Latin Americans who are engaged in Buddhist-Christian dialogue in America), expressed himself critical of quick comparisons and harmonizations of both religions. He appealed to the need to explore the mistaken judgments of each side's polemics against their historical and philosophical background. He argues that in Hinayana *upaya* was not a developed concept, but in Mahayana is presented both as "father of buddhas and bodhisattvas" and in polarity to *prajna* (wisdom), which is regarded as "mother of buddhas and bodhisattvas." *Upaya* was identified with *karuna* (compassion), which stems from *upaya*. But, argues Cabezon, *upaya* was above all the means by which Mahayana Buddhism could understand other religions. For example, in China Hui-yüan (fourth century C.E.) and in Japan Rennyo (1415-99) used the concept of *upaya* to classify teachings that did not directly contradict the higher truth of Mahayana. In this way it was possible to integrate other teachings and religions. This was especially effective because it was not necessary to deny their difference from Mahayana but did not encourage persecution

---

[60] M. J. Augustine, "The Buddhist-Christian Monastic and Contemplative Encounter," *Buddhist-Christian Studies* 9 (1989): 248-55.

[61] R. J. Corless, "The Hermeneutics of Polemic: The Creation of Hinayana and Old Testament," *Buddhist-Christian Studies* 11 (1991): 59-74.

and destruction of the foreign teaching as falsehood, which is shockingly prevalent in the history of Christianity.[62]

When we evaluate the dialogue of recent years, we can assert that Buddhism has understood Christianity in this sense mostly as *upaya*. One must ask whether this could be a general model for interreligious dialogue. At any rate it is clear that *upaya* comes very close to the Christian position of inclusivity: other religions are incorporated into a ladder of understanding-levels and thus possibly taken into the fold. Whether the Buddhist is described as a Christian who just does not (yet) know it, or the Christian appears as a pilgrim on the way of Buddha really makes no great difference. Perhaps this inclusivity is unavoidable. In any case there appears to be no indication today that the majority of Buddhists go beyond the sort of "cautious respect" toward Christianity that is connected to the concept of *upaya*.

Who May Interpret Religion?

Connected to the *hermeneutic questions*, Christian Joachim (California State University, San Jose) gave a much-discussed lecture: "Homo Religiosus: Beyond the Insider-Outsider Paradigm." It is a contribution to the relationship between detached religious studies and theologically engaged dialogue. The historian regards temporal reality as a uniform flow, while the believer values some periods qualitatively higher than others, that is, assesses them as *kairos*: the time of Jesus' life and the life of Gautama are for Christians or Buddhists *prominent* history, the middle of the age, and so on. This differentiation between *chronological* and *kairological* time is, argues Joachim, more suitable than the usual distinction of profane versus holy time. Even less meaningful is the beloved dichotomy of linear and cyclical time, or indeed Rudolf Bultmann's distinction between history and narrative.

Joachim's contribution elucidated the difference between descriptive historical writing and normative historical interpretation, as has been carried out by Christian or Buddhist historians from the perspective of faith. From the kairological perspective comes the distinction between "outsider" and "insider." Joachim believes that this designation of "insiders" is by no means the *sine qua non* of religious humans but marks a form of exclusivism. For the assumption implies that only a Hindu of particular caste or a confessing Christian is a true Hindu or living Christian, and thus only they may interpret the tradition in dialogue. We are, however, "insiders" in relation to all traditions, argues Joachim. Just as no person, as *homo aestheticus*, needs an "insider status" in order to be accepted as a partner in dialogue about art (one need not be a painter to understand and judge painting), so every person as *homo religiosus* (the preceding latent or active religious socialization is another issue) can take fully accepted part in religious discourse.

---

[62] Our source is the manuscript of the lecture, from the conference materials. The significance of the concept of *upaya* for Mahayana Buddhism as an aid to understanding other religions is clearly worked out by M. Pye, "Skillful Means and the Interpretation of Christianity," *Buddhist-Christian Studies* 10 (1990): 17-22.

The distinction between "insider" and "outsider," is, however, problematic.[63] Such a division comes near to arguing in relation to one's own tradition with the submission of an "insider," but reacting to the other tradition with the distance of the "outsider." According to Joachim, the difficulty appears at the point where, for example, the Judeo-Christian tradition regards the "insider" as chosen and the "outsider" as heathen, a difference that does not occur in Hinduism and Buddhism. For Buddhists, every non-Buddhist is an unconscious or "anonymous" not-yet-Buddhist.

The debate is open and important for current dialogue. Joachim at any rate sees the problem as leading back to the dialogue between the person as *homo religiosus* and the object of the religion as a *dimension of culture*. The religious is for him the "final reach of the mind," a highest level under which many lesser and changeable levels of mind unfold for a religious person. A human being seeking after sense can reach from the naive realism of the *homo pragmaticus* to the final desire of the *homo religiosus*. Each of these levels uncovers the same form or the same region, but in different ways: the *homo oeconomicus* sees the same circumstance with other eyes than the *homo religiosus*—religion is fundamental and life-enriching, but not absolutely necessary for survival.

Thus, for Joachim, interreligious dialogue is a community of communication between religious people about problems of spiritual values, without being able entirely to divide "insider" from "outsider" or religion from the other cultural accomplishments of humankind. In this humanistic horizon interreligious dialogue would be freed from its theocentric foundation and aimed toward a *universally freeing goal*.

The Catholic theologian Paul Knitter makes a similar argument.[64] And this seems to be the direction in which Buddhist-Christian dialogue in America is developing in general.

THE INTERNATIONAL BUDDHIST-CHRISTIAN THEOLOGICAL ENCOUNTER GROUP (COBB-ABE GROUP)

After preparatory talks at the first international dialogue conference held in Hawaii in 1980, Abe Masao and John Cobb at the second Hawaii conference in 1984 founded an ongoing work group, such as had appeared nowhere in the world before. Twenty-four Buddhist and Christian scholars, it was planned, would discuss theological and religious questions of common interest over a fixed period of nearly five years. Each of the participants pledged to take part in all the meetings, so that the conversations could gain consistency. The project in the end proved to be so successful that three further meetings were added, leading the dialogue into the 1990s. The participants, chosen and invited by Cobb, are well-known and respected theologians or Buddhist philosophers in their own

---

[63] See R. Reat, "Insider and Outsider in the Study of Religious Traditions," *Journal of the American Academy of Religion* 51 (1983): 459-76.

[64] P. Knitter, "Author's Response," *Horizons* 13/1 (1986): 130-35.

confessions, who did not necessarily have any specialist's knowledge of the other religion. The continuity in this work has made it possible for each side to improve basic knowledge, upon which foundation specific themes could be handled in a new and independent way. John Berthrong, a Canadian theologian and participant as well as observer over the years, reports that the Christians have above all learned to appreciate the long and important tradition of ethics and social-ethical responsibility in Buddhism. Buddhists for their part have learned that the Christians do not have a simple theistic understanding of God, but know how to express the non-duality of God and human as well as the eschatologically believed unity between the two in subtle fashion, so that the personal relationship between the two is integrated into unity. As Berthrong says, "Both traditions have learned that a religion that remains uncritical in its views of other religions is a dangerous artificial product in the modern world, where religions have the task of reducing communal conflicts."[65] Besides Abe Masao and John Cobb, the following took part in the three-day deliberations of the first meeting of the work group in 1984 on the Christian side: John Hick, Gordon Kaufman, Langdon Gilkey, David Lochhead, Schubert Ogden, John Berthrong, David Tracy, Hans Küng, and Yagi Seiichi. On the Buddhist side were Francis Cook, Rita Gross, Tokiwa Gishin, Unno Taitetsu, David Kalupahana, and David Chappell.[66] The theme, "Suffering," formed the basis for these conversations.

The second meeting[67] of the theological encounter group took place at the Vancouver School of Theology (Canada) in March 1985. The theme was "Transformation in the Personal and Social Dimensions." Besides the closed sessions, there were also public lectures and discussions that were prepared and supported by local Buddhist and Christian organizations. This led to the development of local dialogue contacts that are still ongoing today. The discussions revolved especially around the concepts of *karma* and liberation. Buddhists and Christians agreed that both concepts must be understood socially as well as individually. And on exactly this point both religions were subjected to a feminist critique, because both had understood liberation within their own patriarchal structures: Buddhism inasmuch as (most) women must be reborn as men before

---

[65] J. Berthrong, 138.

[66] On the not yet introduced participants: John Hick (professor of philosophy of religions at Claremont School of Theology), Gordon Kaufman (professor of systematic theology, Harvard University), Langdon Gilkey (professor of systematic theology, Chicago University), David Lochhead (professor of systematic theology, Vancouver School of Theology), Schubert Ogden (professor of systematic theology, until 1993, at Southern Methodist University), David Tracy (professor of Catholic fundamental theology, Chicago University), Francis Cook (professor of Buddhist studies at the University of California), Rita Gross (professor of Buddhist studies, University of Wisconsin at Eau Claire), Tokiwa Gishin (professor of Buddhist studies, Kyoto), Unno Taitetsu (professor of Buddhist studies, Smith College), David Kalupahana (professor of philosophy, University of Hawaii at Manoa).

[67] A short report on the meetings can be found in J. Berthrong, "The Buddhist-Christian Theological Encounter," *The Catholic World* 233/1395 (May/June 1990): 122-25.

they can attain final liberation, Christianity inasmuch as women have been excluded in language, liturgy, and institutions.

The third encounter meeting had the theme "Concepts of Final Reality in Buddhism and Christianity." It took place in October 1986 at Purdue University (Indiana). The Buddhist contributions were offered by Francis Cook and Jeffrey Hopkins, with corresponding Christian answers by Hans Küng and Yagi Seiichi as well as Julia Ching and Durwood Foster. John Cobb and Gordon Kaufman gave the Christian presentations with responses by Abe Masao, Reginald Ray, Takeda Ryusei, and Rita Gross. Feminist questions touching both religions were also discussed again (Rita Gross, Rosemary Ruether).[68]

The fourth meeting occurred in August 1987 in conjunction with the third International Buddhist-Christian Conference in Berkeley on the theme "Being in the World: Ethical and Communal Perspectives in Buddhism and Christianity." Not only theologians and philosophers but for the first time also the lay Buddhist Sulak Siverak considered new formulations of the political and social order and the contingent ethics in Buddhist and Christian terms. Feminist questions as well as the problem of the quest for community in the modern world were also included on the agenda. Again the participants tackled the theme of suffering; Buddhism and Christianity have thoroughly different attitudes toward suffering, despite all points of contact. While the Buddha overcame suffering in tranquil rest, Jesus gave himself over to agony that would take the suffering of others upon himself, only then to die in the rest of self-surrender in the hands of God ("it is accomplished"), as the Buddhist Reginald Ray emphasized.

Ray ended this dialogue with the words: "We are not engaged in dialogue in order to emphasize differences, still less simply to agree, but in order to see and to make it possible that we are seen, to be challenged and to challenge."[69] In other words, communication does not only consist of explaining what the religions have said in the past, but above all in presenting perspectives that Buddhism and Christianity have to offer for the questions of the present and the future.

The fifth meeting of the Cobb-Abe group was in March 1989 at Hsi Lai Temple in Hacienda Heights, near Los Angeles. It dealt with the theme "The Buddha and Christ." This is the first time the dialogue group was hosted by an American Buddhist institution. At this meeting the question was raised anew of the significance of history in general and in accordance with criteria for judgment of individual events in view of the historicity and the historical uniqueness of each religion's "cumulative traditions" (W. C. Smith). With this expression, Smith

---

[68] Lectures and summaries are printed in *Buddhist-Christian Studies* 9 (1989): 124ff. On the not yet introduced participants: Jeffrey Hopkins (professor of Tibetology, University of Virginia), Julia Ching (professor of religious studies, University of Toronto), Durwood Foster (professor of systematic theology, Pacific School of Religion [Graduate Theological Union], Berkeley), Reginald Ray (professor of Buddhist studies, Naropa Institute, Boulder), Takeda Ryusei (professor of Buddhist studies, Ryukoku University, Kyoto), Rosemary Radford Ruether (professor of systematic theology, Garrett Evangelical Theological Seminary, Northwestern University).

[69] R. Ray, "Response to Mitchell," *Buddhist-Christian Studies* 13 (1993): 177.

offers the insight that each religion is constantly changing and undergoes new developments in the course of its history that were not foreseen at an earlier point in time. Hans Küng referred to the analytical concept of shifting paradigms, behind which the constants can be grasped beyond the historical change. He pointed out that paradigms are, as explained by the historian of science Thomas Kuhn, "full constellations of beliefs, values, methods, etc., that are shared by the members of a given community."[70] Paradigm shift becomes necessary if scientific developments break up such a generally accepted model of explanation. Similarly, religions, argues Hans Küng, pass through different paradigms (full constellations of beliefs, concepts, organizational forms, and methods). One should be aware of this when making comparisons, so that in dialogue one does not compare a "medieval paradigm" in one religion to an enlightenment-critical paradigm in the other religion and regard the difference as the fundamental difference between "the" religion of each side.

It remained a controversially discussed problem whether parallels in the paths of salvation can be described separately from their historically unique actualization in order to simplify the contemporary encounter between the religions.

This closed the originally planned series of encounters. Because all the participants had found this sort of dialogue extraordinarily stimulating, they agreed to hold further meetings when opportunity offered.

Thus the sixth meeting took place in conjunction with the fourth International Buddhist-Christian conference in the summer of 1992 in Boston on the theme "*Upaya* and Truth." The participants again asked whether *upaya* could be a model for a calmer way to approach the question of truth in dialogue. It is not clear, though, that progress was made beyond the state of the discussion in Berkeley in 1987.

The dialogue group's encounters continue, even though the membership of the group now changes continually. The group accepted an invitation from the Rissho Kosei-kai for a meeting in July 1994 in Tokyo. The goal of further work is to anchor the dialogue dimension more firmly in the theological education of confessional Christian seminars as well as America's ecclesiastical institutions.

JOHN COBB'S DIALOGICAL THEOLOGY IN THE CONTEXT OF PROCESS PHILOSOPHY

American dialogue in the 1980s was, as we have mentioned several times, inseparably linked with the names John Cobb and Abe Masao. Cobb and Abe met in Claremont, California. Abe Masao is a representative of the Kyoto school, taught for many years in Nara (Japan), and since the late 1970s has continued the line of the Kyoto philosophers in America. These philosophers (Nishida, Tanabe, Nishitani), however, were much more closely linked to German philosophy than to Anglo-American. Contact with process philosophy and its wider development in American process theology has only come with Abe's activity in

---

[70] T. Kuhn, *Die Struktur wissenschaftlicher Revolutionen*, 2d ed. (Frankfurt: Suhrkamp, 1976), 186.

the United States. But as a matter of fact, most Americans who engage in philosophical Buddhist-Christian dialogue belong to the process-philosophical school of Whitehead.

Alfred North Whitehead (1861-1947) was born in Great Britain. He was a mathematician and philosopher. Whitehead was a friend of Bertrand Russell (1872-1970), and at first they worked together in the field of mathematical logic. Their ways divided on account of their later philosophical theories. More even than William James (1842-1910) and the later proponents of pragmatism, Whitehead laid the groundwork for a new non-substantialist mode of thought that distanced itself from historical European philosophical roots. He developed an alternative metaphysics (even though he did not like to be identified as a metaphysician) that, although it was not accepted by many other philosophers, became popular with American theologians. John Cobb is now accepted as the leading proponent of this theological-philosophical process theology.

Process philosophy is so called because it moves away from the Aristotelian interest in being and substance toward a dynamic of becoming and process. That means a close relationship to Buddhism, which surmounts fixation on being and substance *(atman, sat)*.[71] Process philosophy takes positions that are similar to certain assertions of Buddhism, without being historically dependent on Buddhism. Whitehead understands Christianity as a religion that has turned into metaphysics, and Buddhism as a metaphysics that has transformed itself into a religion. This distinction is interpreted by contemporary Whiteheadians as more unifying than divisive for dialogue. They lead a group of dialogically thinking theologians who want to establish a union of Buddhist emptiness *(sunyata)* with existential or postmodern deconstructionist concerns, in order to bring traditional metaphysics to an end.

A lecture of John Cobb's illustrates well the historical development of process theology in Chicago. This lecture was given at the invitation of the Center for Metaphysics and Philosophy of God at the Institute for Philosophy and the Theology Department at the University of Löwen in March 1980 on the theme "Process Theology and the Doctrine of God." This lecture is a synopsis of the history of the Chicago School of Theology and an introduction to process thought.[72] It is essential for us to sketch some of the basic lines of this history briefly, in order to make the great influence of process theology on contemporary Buddhist-Christian dialogue in America comprehensible.

---

[71] For example, C. Hartshorne, 1-13. Other names are T. J. Altizer and David A. Dilworth. On them, see R. C. Neville, "Buddhism and Process Philosophy," in Inada and Jacobson, eds., 120-42. For a very short introduction to process theological thought, see P. Ingram, *The Modern Buddhist-Christian Dialogue: Two Universalistic Religions in Transformation* (Lewiston, N.Y.: Mellen, 1988), 6ff.; a detailed presentation of Whitehead's process thought can be found in W. S. Christian, *An Interpretation of Whitehead's Metaphysics* (New Haven, Conn.: Yale University Press, 1969).

[72] J. Cobb, "Process Theology and the Doctrine of God," *Bijdragen* 41, *Tijdschrift voor philosophie en theologie* (Antwerp, 1980), 350-67.

In his lecture John Cobb recalls the liberal background of Chicago theology, which at the end of the nineteenth century was the home of the Social Gospel. Chicago scholars stressed the sociohistorical aspect of Christian history. Shailer Matthews gave social realism a cosmic dimension, by extending the question of God beyond the New Testament, the church, and traditional theology, even beyond Christianity as a whole. For him, God was that which humankind in its history had regarded as worthy of veneration—the element in the cosmos that encourages personality, answers personally, and with which we were originally united.[73] To this naturalistic belief, which had as its content the process of creating the person through the inherent powers of nature itself, the still more influential Henry Nelson Wieman (member of the Chicago theology faculty, 1927-47) added a new interest in *mysticism*, which had hitherto played little role in Protestant theology. For Wieman, God was the element of *creativity* in the cosmos.

Chicago theology fell to one side as the foundations of liberal theology were shaken by Karl Barth's and Emil Brunner's so-called dialectical theology, which was a neo-orthodoxy. Their stress on the radical difference between sinful humanity and an absolutely transcendent God was for the Chicago School a step back toward conservative authoritarianism, supra-naturalism, and exclusivism. For their part, the conservatives reproached the Chicagoans' unbounded optimism in regard to the fallen world and their lack of consciousness of sin. The Chicago theologians were stigmatized both ecclesiastically and theologically. This led some of the theology professors to turn to Whitehead's process philosophy in their quest for a new foundation for a naturalist and truly American theology.

Whitehead in 1926 was already a professor at Harvard University. He was invited to Chicago, and his lectures were published under the title *Religion in the Making*.[74] One of his auditors and students was Charles Hartshorne, who was active in Chicago from 1943 to 1955, first in the philosophy department and then also in the Divinity School. And this laid the foundation for the development of process theology.

Hartshorne's book *Beyond Humanism: Essays in the Philosophy of Nature* (1957) interprets the universe as a universe of "feeling" in different degrees of subtlety that range from molecules and insensate rocks to the upper realms of spirits. Hartshorne sees an "organic sympathy" among all beings, and that means for him that truth can be recognized through intuition. This assumption, however, is based on the rational argument that a pan-psychic theory of this sort can have a special priority: it can, like none other, serve as the basis for an all-encompassing theory.

As a matter of fact, such reflections lean in the direction of Buddhism. In Buddhism, too, a fundamental category for describing reality is feeling *(vedana)*. The Buddhist path is preached for all "feeling beings" from the hungry spirits

---

[73] S. Matthews, *The Growth of the Idea of God* (New York: Macmillan, 1931), 226; cited in Cobb, 355.

[74] A. N. Whitehead, *Religion in the Making* (Cleveland: World Publishing, 1926).

through animals to humans. Being *(sattva)* is endowed with feeling and consciousness, and beings gradually are differentiated from one another according to their subtlety in regard to these qualities.[75]

The entire range of parallels between the Buddhist concept of *pratityasamutpada* (origination in mutual dependence) with process thought was not immediately apparent in Buddhist-Christian dialogue. At first, Suzuki Daisetsu's philosophy of emptiness *(sunyata)* was understood rather in the sense of radical negation than as complete interdependence—at least Suzuki's thought was interpreted in this fashion.

Thus it should not be surprising that the next epoch-making attempt at a theological appropriation of the Buddhist philosophy of emptiness *(sunyata)* should have built upon Nagarjuna's *Madhyamaka-Karika.* This was the work of Frederick Streng, presented in his book *Emptiness: A Study in Religious Meaning* (1967).[76] Streng proposed a new interpretation of *sunyata* as *religious symbol* that went beyond the earlier efforts of T. Stcherbatsky and T. R. V. Murti.[77] His starting point was the *function* that *sunyata* takes on within the wider context of the debate within linguistic philosophy. With this, Streng was the first theologian to write an entire book about Nagarjuna. Process philosophy did not yet play a role, but rather Wittgenstein's linguistic philosophy. Nagarjuna's critique of the abstractionism *(prapañca)* that thwarts every substantial thought and thus every ontology appeared to touch Wittgenstein's revelation of language games.

It was only in the 1980s, as American authors began to take up the thought of the Chinese Hua-Yen school,[78] that the positive depiction of emptiness *(sunyata)* as mutual dependence *(pratityasamutpada)* became generally known and interesting for process theology. A first fruit of this synthesis was John Cobb's book on the mutual transformation of Buddhism and Christianity, *Beyond Dialogue* (1982). *Pratityasamutpada* now has come to be understood as a synonym for *sunyata* and is no longer overshadowed by the negative linguistic form of "nothingness." "All is empty" is now expressed as "everything stands in relationship with everything." The latter expression, to be sure, corresponds better to Hua-Yen philosophy than to Nagarjuna's original ideas. But Hua-Yen studies, which

---

[75] In the language of myth these are, for example, the six realms of rebirth: from hell beings through hungry spirits *(preta)*, animals, and humans, to demonic *(asura)* and godly *(deva)* spiritual beings.

[76] Nagarjuna (second and third centuries C.E.) created the philosophical foundation for the identification of *sunyata* (emptiness) and *pratityasamutpada* (origination in mutual dependence), especially through a critique of the contemporary ontology in conjunction with the analysis that every concept is an epistemological construct *(prapañca)*.

[77] T. Stcherbatsky, *The Conception of Buddhist Nirvana* (Delhi: Motilal, 1968; first appeared 1927); Stcherbatsky, *Buddhist Logic*, 2 vols. (New York: Dover, 1962; first appeared 1930 in the series Bibliotheca Buddhica); T.R.V. Murti, *The Central Philosophy of Buddhism* (London: Allen & Unwin, 1955).

[78] This school of Chinese Buddhism (founded in the seventh century C.E.) teaches "totalism," that is, the mutual penetration of all appearances, by which every appearance is a reflection of all others.

are built on the complete interrelationality of reality, now shape the debate.[79] The connection to Hua-Yen has enriched Buddhist-Christian dialogue through a fruitful and further-leading exchange between process theology and Mahayana Buddhism.

RESULTS AND PROSPECTS

• Dialogue in America is rooted in the confessional pluralism of American history, the unique relationships of the United States with Japan, and the new multiculturalism caused by Asian immigration after World War II. Especially the situation at universities and colleges is such that Buddhist-Christian relations can also be experienced in practical terms in a predominantly pluralistic structure.

• Dialogue in America is for the most part limited to communication among individuals who are scholars. This is because, unlike other English-speaking lands (Canada, England) where cities and communities with a multireligious population initiate and promote dialogue for the sake of practical coexistence, in the United States governmental institutions are not involved in such interreligious and ecumenical efforts because of the separation of church and state. The universities are among the few public institutions that have both the necessary intellectual freedom and the competence to discuss differences between various U.S. religious groups, and thus to make freedom of religion a reality in intellectual debate, too.

• Academic exchange has until now concentrated especially on dialogue with the philosophical Kyoto school. This has been extraordinarily fruitful, especially in the context of American process philosophy. The high degree of institutionalization (Cobb-Abe Group, Society for Buddhist-Christian Studies) has made a thematic and personal continuity possible, which has not yet been attained in other countries.

• The almost overwhelming breadth of dialogue is articulated in a new conference culture that reflects back to influence Christian theological work at universities and seminaries. In many cases Buddhist philosophy has already become an obvious framework in which Christian theology is articulated.

• Unlike Germany, where Buddhist meditation methods are also practiced in ecclesiastical institutions, most Protestant churches in the United States remain detached from practical dialogue with Buddhism. Instead, in America a network of Buddhist-Christian groups has grown up that practice a spiritual exchange

---

[79] The first book in English about Hua-Yen was written by Garma C.C. Chang, *Buddhist Teaching of Totality* (University Park, Pa.: State University of Pennsylvania Press, 1971), a historian of Buddhism with a Tibetologist education. Inaccurate in some details, this study has been displaced by Francis Cook, *Hua-yen Buddhism: The Jewel Net of Indra* (University Park, Pa.: State University of Pennsylvania Press, 1977). But it is above all Thomas Cleary's monumental translation of the *Hua-yen-Sutra* (*Avatamsaka-Sutra*) (Boston: Shambhala, 1984-87) that has quickened dialogical debate. It was continued by Steve Odin, *Process Metaphysics and Hua-yen Buddhism* (Albany, N.Y.: SUNY, 1982), and many others.

between the two religions and overthrow classical boundaries between the confessions. Catholic nuns and monks are also integrated into this network.

• Buddhist-Christian dialogue is an aspect of the liberal heritage of intellectual culture in America. It is to a great degree a theoretical conversation between American Buddhists and American theologians who teach at the same universities. It is supported by an intellectual avant-garde that has up to now found little resonance in politics or the great ecclesiastical organizations. While the liberal church confessions continue to lose members, America's conservative and evangelical churches are growing. It is an entirely open question whether or not it will be possible to make the concerns of Buddhist-Christian dialogue known and comprehensible to these groups. That will decide whether the understanding between the religions in America's multireligious cities and communities can also become socially and politically effective. This is an urgent task.

Conclusion

Hermeneutical Aspects of Future Encounter

That which is taken for granted only becomes a problem or a question when it encounters something different. We experience this when we learn a foreign language. For it is then that the self-explanatory structure of the mother tongue appears as only one quite specific window onto reality, beside which others exist. It is the same with religions. It is through encounter with the Other that understanding comes about, in which the Other is partially made "Us." "Us" and "Other" are abstractions of a process that history shapes. Thus dialogue between "religions" is the place where "religion" has been created, not just a supplementary dimension of an otherwise existing religion. This means:

> Where new thoughts come into being, they belong neither to me nor to the Other. They come into existence between us. Without this Between there would be no inter-subjectivity or interculturalism that is worthy of the name. Matters would be left with the mere expansion or multiplication of the Self; the foreign would always be reduced to silence.[1]

Understanding of the foreign comes about through translations into one's own linguistic and imaginative world. If we regard cultures or religions as a "text," we could say: Translations of a *text* occur in a *context* that produces a new *texture* that will be conditioned by the historically created circumstances of the side that has perceived as well as that which is perceived. In dialogue the circumstances are still more complicated, because both sides are equally perceiving and perceived subjects, or "two immanent self-understandings."[2] In other words, *dialogue is a spoken creative process*. It does not only portray the obvious but creates new modes of perception and communication in dependence on the history of each tradition. In other words, interpretation (or translation) of religion changes religion. We do not mean by this a *radical* constructivism that would argue that there is no reality at all beyond our perception and interpretation. But this view

---

[1] B. Waldenfels, "Das Eigene und das Fremde," *Dtsch. Z. Philos.* 43/4 (1995): 620.
[2] J. May, "Vom Vergleich zur Verständigung: Die unstete Geschichte der Vergleiche zwischen Buddhismus und Christentum, 1880-1980," *ZMP* 66 (1982): 63.

also prohibits the sort of naive realism that believes it can portray reality "as it is." Rather, we proceed from a *relative constructivism* that assumes that we can in fact perceive phenomena that are given outside of our own self. This perception, however, is always interpreted intersubjectively on the basis of different and historically constantly changing traditions. Interreligious encounter or dialogue consists of achieving a (chronologically bounded) intersubjective *consensus of perception* between different traditions. Whether a consciously willed *consensus in interpretation* follows from this is a second question, in which at least, as we saw, there is no uninterpreted perception.

An important result of Buddhist-Christian dialogue is the realization that there is neither *the* Buddhism nor *the* Christianity, and certainly not an *essence* of each, but always just a web of communication processes and shifting images. What a religion *is* is decided in the interaction of different partners who refer to this religion! This is because a person first comes to the essence through its opposite, rather than because he or she experiences it.[3] We do not enter into communication only secondarily, after we already "are"; instead we "come to pass" *intersubjectively* through a communication with the Other that confronts the past of our "own" tradition as it does the current encounter with the Other as *possibility* for our own future. Being human *is* this "between." From this it follows for a hermeneutics of dialogue that the Other be perceived as Other, even and inasmuch as it enters the field of the Self, which through this will be changed. The Other (the other religion) should be perceived in the same way that it understands itself.

That is an important challenge: to avoid premature transmission of our own wishes, objectives, and interests that would make any understanding of the Other impossible. But, to be sure, if the Other were entirely different we could know nothing of it, and if it were completely identical to us, then we would not perceive it. Being "other" is relative to us. Thus we do not remain with the otherness of the Other, and dialogue consists of a "fetching in" of the Other into our own accustomed paradigm for understanding, which in any case changes in the process of interpretation. That is understanding and being understood, and thus *mutual transformation*.[4]

Religious and philosophical conflict consists of the fact that religions assert an absolute claim and want, indeed need, to make this universally valid, at the same time that they are particularly and historically determined and thus undermine their own claim. Does recognition of this dilemma already contain a solution in itself?

On the basis of the experiences that we have presented in the preceding chapters, we wish to discuss the issue from the point of view of certain pragmatic considerations.

---

[3] Martin Buber's *dialogical principle* applies not just to interreligious dialogue but to *every* humanizing development (see M. Buber, "Ich und Du," in *Werke*, vol. 1, *Schriften zur Philosophie*, 77-170 [Munich: Kösel, 1962; first appeared 1923]). Buber's model is an "ontology of the between" (M. Theunissen).

[4] John Cobb, *Beyond Dialogue: Toward a Mutual Transformation of Christianity and Buddhism* (Philadelphia: Fortress Press, 1982).

PRACTICAL CONSIDERATIONS

DIALOGUE AND MISSION

On this theme the (mostly concealed) hermeneutical assumptions of religious encounter manifest themselves. Is there a (transcendental and phenomenological) unity of religions? Are there several truths or one? How can this be decided, and how can contact with several claims of truth be managed—with tolerance or with missionizing the Other? Expressed in theoretical terms: What is the relationship between descriptive religious studies and normative theology? Is there a hermeneutics that integrates the contraries of positions and methods in such a way that a fruitful discourse between the two can bring an increase of knowledge for both rather than an increase in power for one side or the other?

We wish to mention beforehand several historical issues. With the exception of Judaism and Islam, the various religions and cultures for the most part only entered Europe's field of vision in the fifteenth and sixteenth centuries, and only since the nineteenth century have been regarded as grounds for critical self-distancing. At the end of the nineteenth century, especially through linguistic studies, studies in Sanskrit and Eastern languages, corresponding institutes and university chairs were founded to study the culture of individual lands. Also within both Protestant and Catholic schools institutes and chairs were created that were concerned with other cultures and religions. This new interest for its part came to pass under the purview of the missions. And the missions were joined together in an entire concept of European self-understanding that was expressed through optimism about progress and the self-evident drive to expand the apparently superior European-American model of knowledge and culture. This self-image changed radically after the two world wars, especially after World War II. Eurocentrism was at least in principle surmounted, and Christianity too had to find its place in this transformed world. Every "claim of unity" or "world history" was broken on this self-relativizing history.

Religions that impart a universal meaning to the world and a corresponding demand upon life, such as Buddhism and Christianity, have always made inroads into other cultures. Every religion of this sort has, according to its own self-understanding, not only the right but the duty to show itself and to present itself to other people. The history of Christian mission must thus be regarded from two viewpoints:

• On the one side it reflects the legitimate witnessing of Christian faith in the world as an offer of salvation for all humankind.

• On the other side, however, it is indivisibly linked to the colonial history of Europe and North America, which, as we have seen, has left deep wounds in the Buddhist world.

For this reason "mission" has become problematic. Because of the second point, mission has instead obscured and hindered what it has been commanded to do dialogically, namely, to give witness to the basic fact of Christian history, God's unconditional love in the person of Jesus Christ. If the Christian churches hold fast to this mission history because of power or identity interests and refuse to acknowledge the guilt that is linked to it, the Christian partners in religious dialogue will not be able to bring to it what they ought to bring as a specifically Christian contribution: the conviction that God's salvation is promised to all humans and is indeed *unconditional*.

In the Greek Bible the idea of witness and sending out for all humankind has a central significance in the sense of a universal claim to validity of truth as it is believed in Jesus Christ. The universal claim to validity is not abstract, however, but linked to a specific and culturally determined view of the world. It must thus be brought to utterance in another way, so that what it means *theologically* can be expressed hermeneutically in conditions of interreligious communication, or else the danger of confusion between idea and conduct will become acute.

The world was relatively small for the early Christians; their view of the world meant knowledge of the cosmos of that time, in essence the Mediterranean basin. These early Christians had no notion of what lay beyond that, certainly not of the Indian, Chinese, and still more distant cultures. This changed. Then as now, it was accepted that the message of the gospel is a message for all humankind. But that cannot mean that the forms of thought, language, and institutions, in other words the development of church and theology, as they were created above all in Europe over the past two thousand years, are binding and universal for the rest of the world—or even for *contemporary* theology in Europe.

That means that in essence the *message* of God's unconditional love, as it is shown in Jesus Christ, is meaningful for all people. But that does not mean that the *specific form of Christianity*, as it has developed institutionally and theologically, is also universal. Perception is particular and linked to a quite specific tradition and language. Insofar, however, as the interpretation field becomes *interreligious*, as is the case today, hermeneutical methods—the possible conditions for perceiving the truth—are necessary.

Precisely because in Christianity Christ is understood as truth itself this cannot be identified with claims of truth that are limited by space and time, because otherwise the conditional would be accepted as absolute. This would be expressed by a Buddhist as a form of enslaving adherence and from the Christian point of view would be making concepts and human forms into idols. Belief, cultic praxis, or even meditation or prayer are often misunderstood as *means* of salvation in Christianity, and also in Buddhism.[5] However, in both religions such an objectification of religious experience has been criticized. Both Luther's and Shinran's doctrines of grace argue that belief is the answer to an *ineffable* occurrence. This view also marks Zen experience, in which the prevenient reality of *original* enlightenment is grasped unconditionally so that the "I" can leave itself. This also means that if salvation or liberation depended on a specific human spiritual state or exercise of will it would be uncertain, because spiritual factors and the will are relative and limited in time, so that one can never be completely certain of his or her own spiritual purity or singleness of motivation. Only when salvation depends

---

[5] For the following line of thought, see especially J. Cobb, "Can a Buddhist Be a Christian, Too?"

on *no* human demeanor or action is it certain. Belief or a meditative conscious-ness is the *opening* to receive the *unconditionally* granted love of God. For Chris-tians this is actualized in the communion of love in Christ. For Buddhists it is the experience of transrational unity in which the Buddha nature becomes manifest.

In Christian terms the argument comes to a point thus: If God loves uncondi-tionally, this love cannot only be concerned with some people while closing oth-ers out. If this were the case, the love would be conditional. Thus, according to the logic of salvation based on unconditional love, salvation must in fact be uni-versal. Because in consequence God's love also precedes all human perception, all humans *are* saved whether they know it or not. *Perception* is the surmounting of doubts and the existential realization of this unity of salvation. This can be expressed symbolically, for example, using the particular symbols of the mysti-cal body of Christ or the universal Buddha nature. For Christians this gift of God appeared unambiguously in Jesus Christ, but not only there. This is taught by the logic of salvation and also the actual history of Christ's passion before, after, and outside of Christian interpretation of salvation. Thus

> Belief in Christ means being open to all truth and all reality—not to adhere
> exclusively to a single truth and a single reality. Trusting in Christ means to
> abandon all prejudices as well as defensive positions and to receive all that
> can be received. Buddhists can only be commended to *this* belief in Christ.[6]

The same insight can be found in Buddhist language, for example, in the con-cept of emptiness *(sunyata)* and in the famous Zen-Koan "open wideness—noth-ing of holiness," both of which signify non-adherence to any concept that is only possible. Even emptiness, when it coagulates into an image or concept to which one wants to adhere, must be further emptied. Buddhism has therefore desig-nated all religious expressions, cultic forms, and so on as *upaya*, as skillful and provisional means that attest to the reality of the final validity but are not identi-cal to it. Buddhism in the history of its expansion was in general correspondingly flexible, tolerantly inviting, and not aggressively assertive. This could be a model for the current interaction of religions with one another. Not from opportunistic adjustment to the "spirit of the time," but from insight into the inner dynamic of both religions, which in the last decades has become possible in dialogue.

Does this mean a cultural relativism that will only be held together by refer-ence to a general and humanistically signified "essence" of religion or to a less-defined "numinous"? Is it indeed hermeneutically possible to assume a funda-mental experience that is common to all religions, that could be of use as the starting point for communication in dialogue?

A COMMON FOUNDATION OF ALL RELIGIONS?

The question may be answered neither yes nor no, because every interpreta-tion of this problem has its roots in a specific tradition, in a specific language and

---

[6] Ibid., 49.

tradition of thought. This acts as a matrix through which the world is perceived automatically from one perspective, that is, specific and circumscribed. Even what can be expressed about the transcendent, the numinous, or God always appears only from a specific perspective. There is no meta-perspective from which a human being could look down as if hovering above the world or from God's perspective *(sub specie Dei)* upon the world of religious multiplicity, and thus be able to evaluate the relativity of different religions from the outside. On the other hand, the observing and interpreting consciousness also perceives that there are other perspectives, which can be just as coherent and authentic as one's own.

Of course there are basic experiences[7] that are common to all people—humans are physically very similar to one another, and corresponding impulses are universal. The yearning for a fulfilled life can also be accepted as universal. But these are very general assertions. In which spiritual images humans experience "fulfilled life" and what they understand by that is differently interpreted in different cultures according to the linguistic and religious context of each. Languages and religions are different from each other and cannot be reduced to a common denominator.

But they are also not so different from one another that they cannot be linked to one another. The history of religious encounter teaches that they can be made understandable and thus one can gain knowledge, that languages can be translated, and religions can be compared with one another. The effort to discover what different religions understand by "God" and what the functional equivalent of this concept might be in Buddhism has not led to a solution fixed for all time. Still, it has brought knowledge that for both dialogue partners has deepened understanding of their own presuppositions as well as those of their partners: that the concept concerns something that portrays an ultimate value, an absolute, upon which one can rely unconditionally. True, this "text" is conceived and given shape in differing "textures" in each individual religion. Thus it would be problematic to claim that there is *a* common basis, while the different religions are only the differing outer forms of it. Even this statement is expressed again in a specific language, and thus remains perspectivally circumscribed.

The "unity of reality" does not lie in appearances themselves, but appears in a transrational consciousness experience (mystical experience) that again appears, dependent on its context, in different images and is formulated in differing ways.

LANGUAGE AND POWER

Overall, as we have seen, dialogue between Buddhists and Christians has made progress. But also overall, it has been met with mistrust. What are the reasons for this? Is it the fear of each partner that it will be absorbed, or the fear of falsifying

---

[7] See P. Schmidt-Leukel, *Den Löwen brüllen hören*, 675ff. The author deals with the human foundational experiences as *starting point* of communication, which appears more unified as abstracted concepts that themselves relate back to human fundamental situations. He does not argue that the fundamental experiences in all religions are the same.

its own cultural identity, often articulated as a warning against syncretism[8] or blending of religions? Or are the hermeneutical and linguistic difficulties the insurmountable barrier, because one recognizes increasingly that the construction of linguistic structures that claim to be general stand under ideological condemnation, since they declare specific positions (as, for example, secular humanism) to have universal validity?

There is no interreligious Esperanto, just as no intercultural Esperanto language has been accepted or can be accepted, because Esperanto must be explained again in a specific language. So too with religions: we cannot create a single unified religion and should not want to do so, because this would be a spiritual impoverishment. It would be an abstraction from the concrete myths, histories, life experiences, and claims of different peoples and cultures—a pitiful surrogate.

But one can learn and understand both languages and religions, with expense and effort. How far someone can penetrate into another religion depends on many factors, especially on that person's own personal biography and hermeneutical consciousness. In any case, this is a difficult learning process, collecting new experience and changing the person. All those have such experiences who have ever lived for a long time in a foreign land or lived among foreigners in their own city—they do not remain the same, because values, including their own religion, become relative. They become aware that there are other possibilities and interpretations of life.

This is therefore also an enrichment promoting the process of maturation, because in this way the unique qualities of one's own language and religion become known in a very special fashion. Change in relationship to the Other is the history of every religion that has itself developed and changed through encounter with the Other. One need only consider the history of Christianity, how it changed from its beginnings in Judaism and exposure to the Hellenistic environment through the influence of Platonism, neo-Platonism, and so on. Then in the Middle Ages it was enriched by Islam, inasmuch as high scholasticism could develop through the rebirth and reclamation of Greek antiquity mediated by Islam. Then for the past hundred years increasingly it has also been enriched by other cultures and lands in which a non-European Christianity is being created. (Similar points may be made of Buddhism up to the current transformation that it is experiencing through its spread to Europe and America.)

Here an important consideration arises: Through dialogue will the non-European cultures, first materially pillaged by the colonial powers, now also be spiritually plundered? This is a very serious question, and there are indeed corresponding tendencies. It is dangerous but can only be avoided especially if the currently dominant religions no longer persevere in their own positions but

---

[8] The concept of syncretism has become a polemical catchword. Every religion is syncretic, but in the history of religions it is necessary to differentiate between different forms of melting together what was originally divided. See on this the overview article "Synkretismus" by Chr. Bochinger, in *Wörterbuch der Religionssoziologie*, ed. S. R. Dunde (Gütersloh: Gütersloher Verlagshaus, 1994), 320-27.

become ready to change. In other words, if people in the other religions are not *objects* of missionary work but are seen as partners. In a partnership both sides change insofar as both traverse a common path. They learn from one another, take from one another, but also give to one another. Only through the exchange process of give and take can one partner be prevented from dominating and robbing the Other, pillaging the Other psychically, materially, and also spiritually. Thus we speak of an *identity partnership*. But the danger of dominance and pillaging is great. And it is especially a problem for Christianity, because the churches are in the by no means entirely fortunate situation of being rich and able to dominate because they have at their disposal the apparent world language, English. Even the dialogue described in this book, as well as the hermeneutics of dialogue that want to make these problems conscious and avoid the belief that Christians or Christian-shaped thought and lifestyle are lords of the world, is mostly formulated in English. In this linguistic dominance itself an immense problem lies hidden.

LANGUAGE AND SPIRITUAL PRAXIS IN DIALOGUE

It is often maintained that Christianity understands itself as a religion of the word and thus to a high degree identifies itself with its spoken form, while Buddhism finds itself more at home in silence. This generalization, however, is not universally applicable. Indian Buddhist philosophy (from which Tibetan also stems) and in their own fashion also the Chinese, Korean, and Japanese traditions have developed extremely different spoken images and conceptual systems. In the process they have not only found or reinterpreted language but have also created a new language. Rhetorically gifted and hermeneutically trained, especially the Indian Buddhists in early Buddhism as also later in Mahayana led philosophical controversy debates to a flowering the like of which has hardly been seen in the world. In these traditions Christian theology can find language-conscious partners, as long as the conversation is not ended before it even begins thanks to the spoken or unspoken missionary intent of many Christians. Also, Christianity worldwide makes much more use of the power of the media than other religions, which often arouses a justifiable mistrust.

Language enables especially (but not solely) verbal dialogue. Verbal dialogue is important, but it comprises only *one* level of interreligious communication. Spiritual praxis, which intensifies or changes motivations and states of consciousness, leads mostly into deeper levels of the human and thus also of the understanding. Christians increasingly practice Zen and Yoga, they follow Sufi meditations or study the Kabbala. This is a great chance for deepening of religious perception, because through meditation what has only been learned through reading or externally transmitted (values, beliefs, and so on) can become one's own individually imprinted experience that is a unified whole, because it incorporates and transforms the body as well as the realms of feeling and thought.

However, the desire to play out the linguistic conceptual dialogue against the encounter in the imagination of symbols and images and with the meditative level of silence does not correspond to experiences in Buddhist-Christian encounter. For meditative praxis concludes in "return to the marketplace," as it is called in Zen. That means that the meditative consciousness is embodied in spoken expression. Language can thus gain deeper qualities—a goal that seems urgently necessary in the face of so many emptied images, conceptual word husks, inflationary imperatives, and ideological catchwords. Even more, in face of the wave of manipulated images in the mass-media society, through which a power is practiced that undermines the personal responsibility and freedom of the individual, the meditative freedom from images and words is a psychic and spiritual hygiene that could become necessary for life itself. The silent and spoken dialogue between religions could, we hope, create a critical counterweight to the manipulative web of spoken and imaged structures in the media industry, which is subject to an ever-stronger concentration and runs counter to the hermeneutical principle of unity and multiplicity that is necessary for the existence of different cultures and religions. That this hope is justified can be seen from developments in Buddhist-Christian exchange programs or "engaged Buddhism" as well as in Christian-Asian liberation theology.

In dialogue thus comes to pass what can be designated in Buddhist terms as a progressive freeing from dependence on concepts and prejudices, or in Christian terms as the liberating action of the Holy Spirit.

HERMENEUTICS OF IDENTITY: THE SELF, THE OTHER, AND THE FOREIGN

We differentiate the categories of "other" and "foreign" in the following way. The Other is that which enters into the field of perception and perspectivally is set into relation with the self. The foreign partially avoids this relation—it cannot yet or can no longer be integrated. Perspectives are projections. Perspectives change many times when measured, that is, measured on "opposition" and not only on "I" so that understanding may occur. Perception by which the Other is neither rapidly assumed into the self nor distanced, but instead is understood, requires the delicate balance of nearness and distance in a contextually ever-new creative process of perception. Understanding is a resonating phenomenon. One must become empty to understand the Other. Only thus can the necessary perspective-change of perception come to pass, which makes possible what has taken place "between" me and the Other.

The creation of tradition in cultures is a process of self-identification through *demarcation* of the Other. In individual development, at a certain stage the symbiotic unity with the mother is broken, and the "I" develops through discovery of the Other, which it can summon and also manipulate. The Other is thus *relationally* the mirror through which self-understanding first becomes possible; it is a necessary opposition. Later the individual needs membership in a group. The "we" feeling (including spoken and mental consistency) also develops itself in both appropriation and demarcation, that is, "we" stands in opposition to "the other." The group is conceived as a unity with a relatively stable structure through generalization of attributes. And this structure is not only marked by cognitive elements, but above all occupied by affective valuations.

There is a still more essential psychological factor involved: the opposite experienced as the "other" is to a high degree one's own shadow, that is, the sum of repressed and non-realized realms of reality of one's own being. This repression can derive from the individual biography or from the discrepancy of one's own claims to the existing cultural standard. The Other as the repressed is then the more rejected the closer it lies to one's own identity attributes.

In order to simplify identification and communication, often *an* attribute is made absolute. Thus, *the* German, *the* Jew, *the* Muslim should then exhibit *this* specific character. Cultural or religious identity is transmitted in the acceptance of such often-simplified perceived cultural standards, which can only appear as such if one's own is experienced as different from the praxis of the Other. In other words, identification comes to pass through demarcation. The Other is thus source of self-knowledge and self-validation—one knows who he or she is, if one is able to say who he or she is not or may not be. Social or religious judgments see the Other through the lens of this self-confirmation, and the entire process can be conceived as a reciprocal identity building.

In two circumstances the Other appears as *foreign*: (1) when an understanding of the Other is fundamentally impossible, because there are no analogous or contrasting experiences in one's own social world; and (2) when the Other is perceived, individually or politically, as being no longer "tremendous and fascinating" but instead as so "threatening and abhorrent" as to be repulsive (Otto Rudolf). The foreign does not arise from demarcation but from *fencing off*. For then it is no longer the Other, which in the process of self-identification stands in relation to the self. Instead, it is the fundamentally incomprehensible, with which relationship is destroyed. In this way the identity formation of both the Self and the Other is endangered.

The foreign or the foreigner appears very frequently in myths and tales in religious history as an ambivalent guest, who knocks unexpectedly and later reveals himself as divine. This is the motif of the ambivalent *other;* it is not comfortable. In other words, it compels people to go beyond it or grow beyond it, to surmount their own identity and to show themselves to have grown in the new situation. If it is not possible to accept the foreign as an opportunity for the realization of the self, in other words to receive "God" fittingly, the foreigner or the foreign shows itself as destructive and turns out to be one's own damnation; that is, it has become an enemy.

The foreign becomes "enemy" when the Other is not regarded as opportunity, but when the subject believes it must demarcate or when, reversed, the Other opposes the above-described individual or collective manipulation and reacts with counter-projections. To *stabilize* the now-endangered identity, above all the solidarity of groups, *enemy images* are then constructed that have their own dynamic in the above-signified sense. That means that in the perception of the enemy image one perceives precisely what one wants to in order to stabilize one's own identity, which had been threatened by the conversion of the Other into the foreign.

PLURALISM, IDENTITY, AND FUNDAMENTALISM

In the debate on the character of interreligious encounter, pluralism and identity often appear as contradictory. Pluralism means giving equal validity to what is different, while identity seeks continuity in demarcation, which often appears as devaluing of the foreign. But are not all religions syncretic—that is, syntheses from originally different strands of tradition?[9]

If someone wanted to synthesize a religion artificially based upon a theory of unity, this religious synthesis would certainly have no life. But religions are grown syntheses, and they only remain alive when this process of synthesis (which also includes repulsion and subduing of one's own old thought and behavior patterns as well as the foreign) continually proceeds. What we can recognize as religious currents and movements over the centuries always have a root somewhere that is multi-branched. All religions known today have their roots in several cultures or several original situations. Obviously this includes Christianity. What we know today as Protestant, Catholic, or Orthodox Christianity has many roots and has experienced differing spiritual influences, as the confessional plurality itself reveals. Religions are predominantly integrative, while ideologies on the contrary are a complete self-identification through demarcation and fencing-off. Religions die, then, when they become ideologies, when their identity becomes fixed and they can no longer change and adopt anything new. We call this analogue to biological processes the concurrent process of dissimilation and assimilation. A spiritual movement, a culture, a religion can assimilate what corresponds to it, what at the same time corresponds to the unfolding of its spiritual dynamic or its own "center."[10] That can mean at times incisive corrections, reformations, and fundamental transformations for religions in the sense of discovery or rediscovery of what lies in the dynamic of this religion. However, a religion will dissimilate that which is diametrically opposed to it. Let us suppose that for some reason we wanted to adopt again the practice of human sacrifice—and there are certainly equivalent modern forms of disregarding and destroying humans. This would not be possible in Christian belief, because it would be at variance with the thought that humans are created in the image of God, and also with Christian emphasis on love of neighbor. Thus it could never be assimilated. Buddhists could argue similarly: human and animal sacrifices are unacceptable because they are at variance with the Buddha nature of all living beings, and also contradict the karmic interdependence as well as the personal responsibility of all beings.

---

[9] See C. Colpe, "Synkretismus, Renaissance, Säkularisation und Neubildung von Religionen der Gegenwart," in *Handbuch der Religionsgeschichte*, ed. J. P. Asmussen et al. (Göttingen: Vandenhoeck, 1975), 441-523; K. Rudolph, "Synkretismus—vom theologischen Scheltwort zum religionswissenschaftlichen Begriff," in his *Geschichte und Probleme der Religionswissenschaft* (Leiden: Brill, 1992), 193-215; U. Berner, *Untersuchungen zur Verwendung des Synkretismus-Begriffes* (Wiesbaden: Harrassowitz, 1982). See also note 8 above.

[10] In the sense of Ernst Troeltsch. See M. Pye, "Comparative Hermeneutics in Religion," in *The Cardinal Meaning. Essays in Comparative Heremeneutics: Buddhism and Christianity*, ed. M. Pye and R. Morgan (The Hague/Paris: Mouton, 1973), 1-58.

Every tradition wrestles historically with its ever newly to be created identity, and it can thus adopt the Other and repel as false that which is perceived. This is precisely what is now occurring around the world. The religions find themselves in a fundamental crisis in face of secularism or the economically based culture into which the world has developed. This is no different in India than it is in Japan or Europe. All religions face the question of what their unchangeable and indispensable contribution to humankind is, not only to legitimize and strengthen religious institutions, but to achieve a selfless contribution to humanity that will correspond to the original impulse of each religion. From this arises the hermeneutical task. For example, how can the life and fate of Jesus and the life and fate of the Buddha be understood today not simply in opposing delimitation, but in the form of common quest for answers to the uncertainty, fear, and frustration of modern people?

What is usually meant by the scintillating and ambiguous catchword *fundamentalism*[11] represents a denial of the sort of self-reflection and relativizing of one's own knowledge that we have examined. One must distinguish first between different forms of fundamentalism, including those that are politically motivated and supported. Totally different movements in the Islamic world, in Hinduism, and in the Christian confessions vary so greatly psychologically, sociologically, and historically that they cannot be adequately grasped under the umbrella term *fundamentalism*. The forms of denial in regard to self-relativation, change of life, and recognition of possible truth and possible salvation in other religions have essentially two reasons.

One reason is of a more individual sort: *fear*. It is the fear humans have that they will lose something. People hang onto what can be formulated because they are perhaps not completely certain of their own belief or salvation. Clinging to traditional forms and to rigid institutions is a behavior of the weak. The person who, to speak with Paul, "nothing can separate from the love of God" (Rom 8: 38-39) does not need the demarcation that comes from fear that one's identity is jeopardized.

The other reason is social: *grasping for power*. The just-described longings for security and certainty can be used politically. Individual parties or groups make political capital from the quest for identity, if they try to erect purposeful fixed identities from interests of rule. That is the ideologization of the question of identity.

The concept of identity must be differentiated; we live concurrently in completely different identities. One need only consider that, for example, regional identity or national identity is important in different situations. Bavarians thus have a specific identity in relation to people from the other states of Germany, but at the same time they all have a single national identity. Other identities, such as confessional, are superimposed on this determination. When we see ourselves from the perspective of Europe, then we regard ourselves more in the

---

[11] V. N. Makrides, "Fundamentalismus aus religionswissenschaftlicher Sicht," *Dialog der Religionen* 4 (1994): 2-25; M. E. Marty et al., eds., *The Fundamentalism Project*, vols. 1-3 (Chicago: University of Chicago Press, 1991-93).

wider identity as Germans. If we look from the perspective of all humankind, then we identify ourselves as Europeans, and so on.[12]

A similar pattern is also true of religious identity: confessional identifications lose significance in the context of encounter with another religion, and the divisions between religions lose at least part of their function in a secular-atheistic context—here it only matters whether one "believes." Identities also change according to systems of relativity. They are not arbitrary or interchangeable, but indeed the identity pyramids place the subject in a wider context.

The process of identity formation is more complex in the history of religions than we can describe here, because in a religion, culture, or nation different identities are superimposed on each other, and in varying systems of relativity each different identity form will become dominant.

One must consider how there can be a repercussion to suppression: the person who is frustrated at work takes his or her frustration out on the family; the religious minority suffering discrimination may in turn react violently and suppress dissidents in its midst.

If today we perceive ourselves in a global situation of responsibility in crisis as a single humanity in "Spaceship Earth," or on a single storm-tossed boat, and, in Christian terms, recognize that we are all children of God, the traditional religious identities that up to the present have marked off individual cultures from each other become relative. This is occurring to a degree that is without parallel in human history. Tribal religions as well as the so-called high religions (whose origin lies in the development of urban cultures that are separated from each other or ethnic religions) underlie a dramatic shift in the identity matrix, against which each religion's institutions strive on the basis of their ruling interests. Despite this, besides all concurrent tendencies toward demarcation there is growing a consciousness of global unity. This presents itself as the *lived* and *experienced* identity that is the heritage of all people as a single humanity and the belief that all people are creations of one God. Or, if one does not care to use the concept of God, that all human beings are responsible to an inexpressible secret of life. Different identities show themselves as increasingly related to one another. Thus they enter an *identity partnership*, in which this analogy to the modern political-military concept of the "security partnership" is not coincidental, but instead shows the sweeping restructuring of old social forms.

This means that in the partnership of religions at all levels of human expression and form, that is, in interreligious dialogue, a common identity is being formed. However, this does not mean that each religion's special religious identity has been lost or must be lost—quite the contrary. On the basis of all the experiences that we have portrayed above, we can assert confidently that Christians, for

---

[12] One can make the attempt. If a European on a Pacific island encounters another European, he will perceive kinship, that is, similarity, and greet the other as a neighbor, that is, as a European. He would never do this, however, in circumstances where everyone was European, but in that case would hear German or more likely the Bavarian dialect and identify himself in that way.

example, discover their specifically Christian identity in a new way through encounter with Buddhists. Certainly the new form is without the compulsion to demarcate, and lacks the sort of superiority complex that would be involved in aggressive claims to truth and mission.

It is bitterly necessary to overcome these superiority complexes. For at present the world is experiencing demarcation movements that are legitimized nationalistically, racially, and religiously, and are linked to force. Unfortunately, in this movement religions often play a discreditable role precisely because as religion they lay claim to an absolute and uncircumscribed level of reality. Ideologically recoined, this assertion is misused to legitimate power. The finite-relative partial identity is issued as an infinite-absolute claim. According to the biblical view, this is the foundation of sin, of idolatry, of turning what is relative into a false god. But Christian churches have become guilty of this. And this is linked to what was said above about mission. When the ineffable presence of God or God's coming to humankind *(missio Dei)* is confused with human-institutional self- and mission-consciousness, the fundamental hermeneutical mistake appears of regarding the finite as absolute. That will always be the case, as long as people cannot accept that an Other is different, or if the Other is only accepted as worthy of association when through conversion the Other has been made the same as one's self. In other words, the situation will exist as long as belief is lacking that God in creation not only allowed very different sorts of people, cultures, and religions, but apparently wanted them!

Relativizing religious claims in dialogue means neither leveling nor arbitrariness. Rather, the religious formation processes that are going on worldwide today will be experienced as interactive and rational questing movements. Or to express it another way, with the dialogical relativization of traditional theological positions, certain important accompanying points of view are experienced. Following the American theologian Paul O. Ingram, we can express these on the basis of differentiation between a trusting experienced basis of belief *(faith)* and relative expression of belief *(belief)*:[13]

1. One must distinguish between trivial and profound religious assertions, on account of which the dialogical common search for criteria is essential.

2. Relativized claims do not become false, but are placed in a fuller context. It is valid to consider that images and concepts that have stamped the imagination of entire peoples over long periods are indeed effective.

3. Relativizing of knowledge can and should go hand in hand with decisive actions (for non-action in a given situation on the basis of doubt about the general validity of one's own maxims of action is a form of action). Relativizing means the readiness to change action, when the circumstances and contents of perceptions change.

4. All belief assertions can be reformed, because there can be no final or absolute formulation of belief claims, insofar as the basis of belief never becomes fixed.

---

[13] P. O. Ingram, *The Modern Buddhist-Christian Dialogue: Two Universalistic Religions in Transformation* (Lewiston: Mellen, 1988), 15f.

5. Encountering other religious claims in dialogue creates the opportunity to reformulate one's own tradition more clearly and adequately and in relation to the contemporary context. In the continual process of dialogical crossing-over into the other's symbolic and conceptual world, as well as in returning from that point, lies the possibility to give religion new life at the level of the last secret of life.

PERSPECTIVES

So long as the unity within the multiplicity of all historical occurrences is not accepted, which in the final analysis is only possible from the basis of a fundamental religious trust, we will continue to try to make the Other into what we ourselves are, because we feel threatened by the Other as foreign. This is a cause of conflict, force, and war that is connected to economic and political interests.[14] The lack of trust is also reflected in European and American identity fears in face of the aspiring peoples of the South, and these fears will be compensated through attempts at force.

This syndrome can only be overcome if the unity of reality within multiplicity is experienced as a *salvific* mutual interpenetration (cf. the *pratityasamutpada* model). In other words, this will come to pass when on the one side trust in the goodness of God's creation is cultivated—this is a deeply Christian concern— and on the other side the awe at the multiplicity of life remains untouched. In Christian theological terms one can argue that God wanted differing people, languages, and religions, that through their very otherness they could learn from one another and in this way become able to surmount their egocentrism and their own institutional self-centeredness.

We wish one more time to illustrate the consequence of our hermeneutical model on the problem that is fundamental for both religions: suffering or the frustration of existence. Starting from the Christian-Buddhist analysis of suffering, we can say that the sense of the dialogue is that our suffering does not consist of the fact that we find no language for that which goes on unconditionally, but only with a new language can we discover what in fact it is that we must search for.

Although religious encounter can perhaps also contribute to a confusion of language, in the longer view this healthful confusion might lead to the birth of a new linguistic and conceptual consciousness. It is thus important that Christians do not disqualify Buddhism as impersonal, nonethical, atheistic, and ahistorical, while they conceive of Christian views of personhood, God, ethics, and history in an extraordinarily strong position themselves. Vice versa, it is not helpful when Buddhist philosophers are so completely convinced that the abstractness of Buddhism can describe reality as it is—so one can then, comforted, carry the classical conceptual systems home again as dogma. Both traditions find themselves in a semantic confusion, as our report about the various dialogue fields has shown.

---

[14] As in recent times one can observe again in India, Sri Lanka, and many other parts of the earth.

But how can we free ourselves from hurling words and concepts at one another? Perhaps this can be accomplished by returning to the foundations of our human limitations and moral guilt. This must, however, be done without the conceptuality of dogma, which believes it has the whole tight in its grasp, divided into the metaphysical drawers of *karma* and *samsara* or *guilt* and *damnation*. Then the images and insights of both religions could be brought together for a new world of religious consciousness that corresponds to our real situation. But for this the courage is necessary to accept the inherent boundaries of *each* religious conceptual system and also to recognize the richness of each other's tradition.

How much in world history these two traditions have developed, encountered one another, penetrated one another, and exchanged their piety shows itself clearly for the first time in the current encounter. Christianity, too, cultivates in its mystical traditions an experience of losing the self. For its part, Buddhism knows the failure of the moral will in the face of eschatological despair and the hope by which Buddhists too can accept the promise of grace.

When we proceed from an understanding that both religions answer the fundamental fears and hopes of the same human species, such an interreligious reconnaissance should lead further toward mutual humility and sharing of insights. Thus one can recognize in the belief of the Other, at least allusively, certain neglected aspects of one's own traditions. By this means one can be moved to accept a more comprehensive human praxis, one that feeds from the great and liberating insights of Gautama the Buddha and Jesus the Christ.

We may answer in the affirmative the question of whether there is an interreligious hermeneutics. Its structures and contours are already visible; however, it can only be worked out in a pluralistic context. Thus interreligious hermeneutical praxis will also remain pluralistic. It may well come in each case *mutually* to advocate what is *known to be true* argumentatively, and to live in a way that gives witness to it as *sustained belief*. The first point is a critical corrective, the second constitutes the existential deepening that all religions urgently need.

CLOSING ARGUMENTS

This investigation sought to show how and why understanding and encounter between Buddhism and Christianity have succeeded or failed. Upon this basis certain general conclusions can be drawn for future encounters between religions in general, but especially between Buddhism and Christianity. These arise from a weighing of the encounter history of Buddhism and Christianity up to the present:

Retrospect

• The Western-Christian missionary movements as well as the European and American assertions of superiority and imperialism, shaken in the two world wars of the twentieth century but not yet fully overcome, had different effects on Christianity and Buddhism.

Christianity is concerned to clear away its past and to surmount developments that have clearly been mistaken according to the standard of the gospel. Intra-Christian ecumenism as well as openness toward other religions are results of this self-critique. Both intra-Christian and interreligious ecumenism are, in world historical perspective, the sign of a new orientation of the Christian tradition in a post-Constantinian epoch, which is, to be sure, contested within Christianity. Intra- and interreligious ecumenism are two aspects of one and the same process. The acceptance of guilt was in this way the precondition for the beginning of renewal. In this context the relatively great openness of many Christian groups to integration of Buddhist meditation traditions can be put into place historically—it serves for the construction of a renewed Christianity.

The Buddhists were only united in political and religious-ideological terms for a short time during the anticolonial struggle against the Christian West. This is because Buddhism in the Theravada lands is given coherence through national loyalties. In Mahayana it has only been possible in a rudimentary fashion (especially in Japan) to prepare the way for a comprehensive Buddhist ecumenism through a historical critique of tradition and inquiry into the historical Buddha. For these reasons, not even the trauma of World War II and the Vietnam War has led to a critical confrontation with the political history of Buddhism or to a Buddhist unifying movement in East or South Asia.

• To be sure, Buddhist peace movements arose in East Asia (for example, Rissho Kosei-kai in Japan). But they base themselves solely on the traditional Buddhist ethic of freedom from force, without regarding the formerly institutional consequences in regard to the organization or national fragmentation and the national loyalties of the *samgha*. In other words, these movements did not lead to talk of reform of the tradition itself. Some exceptions are the XIV Dalai Lama, Bhikku Buddhadasa and Sulak Sivaraksa in Thailand, and Thich Nhat Hanh from Vietnam, whose sphere of activity has mostly been Europe and America.

• It is important to note the basic assumption of most Buddhists of all schools that Buddhism is self-sufficient and needs interreligious dialogue for practical political reasons, but not for renewal of Buddhism's own religious self-understanding. The weakly impressed critical perception of their own history means that up until now modernism has only been recognized as problem and challenge in specific cases. Thus Buddhism in its Asian homelands—with the exception of Sri Lanka and the new Buddhist lay movements in Japan—exists in a certain isolation as far as the problems of modern and industrializing societies are concerned.

SHORTCOMINGS

• Understanding of the other's religious traditions was always lacking when other religions were perceived very selectively. In reality, the political, spiritual, dogmatic, and cultic dimensions of religions form a web, in which the religion translates itself into reality as the lifestyle of the individual as well as of the entire society. The isolation of specific elements has thus led to false assessments and lack of understanding in Buddhist-Christian dialogue. This occurs, for example, if one believes it is possible to view Buddhism separately from its political and social history, instead regarding only the meditative tradition. Similarly, too often people have focused one-sidedly in looking at Christianity on the personal nature of the concept of God, without paying attention to mystical theology or the dynamizing of the concept of person in the doctrine of the Trinity, or its corresponding actualization in Christian social history. To remedy this lack, dialogue must go beyond intellectual understanding and encourage participation in the spiritual praxis of the other as well as promoting interreligious communal life.

• To this point, in encounter the two religions have both given a central position to academic comparison of ideas and to meditation. But neither the church nor the *samgha* can be reduced to these dimensions. The meditation movement was indeed able to correct the one-sided intellectualization of dialogue. Still, however, the popular Buddhism of the village, its social dimensions, and its local political conflicts play a subordinate role. Nevertheless, there have been the first steps toward an interreligious learning process. Simplified, it can be characterized thus: meditation is revivified in a strongly despiritualized Christianity; and Buddhist ethics, meditation, and social practice are increasingly transmitted consciously in the day-to-day world of Buddhist laypeople.

• A great shortcoming of dialogue is that, so far, there are still very few representative speakers for Buddhism who have become engaged in dialogue from the midst of Buddhist belief and responsibility in the *samgha* (the fourteenth Dalai Lama and Thich Nhat Hanh are among the few exceptions).

PROSPECTS

• The *otherness of the Other* (the other religion) is not an evil that can be veiled or set aside through conceptual imperialism. Instead, it is the *source of inspiration and understanding*. For encounter with the Other awakens us from the lethargy of what is accustomed and generates wonder and astonishment, perhaps also fear. Astonishment (Plato) or fear (Epicurus) are, though, the beginning of philosophy. And even opposition to the Other, which prevents rapid understanding, must be endured, so that in dialogue a knowledge of the new can come to maturity, a knowledge that is more than the simple repetition of what is already known, or what is thought to be known.

• There is no alternative to dialogue between the religions. It is a precondition for the success of dialogue that the partners regard one another as equally valid, both politically and in religious-theological terms.

• Because religions are never solely the expression of inner spiritual experience but are always also institutions with political significance and power, dialogue can only succeed if the plurality of religions in society is recognized. Missionizing the Other in the sense of aiming to incorporate the Other into one's own institutions by means of overt or hidden pressure must be forbidden and abandoned by all sides. Only then can the partners in dialogue bear witness to and live exemplarily what they recognize as true.

• In the encounter with other religions the relativity of confessional-institutional and dogmatic systems becomes apparent. Christians can perceive in this the unforeseeable and inconceivable creative working of the Holy Spirit and thus be led more deeply to their own roots. Buddhists, too, can perceive, stimulated through the Christian historical-critical attitude toward tradition, the relativity of how their own tradition was created, and open themselves to other Buddhist schools as well as other religions. The historical-critical relativizing of one's own as well as another's standpoint can be conceived of as *upaya*, as clever means to free oneself from attachment to one's own tradition. This is, of course, an essential Buddhist concern.

• In dialogue there must be discussion of the values and lifestyles of future human societies, both factually and with the partners looking back to the *origin* of their traditions. This clears the way for reciprocal critique of the religions, which is necessary because a goal of dialogue is to contribute to the democratization of religious institutions. Agreement in this is not a requirement, but a possible result of dialogue.

• Dialogue does not need fixed dogmas about the methods and content of interreligious communication. More necessary are *rules* built from consensus, in accordance with which the necessary struggle for meaning can be carried out. For this to occur requires the national and international institutionalization of interreligious communication.

• In order to avoid a "cultural war" in the twenty-first century, which would not primarily revolve around economic or political power but rather the security and identity of the various cultural/religious lifestyles, the *identity partnership* of religions must be practiced and fostered in dialogue. Dialogue in this way expands each partner's traditional identity through the process of *mutual* deepening of the religions according to criteria that must themselves first be worked out in dialogue.

• So that future prejudices, false perceptions, and false interpretations of religion can be surmounted in dialogue, all possible efforts must be made in the realm of education and information about other religions and in interreligious communication.

• Buddhist-Christian dialogue in the twenty-first century should act in accordance with an ecumenical spirit, in which the dialogue partners mutually enrich each other in the broad perspective of encounter with various world cultures. This could be accomplished through a renewed Christian spirituality, created with the help of Buddhist experience; and through a renewed social organization of Buddhism, attained with the help of Christian experience.

The two traditions, by doing this, do not melt into one another, but creatively reinterpret their own tradition in light of the other. Dialogue offers the opportunity to develop and to live unity within the diversity of different religious traditions.

Index

Other Titles in the Faith Meets Faith Series